The Nature of Demography

The Nature of Demography

Hervé Le Bras

Princeton University Press

Princeton and Oxford

ISBN: 978-0-691-13943-2 (cloth)
ISBN: 987-0-691-12823-8 (pbk.)

Library of Congress Control Number: 2008930612

British Library Cataloging-in-Publication Data is available

This book has been composed in Times

Typeset by T&T Productions Ltd, London

Printed on acid-free paper ∞

press.princeton.edu

Printed in the United States of America

10 9 8 7 6 5 4 3 2 1

Contents

II Populations 137

Preface

The techniques and findings of demography are of interest to a wide range of social science disciplines. Population questions occupy a central position in the research of economists, sociologists, geographers, historians, and biologists, and it is to these researchers and students, as much as to professional demographers, that this book is addressed. In its conception, therefore, it has been designed to present a coherent overview of demography as a field that can engage with these diverse preoccupations and supply methods for handling them. In this sense, while not precluding a detailed examination of the fundamental population phenomena, the book is really a general introduction to demography. For experienced researchers as well as for students starting out in the social sciences, it will serve as a guide to recent research of relevance to their particular subjects of study, including the marriage market, migration fields, human capital, settlement models, life-cycle models, migration contributions, retirement pension systems, ecological constraints, population aging, and population projections.

Population questions have evolved rapidly in the last twenty years. Every branch of demographic analysis has to some extent been renewed. This is true first of all for fertility. A major transformation has been the weakening of the connection between marriage and fertility and the delaying of first childbearing. One consequence has been a change in how fertility trends and their determinants are interpreted. Whereas up to 1990 the emphasis was placed on cultural factors, the dominant position is now occupied by microeconomic models of the family, based on the work of Gary Becker (1993) and George Schultz (1974). Extended by the recent research of Peter McDonald (2006), these models are providing material for the debate over the family policies that successive developed countries are introducing to combat forecast declines in their populations, the growing burden of their elderly populations, and the impoverishment of their young people.

Equally important changes are observed in the area of mortality. The resumption of the decline in mortality has been both sharp and unexpected. It is now affecting the older and oldest ages as stated by Shaw (2007), with the result that research is focused on the end and ultimate limit to human life. New concepts, such as avoidable mortality and healthy life expectancy, have been developed (Schoeni et al. 2006; Bongaarts 2006). The final stage of life also connotes retirement and old-age pensions. Population aging has replaced the population explosion as the number-one preoccupation of demographers, forcing new issues onto the agenda and leading to the adoption of new tools borrowed from economics, sociology, and biology. Lastly, the decline in mortality, like that in fertility, modifies the estimation of demographic indices, in this case life expectancy. Debate is currently raging in the specialist journals—*Population Studies*, *Population and Development Review*, and *Mathematical Population Studies*—over "tempo" effects in mortality (Inaba 2007; Goldstein and Wachter 2006), which accordingly are the subject of chapter 6.

Migration studies have also been transformed. Fears of invasion, requests for regularization, the shift from immigration for survival to immigration for personal fulfillment, ethnicity, globalization of migration flows, the role of human capital, immigration as the remedy for population aging—all these issues are now subject to analyses that will be considered here in relation to the models from economic geography and quantitative sociology (Van Dalen and Henkens 2007; Massey and Taylor 2004).

The recent changes have not only affected demography's three determinants—fertility, mortality, migration—they have also modified the scale on which the study of populations is conducted. Demography was by tradition structured around nation states, but, with the rise to prominence of ecological and environmental concerns, both local and global scales have assumed a new importance. The models for population dynamics and forecasting have in consequence had to be adapted to incorporate constraints, notably those of bounded space and limited resources of food, minerals, and energy. Chapter 9 is devoted to showing how populations react to these new limits. That standard demographic theory has been able to integrate these changes without running into serious contradictions or undergoing fundamental revisions illustrates the power of its theoretical model, that of stable-population theory, which constitutes the core of the book (chapter 8).

Acknowledgments

This book is the product of a large body of research work. It owes a great deal to my first mentors, Louis Henry and Peter Laslett. It owes an equal debt to my colleagues, including Ken Wachter, Jim Vaupel, and Philippe Fargues, and to my first students, now established researchers, Alain Blum, Catherine Bonvalet, and Maurizio Gribaudi. Gérard Jorland and Odile Jacob made possible publication of the French version of the book (Éditions Odile Jacob in 2005), and Richard Baggaley did the same for this English edition. Godfrey Rogers has been a careful and conscientious translator. Jon Wainwright at T&T Productions Ltd was precise and meticulous in his editing and typesetting. I would also like to thank the Institut National d'Études Démographiques (INED) and the Institut de Recherche et Applications Démographiques (IRAD) for their assistance with funding. Finally, to my wife and children, who saw little of their spouse and father during the writing of this book; I hope that it will show them that it was in a good cause.

The Nature of Demography

Introduction

The Dynamics of Change in Demography

Demography has often been contrasted with psychoanalysis. Both are studies of man and society: one is concerned with populations, the other with individuals. One makes use of mathematics, the other focuses on language. For one the individual is an anonymous and isolated gambler who draws the events of his life as in a lottery; for the other, society remains a shadowy multitude governed by the primary drives of life and death. To these differences I would add another that appears to me to sum them all up: demography has one and only one theory, one and only one paradigm, whereas the many competing schools of psychoanalysis defend rival and mutually incompatible theories. An analyst will be labeled as Freudian, Jungian, or Lacanian, and will invoke such and such a master when defining his or her position and clinical methods. A demographer will be described simply as a demographer and will make reference to no master.

One may object that the reason for this is obvious. Demography operates in the real world of people and places, psychoanalysis in the realm of interpretation. In demography, people are born, they get married, have children, migrate, not necessarily in that order, and finally they die. These events are real, factual; each one is unique. In psychoanalysis, individuals have dreams, commit slips of the tongue, suffer from psychoses or neuroses, recollect early or even infantile experiences. These are mental representations; they are countless. It is a science of nature versus a pseudoscience of the mind. Such a conclusion is inaccurate. Even though one of the two disciplines has a single theory and the other many, both are based on theory, and hence on a construction, a codification, an abstraction of reality—on conventions whose main rationale is coherence. For theory implies coherence. There is no such thing as an incoherent theory: at most there are theories that are incomplete.

In saying this I risk offending the positivism laid claim to by demographers and analysts alike—the former openly, the latter more discreetly. Both own to accepting a few conventions but both claim to have a strong grasp on reality. This is the reality of death or of dreams, of course, but most importantly the reality of their respective instruments and concepts: mortality, with its age-specific mortality rates and life expectancies, and the unconscious, with its desires and impulses. Yet instruments are not part of nature. They have not lain hidden since the dawn of time waiting to be discovered by demographers and analysts, like fossils by paleontologists or galactic clusters by astronomers. They possess a history, a rationale; above all, they have been shaped in relation to each other to produce a coherent whole. If this is the case, can we not simply say that theories are social constructions and that their instruments constitute the equipment? That would be to go from one extreme to the other and gain nothing in the process. Apart from the fact that all theoretical constructions, being mediated by language, are social by definition, the expression itself reveals a woolly cultural relativism. Clearly, the fact that demography and psychoanalysis existed in the twentieth century, rather than at the time of Athens, Rome, or Xian, was thanks to particular social—but also political, economic, and intellectual—conditions. But these do not explain why the disciplines have stabilized in their exact present form. The erratic evolutions of the economic, political, and social systems do not mysteriously create order in the form of demographic theory or a particular psychoanalytic theory. Theoretical order is achieved only after lengthy and collective intellectual effort during which the early propositions, formulated independently and giving rise to contradictions, are gradually solved by new conceptual choices, which in turn raise new difficulties. The remarkable point—and perhaps the one true mystery of nature—is that such a process results in virtually stable situations, theories that are few in number, and in some cases unique, for example, those by which we understand the evolution of living organisms, the formation of crystals, the Platonic solids, or the regular divisions of the plane.

Learning and understanding demography is thus to penetrate deep into the theory that it constitutes, and this is the necessary condition for its existence as an independent discipline; it means isolating its primary constituents and their basic relations, and highlighting the conceptual choices and the bifurcations that had to occur in the course of its elaboration for it to attain its current stability. Only with this approach can we identify the still-unresolved problems and trace the dynamic development of the theory faced in particular by the new social, economic, and political situations that gradually undermine its original foundations. The theory is not cut off from present reality, but its structure was achieved with difficulty and is highly resistant to change. A knowledge and understanding of the form taken by demography as an organized whole is the only way to make it evolve. But this is always difficult, since once a certain expertise has been established, the tendency is to protect and defend it like a capital, not to seek to reach beyond it.

Is this not a commonplace situation that all disciplines know how to deal with? A look at the recent treatises and encyclopedias of demography—whose quality is not in question, merely their epistemological orientation—makes this seem doubtful. What they frequently have in common is a preference for practical formulas—which the seminal work by Graunt and Petty (1661) had already described as "shopkeeper's arithmetic"—and a conviction that the established instruments will remain forever. After reading such books, leaving aside the standard typologies such as longitudinal/cross-sectional, first- and second-order rates, renewable and nonrenewable events, you do not know what constitutes the discipline, or the position of its boundaries. Demography's general form, its overall structure, in a word, the coherence that is the fundamental reason for its existence—these remain concealed. Yet there is no reason why a set of formulas and typologies should coalesce as a particular discipline. And to say, as is customary, that demography is the scientific study of populations, solves nothing. Populations are everywhere and nowhere. Ironically, it could be argued that their discovery came after that of demography (this is true of the term "population," which did not come into use until a hundred years after publication of Graunt's and Petty's works). The geographer Hartshorne (1939) chose an admirable and simple title for his book *The Nature of Geography*. We would gladly adopt it for our purposes and say that what we are seeking to capture here is the nature of demography, not from esthetic or philosophical motives, but on the contrary from practical necessity. To engage in the major contemporary debates over demographic issues—population aging, exploding birth rates, abortion, retirement pension systems, urban concentration and dispersion—one needs to know exactly how they are interrelated and how they are formalized. The weapons of critique must be forged before they can be used.

This does not mean that we shall have our heads in the clouds. Even if demography uses numbers and mathematical reasoning, it need not take this to excess. Its objective is not to become a part of the corpus of mathematics but to use it in the simplest and most concrete way, along the lines Richard Feynman sets out in his treatises on general physics. When all is said and done, demography employs mathematics to handle problems that in essence come down to those of taps, tanks, and bathtubs. There is no point in adopting technically tortuous methods to resolve them. Every now and then a major mathematical theory will be encountered and pointed out, but the rest of the time we shall be working at the level of a secondary-school student in his/her final year. What matters is to make the approach used comprehensible, not to fix demography in the camp of mathematics.

To address these theoretical preoccupations and practical intentions, the book is divided into three parts, corresponding to three stages of increasing complexity: individuals, populations, and networks. We begin by setting up a simple and general model of behavior, personified by *homo demographicus*. He is a gambler who must contend with various risks—those of dying, having a child, migrating, getting married. He and the lifeline linking the events he has experienced are the necessary starting point for demographic analysis: aggregating individual behaviors represented by a probability set, we get results at the population level which are summarized in the form of indices such as life expectancy or total number of children ever born, before subjecting those changes of behavior to analysis. The more precisely analysis relates behavior to observations, the greater its capacity in the other direction to infer changes in behavior from variations in observations. This will be verified in the last two chapters of part I, which are given over to changes in the pace—in the timing or tempo to use English demographic terminology—of fertility and mortality, the effects of which are far from obvious.

At the end of part I we run up against two questions. First, how can change in the size and age structure of populations be related to the fertility and mortality behavior of *homo demographicus*? Second, how can the overly simple model for the life and death of *homo demographicus* incorporate marriage and migration, and how can these be associated with fertility and mortality? The answer to the first question constitutes the core structure of contemporary demography. Part II is thus devoted to the passage from the behavior of individuals to that of populations, a question that has been the focus of attention in demography for nearly a hundred years. This approach was adopted in the 1920s as a result of the first population projections. Its effect was to orient demographic theory strongly toward the mathematical theory of stable populations, of which projections were an application. There is no mystery about this latter theory's neglect of migratory movements (although it can accommodate them, it usually reasons in terms of "closed" populations) and especially of nuptiality (fertility is defined uniquely by the age of mothers at childbearing). Stable-population theory assured a coherent relation between mortality and fertility on the one hand, and between population growth and age structure on the other, by supplying a model of population change based on the measures of behavior defined in part I. Stable populations and their generalization to populations in which fertility and mortality vary over time can be used to analyze a wide variety of social and, particularly, economic phenomena. These include financial equilibria over the life cycle, sustained long-term fluctuations in fertility and in the size of the labor force or in local population structures, population aging, decisions over retirement pensions (pension schemes or pay as you go), population regulation, and the relationship between economic growth and population growth, to mention just a few examples that we shall be examining.

The second limitation of contemporary demography derives logically from the choice in favor of stable populations. These are fundamentally closed populations in which the pace of events is dictated by the age of the individuals, independently of the other people with whom they live or interact. *Homo demographicus* is a Robinson Crusoe-like figure, cut off from his fellow men. When we wish to take account of ties of family or locality, demographic theory quickly loses its effectiveness. The third and last part, however, will attempt to push back the limits set by the second by examining the domain of marriage, then that of internal migration, and, finally, the spatial distribution of population. Models of social ties based on competing choices under simple constraints will be proposed. The preferred partner is chosen from among a set of possible partners; the nearest migration destination is chosen from among several opportunities. But competition inevitably arises between those in a position to choose the same person or the same place. This brief description explains why research has turned toward marriage-market and spatial-allocation models. We review these and in a number of cases extend them by using documented examples. The final part will thus remain exploratory, for although nuptiality or "partnership formation" determines fertility and the influence of migration on numbers is greater at lower scales, there are still many obstacles to their integration into population theory.

An account along these lines produces a strong image of demography with its central core of stable populations and its potential for extension in the areas of nuptiality, migration, and spatial population distribution. But it must also be admitted that, like any theory, demography exists and can only exist as a result of major and deliberate restrictions. Outside the frontier of the discipline, therefore, we have left a fringe that contains, among other topics, animal populations, the family, and kinship. The reasons for these exclusions can be stated briefly.

The demography of animal populations is central to biomathematics but it has different objectives to human demography and uses different methods. The elegant models of predation, competition, and spatial dispersal have no equivalent in human societies except at the level of metaphor. Conversely, changes in behavior in respect of fertility, mortality, migration, and nuptiality are alien to biomathematics, which postulates animal populations that are history-less and species-bound, and envisages change only at the level of an evolutionary theory, hence of selection and of competition between species.

Family demography has been left aside for other reasons. It seems to me that it is still unsure about its choices and concepts, not due to vagueness in sociology or multiple theories in anthropology—we pass no judgment on other disciplines— but because its construction requires mastery of the formalization of nuptiality and migration, which is not realized at the moment, as will become clear in the course of part III. Valuable models for the simulation of kinship and family exist—and we have contributed to them—but they are not yet at the stage where they can account for very general regularities such as the relatively high proportions of both sexes never marrying in Europe since the Renaissance, or the reproduction of household structures across cohorts through their life cycle. In these areas we are still at the stage of observation. Demography might well extend in these directions in the years to come, but since all the elements are mutually interdependent this is likely to involve a challenge to its current form. For the present that eventuality is still remote. Accordingly, we will confine ourselves to the strong core theory that dominates the discipline today and not roam beyond its immediate extensions.

Part I

Individuals

1
Mortality

Every group of inanimate objects and living organisms, including human beings, undergoes diminution through a gradual loss of its members. The houses standing in a given year are later destroyed through fire, landslides, or renewal programs; the cars manufactured in a given month disappear from circulation as a result of accidents or because they wear out or become obsolete. The humans born in a given year or present at a place on a particular date are no exception: death reduces their number day after day. The study of mortality seeks to formalize, standardize, and summarize this ineluctable process. Not merely from a concern with description and general knowledge, but also to compare the destinies of different groups and to draw general conclusions on which to base predictions about the futures of groups engaged in this process of attrition.

We will begin with the most obvious case, where a group is observed up to extinction, until the last of its members has died off. We will show how information about the length of each life can be summarized in a life table made up of three series: the survival or proportion of members still present after a time t; the distribution of deaths or departures by length of time; and lastly the risks of exiting or dying at any point in time. Construction of life tables reveals consistent structural features in the form of mathematical laws of mortality or statistical regularities that are used to determine the structure of mortality when observation of death or departure is incomplete. Knowledge about the mortality of a group can be applied in actuarial science—life insurance and annuities—and reliability analysis.

1.1   The Survival Curve

The most complete information about the depletion of a group is supplied by the list of the lengths of life (or duration of stay) of the individuals since they entered the group. For example, in a group of nine elderly persons, the lengths of life observed for each are 66, 49, 80, 22, 52, 56, 111, 28, and 70 months respectively. To make things clearer, we begin by arranging these lengths of life in order and representing them in a particular way. Each one is assimilated to a segment of the same length as the length of life being considered. The segments are placed on top of each other,

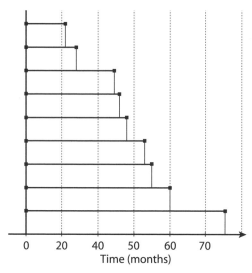

Figure 1.1.   Lengths of life of nine persons in a group
observed from time $t = 0$ up to the last death.

longest first, and aligned on the left, where the common starting point is the date of
the start of observation of the group (figure 1.1). The number of persons surviving at
any age is given by the upper limit of the stack and can be simply read off the vertical
axis. This is called the *survival function* rather than simply the "survivor's curve."
The reason is not terminological fussiness or linguistic archaism: it is to express
a very general property that two statisticians, Kaplan and Meier, demonstrated in
1958.

1.2   Estimating the Survival Function by the Kaplan–Meier Method

There are two ways of considering the mortality of a group of persons (often referred
to as a *cohort* to emphasize the aspect of following over time or *longitudinal observation*). Either this group represents a unique experience in history, in which case
figure 1.1 describes the situation adequately, or this group is one among many other
possible groups that had or could have had a similar experience but whose dying out
went unrecorded. In this situation the survival curve provides a means of approximating, or more exactly of estimating, a distribution of deaths within these groups.
Mortality is no longer known only at the exact date of death observed for the members of the group, but is defined for every time t, hence by a continuous curve, which
is that for the survival of the group since the nine lengths of the example are not
the only possible lengths of life in the other groups, even if mortality conditions
obtaining in them are similar.

Kaplan and Meier overcame this problem by establishing a fundamental property. The stepped survival curve of figure 1.1 is the most likely of all the possible curves or functions that can be defined from the individual durations to death. More exactly, at each age, the survival value given by the curve is the most likely possible for the sample observed. It is said to correspond to the "maximum likelihood." This is easy to prove.

Let $S(t)$ be the probability of surviving to time t. The probability of observing the sample actually observed is $L = S(t)^{n(t)}(1 - S(t))^{N-n(t)}$, where N is the number of persons at the origin and $n(t)$ is the number still alive at time t.[1] The maximum likelihood is the value of $S(t)$ that maximizes this probability L for the sample. It is obtained by setting the derivative of L (or rather, which is equivalent, its logarithm) to zero for $S(t)$:

$$\frac{\partial \log(L)}{\partial S(t)} = \frac{n(t)}{S(t)} - \frac{N - n(t)}{1 - S(t)}.$$

Hence,

$$S(t) = \frac{n(t)}{N}.$$

This will be recognized as the classic result for the binomial distribution, but it has added interest in this context since it holds whatever the time t. This property might appear obvious—why should some deaths be more important than others?—but it is in fact curious. At first sight it is tempting to select a survival function that is more rounded than the angular stepped form of figure 1.1, since it seems reasonable that the chances of surviving decrease in a fairly linear fashion and not in abrupt steps. That would be contrary to the underlying logic of nonparametric statistics, which consider only the observations while excluding the assumptions that, by contrast, are employed in parametric statistics, in particular, the existence of predetermined distributions to which the observations are made to fit. It may then be tempting to avoid the stepped function by reverting to the relativism that treats the mortality of each group as unique and described uniquely by the list of lengths of life of its members. That choice would remove the possibility of comparing mortality in two different groups, or following the evolution over time of mortality in a particular type of population (for example, in successive annual birth cohorts), or, as will be seen shortly, calculating the instantaneous mortality risks often called *forces of mortality*.

The postulate of a survival function establishes *homo demographicus* as a probabilistic being, subject uniquely to various probabilities—in this instance of dying, later of having children, of migrating, of marrying or divorcing. The individuals whose lengths of life are represented in figure 1.1 are alike in their identity to none other and are, at the same time, one realization among others of a stochastic process whose construction can be specified by defining the risks or probabilities of dying.

---

[1] The use of the letter "L" as an abbreviation for likelihood was introduced by the English statisticians of the journal *Biometrika*, who pioneered this way of reasoning.

1.3   Mean Length of Life and Life Expectancy

The set of different durations can be summarized by a single indicator. In the case of figure 1.1, the simplest is to compute the mean length of life, i.e., divide the sum total of the durations by the number of individuals. If the group of persons has been observed since birth, this mean is called the *mean age at death*. Of greater interest is the case of the survival function. It can immediately be seen that the sum of the lengths of life represents the area between the survival function and the two axes divided by the length selected for the base (i.e., for survival from time 0). Any of the methods for approximating plane surfaces (calculation of definite integrals) can be used for this purpose. The approximations encountered in the technical literature are all based on estimation of this area.[2] The difference between the *mean age at death* and this new value termed *longitudinal life expectancy* (and *life expectancy at birth* when observation begins at birth) is the same as that between an empirical mean and a mathematical expectation. The survival function is no longer a juxtaposition of lengths of life but a distribution defined for each age, and of which the observed sample is merely one of the multiple possible realizations.

The number of survivors at the origin is called the *life table radix*. Here we have set it to 1 because the survival function has been used as a probability changing over time, but the initial number of individuals (9) could have been kept as the scale. A round number of individuals—1000, 10 000, or 100 000—is usually chosen for the radix. In any large population subject to the mortality defined by the survival function, the mean age at death will tend to be very close to the life expectancy given by this function, which is why the two terms are frequently confused.

We might also consider survival from a certain time onward. This is equivalent to reducing the survival function to the section beyond this time. The rule then applies in the same way as from the origin: life expectancy from time t is equal to the area between the survival curve and the horizontal axis beyond the line drawn vertically at t divided by the survival function value at t, $S(t)$, which is the new radix of this reduced life table. We can draw the curve of variation in life expectancy from time t

---

[2] For example, if the ages at death are grouped in five-year periods, survival is determined only every five years. The trapezoidal (or Riemann) method then gives the conventional formula for life expectancy:

$$e(0) = 5 \cdot \tfrac{1}{2}(S(0) + S(5)) + 5 \cdot \tfrac{1}{2}(S(5) + S(10)) + \cdots + 5 \cdot \tfrac{1}{2}(S(120) + S(125)),$$

where 125 years is higher than the highest age reached $S(125) = 0$. The formula is also written by grouping the terms:

$$e(0) = 2.5S(0) + 5(S(5) + S(10) + \cdots + S(120)).$$

If, as is sometimes the case, the ages are divided irregularly, for example, by separating the first age group from the next four due to the heavy mortality among children under one year (referred to as *infant mortality*), the formula becomes

$$e(0) = 0.5S(0) + 2.5S(1) + 4.5S(5) + 5(S(10) + S(15) + \cdots + KS(120)).$$

as a function of this length of time (figure 1.2). It is seen that life expectancy declines at the same pace as time when the survival function is horizontal (constant) and that it cannot fall faster. On the other hand, over certain time intervals life expectancy can increase with duration.[3] This occurs inevitably at the precise moment of each death.

The survival function can be summarized in other ways, for example, as the median length of time or life, which is the value such that as many individuals die before attaining it as after. In figure 1.1 this length of time corresponds to the fifth lifeline, or 56 months. Another measure sometimes considered is the half-duration or half-life, which is such that as many years have been lived before as after, so that the line drawn at this level divides into two equal surfaces the area between the survival function and the two axes used to calculate life expectancy. These indicators must not make us lose sight of a remarkable property of the mean or mathematical expectation: it is the value that minimizes the squares of the deviations of all the individual lengths of life.[4] The median is a less refined indicator, which in the case, for example, of an even number of observations $2n$, is not known exactly but is situated between two values, the nth and the $(n + 1)$th values.

1.4 Deaths and Probabilities of Dying

Instead of representing the individual lifetimes by lines, we could have used the simplest and most widespread method—a histogram representing the distribution of the deaths by time elapsed (figure 1.3, using the same data as figure 1.1). It will be recalled that in a histogram it is the areas of the rectangles, and not their heights, that are proportional to the item frequencies (in this case deaths).

As with any frequency distribution of events, the proportion of events per class can be interpreted as a probability. In the present case this will be the a priori—i.e., at the moment where the counting of the times begins—probability of dying in the time interval selected, for example between 6 and 8 years or between 1 and 4 years. These probabilities are denoted $d(t_1, t_2)$ and this is described as the *probability of death*. The number of deaths is denoted $D(t_1, t_2)$. Generally speaking, these probabilities

---

[3] Thus, if life expectancy at one year is 30 years, but half of the individuals die before one year, the life expectancy at birth is $0.5/2 + (30 + 1)/2 = 15.75$ years.

[4] This minimum sum of the squared deviations is n times the variance. The demonstration of the property is simple: we look for the value m that minimizes the sum of the squared deviations and thus equates its derivative to zero at m:

$$\text{SC} = \sum_i (x_i - m)^2 \qquad \frac{d\text{SC}}{dm} = 2\sum_i (x_i - m) = 2\sum_i x_i - 2nm = 0.$$

Hence,

$$m = \sum_i \frac{x_i}{n}.$$

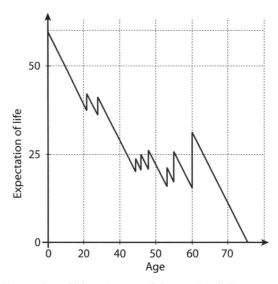

Figure 1.2. Expectation of life at the ages of the sample of nine persons in figure 1.1.

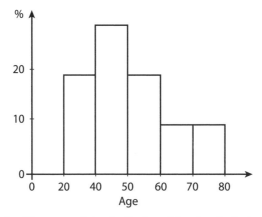

Figure 1.3. Histogram of the distribution of the nine deaths in figure 1.1.

are not very meaningful because they do not relate to a context. With rare exceptions each of us knows that we are going to die at one time or another. By contrast, we are more aware of close risks, and thus of the probabilities of dying in a near future when we have already attained a certain time or a certain age. These probabilities conditional on attained time are called the *probabilities of dying* or *quotients of mortality*. The probability or risk of dying between time t_1 and time t_2 when t_1 has been attained is thus the probability of death between t_1 and t_2 divided by the probability of living to time t_1, i.e., by survival at t_1:

$$q(t_1, t_2) = D(t_1, t_2)/S(t_1).$$

Table 1.1.   Life table for the nine durations in the example shown in figures 1.1 and 1.3.

Times (year)	Interval	Survivors	Deaths	Probabilities
0		1		
	0–1		0	0
1		1		
	1–4		0.22	0.22
4		0.78		
	4–5		0.34	0.43
5		0.44		
	5–6		0.22	0.50
6		0.22		
	6–8		0.11	0.50
8		0.11		
	8–10		0.11	1.00
10		0		

The risk of dying during the first year of life is called the *infant mortality rate*. We see that the risk of dying in the last period of life is equal to unity: death is certain. Using the definitions of the survival function, the number of deaths, and the mortality probabilities, it is now possible to construct a life table.

1.5   Life Tables

A life table does not introduce any new elements, rather it brings together the previous series and presents them in a tabular framework that came into use in the mid eighteenth century. The life table corresponding to the data shown in figures 1.1 and 1.3 is presented in table 1.1.

The first column shows the times elapsed since the start of observation, and the second, arranged in quincunx, the resulting division by time intervals. The third column contains the survival function with a radix of 1 ($S(0) = 1$). In the next column, also in quincunx since it corresponds to times, the deaths in the table $d(t_1, t_2)$. Then, at the same level in the last column, are the probabilities of dying, $q(t_1, t_2)$.

With any one of the three series we can derive the other two by a set of simple relations that hold between them:

$$d(t_1, t_2) = S(t_1) - S(t_2),$$
$$q(t_1, t_2) = d(t_1, t_2)/S(t_1),$$
$$S(t_2) = S(t_1)(1 - q(t_1, t_2)).$$

Table 1.1 makes clear the advantage of the risks of mortality. Their value increases with time, whereas the deaths, whose number falls, cannot be used to establish the risks of dying at high survival durations. However, for comparisons between risks of mortality to be pertinent, they must be made over equal time intervals. A probability of dying over three years is not directly comparable with a probability over one year. How can we compare two mortality probabilities for different time intervals? Answering that question leads us to the notion of instantaneous death rate or *force of mortality*,[5] which no longer depends on the length of a period, and hence on two limits (t_1, t_2), but is a direct function of age t in the same manner as the survival function $S(t)$.

1.6   Comparison of Mortality and Instantaneous Probabilities

Up to this point no hypothesis has been made about the data. Yet for comparison to be possible, one must be made, being required by the very idea of comparison: if two terms can be compared, the assumption is that they can be reduced to a common reference. Let there be a probability Q over an interval (t_1, t_2). We divide this interval into n subintervals of equal length and assume that q is the probability over each. The proportion surviving from one subinterval to the next is $1 - q$, so that survival after n subintervals is $(1 - q)^n$. Since these subintervals put end to end make up the whole interval (t_1, t_2) at the end of which the proportion surviving is $1 - Q$, we have

$$1 - Q = (1 - q)^n,$$

or, equivalently,

$$q = 1 - (1 - Q)^{1/n}.$$

To compare two probabilities for intervals of different lengths, all we need do is divide them by a common subinterval such that the first contains n_1 times the subinterval and the second n_2. In both cases the previous formula is applied that gives the probability of the common subinterval from the probability of the first interval and from the second. The two values are now comparable since they pertain to the same duration.

In the example used at the start of the chapter, reading off from table 1.1 we have

$$q(4, 5) = 0.43 \quad \text{and} \quad q(6, 8) = 0.50.$$

The common subinterval is 1 year and the two values for the probability are

$$q_1 = 1 - (1 - q(4, 5)) \quad \text{and} \quad q_2 = 1 - (1 - q(6, 8))^{1/2},$$

that is,

$$q_1 = 0.43 \quad \text{and} \quad q_2 = 0.29.$$

Reduced to the same time interval, the probability for the period 6–8 years is now less than the probability for the period 3–4 years.

---

[5] The term "hazard" is also used in the literature.

Instead of a common subinterval of 1 year, a much smaller interval could have been used—1 month, 1/100th of a year, or even 1/10 000th of a year. This does not alter the result of the comparison but gives increasingly small probabilities. Hence, for 1/1000th of a year the two previous probabilities become

$$q_1 = 0.000\,56 \quad \text{and} \quad q_2 = 0.000\,34,$$

and, for 1/10 000th,

$$q_1 = 0.000\,056 \quad \text{and} \quad q_2 = 0.000\,034.$$

A simple relation becomes apparent at very small intervals. The probability divided by its length tends toward a constant μ, which is written[6]:

$$q(t, t + dt) = \mu \, dt.$$

For any time t, there is thus an associated instantaneous probability $\mu(t)$. The probability is no longer the characteristic of an interval but a value for the instant in time. We can speak of the mortality function in the same way that we speak of the survival function.[7] The instantaneous probabilities are in general expressed as annualized values, which gives the relation

$$\mu = -\frac{\log(1 - Q)}{t_1 - t_2}.$$

This procedure frees us from the constraints of the two limits of the interval on which the finite mortality probability was calculated. From the instantaneous probability, the instantaneous deaths are inferred by using the life table formula:

$$d(t) \, dt = s(t)\mu(t) \, dt$$

thus

$$d(t) = s(t)\mu(t).$$

---

[6] Assuming that dt divides the interval, put $1 - Q = (1 - q)^{(t_1 - t_2)/dt}$. Changing to logarithmic notation, we obtain

$$\log(1 - Q) = \frac{t_1 - t_2}{dt} \log(1 - q).$$

For small values of q, the logarithm can be replaced by $-q$, which gives

$$\frac{q}{dt} = -\frac{\log(1 - Q)}{t_1 - t_2}.$$

q/dt has thus become independent of the interval dt and it can be named μ or the instantaneous probability. Contrary to what it seems, the instantaneous probability does have dimension. It must be expressed in the same units as dt, for example, annual. An instantaneous probability in monthly units will thus be 12 times smaller than in an annual unit.

[7] The finite mortality probability is expressed exactly as a function of $\mu(t)$ by the formula

$$-\log(1 - Q(t_1, t_2)) = \int_{t_2}^{t_1} \mu(t) \, dt.$$

By simple operations on a limited number of age intervals, an underlying structure $\mu(t)$ has thus been identified. Compared with the survivor function estimated by using the Kaplan–Meier method, however, the form of $\mu(t)$ may appear disappointing. The function is nil almost everywhere and infinite at each exact date of death.[8] This conclusion is scarcely acceptable. Extended to a larger population it would mean that some ages are very dangerous and others not at all. Such beliefs predominated at the time of the Renaissance, with the "climacteric" ages divisible by 7 or 9, but have lost all basis. Postulating a degree of continuity and regularity in the probabilities leads us to make parametric assumptions. Implicitly this step was taken a few lines back by assuming a probability that is constant over the whole period of comparison. What was there merely a procedure can be taken as reality and leads to the very general notion of rate.

1.7 Instantaneous Rates of Mortality

Assume now that the risk of dying, μ, is constant over the whole observation period, between 0 and 5 years in the initial example, for example. The Kaplan–Meier estimation is no longer valid. The likelihood function L must be calculated with this new hypothesis and its maximum sought. L is the product of the individual probabilities that each observation (each duration) has the observed value. The probability of one of the n deaths observed in the period occurring at time t_i is the product of the probability of surviving up to t_i at constant probability μ, thus the exponential of $-\mu t_i$ by the probability of dying at t_i. The logarithm of this probability has the value: $\log(\mu) - \mu t_i$. The probability of one of the $N - n$ other persons not dying over the period is only the exponential of $-\mu t_i$ and its logarithm thus has the value $-\mu t_i$. The logarithm of the likelihood L that we are seeking to maximize is the sum of these logarithms for the n individuals who die in the period and the $N - n$ who are still alive:

$$\log(L) = n \log(\mu) - \mu \sum_i t_i.$$

The sum is extended to all the observations. The derivative at μ can be calculated immediately and gives the value of the maximum:

$$\mu = n \Big/ \left(\sum_i t_i \right).$$

This simple and general form shows that the rate is the number of deaths divided by the sum of the age intervals lived by all the individuals in the group. It is also the inverse of the mean time to occurrence of an event for an individual. This very broad formulation can be applied to any observed phenomenon: death, migration, birth, marriage, etc. Note that the mortality rate is more sensitive than the instantaneous

---

[8] According to a Dirac function of value $1/(n - p)$ for the pth death.

Table 1.2. Life-table calculated from mortality rates. (The third column is the inverse of the second, the fourth follows the formula $Q = 1 - e^{-12\mu}$. Multiplication by 12 is performed because μ is by month and Q by year.)

Time (years)	Number of deaths	$\sum_i t_i$	m (monthly)	Probabilities Q (yearly)	Survivors
0					1
1					1
	2	278	0.0072	0.083	
4					0.77
	3	61	0.049	0.45	
5					0.43
	2	28	0.071	0.57	
6					0.18
	1	32	0.031	0.31	
7					0.09
	1	15	0.067	0.55	
10					0.02

probability calculated using the Kaplan–Meier method: this is because it depends on the distribution of deaths during the period and not just on their number. Taking an a priori division by age, as was done for table 1.1, and assuming instantaneous probabilities are nearly everywhere nonzero, and thus mortality is a continuous process, the best way of calculating the life table is to use the rates. Doing the calculation with the same data and the same age groupings as in table 1.1 gives table 1.2.

The discrepancies with table 1.1 are greater at the higher time intervals, because the individual fluctuations (the position of the deaths within the age group) become large here. Note also that the table does not end with extinction since for that to be reached the rate would have to become infinite, something that cannot happen here given its method of estimation. The discrepancy between the two methods of calculation, based on a difference of hypothesis regarding the instantaneous probabilities, is not too serious, since with large numbers of observations, the mortality rate tends toward the instantaneous probability. The demonstration is given in the appendix (section 1.11.1) since it introduces a confirmation, not a new idea. The differences between the life tables in table 1.1 and table 1.2 are thus due primarily to the extremely small numbers used (nine deaths).

Although the exact formula for going from rates to probabilities (in the case of large numbers, thus with convergence of the rate on the probability) uses exponentials, and going in the opposite direction, logarithms, demographers often use an approximate formula:

$$\mu = q/(1 - \tfrac{1}{2}q).$$

This formula results from the similarity between the limited development of μ from the logarithm of $1 - q$ and the limited development of $1/(1 - \tfrac{1}{2}q)$:

$$\mu = -\log(1 - q) = q + \tfrac{1}{2}q^2 + \tfrac{1}{3}q^3,$$
$$q/(1 - \tfrac{1}{2}q) = q(1 + \tfrac{1}{2}q + \tfrac{1}{4}q^2) = q + \tfrac{1}{2}q^2 + \tfrac{1}{4}q^3.$$

The difference between the two expressions is $q^3/12$, or less than $1/10\,000$th when $q = 0.1$, which in practice represents a negligible quantity. There is, however, no reason to prefer an approximation to the exact formula.[9]

Postulating a constant rate between some ages is the first step toward looking for functions to represent deaths, probabilities, or survivors over large age ranges. It is all the more tempting to enunciate "laws of mortality" since remarkable regularities are observed in the many life tables constructed over the last three hundred years.

1.8   Exponential Functions: Gompertz, Makeham, Weibull

The most common "mortality law" in the universe is also the simplest. It is the exponential function in which the instantaneous probability $\mu(t)$ remains constant. This is the law followed by all radioactive atoms when they disintegrate. It derives from an important property: at any given time, the life expectancy of an atom is the same, which also means that its survival during a certain time does not alter its subsequent life expectancy. The survival function is thus exponential, as is the distribution of deaths. A remarkable particularity of the exponential law is that life expectancy remains the same regardless of duration.[10] Thus it is said that atoms never age, since their survival function does not change over time. The same is not true for people, rather the opposite, a fact that has been known ever since an actuary, Benjamin Gompertz (1825), noticed that, above the ages 35–40, the probabilities of dying followed an exponential function by age[11]:

$$\mu(x) = ae^{rx},$$

which is *Gompertz's law*.

Figure 1.4 displays the mortality probabilities for completed years of age between 0 and 105 years observed in France in 2000. The probabilities are plotted on a logarithmic scale, which transforms an exponential into a straight line. It is seen that after around age 40 the probabilities increase in a steady, almost linear, fashion.

---

[9] Especially since the reasons usually given to explain the approximation are incorrect, notably the equal distribution of events, since the survival function over the interval is negatively exponential.

[10] Life expectancy is written:

$$e(0) = \int_0^1 xe^{-rx}\,dx \Big/ \int_0^1 e^{-rx}\,dx = \frac{1}{r}.$$

As the survival at time t is e^{-rt}, life expectancy at t has the same value, since the survival function S_1 from t is the same as from 0:

$$S_1(x) = e^{-r(x+t)}/e^{-rt} = e^{-rx} = s(x).$$

[11] The Gompertz function gives a less good fit at the oldest ages, over age 90, where the increase in mortality probabilities slows down and, according to some authors, may even become constant (Le Bras 1976; Vaupel 1997).

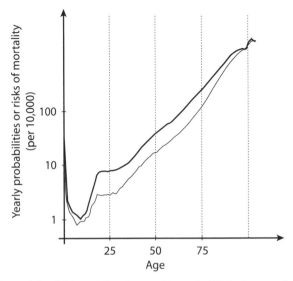

Figure 1.4. Male and female mortality probabilities by completed
years of age, France, 2000 (logarithmic scale on vertical axis).

There is a plateau preceding the exponential increase in the probabilities, and in
1860 another actuary, Makeham (1860), suggested adding a constant to Gompertz's
formula to adjust the probabilities after age 25:

$$\mu(x) = ae^{rx} + b.$$

Gompertz's law seems to be followed by all mammals,[12] though the situation is
less clear for the other forms of life. By contrast, machines and manufactured objects
(electric light bulbs, for example) follow instead a Weibull distribution, named after
its discoverer:

$$\mu(x) = Kx^{m}.$$

The explanation for the Weibull distribution is quite simple. It is the probability
function for the failure of the first component. There have been attempts to explain
Gompertz's law by the failure of the last component, but they are unconvincing.
A good example of the argument justifying the Weibull distribution is provided by
electric light bulbs: the assumption is that their filament is composed of a chain of
thousands of tiny segments, each of which has a probability $p(t)$ of failing at the end
of a time t. The failure of just one segment cuts the chain and hence the current, and
renders the bulb useless. The probability law for the first failure is easily calculated.
It has the form of a power of the length of time t. The discipline of reliability theory
has been established for studying the survival of machines and institutions.

---

[12] It seems that Gompertz's law does not hold at the oldest ages, which opens the possibility of extending
human life.

The Gompertz function is commonly used to estimate the mortality differences between regions or social groups for which the age-specific probabilities of dying are not all available, due to inadequate or incomplete information. Fortunately, using the maximum likelihood method the parameters of the distributions can be estimated directly from the individual lengths of life, and hence with relatively small samples. The method is developed in the appendix (section 1.11.2) for the most common cases, the exponential and the Gompertz. This is an important result because it can be obtained from a sample containing just a few dozen lengths of life, where the division into age groups to construct the life table would introduce large random fluctuations thereby masking the underlying regularity of a Gompertz function. Can we be sure that it really is underlying? It is advisable to check this by comparison with analogous cases: if the Gompertz function is observed in the life tables for all the countries of the world between ages 40 and 90, there is no reason that a regional or occupational subpopulation, for example, should be any different. If a doubt persists, however, a goodness-of-fit test, such as chi-square or Kolmogorov, may be used. To get an idea of the goodness of fit it may also be useful to compare graphically the survival function estimated by the Kaplan–Meier method with the theoretical curve estimated by maximum likelihood. The above may appear all very empirical, but let us remember that it is essential not to lose contact with the data.

1.9 Model Life Tables

The study of mortality is the oldest topic in demography, emerging in the second half of the seventeenth century in the work of Petty, Graunt, de Witt, and Huygens. Laws of mortality were first proposed in the eighteenth century (see, for example, Simpson 1742), and they appeared with accelerating frequency in the course of the nineteenth and twentieth centuries (Quetelet, Pearson, Fréchet, for example). None, however, gives an accurate description of mortality over the entire lifetime. But between an absolute empiricism that assumes no a priori structure, and the mortality laws that on the contrary postulate a rigid relation of dependence, an intermediate solution exists: *model life tables*. The idea behind these is to exploit the similarities observed between all known life tables. It is very likely that a table constructed with new data will be similar in form to previous tables. This nonformalized knowledge can be integrated using two possible methods: biometric standards and multivariate statistical estimation.

Biometric Standards

Let us return to the Gompertz function. By assumption there exists an ideal life table such that $q(x) = Ae^{Rx}$. Any other table in which the probabilities $q_1(x)$ also follow a Gompertz function $q_1(x) = ae^{rx}$ can be inferred from it by putting

$$e^x = (q(x))^{1/R}/(A)^{1/R}$$

from the formula giving the reference $q(x)$. Substituting for $q_1(x)$ into the formula gives

$$q_1(x) = a(q(x))^{r/R}/(A)^{r/R}$$

and, putting $a_1 = a/A^{r/R}$ and $r_1 = r/R$, gives

$$q_1(x) = a_1(q(x))^{r_1}.$$

The probability for any table is thus obtained from the probability of the reference table by a simple (log-linear) transformation. This new formulation has the advantage that an empirical, as opposed to a theoretical, life table can be used as the reference. In the case of Gompertz's law, this allows the range of ages for which the fit is good to be extended to the younger ages. A widely used method of this type is that of "standards" introduced and made popular by Brass in the 1970s. Brass (1971) replaces the probabilities in the previous relation by the ratio $g(x)$ of the dying to the living at age x in the table

$$g(x) = (1 - S(x))/S(x)$$

and then postulates that $g_1(x) = a_1(g(x))^{r_1}$.

The method is used and has chiefly been used in cases where data for some ages are missing. Parameters a_1 and r_1 are obtained by linear regression of the logarithms of the observed $g_1(x)$ on the logarithms of the reference $g(x)$. These logarithms are called the "logits" of the survival function since they correspond to the inverse of a logistic function (in other words, age is a logistic function of the logits).

Multivariate Statistics

A further step toward an empirically based approach is to do without the parameters a_1 and r_1 and estimate the probabilities directly by reference to one or several specific indicators (for example, life expectancy, infant mortality, or the probability of dying at ages 0–20) that are calculated from observations or by reference to the available probabilities if some are missing. This is a general problem of estimation: in the universe of known tables, the risks, the numbers dying or surviving at each age, and specific indicators—the "entries"—are all available. In the population being studied, only some particular entries are available. The probabilities have to be estimated from them while respecting the relation that links these probabilities to the entries in the universe of known tables. This problem is usually overcome by multiple regression of functions for the probabilities or the survivors (logarithms or logits) on the same functions for the entries. For each age, therefore, a particular relation is obtained linking the function for the probability to that for the various entries. For example, in the "network 202" of the model life tables constructed by Sully Ledermann,[13] the probability for each five-year age group is estimated by the

---

[13] With the new United Nations model life tables, they are the most rigorous as regards sample and method, but are old and hence do not include the low-mortality regimes.

formula:

$$\log(q_1(x, x+5)) = ax + bx \log(q_1(0, 15)) + cx \log(q_1(20, 50)).$$

The coefficients ax, bx, and cx are estimated by multiple regression on the sample of 157 tables selected by Ledermann, and thus vary for each age x. The probabilities over 15 years from birth ($q_1(0, 15)$) and between 20 and 50 years ($q_1(20, 50)$) were collected or calculated for the population studied and are thus obtained empirically and can take any reasonable value. The method can be used to determine, or more exactly to estimate, all the other $q_1(x)$ while respecting the overall structure of the known tables.

There are many other methods besides Ledermann's for construction of model life tables (Ledermann 1969; United Nations 1982; Coale and Demeny 1966; Gabriel and Ronen 1958; Le Bras 1968). None is very accurate since mortality varies between different societies, historical periods, and ecosystems. With standard regression software now available it is preferable to generate one's own set of model tables from known tables for situations close to that being studied. For example, if the aim is to know the state of mortality in a fairly limited area or for a particular occupation, we collect together the available life tables for a larger geographical or occupational scale that encompass the area or occupation being studied and the period being studied, and calculate the regression coefficients on this sample of tables.

The same procedure is used for population forecasting. To forecast mortality at each age for the years ahead, an assumption is made about life expectancy and perhaps also about the reduction of risks at some ages, then multiple regressions of the logarithms of the probabilities are performed on these quantified assumptions, described as "entries" by using the available life tables for the previous years. The entries are then extended into the future (for example, the rate of increase in life expectancy), and the regression formulas are applied to obtain the probabilities at each age in the years to come. Some official statistical agencies simply perform separate regressions of the probabilities at each age (or their logarithms) for the future years on those for past years at the same age. This approach better captures the temporal evolution at each age but it sacrifices the coherence of mortality at different ages, which is a remarkably constant feature of the phenomenon.

1.10   Life Insurance and Annuities

One of the reasons advanced to justify life tables and to account for their introduction is their usefulness for calculating annuities and life insurance. In fact, history did not follow such a simple utilitarian course. Annuities, for example, were already common in Holland by the thirteenth century without attempts being made to calculate mortality. But once the techniques of life-table calculation had been mastered (in the mid eighteenth century, through the contributions of Wargentin and Deparcieux) and the first private insurance companies founded, actuaries came on the scene and started using life tables.

Two operations are symmetrical. In annuities, the beneficiary makes a single payment to the insurer, who in return undertakes to pay him a sum annually up to his death or that of a nominated person. Conversely, in life insurance, the person makes an annual (or monthly) annuity payment in return for a predetermined amount to be paid on his death to the person of his choice. The key issue is to make the amount paid A proportional to the annuities a, and thus to compare the amounts over time. Let us first deal with the simple case where the annuity is taken out for n years only, and is thus in effect a fixed-term loan. Note that an amount a paid in p years has a present value of $a/(1 + i)^p$, where i is the rate of interest. For if we have an amount b, it could be immediately invested at rate of interest i, and p years later, with continuously compounded interest, would be worth $b(1 + i)^p$. Let a be this amount paid back after p years: $a = b(1 + i)^p$. The present value of a is thus the same as b, i.e., $a/(1 + i)^p$, as announced. We say that a has been *discounted*. The discounted payments p must therefore be equivalent to the amount loaned:

$$\frac{a}{(1 + i)} + \frac{a}{(1 + i)^2} + \frac{a}{(1 + i)^3} + \cdots + \frac{a}{(1 + i)^p} = A$$

or, expressing a in term of A,

$$a = \frac{Ai}{1 - 1/(1 + i)^{p+1}}$$

according to the sum of the geometric series.

If date p becomes infinitely large, we speak of a perpetual loan and the relationship is simpler still since the inverse of the power of $1 + i$ which is part of the denominator tends toward 0:

$$a = Ai.$$

Now assume that the annuity is paid only if the person is still alive. If he paid the initial amount at age t, his probability of being alive at $t + x$ is equal to $S(t + x)/S(t)$, where S designates the survival function of the life table corresponding to his case. On average, therefore, he can hope to recover the amount invested A by setting a such that:

$$\frac{S(t + 1)}{S(t)}\frac{a}{(1 + i)} + \frac{S(t + 2)}{s(t)}\frac{a}{(1 + i)^2} + \cdots + \frac{S(t + p)}{S(t)}\frac{a}{(1 + i)^p} + \cdots = A$$

or

$$a\left(\frac{S(t + 1)}{(1 + i)} + \frac{S(t + 2)}{(1 + i)^2} + \cdots + \frac{S(t + p)}{(1 + i)^p} + \cdots\right) = AS(t).$$

In the opposite direction, in the case of life insurance, if the person dies at the end of p years, his investment is

$$\frac{b}{(1 + i)} + \frac{b}{(1 + i)^2} + \frac{b}{(1 + i)^3} + \cdots + \frac{b}{(1 + i)^p} = \frac{B}{(1 + i)^p}.$$

The probability of dying at the end of exactly p years being $D(t + p)/S(t)$, where $D(t + p)$ designates the deaths in the life table for the age between $t + p$ and $t + p + 1$, by summing all the possible ages at death after t, we obtain

$$\frac{S(t+1)b}{(1+i)} + \frac{S(t+2)b}{(1+i)^2} + \cdots + \frac{S(t+p)b}{(1+i)^p} + \cdots$$

$$= \frac{D(t)B}{(1+i)} + \frac{D(t+1)B}{(1+i)^2} + \cdots + \frac{D(t+p-1)B}{(1+i)^p}.$$

The symmetry is not complete: two groups of persons cannot exchange the annuities held by the one for the life insurance held by the other, without going through a financial intermediary, since amount A is paid immediately and amount B at the end of the period. The two situations have one point in common: investors transfer to the insurer the risks associated with their demise. The insurer can assume this risk when the contracts are numerous because the law of large numbers allows him to balance the sums paid out by the sums received. However, the risk is not eliminated entirely since fluctuations still occur and mortality for the investors as a group is not known exactly and may change. In addition, the insurer is providing a service to the insured person and may consider it reasonable to charge for this service that relieves the client of a serious uncertainty. From these points plus the fact that interest rates vary over time, it can be seen that mortality is only one of many factors in play, which probably explains why insurers were slow to start using life tables.

There is an ethical difference between life insurance and annuities. The person who buys a life annuity can be described as selfish: he calculates so as to leave nothing for his heirs. By contrast the person who takes out life insurance is being altruistic since he wishes to pass on a lump sum to a third person, usually his surviving partner or children, after his death. Lorraine Daston, who has written on the history of probability (Daston 1988), highlights this contrast and shows that life insurance was tending to replace annuities in the second half of the eighteenth century. She infers from this a rise of family or at least parental sentiment at this time, preparing the way for changes in family structures and, shortly, in fertility. The idea is attractive but deserves further discussion, for in the case of an annuity placed on the life of a third person, usually someone younger, they outlive you and it is your children who benefit, so that altruism is combined with selfishness.

1.11   Appendix

1.11.1   Convergence of the Estimation of the Mortality Rate to the Instantaneous Probability

Let μ be the mortality rate, q the mortality probability, t_i the length of life before the ith death, n the number of deaths in the period, N the number of individuals observed in the period. In addition, without loss of generality, the length of the period may be set at 1.

We know that $q = n/N$ and $\mu = n/(\sum_i t_i + N - n)$. At the end of the period, survival is thus $1 - n/N$ when computed using the finite probability q and $e^{-\mu}$ when computed with the instantaneous probability. It must be shown that these two quantities tend to converge when N is large.

We write

$$\sum_i t_i = n \left(\sum_i t_i \right) \bigg/ n = n \times \text{the observed mean of the } t_i.$$

The law of large numbers tells us that the observed mean m tends to the mathematical expectation, thus to:

$$m = \left(\int_0^1 x e^{-\mu x} \right) \bigg/ \left(\int_0^1 e^{-\mu x} \right)$$

since the deaths between 0 and 1 are distributed proportionally to the survival function $e^{-\mu x}$. Integrating the numerator by parts yields

$$m = \frac{-e^{-\mu}/\mu + (1 - e^{-\mu})/\mu^2}{(1 - e^{-\mu})/\mu},$$

which simplifies to $m = 1/\mu - e^{-\mu}/(1 - e^{-\mu})$.

Substituting this expression into the formula for estimating μ yields

$$\mu = \frac{n}{n/\mu - ne^{-\mu}/(1 - e^{-\mu}) + N - n}$$

$$= \frac{n}{n/\mu + N - ne^{-\mu}/(1 - e^{-\mu})}$$

or

$$n + N\mu - \frac{n\mu e^{-\mu}}{1 - e^{-\mu}} = n.$$

Simplifying and dividing by μ, we get $N(1 - e^{-\mu}) = ne^{-\mu}$, that is, $e^{-\mu} = 1 - n/N$, a formula that expresses the equality of survivals by the two methods, hence the coherence of the calculation of rates and that of probabilities.

1.11.2 Maximum Likelihood Principle

The maximum likelihood principle is simple: we take the formula that gives the probability of obtaining the sample obtained and look for the values that maximize this probability. In most usual situations, the estimation obtained is robust and converges to the real values as sample size increases. Since it can generally be assumed that the observations are independent of each other, the sample probability is the product of the probabilities for each observation, which in the present case are none other than the probabilities of dying:

$$L = \prod_i p_i,$$

where L designates the sample probability or likelihood, and p_i that of the ith observation.

For example, in the exponential case it was seen that $p_i = re^{-rt_i}$. For a sample of n observations, the likelihood will be

$$L = \sum_i re^{-rt_i} = r^n \exp\left(-r \sum_i t_i\right)$$

and the value of r is chosen that maximizes L, thus equating the derivative to zero. Usually, for ease of calculation, the logarithm of the likelihood L is used, whose maximum has the same value r:

$$\frac{d\log(L)}{dr} = \frac{n}{r} - \sum_i t_i = 0,$$

where $r = n / \sum_i t_i$; the rate of increase of the exponential that gives the best fit to the observations is thus the inverse of the mean length of life or the mean age at death. For the Gompertz function that depends on two parameters, a and r, it is not as quick but does not present difficulties. It results in two equations for the two parameters:

$$a = \frac{r}{\sum_i e^{rt_i}/n - 1} \quad \text{and} \quad \frac{n}{r} = \frac{\sum_i i\, e^{rt_i}}{e^{rt_i}/n - 1} - \sum_i t_i.$$

The second equation is solved by considering it as a sequence of values r: beginning from a first value, the second member is calculated, from which the value of n/r is inferred and thus a second value for r, which is substituted into the second member, and so on. Convergence is rapid. Equation solving software, using the Newton–Raphson technique for example, may also be used. If several maximums appear (as is the case here where one of them is very close to $r = 0$), the one giving the highest value of L is selected.

2

Fertility

Fertility describes and measures the reproduction of a population. It is usually distinguished from fecundity, which refers to the biological capacity for reproduction regardless of whether any actual reproduction takes place. The opposite of fecundity is sterility, whereas fertility has no opposite, merely a large array of indices that measure its different aspects. To show how these indices combine to produce an overall representation of the process, we start from the most immediate but most complete data possible: the life histories of women observed between ages 10 and 50 for which the age reached by each at the birth of her children or age at maternity is known to within one month. It will not take long to see that this set of life histories can be simply summarized. But if we want to understand the large differences in fertility observed between populations, we must go beyond the stage of biographical description and ask how these series of births are determined and how the intervals between the births are distributed. We do this by examining the intermediate determinants or components that lead to fertility as it is observed: the probability of conceiving, the probability of intrauterine mortality, the nonsusceptible periods after live births or miscarriages, age at onset of permanent sterility. These parameters regulate fertility and in the recent past provided the basis for the controversial notion of "natural fertility." Controversial, because from time immemorial fertility has been controlled through individual and social procedures: age at marriage, widowhood, divorce, and remarriage; pregnancy termination or induced abortion, contraception, temporary or permanent sterilization. By introducing these modes of control into the natural fertility model, it is possible to describe the fertility regime of any actual or historical human population with great precision; numerical simulations are necessary given the multiple and complex interactions between the various modes of control and components of fertility. However, it will be seen that the black box of the computer can be avoided by establishing a relatively simple formula that integrates the biological and volitional parameters of fertility at the macroscopic level.

2.1   Measures of Fertility in the Absence of Mortality

Figure 2.1 shows a simple drawing of a series of eight female life histories starting at age 10 and ending at age 50. Each is made up of a separate line on which dots

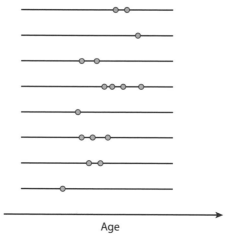

Age

Figure 2.1. Representation of eight female life histories for total reproductive period (ages 10 to 50). The dots indicate births. The vertical order of the biographies is not significant.

represent the exact ages of the mothers at the birth of each child. All the lines reach 50 years, the upper age limit of fertility, which supposes that all the women were present and thus alive at this age. If some women had died before age 50, their lifelines would be interrupted at the exact date of their death. In this case we would say the data were "censored," in the sense of "cut," because an event had impeded observation. Fertility will be considered here in the absence of mortality. In the next chapter, mortality will be introduced, making it possible to study the impact of its censoring of fertility.

The lifelines from figure 2.1 are used to plot a cumulative curve of the births occurring before age x (figure 2.2). At the date of each birth, the cumulative curve jumps by a step of height $1/n$, where n denotes the total number of lifelines (eight in the example). Thus it is simple to read off the average number of children per woman at each age (the number of children born before the age considered is divided by the number of women, eight here). This is described as *cumulative fertility at age x*. When the women have gone beyond the age of childbearing, the curve stays horizontal at the level of the *completed fertility*, the final fertility attained by this population, which is 2 children per woman in figure 2.2 (16 births for 8 mothers). Designating as $E(x)$ total fertility at age x, we can infer from it the number of children per woman born between two ages x_1 and x_2 of the mothers:

$$F(x_1, x_2) = E(x_2) - E(x_1).$$

This number will be higher, of course, the longer the interval used. To obtain a measure of fertility that is independent of the interval selected, the interval (x_1, x_2) can be divided into m intervals over which the mean number of children born is assumed to be the same. Over an interval $(x_2 - x_1)/m$ located between x_1 and x_2,

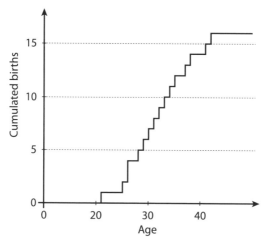

Figure 2.2. Cumulated births occurring before each age x for the sample of eight lifelines in figure 2.1. (Dividing this number by eight gives cumulative fertility at age x.)

we then have an average of $F(x_1, x_2)/m$ children. It is simplest to measure fertility in the selected unit of time by putting

$$f(x_1, x_2) = F(x_1, x_2)/(x_2 - x_1).$$

By convention, $f(x_1, x_2)$ is called the *fertility rate between ages x_1 and x_2*. If we represent these fertility rates by age, we obtain a histogram of exactly the mean number of children per women by age. Ultimately, when x_1 and x_2 are very close, we can write

$$\mathrm{d}x = x_2 - x_1 \quad \text{and} \quad f(x)\,\mathrm{d}x = F(x_1, x_2) = F(x_1, x_1 + \mathrm{d}x).$$

We call $f(x)$ the *instantaneous fertility rate at age x*. Up to this point we have avoided speaking of risk and probability, since over quite a long period a woman may give birth to several children, which is why the mean number of children is used. But over a very short time interval, a woman can have only one child or none. $f(x)\,\mathrm{d}x$ may then be considered as the probability of a birth during the time interval $\mathrm{d}x$ spanning age x. It is also a risk of birth, though this term is not generally used.

It will be seen immediately that completed fertility DF is the sum over the total reproductive age span (ages 10 to 50) of the fertility rates multiplied by their defining intervals:

$$\mathrm{DF} = (x_2 - 10)f(10, x_2) + (x_3 - x_2)f(x_2, x_3) + \cdots + (50 - x_k)f(x_k, 50).$$

When the age intervals are annual, completed fertility is simply the sum of the annual fertility rates since the intervals have a value of 1. To go further in the description of fertility, attention must now turn to the distribution of births along a single lifeline, which forms the subject matter for models of reproduction. The Italian statistician

Corrado Gini laid the foundations for such models in 1924 by defining *fecundability* and showing how this can be modeled simply to describe the distribution of first births in a population.

2.2   Gini and Fecundability

It was in the somewhat unlikely setting of the Toronto Mathematics Congress in 1924 that Gini presented the first model of reproduction. His paper (Gini 1924) begins with a definition that still holds: "I call female fecundability the probability of a married woman conceiving in a month, in the absence of any Malthusian or neo-Malthusian practice." At that time, *neo-Malthusian* signified "contraceptive," in contrast to the *Malthusian* practice of delayed marriage or voluntary abstinence within marriage. Saying that the woman is married makes the assumption that she has regular, not occasional, sexual relations. Gini therefore directed his attention to the timing of first births after marriage. For this purpose he had access to precise Italian statistics giving the monthly frequency of first births after marriage by region. The frequency of these births peaks 10 months after marriage and then decreases steadily. Thanks to the notion of fecundability, Gini proposed a simple generator to account for this phenomenon: denoting fecundability by ϕ and assuming that conceptions begin 1 month after marriage (because, Gini says, of the unusual conditions produced by the honeymoon trip), ϕ children will be engendered in month 2, giving ϕ births in month 10. A proportion of the women, $1 - \phi$, will not conceive and will try again the next month, 3, when once again a proportion ϕ will conceive, equal to $(1 - \phi)\phi$ of the original number, and will give birth in month 11 after marriage. Once again, of the women who reach month 3 without conceiving, $1 - \phi$ will try in the next month and ϕ will succeed, resulting in $(1 - \phi)(1 - \phi)\phi$ births in month 12. More generally, the births will follow a negative binomial distribution, those corresponding to the nth month after marriage being in the proportion of $(1 - \phi)^{n-10}\phi$. When Gini compared this theoretical pattern with the data, he found that the observed distribution declined more slowly than the theoretical distribution predicted by his model. From this he cleverly deduced that fecundability is heterogeneous: some of the more fecund women conceive quickly, others are less fecund and have to wait a long while to conceive. This was in fact the result he wanted to find, since the heterogeneity of fecundability enabled him to defend a biological theory of the cycle of nations based on the idea of a gradual degeneration of reproductive function. Gini's model has outlived his fantastical theories and has provided the core for subsequent microsimulation models of reproduction.

2.3   Models of Reproduction

In Gini's model, the births are distributed month by month according to a geometric progression with a frequency of $(1 - \phi)^{n-10}\phi$ for the nth month. Dividing this expression by 12 (interval of one month, counted by year), these frequencies are the fertility rates as defined earlier. More exactly, they are fertility rates for first births, not for all births. Would it not be possible to follow the first birth with a second, then a third and so forth, and thus reconstitute fertility for all birth orders together? Louis Henry developed this idea in 1953 by assuming that after the first birth there is a fixed delay or *nonsusceptible period* between two successive conceptions due to the pregnancy and a temporary postpartum sterility, after which the possibility of conceiving, and hence fecundability, is restored. A second birth can occur according to the same process as the first, that is, according to the Gini model, the date of the end of the nonsusceptible period having the same role as marriage for the first birth. Then, in the same conditions, a third birth and so forth, until the onset of permanent sterility.

Using these simple elements, Henry defined a process—in effect a "machine"—for building families, if the word *family* is used to mean merely the list of dates of the marriage and the births of the children.[1] The results from this new model cannot be obtained directly by calculation. This requires a microsimulation: events are simulated by computerized random drawings analogous to throwing dice or drawing balls from an urn. In Henry's first model, p black balls and q white balls are placed in an urn, so that fecundability has the value $p/(p + q)$, and a ball is drawn each month when ovulation occurs. If the ball is white, conception does not occur and we go on to the next month. If the ball is black, conception occurs, followed 9 months later by a birth, and after the nonsusceptible period of length T_m the drawings begin again until another black ball is drawn. The computer simulates these drawings by generating a number evenly distributed between 0 and 1. If the number generated is less than the fecundability ϕ, conception does not occur and we advance to the next month where drawing is repeated for as long as the end of the reproductive period has not been reached. All these stages can be summarized in a flow diagram showing the successive states occupied (figure 2.3), the assumptions being that marriage occurs at age 15 and that fecundability ceases at age 50. In this way complete fictitious family histories are generated, from which to calculate the fertility function.

Table 1.1 gives an example of the successive drawings performed to simulate the construction of a family following a marriage at age 25 (i.e., age 300 months), and taking a fecundability of 0.2 and a nonsusceptible period of 12 months. The first conception occurs 11 months after the marriage since the first 11 random numbers drawn are higher than fecundability, 0.2. The twelfth (0.064 71) being lower, conception occurs, followed by the birth 9 months later. To this is added the nonsusceptible period of 12 months, so that the possibility of a conception does not return until month 332. The process continues up to conception number 12 in month 591, which is the last one, since, when the pregnancy and the nonsusceptible period are

---

[1] This model served as the prototype for the family reconstitution forms ("fiches").

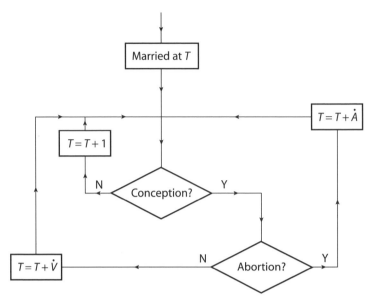

Figure 2.3. Flow chart of Louis Henry's microsimulation of reproduction. Marriage takes place at T. The rectangles indicate the progression of time and the lozenges the decisions made using random numbers equally distributed between 0 and 1. (N, no; Y, yes; A is the length of the nonsusceptible period after a conception leading to a spontaneous abortion; V is the length of the nonsusceptible period after conception leading to a live birth.)

ended, month 612 has been reached, which is beyond the end of the reproductive life at 50 years. This example is easy to implement and is already quite realistic. It shows, for example, a wide disparity in the intervals between births. Thus it is tempting to introduce other factors to make the model still more realistic.

2.4   Variation in Fecundability with Age, Intrauterine Mortality, and Permanent Sterility

A more precise picture of fecundity, that is, the capacity of couples to conceive children (in contrast to fertility,[2] which is a measurable consequence of fecundity), has been built up from sample surveys, analysis of life histories for historical populations reconstituted from parish registers, and from medical observations. First to be brought to light was the variation in fecundability over a woman's lifetime. Somewhat lower in youth, it remains more or less constant between ages 20 and 35, then declines quite rapidly before disappearing at age 50. Simultaneously, or in conjunction, with this, the proportion of permanently sterile women increases after age 25, rising from around 3% to 100% at age 50. Furthermore, conception does not necessarily lead to a live birth. A miscarriage occurs in roughly one quarter of cases.

---

[2] An overview of the factors influencing fertility is given in Bongaarts and Potter (1983).

Table 2.1. Simulation of a fertility history using random numbers.

Random number	Month	Cumulative conceptions	Random number	Month	Cumulative conceptions
0.498 13	300	0	0.124 47	366	2
0.217 43	301	0	0.133 25	387	3
0.695 10	302	0	0.146 87	408	4
0.917 34	303	0	0.166 70	429	5
0.850 90	304	0	0.031 07	450	6
0.875 35	305	0	0.959 82	471	7
0.230 79	306	0	0.148 79	472	7
0.718 00	307	0	0.050 30	493	8
0.868 15	308	0	0.890 48	514	9
0.532 28	309	0	0.710 83	515	9
0.924 16	310	0	0.429 21	516	9
0.064 71	311	0	0.259 68	517	9
0.288 10	332	1	0.589 34	518	9
0.908 56	333	1	0.350 64	519	9
0.643 19	334	1	0.422 78	520	9
0.517 70	335	1	0.307 01	521	9
0.284 50	336	1	0.774 51	522	9
0.248 17	337	1	0.449 38	523	9
0.997 89	338	1	0.446 06	524	9
0.983 11	339	1	0.182 98	525	9
0.729 78	340	1	0.478 96	546	10
0.930 70	341	1	0.542 50	547	10
0.534 57	342	1	0.016 28	548	10
0.086 16	343	1	0.629 95	569	11
0.816 54	364	2	0.098 34	570	11
0.305 06	365	2	0.110 43	591	12

Lastly, the duration of the nonsusceptible period after a live birth or miscarriage varies. All of these elements have been incorporated in the simulation. The variation in fecundability with age appears in table 2.2. For the proportion of sterile women we have used an exponential distribution starting from 3% at age 25 and reaching 100% at 50. Also indicated in the table are the distributions of nonsusceptible periods after live birth and spontaneous abortion.[3]

2.5 Natural Fertility

A simulation performed using the mechanism in figure 2.3 produces the fertility function by age in figure 2.4. This is a maximum fertility since it is assumed that all

---

[3] The numerical values are given to allow the reader to perform the same simulations using the flow diagram in figure 2.3.

Table 2.2. Fecundability by age and distribution of nonsusceptible periods by duration.

| Age (years) | Fecundability | Duration (months) | Distribution of nonsusceptible periods after | |
			Spontaneous abortions	Live births
15–19	0.172	1	0	0
20–24	0.242	2	0.08	0
25–29	0.250	3	0.25	0
30–34	0.240	4	0.34	0
35–39	0.200	5	0.25	0
40–44	0.115	6	0.08	0
45–49	0.022	7		0
		8		0
		9		0
		10		0.02
		11		0.03
		12		0.07
		13		0.14
		14		0.14
		15		0.20
		16		0.14
		17		0.14
		18		0.07
		19		0.03
		20		0.02

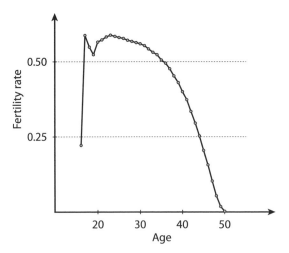

Figure 2.4. Age-specific fertility in a population practicing no fertility control ("natural" fertility). Results from microsimulation.

the women are exposed to the risk of conception between ages 15 and 50. The peak at the start of the curve, corresponding to the birth of the first child, is artificial. It arises from the fact that all the women experience the onset of reproductive capacity at exactly age 15. In reality there is variability in age at first ovulation. Thereafter, however, the curve becomes smooth, as the random variations in fecundability, in the length of the nonsusceptible period after live birth, and in intrauterine mortality spread births of the same order over an increasingly wide age range. Overall, in these conditions of maximal fertility, a woman exposed to the risk of conception between ages 15 and 50 (remaining married during this time, for example) gives birth on average to 14.8 children (this is the area under the fertility curve), and between ages 17 and 35, each year, the woman has more than a one-in-two chance of having a child. Regarding this curve, reference has been made to a "natural" fertility, that is, the absence of any attempt by couples to control their family size. That view was too hasty since the results from observation of populations and societies presumed not to control fertility (the Hutterites in early-eighteenth-century France) are both different—the average number of births per woman never exceeds 10 among the Hutterites and 6 in historical France—and contradictory, which would suppose more than one level of natural fertility and thus differences between populations in the biological capacity to reproduce. In fact, confusion had occurred between maximal fertility, which is a biological limit, in the same way as man's maximal height or maximal length of life may be, and a natural fertility that was held to prevail in actual populations. Yet after the admirable study by Frank Lorimer (1954), it is legitimate to think that throughout human history every population has employed means for controlling fertility, and that consequently there has never been a population whose fertility was, if not actually controlled by couples, at least codified by customs and social practices. The fertility represented in figure 2.4 thus marks an upper limit that no human population can exceed. It provides a reference against which to judge the impact of the various modes of fertility control employed by human populations. A set of mechanisms—both social and volitional—bring about a very large reduction in reproductive capacity, since, outside of a few small and special groups, completed fertility in historical populations has invariably ranged between 4 and 7 children, well short of the 15 possible under maximal fertility.

2.6   Fertility Controls

For each stage of the process represented on the flow chart in figure 2.3, there cor-responds a particular fertility control. In the order of the diagram these are: age at marriage, which in populations where relations between the sexes are confined to marriage virtually eliminates reproductive risk from the period before marriage; then contraception, which reduces fecundability and hence the probability of con-ceiving in the course of a cycle; then abortion, which is equivalent to an increase

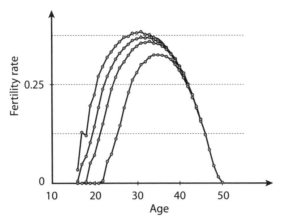

Figure 2.5. Age-specific fertility for different values of mean age at marriage: in order of curves, 50% of women married at ages 19, 21, 23, and 27 (microsimulation).

in intrauterine mortality; then medical sterilization; and finally the lengthening of the nonsusceptible period after live births, notably through extended breastfeeding. None of these controls operates alone. They are combined in characteristic fertility regimes dominated by one of the modes of control: late marriage if it is age at marriage, contraception if it is control of fecundability, induced abortion, and extended breastfeeding. We shall see that each of these controls has a different action and that combining them is not simple. To do this we use the month (or period) by month microsimulation mechanism and start from a composite reference situation of relatively early marriage (50% of women married at age 21) and short mean nonsusceptibility (12 months after birth), negligible abortion and no contraception. Such a regime is not unlike that in Eastern Europe before the nineteenth century. Within this basic regime, we will introduce the four main means of control and measure their impact.

2.7   Effect on Fertility of Age at Marriage

In societies where extramarital births are socially frowned upon, and hence quite rare, postponing marriage for women to higher ages reduces exposure to the risk of conception and hence fertility. This method—that Malthus recommended under the label of "moral restraint"—was widely practiced by the populations westward of the Dubrovnik–Saint-Petersburg line (as demonstrated by John Hajnal) from the Renaissance onward and pushed the mean age at the first marriage of the women above 30 years in some parts of Northern Europe in the mid nineteenth century since when it has spread to become general throughout the world. The impact of delayed marriage is studied by drawing at random the age of entry into reproductive life using a known probability distribution, and then shifting this distribution by a

Table 2.3.

Age at which 50% of women are married	Completed fertility
19	9.0
21	8.2
23	7.5
25	6.6
27	5.8

certain number of years depending on the case. Figure 2.5 represents the fertility curves obtained with this assumption. This control is introduced into the model by a distribution of the women's ages at first marriage, from which we select at random the age at marriage that we use as the start point for the family-building process. The four curves correspond to the nonsusceptible periods from table 2.2 increased by 6 months in the case of live births, and to a distribution of the reference marriages (50% of marriages at age 21), then moved forward by 2 years, and delayed by 2 years and 6 years. We see immediately that the fertility curves converge once most of the unions have taken place. The importance of the Malthusian control is reflected in the variation of completed fertility (see table 2.3).

If in addition to delayed age at marriage we take into account the sizeable proportion of women never marrying (between 10 and 15% in western Europe in the eighteenth century), completed fertility goes down to 5.5 children for a mean age at first marriage of 25 years. With half of all children dying before their fifth birthday, slightly more than two children per woman eventually reached the age of marriage, a proportion that in the absence of major mortality crises would ensure moderate population growth. Except for western Europe, we possess no example of this model of regulation in other major cultural zones. In many premodern societies, the control of fertility through marriage—in the opposite direction—was achieved by a relatively rapid dissolution of marriages, due either to widowhood (because of too large an age gap with the husband) or to repudiation or easily available dissolution with no subsequent remarriage (the case of some populations in Southeast Asia).

2.8 Length of Nonsusceptible Period after Live Births and Fertility

Little attention was at first given to this factor since nonsusceptible periods, and hence the intervals between successive births, are fairly short in Europe. But as knowledge about the fertility of African and Asian populations increased, it was realized that this factor had a primordial role. This is clear from figure 2.6, which displays the fertility curves by age produced by four microsimulations in which

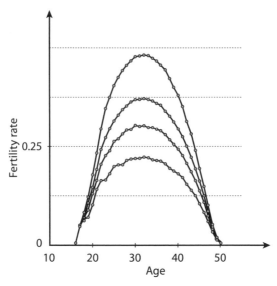

Figure 2.6. Age-specific fertility for different values of mean duration of nonsusceptible period after live birth: in order of curves, 6, 12, 18, and 30 months (microsimulation).

only the mean length of the nonsusceptible period differs, all other parameters of the reproductive mechanism remaining the same. Between the highest fertility (corresponding to a mean nonsusceptible period of 6 months after the birth) and the lowest (nonsusceptible period of 30 months, or two and a half years), fertility is halved. More precisely, we obtain the values in table 2.4 for completed fertility (with the age at marriage distribution corresponding to 50% of women married at age 21).

Note that the longer the nonsusceptible period to begin with, the smaller the reduction in completed fertility. An increase of 6 months corresponds to 2.3 fewer children in the first case, and to 0.7 fewer children in the fourth. It is also seen that the fertility curves are parallel or more exactly affine in form, that is to say, the ratio of their fertility rates varies little with age. These regularities will be explained later.

It has been demonstrated empirically that the mean length of birth intervals in any given population varies in the same direction as the mean duration of breast-feeding. Numerous studies have attempted to clarify the physiological basis of the relationship between the two phenomena, though without producing conclusive results. They have ruled out the idea of a relationship between breastfeeding and an absence of ovulation (mediated by blood fat levels, for example). Anthropological explanations have not obtained better results. The lengthening of intervals is observed indifferently among populations that practice a prohibition of sexual abstinence during breastfeeding and among those that recommend the opposite. There remains the statistical evidence of a precise coincidence between the mean duration

Table 2.4.

Mean length of nonsusceptible period (months)	Completed fertility
6	10.5
12	8.2
18	6.8
24	5.9
30	5.1

of breastfeeding and that of nonsusceptibility. The importance of this factor needs to be stressed. As was the case for late marriage, the role of the lengthening of nonsusceptibility is enough to prevent population growth in countries with high mortality, which was the case in Africa and Asia fifty years ago.

The lengthening of the nonsusceptible period cannot be described as volitional. Rather it is customary, imposed on mothers by their family and social environment, but its effectiveness in reducing completed fertility makes it a remarkable fertility control in high-mortality populations. How, in the absence of individual calculation, did the idea of this control appear? It is possible that it is a survival from the era of hunter–gatherers, who are known to have quite low fertility as a result of lengthy intervals between births. Hunter–gatherers practicing nomadism over large expanses of territory are frequently on the move. A mother will thus have difficulty carrying two young children over long distances and must try to avoid this situation by lengthening the intervals between births. How did the hunter–gatherers achieve long intervals? Information about these residual populations, nowadays confined in hostile habitats, is inadequate, but several hypotheses have been put forward: extended breastfeeding, abortion of one in two births, and infanticide.

For as long as mortality in childhood and youth exceeded half of all births, the combination of lengthy nonsusceptible periods with control of marriage durations, and hence of the period of exposure to risk of conception, was quite enough to keep fertility within limits corresponding to stationarity or low population growth. But when mortality declined sharply, enabling the great majority of children to reach adulthood (80% in the early nineteenth century, 95% in 1950, 98% at present in the developed countries), it was no longer possible to regulate fertility through the two traditional means, except by postponing marriage to beyond age 35 or by lengthening the birth interval to ten years, both solutions that were culturally incompatible with family structures and life cycles in the countries—Europe, Asia, and Africa—involved. It was at this time that contraception and abortion, already well-known in specific sections of society (among prostitutes, for example), became widespread, as did sterilization.

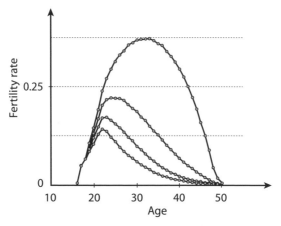

Figure 2.7. Age-specific fertility for different levels of contraception: a priori probabilities of having another child of 100%, 80%, 60%, and 40% in vertical order of curves (microsimulation).

2.9   Contraception

The name *contraception* is applied to any voluntary technique that reduces the level of fecundability. A distinction is made between traditional methods—coitus interruptus, the Ogino (temperature), or rhythm method—and modern methods—the pill, the intrauterine device. The impact of these methods is measured by calculating contraceptive *efficiency*, which is the ratio of the number of averted conceptions to the total number of possible conceptions. Thus, 95% efficiency for the temperature method means that 95% of conceptions are averted, so that the probability of conceiving (fecundability) over the cycle is reduced to 5% of its value in the absence of contraception. The traditional methods are between 90 and 95% efficient, meaning that their use reduces fecundability to 5–10% of its value. The modern methods are more than 99% effective, reducing fecundability to less than one hundredth of its value. Abortion is often used in the event of a failure of contraception, but in certain contexts, such as Japan and the countries of Eastern Europe after World War II, it has also become the main mode of fertility regulation.

The fertility curves for populations using contraception are very different from the curves seen so far. Figure 2.7 gives several examples that have been simulated in the following way. The assumption was made that after each birth, a proportion $1 - k$ of the women decided to stop having children completely, while proportion k continued without contraception. Starting from the standard population used in the previous examples (50% of women married at age 21, mean nonsusceptible period of 12 months), the curves of figure 2.3 correspond respectively to the case with no contraception, then to values for k of 0.8, 0.6, and 0.4 with 99.5% efficiency. Contraception has a marked impact on fertility (see table 2.5).

Table 2.5.

$(1-k)$ a priori parity progression ratio or probability of having at least one more child	Completed fertility
1.0	8.2
0.8	3.8
0.6	2.3
0.4	1.6

The lower the probability k, the smaller are families and the faster they attain their final size. After age 25 the fertility curve falls back and becomes concave instead of convex.

In this example it was assumed, first, that contraceptive efficiency was very high (the women could equally well have chosen sterilization), and, second, that the proportion of women who wished to go on having children after a birth was independent of the number of children they already had. Both of these propositions deserve discussion. Introducing contraceptive efficiency assumes that some conceptions that one wanted to avert have occurred and have then developed toward a spontaneous abortion, an induced abortion, or a birth. So let us consider the demographic effect of abortion.

2.10   Induced Abortion

Start with the case studied in the previous section where the probability of having another child is 0.6 regardless of the birth order (solid curve in figure 2.8) and assume that the contraception used by the women who decided to stop childbearing is 98.5% effective instead of 100%. By microsimulation we obtain the fertility curve represented by the lower dotted line in figure 2.8, which is consistently higher than the first. 0.35 of an additional child is born because of the mere 1.5% of extra fecundability. This is not surprising since between ages 15 and 50 there are 420 months. A tiny risk that is experienced many times eventually produces the event associated with it. If instead of a modern method of contraception a traditional method had been used, the efficiency would have been lower, in the region of 95%. The failures would then be far more numerous. In figure 2.8 we see that in these circumstances fertility is indeed considerably higher than was intended since on average 0.95 of a child was conceived during a period of contraception (the upper dotted line). Can these unintended births be averted by induced abortion? That will depend on the legislative context and on the attitude of the parents toward this procedure. But making the assumption that induced abortion is performed for each contraceptive failure, the number of abortions will exceed that of averted births (the

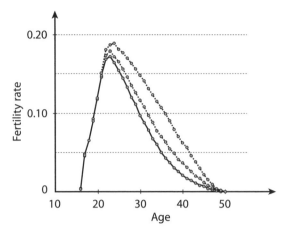

Figure 2.8. Age-specific fertility by efficiency of contraception: 100% for the solid line, 98.5% for the lower dotted line, 95% for the upper (microsimulation).

previous simulations give respectively 0.4 and 1.2 abortions per woman for 98.5% and 95% efficiency compared with 0.35 and 0.95 children averted). The explanation for this difference lies with the periods of exposure to the risk. In the case of an abortion, the mean nonsusceptible period lasts 4 cycles, but in the case of a birth it is $9 + 12 = 21$ cycles. After an abortion, therefore, and compared with a live birth, the risk of conception is experienced for an additional 17 cycles, during which a new conception may occur and thus be followed by a new abortion.

The conclusion from this experiment is that abortion cannot be compared with averted births in the way that opponents of voluntary termination generally do. This point becomes obvious when abortion is used not as a backup to failed contraception but directly as the means for controlling fertility. This was the case in the Eastern European countries and Japan after World War II. Pregnancy termination was easily obtainable whereas the pill was either unavailable or banned by law. By means of microsimulation we can calculate the mean number of abortions per woman that would be necessary to restrict fertility to 2.1 children. It would reach the huge figure of 14.2, or 7 times more abortions than births. The number of abortions in the Eastern European countries and the USSR, though very high, was seldom more than double that of births. The conclusion must therefore be that abortion was not the only means of controlling fertility. Traditional and primitive forms of contraception, plus abstinence and perhaps sterilization, were in use. For the figure of 14.2 abortions we can see more clearly that it is not possible to speak of 14.2 averted births. Without contraception but with nuptiality and nonsusceptibility unchanged, completed fertility would in fact be 8.2 children, as we saw earlier. So the 14.2 abortions correspond to $8.2 - 2.1 = 6.1$ fewer births.

The difference between a completely effective control, either by sterilization or by contraception combined with abortion, and a more lax control during which a conception can occur, is often used to contrast two kinds of contraceptive behavior: contraception for the stopping and the spacing of births. In birth spacing, the woman or couple make efforts to space the births of their children, while in birth stopping their intention is to avoid them occurring. It was often thought that contraception for birth spacing came before contraception for birth stopping, but the historical evidence for this is not convincing. More plausible is that couples initially have recourse to a contraception that is not especially effective but easy to use, before choosing a more radical solution following a failure. Behavior of this kind can be simulated in the modeling of contraception: after each birth, it is postulated that a proportion of women, k, adopts contraception of low effectiveness (90% for example), then, at the next child, completely effective contraception or sterilization. Mixed models can also be imagined, in which, after each birth, one or other mode of contraception is adopted according to a certain probability. But we must avoid introducing too many options, since the simulations derive their strength from a parsimonious reconstitution of the observations, that is, with as few parameters as possible. It may prove necessary, however, to use both stages of contraception (which imposes only one new parameter, the efficiency of the first mode of contraception) to account for the observed lengthening of the interval between the penultimate and last births. Another advantage is that this yields probabilities of having another child with high values for the first and second births, and lower subsequently, which is consistent with the observations made in modern populations, where completed fertility stands at around 2 children.

2.11 Probabilities of Having Another Child and Parity

The probability k of continuing childbearing after the birth of a child may depend on the birth order n. In this case it is denoted k_n. It has a direct influence on the distribution of mothers by the number of children they have borne. Thus in the previous example, where completed fertility was 2.1 children, the women are distributed by number of births (see table 2.6).

In the third column we have indicated the proportion of women who have had at least n children. We can calculate what proportion go on to have an $(n + 1)$th child after the nth child. This proportion appears in the fourth column. For the first child it is 0.89, since some unions are sterile for biological reasons. Thereafter, the values are very close to 0.6. The proportions k'_n are called *parity progression ratios of rank n* and $k = 0.6$ is an a priori parity progression ratio. The values for k'_n are slightly lower than those for k because some women who have continued their reproductive life have not conceived or have become sterile. For an initial approximation, we can equate k'_n with k and speak of parity progression ratios without specifying "a priori." These ratios have been calculated for many populations, and we give examples of them in chapter 5.

Table 2.6.

Number of births	Percentage of women	Percentage having this number of children or more	k'_n
0	11.1	100.0	0.89
1	36.8	88.9	0.59
2	21.9	52.1	0.59
3	13.1	30.2	0.57
4	7.3	17.1	0.57
≥5	9.8	9.8	

The parity progression ratios derived empirically from the distribution of women by the number of children they have had can be used in a microsimulation. More generally, any additional information about reproductive behavior—such as mean interbirth intervals, age-specific variations in intrauterine mortality and number of spontaneous abortions experienced, variations in the nonsusceptible period with the survival or death of the child (in which case breastfeeding ends, unless the woman takes another child to nurse)—can be included in the simulation. Microsimulation is thus a powerful instrument for interpolation, that is, for estimating missing individual data, in particular life histories, when only certain aggregate results are available.

It might be thought that with the growing number of factors for varying and controlling fertility it becomes impossible to establish general results. Not so. Despite the complexity of the reproductive process, a number of simple regularities can be identified.

2.12   Laws of Fertility

When there is neither contraception nor voluntary termination, a simple relation can be established between the general age-specific fertility rate and the parameters of the fertility model. For this we denote as C_t the proportion of women capable of conceiving in period t, and as TA_i and TV_i the distributions of the lengths i of the nonsusceptible periods (in months) after a conception leading to an abortion or a live birth. The proportion C_t of those in a state to conceive can be written as a function of their situation the previous month: already in a state to conceive or in a nonsusceptible state following abortion or live birth, with a the probability of spontaneous abortion and ϕ_i the fecundability at age i:

$$C_i = C_{t-1}(1 - \phi_{t-1}) + \sum_i C_{t-i}\phi_{t-i}(1 - a)TV_i + \sum_i C_{t-i}\phi_{t-i}a TA_i.$$

In part III it will be seen that this is a form of the renewal equation which has the ergodic property of weak convergence, that is, the initial conditions are quickly "forgotten." If fecundability is assumed to be constant over the intervals of the longest nonsusceptible period, C_t will tend toward a constant C that can be determined by writing the sum of the proportions in the different states with a value of 1 using the survival functions TA_i and TV_i in the two types of nonsusceptible periods:

$$C + C \sum_i \phi_{t-i}(1-a)\text{TV}_i + C \sum_i \phi_{t-i} a\text{TA}_i = 1.$$

An approximation can be made by replacing the values of the nonsusceptible periods after live birth and abortion by their means TV_m and TA_m:

$$C_t = \frac{1}{1 + \phi_{t-\text{TV}_\text{m}}(1-a)(\text{TV}_\text{m}-1) + \phi_{t-\text{TA}_\text{m}} a(\text{TA}_\text{m}-1)}.$$

And so for fertility at age t:

$$f_t = \frac{\phi_t}{1 - \phi_{t-1} + \phi_{t-\text{TV}_\text{m}}(1-a)\text{TV}_\text{m} + \phi_{t-\text{TA}_\text{m}} a\text{TA}_\text{m}}.$$

Lastly, it is necessary to introduce the proportion of married women not sterile at the time of the conception, or $N_t S T_t$, finally giving

$$f_t = \frac{N_t S T_t \phi_t}{1 - \phi_{t-1} + \phi_{t-\text{TV}_\text{m}}(1-a)\text{TV}_\text{m} + \phi_{t-\text{TA}_\text{m}} a\text{TA}_\text{m}}.$$

In figure 2.9 the approximation is seen to be good over most of the fertile age span (we have used a case of late marriage with short nonsusceptible period). The formula gives a good fit to the parallel form of the curves in figure 2.6 where only the mean length of the nonsusceptible period, TV_m, changes. It can also be used to estimate quickly the effect of a delay in age at marriage, for since fecundability, and therefore fertility, in marriage is virtually stable up to age 30, the number of children fewer will be the product of the marital fertility rate around age 25 and the value of the delay in age at marriage.[4]

Another simple way of justifying the fertility formula is to say that it is inversely proportional to the mean duration in the state of fecundability, thus to the frequency-weighted mean of the mean durations of each cycle, those of birth (TV_m), abortion (TA_m), and not conceiving (1), a total mean time that is therefore

$$t_\text{m} = \phi(1-a)\text{TV}_\text{m} + \phi a\text{TA}_\text{m} + (1-\phi).$$

Not all of these results can be transposed to populations practicing contraception. However, a way does exist of summarizing the great diversity of fertility functions for contracepting populations.

---

[4] The longer the nonsusceptible period after live birth, the greater the deviation between the formula and the value given by the microsimulation.

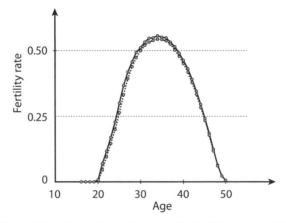

Figure 2.9. Comparison of age-specific fertility calculated by
microsimulation (solid line) and by the convergence formula (dotted line).

Table 2.7. Coale and Trussell coefficients.

Age i	f_i	F_i	F_i^*
20–24	0.460	0	0
25–29	0.431	−0.316	−0.426
30–34	0.396	−0.814	−0.825
35–39	0.321	−1.048	−1.192
40–44	0.167	−1.424	−1.643
45–49	0.024	−1.667	−1.667

2.13 The Coale–Trussell Formula

Ansley Coale and James Trussell (1974) discovered an interesting pattern in the
fertility rates of married women or marital fertility rates (those obtained only for
the sections of life histories between marriage and widowhood or divorce). They
showed that the five-year marital fertility rates $F_{i,j}$ at age i in a population j could
be written in the form

$$F_{i,j} = K_j f_i e^{-v_j F_i},$$

where K_j and v_j are two constants characteristic of the population j, f_i is a rate
of natural fertility at age i, and F_i a series of numerical coefficients valid for every
population. The values proposed by Coale and Trussell for f_i and F_i appear in
table 2.7.

In principle, when the fertility rates of a population j are known, the constants
$\log(K_j)$ and v_j are determined by linear regression on their logarithms. Another
advantage of the Coale–Trussell formula is in providing a set of age-specific rates
for a population on which data are scarce. This second use assumes that one knows

the specific meaning of the two parameters K_j and v_j and of the constants F_i. An interpretation can in fact be proposed, although Coale and Trussell restricted themselves to an empirical derivation.

For this we assume that the fertility function $f(x)$ is continuous and that it indicates the probability of a birth at age x independently of what has previously occurred (for example, a birth one month before). A priori, this assumption is false, but it does not distort the phenomenon greatly. It enables the succession of births to be considered as a Poisson process, a well-known process in probability theory that has several interesting properties. For example, naming $F(t)$ fertility at age t (thus cumulated fertility up to t), we can determine the probability of the first birth, the second, the nth as a function of age t:

$$F_n(t) = f(t)e^{-F(t)}F^{n-1}(t)/(n-1)!.$$

By adding together the different parities we again have fertility $f(t)$:

$$
\begin{aligned}
f(t) &= f(t)e^{-F(t)} + f(t)e^{-F(t)}F(t) + \tfrac{1}{2}f(t)e^{-F(t)}F^2(t) \\
&\quad + \cdots + f(t)e^{-F(t)}F^{n-1}(t)/(n-1)! + \cdots \\
&= f(t)e^{-F(t)}(1 + F(t) + \tfrac{1}{2}F^2(t) + \cdots + F^{n-1}(t)/(n-1)! + \cdots) \\
&= f(t)e^{-F(t)}e^{+F(t)} = f(t),
\end{aligned}
$$

as defined by series expansion of the exponential.

Now assume, as we did in the section dealing with contraception, that after each birth only a proportion k of women still want another child. Then, the probability of the nth parity will be

$$F_n(t) = k^n f(t)e^{-F(t)}F^{n-1}(t)/(n-1)!.$$

And the sum of the births at t, $f_1(t)$, will be, as previously, the sum of the births of all parities n, that is,

$$
\begin{aligned}
f_1(t) &= f(t)e^{-F(t)} + kf(t)e^{-F(t)}F(t) + \tfrac{1}{2}k^2 f(t)e^{-F(t)}F^2(t) \\
&\quad + \cdots + k^n f(t)e^{-F(t)}F^{n-1}(t)/(n-1)! + \cdots \\
&= f(t)e^{-F(t)}(1 + kF(t) + \tfrac{1}{2}(kF)^2(t) \\
&\qquad\qquad + \cdots + (kF)^{n-1}(t)/(n-1)! + \cdots) \\
&= f(t)e^{-F(t)}e^{+kF(t)} \\
&= f(t)e^{-(1-k)F(t)}.
\end{aligned}
$$

The formula obtained is identical to the Coale–Trussell if we put

$$K_j = 1, \qquad F_i = F(i), \qquad v_j = 1 - k.$$

We verify that Coale and Trussell's F_i coefficients are in fact close to the cumulated natural fertility rates F_i^* given in the last column of table 2.7.[5] Coefficient K_j depends on the duration of nonsusceptibility since we saw earlier that the natural fertility curves were affine, that is, inferred from each other by a coefficient of proportionality. Applying the formula with the F_i^* coefficients to the fertility rates from the simulations with contraception (figure 2.7), we obtain values for v_j of 0.81, 0.60, and 0.39, which are practically the same as the values of k used to construct the microsimulations (0.8, 0.6, and 0.4). The Coale–Trussell coefficient that measures the level of contraception can thus be considered as the complement of an a priori probability of having another child or an a priori parity progression ratio. This result is valuable for its simplicity but also because it establishes a link between the models produced so far and the observed data.

2.14   Male Fertility

The foregoing construction of fertility, based on what are known as proximate determinants and intermediate variables, is remarkable in many respects. Yet on the subject of men it is silent. Could a symmetrical model, in which men took the role of women, not be imagined? This idea is generally rejected because of the births outside marriage to fathers of unknown age (when the births are not recognized). This obstacle can be overcome when lifelines are available or if not, with general data, by assuming that the age of father distribution is the same for registered and unregistered births. In France, moreover, registration by the mother is also lacking in the case of the "accouchements sous X" (maternal anonymity), which does not prevent the calculations of female fertility being made on the assumption that the births "sous X" have the same age distribution as registered births. It might also be thought that choosing to make women responsible for reproduction reflected certain ideological presuppositions. This choice was made by statisticians in the late nineteenth century, though formerly reference had been to the fertility of couples. It occurred at a time when demography was developing closer ties with biology under the influence of social Darwinism.

   However, the obstacles to the inclusion of men in the analysis are at two other levels. The first is historical. It is not possible to transpose to male fertility behavior the detailed parameters presented in the analysis of female fertility, such as nonsusceptibility related to breastfeeding, intrauterine mortality, and induced abortions. The historical role and perception of these parameters has been in relation to female behaviors that have no equivalent in the male population. The only ones that can be used for men are nuptiality, permanent sterility, and the parity progression ratios describing contraception. We would be restricted therefore to the Poisson model that

---

[5] The two series of values have been put on the same scale by making their two coefficients equal in the last age bracket, 45–49 years.

was used to explicate the Coale–Trussell formula, a model that can explain the rates for aggregate data but not generate lifelines except by postulating a function for distributing the intervals between successive births to avoid the too closely spaced events of the Poisson process. This would be artificial since this interval function would be inferred directly from the pregnancy and breastfeeding durations of the mothers.

The second obstacle is epistemological. If men and women are considered simultaneously, we can no longer work directly from life histories. A diagram could be imagined on which the life histories of mothers and fathers are represented by lines that converge and run together for the duration of their unions, but such a schema would be impossible to transpose to a Lexis diagram, where, as will be seen later, age and time are represented simultaneously. In any case, a more serious problem arises: assuming—as is possible—that the male and female fertility functions are calculated on the same population, it is not generally possible to make them agree. For example, one sex may have a completed fertility well above 2 children and the other not. The problem is not confined to questions of fertility but also affects nuptiality. We introduced a distribution of ages of women at first marriage but a distribution of ages at first marriage also exists for men. It is difficult to link the two together since the combined age of the man and woman at first marriage depends on the number never married of each age and each sex. In addition, one of the spouses may be marrying for the first time while the other has been previously married. At the present time it is not possible to construct a coherent demography in which both sexes are handled simultaneously. For a single population there are thus two demographies, one constructed on men and the other on women. Historically, the latter has had priority.

The exclusion of the male sex also creates a problem for distributions other than those of nuptiality. The concept of fecundability assumes the availability of a perfectly fecund male partner. Even when she is in a fertile period, a woman cannot conceive without a man or at least not without male semen (leaving aside artificial and therapeutic procreation, still unimportant statistically). Similarly, because fertility is considered uniquely from the female angle, the permanent sterility imputed to the woman is in fact that of the couple. Yet it can originate from either member of the couple or from their interaction. In spite of these criticisms, the microsimulation model of fertility remains one of demography's finest achievements, by its capacity to explain the extraordinary variety of fertility regimes past and present, and also because it links life histories directly to the macroscopic descriptions of the indices, rates, and distributions by age and parity. Up to this point in the discussion, however, fertility has been calculated without reference to mortality or migration. None of the female lifelines has been interrupted before age 50 by death, divorce, or emigration. What happens when these events do occur and how can they be included in the analysis? It is to the question of censored data that we now turn our attention.

3
Censoring

The first two chapters have been devoted to "pure" phenomena that were not per-turbed by other factors. The study of mortality was conducted under the assumption that no observation was missing or interrupted as a result of emigration by or loss of contact with any members of the group being studied. Similarly for fertility, every lifeline reached age 50, the upper limit of the reproductive span, without any individual having died or exited the group under observation. In real-life situations, however, women do die before age 50 and group members are lost to observation. We could decide to retain only complete lifelines, that is, those terminating with an observed death in the case of mortality and those going beyond age 50 in the case of fertility. This is the solution adopted in historical demography, when attention is restricted to family records that are "complete," that concern couples who have been observed all the way from marriage up to the death of the first spouse. In this case we speak of *truncation*. Apart from the loss of information, selection of complete observations has the drawback that no link can be established between the vantage point of the individual (life expectancy, final completed fertility) and the vantage point of the population (population growth, age structure). It is therefore important to keep the lifelines that are interrupted (said to be right censored), those that are known only after a certain age (left censored), and those of which only a segment is available (double censored). This is achieved by making a crucial and far-reaching assumption about the independence of the phenomena. After the relatively intuitive approach of the two previous chapters, the study of censoring introduces a more rig-orous logical and statistical formalization based on two powerful analytical tools. One is the concept of consistency, which formalizes the notion of independence. The other is the maximum likelihood method, already used in the Kaplan and Meier estimation and in estimation of rates.

3.1   Incomplete Observations of Fertility and Mortality

Let us start from the example represented in figure 3.1, where the female life histories can contain light circles indicating births and end with a dark square indicating death. Because the number of women present is no longer constant over time, cumulative

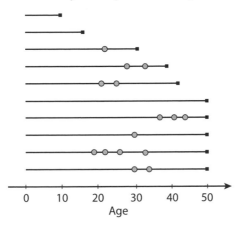

Figure 3.1. Example of right-censored life histories (the light circles represent births, the black squares deaths). Lines arranged by order of age at last event.

fertility at age x cannot be estimated in the same way as in the last chapter. If, however, we consider only the intervals between successive deaths, the number of women observed there is constant, thus enabling us to revert to the method developed in chapter 2 for the case of no mortality and resume estimation of the fertility rate

$$f(x_i, x_{i+1}) = \frac{B(x_i, x_{i+1})}{P_i(x_{i+1} - x_i)},$$

where $B(x_i, x_{i+1})$ is the number of births between age x_i of the ith death and x_{i+1} of the $(i + 1)$th, and P_i is the number of women surviving after the ith death. As long as there are some births that do not coincide with some deaths, this calculation can be done for all the intervals defined by the deaths.[1]

As in chapter 2, final completed fertility (total number of children ever born) DF is the sum of the fertility rates thus calculated multiplied by the interval over which they are calculated starting from the age at the first observed death and terminating at the age where reproduction or observation ends (50 years):

$$DF = (x_2 - 10) f(10, x_2) + (x_3 - x_2) f(x_2, x_3) + \cdots + (50 - x_k) f(x_k, 50).$$

In practice, the calculations are simply organized by calculating the number of lifelines for each age interval between two deaths, and the number of births for each subinterval (or for the interval itself). Dividing this number by the length of the interval and by the number of lifelines present in the interval gives the fertility rate. Table 3.1 displays the calculations for the sample corresponding to figure 3.1.

If deaths had not been taken into account, dividing the 15 births by the 10 women shown in figure 3.1, equal to 1.5, would have substantially underestimated final completed fertility, but we would have obtained the correct total for a population of 10

---

[1] In the case of coincidence (highly unlikely if the dates are measured precisely), the birth can be separated into two half-births placed at $+\epsilon$ and at $-\epsilon$ from the date of the death and the calculation performed as for the case without coincidence.

Table 3.1. Calculation of fertility rates when some lifelines are interrupted by death.

Ages at death	Number of surviving women	Births over the interval	Fertility rate over the interval	Cumulative fertility
10				0
	9	0	0	
16				0
	8	9	0.075	
31				1.125
	7	4	0.071	
39				1.696
	6	1	0.056	
42				1.863
	5	1	0.025	
50				2.063

women. The first figure (2.063) is called *cumulative gross fertility* (with no mortality) and the second (1.5) is *cumulative net fertility* (with mortality). If the calculation had been made only for the 5 women who reached age 50, their final completed fertility would be $10/5 = 2.0$ children per woman, which is very close to the cumulative crude fertility, thus providing support for the assumption of independence between the two phenomena.

3.2 Independence of Fertility and Mortality: Consistency of the Estimation

The crucial hypothesis of independence is defined in probability theory thus: the probability of event A occurring remains the same whether event B occurs or not. Consequently, by symmetry we know that the probability of B is the same whether A occurs or not. In the case of fertility and mortality this property is stated in a slightly special way: had they not died, the women who died at age x would have had the same reproductive behavior as the women who survived beyond age x. This property can be written as a consistency condition for cumulative fertility. The cumulative fertility of the N women at age x, $K(x)$, is the mean of the births observed before age x and the cumulative fertilities between the exit age x_i and age x, for the censorings prior to x, that is, $K(x) - K(x_i)$. The women who died before age x are thus assumed to have the same fertility as the women who survive, which is exactly the independence assumption between the two phenomena of mortality and fertility. Defining fertility by reference to itself as we have just done might be thought to be circular reasoning, but this is not so. The previous definition has a single solution, which is that given in the previous section. The intuitive estimation is thus consistent and is indeed the only consistent solution. This can be demonstrated by formalizing the relationship that has just been postulated between the cumulative fertilities at age x and studying how they change when going past the exact age at which a birth occurs, then when going past the exact age of a death and thus of a censoring.

The definition is written:

$$K(t) = \frac{1}{N}\left(B(0,t) + \sum_i (K(t) - K(t_i)) \right),$$

where $K(t)$ is the cumulative fertility at age t, $B(0,t)$ is the total number of births observed up to age t, N is the total number of lifelines.

The sum is limited to the censoring ages t_i less than t numbering $C(t)$. The formula can be given a more manageable form

$$K(t)\left(1 - \frac{C(t)}{N}\right) = \frac{1}{N}\left(B(0,t) - \sum_i K(t_i) \right),$$

which gives the value of the sum

$$\sum_i \frac{K(t_i)}{N} = \frac{B(0,t)}{N} - K(t)\left(1 - \frac{C(t)}{N}\right).$$

When there is only one birth between t and t_1, the sum $\sum K(t_i)$ stays the same, as does the number of censorings, and the number of births increases by 1. At t and at t_1 we thus have

$$\sum_i \frac{K(t_i)}{N} = \frac{B(0,t)}{N} - K(t)\left(1 - \frac{C(t)}{N}\right)$$

$$= \frac{B(0,t)+1}{N} - K(t_1)\left(1 - \frac{C(t)}{N}\right),$$

which simplifies to

$$(K(t_1) - K(t))\left(1 - \frac{C(t)}{N}\right) = \frac{1}{N},$$

that is,

$$K(t_1) = K(t) + \frac{1}{N - C(t)}.$$

When there is only one death between t and t_1, thus a censoring at t, the sum $\sum_i K(t_i)$ increases by $K(t_2)$, $C(t)$ increases by 1, and $B(0,t)$ is unchanged. Thus we have

$$\frac{B(0,t)}{N} - K(t_2)\left(1 - \frac{C(t)+1}{N}\right) - \frac{K(t_2)}{N} = \frac{B(0,t)}{N} - K(t)\left(1 - \frac{C(t)}{N}\right).$$

That is, after simplification, we have

$$K(t_2) = K(t).$$

This formula shows that, after a birth, cumulative fertility increases by $1/(N-C(t))$ and that, after a censoring, completed final fertility does not change.

This is the same as the result obtained intuitively in the previous section. It is written by grouping the births between two deaths and by setting the number of lifelines present at t, $P(t) = N - C(t)$:

$$K(t) = \frac{N(t_1, t_2)}{P(t_1)} + \frac{N(t_2, t_3)}{P(t_1) - 1} + \cdots + \frac{N(t_{n-1}, t_n)}{P(t_1) - n} + \cdots .$$

For example, for the sample in figure 3.1

$$K(31) = \tfrac{4}{7} + \tfrac{1}{6} + \tfrac{1}{5} = 0.938.$$

Is the independence assumption warranted? Answering that question is problematic, first, by definition, since we will never know how many births the women who died would have had. Next, it may be supposed that those who died were in less good health and, had they lived, would have had fewer conceptions and births. In historical populations, by contrast, mortality depends on fertility through deaths of women in childbirth or maternal mortality. The women who have most children are at greater risk of dying, which operates a gradual selection in favor of less fertile women.

An indirect way of approaching independence is to compare the fertility of the women who died before age 50 with that of the women who reached that age, as was done earlier. However, if the women who died have a lower fertility, this may be due to an impaired state of health that is the cause both of their death and of their low number of births. All these uncertainties argue in favor of disregarding incomplete data. Unfortunately, that is impossible, for censoring is the rule, not the exception, as will be seen in the next chapter. Abandoning use of censored data would mean abandoning cross-sectional (period) analysis.

3.3   Censored Data: The Case of Mortality

Mortality is one cause among others of losses to observation. Some lifelines are also interrupted because the person has moved abroad or cannot be contacted. The way of handling these censorings is identical to that of deaths for fertility detailed in the two previous sections since it is also based on the assumption of independence. Censoring is not restricted to the case of fertility but affects all demographic phenomena, notably the analysis of mortality. Life-table construction must therefore be adapted to the situation where individuals leave the field of observation before their death. As was done in the case of fertility, it will be assumed that those who leave observation would have had the same mortality, hence the same survival function, as those who remain in observation. To estimate survivorship at age t from a set of interrupted lifelines, three methods produce the same result. The intuitive method, already used in the case of fertility, involves dividing the age into intervals delimited by the censoring dates. Since the data inside each interval are not censored, the life-table method of estimation can be applied. Between two consecutive dates of censoring,

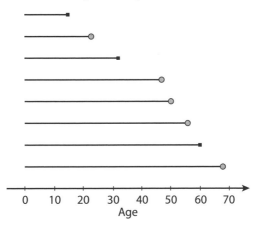

Figure 3.2. Example of right-censored mortality data. The light circles represent deaths and the black squares the censorings or losses from observation. Lines arranged by order of age at last event.

Table 3.2. Calculation of life table with right censoring.

Age (C, censorings)	Number present before event	Probabilities	Life-table survivors	Life-table deaths
0	8		1.000	
15(C)	8	0	1.000	0
23	7	$\frac{1}{7}$	0.857	0.143
32(C)	6	0	0.857	0
47	5	$\frac{1}{5}$	0.686	0.171
50	4	$\frac{1}{4}$	0.515	0.171
56	3	$\frac{1}{3}$	0.344	0.171
60(C)	2	0	0.344	0
68	1	1	0.000	0.344

the probability of dying for each age at death is thus equal to the reciprocal of the number of lifelines still present immediately after the censoring at the beginning of the interval. At the date of censoring, the probability of dying is nil because there is no death. Probabilities are available for all the ages, so the life table is built up from them by means of the usual formulas (giving the life-table survivors and deaths).

An example of this construction is given in figure 3.2 and table 3.2. The censorings shown by dark squares and the deaths by light circles define the age groups (which can also be subdivided or merged once the calculations have been made). We have indicated the number present immediately before a censoring, the probabilities of dying, and the life-table survivors and deaths corresponding to the probabilities.

It is seen that if N designates the initial number of lifelines, at the ith death after j censorings, the probability of dying is

$$q = \frac{1}{N - i - j}.$$

For example, just before the sixth death at age 50, there remain 4 persons, so q is $\frac{1}{4}$. As the survival function previously stood at 0.686, it falls to $0.686 \times (1 - 0.25) = 0.515$ at this age. The formula is identical to that of the consistency rule that states: survivorship at t is equal to the number of survivors plus the sum of the survivorships of those who were censored previously (at $t_i < t$), all divided by the initial number of lifelines N. This result also corresponds to the maximum likelihood of the sample, as we show directly using the Kaplan and Meier method.

The equation that expresses the independence of mortality and censorings or exits from observation is

$$S(t) = 1 - \left(D(0, t) + \sum_i \frac{1 - S(t)/S(t_i)}{N} \right),$$

where N and $C(t)$ mean the same as for fertility, $D(0, t)$ designates the number of deaths before t, and $S(t)$ the survival function on radix unity. The sum of the reciprocals of the survivorships is extended to all the censorings prior to t. We first find $\sum_i 1/S(t_i)$,

$$\sum_i \frac{1}{S(t_i)} = \left(1 - \frac{1}{S(t)} \right) N + \frac{D(0, t) + C(t)}{S(t)},$$

and examine the variation in $S(t)$ when an event occurs.

If this event is a death, the sum does not change, nor does $C(t)$, but $D(0, t)$ increases by one unit. We express the sum just before (at t) and just after the death (at t_1) without any other event occurring:

$$\sum_i \frac{1}{S(t_i)} = \left(1 - \frac{1}{S(t)} \right) N + \frac{D(0, t) + C(t)}{S(t)}$$

$$= \left(1 - \frac{1}{S(t_1)} \right) N + \frac{D(0, t) + 1 + C(t)}{S(t_1)},$$

that is,

$$N \left(\frac{1}{S(t_1)} - \frac{1}{S(t)} \right) = \frac{D(0, t) + C(t) + 1}{S(t_1)} - \frac{D(0, t) + C(t)}{S(t)}.$$

Putting the probability $q(t, t_1) = (S(t) - S(t_1))/S(t)$, we obtain

$$Nq(t, t_1) = (D(0, t) + C(t) + 1) - (D(0, t) + C(t))S(t_1)/S(t)$$

$$= (D(0, t) + C(t) + 1) - (D(0, t) + C(t))(1 - q(t, t_1)),$$

whence we can now derive $q(t, t_1)$:

$$q(t, t_1) = \frac{1}{N - D(0, t) - C(t)},$$

which is, of course, the formula found in the intuitive approach.

If the event is a censoring, the sum increases by $1/S(t)$, $C(t)$ increases by 1, and the other parameters remain unchanged. By again equalizing the two expressions of the sum of the reciprocals of the survivorships at the censoring dates, $\sum_i 1/S(t_i)$, we get

$$\left(1 - \frac{1}{S(t_1)}\right) N + \frac{D(0, t) + 1 + C(t)}{S(t_1)} - \frac{1}{S(t_1)} = \frac{1}{S(t)} N + \frac{D(0, t) + C(t)}{S(t)}.$$

When the two terms of $1/S(t_1)$ are removed from the first side, the two sides become identical and $S(t) = S(t_1)$.

This last is the most powerful proof of the formula since it is based directly on mathematical statistics. Its validity does not therefore have to be proved through demographic arguments but depends on the status of the maximum likelihood estimation and on its properties, notably when sample size is very large (bias, efficiency, confidence interval). As concerns demography, all that must be verified is that the conditions of application are satisfied, notably the independence assumption of which the consistency rule is an expression. It is noted, however, that the fertility rates have not been estimated by the maximum likelihood method and, in practice, they cannot be since they are not mutually independent. This important point will be discussed at the end of the chapter.

3.4 Multiple Life Tables

The censorings and deaths of figure 3.2 are readily interchangeable, so the same calculations could be conducted on the censorings as on the deaths. In this case we would obtain an exit or "decrement" table analogous to a life table for mortality experience. The reasoning used to calculate deaths with no censoring can thus be used for a table of censorings or of exits with no deaths. We have computed such a table (table 3.3) again based on the example in figure 3.2.

A table can also be constructed for all causes of exit, whether censorings or deaths. Its structure is analogous to that of the table calculated in chapter 1 in which the ith probability was $1/(N - i)$, where N was the total number of lifelines. In this case, every lifeline does of course end with an exit. Very simple relations hold between the table of deaths, that of censorings and the table for both modes of exit or decrement treated together. Call the first two (S_1, D_1, q_1) and (S_2, D_2, q_2) and the third (S, D, q). By juxtaposing them or by applying the independence property, we see that

$$S(t) = S_1(t) S_2(t)$$

Table 3.3. Table of exits from observation calculated by the same principle as the life table in table 3.2.

Age (D, death)	Number present before death	Probabilities	Life-table survivors	Life-table deaths
0	8		1.000	
15(D)	8	0	1.000	
23	7	$\frac{1}{7}$	0.857	0
32(D)	6	0	0.857	0.143
47	5	$\frac{1}{5}$	0.686	0
50(D)	4	0	0.686	0.171
56(D)	3	0	0.686	0
60	2	$\frac{1}{2}$	0.343	0
68(D)	1	1	0.000	0.343

and that

$$1 - q(t) = (1 - q_1(t))(1 - q_2(t)).$$

Applying the formula for the instantaneous probability μ, we derive

$$\mu(t) = -\log(1 - q(t))/L = -\log(1 - q_1(t))(1 - q_2(t))/L$$
$$= -\log(1 - q_1(t))/L - \log(1 - q_2(t))/L$$
$$= \mu_1(t) + \mu_2(t).$$

The instantaneous probability of exit is thus the sum of the instantaneous probabilities of death and of censoring. The two causes of exit, which at first sight appear to operate in an uncoordinated fashion, are combined very simply when we work at the level of very short time intervals or, preferably, of the infinitely small. This is no chance result but a fundamental property of the processes, for which Kolmogorov first supplied the explanation. Their action is continuous and, contrary to the initial impression, is easier to understand and model over infinitesimal durations than over finite time intervals.

3.5 Cause-Specific Mortality

The distinction made above was between deaths and censorings, but we could equally have separated cancer deaths from other deaths in a cohort where all the lifelines are observed up to death. A life table can then be computed for cancer deaths only, though this is of limited interest, and a life table omitting cancer deaths, which is of more practical significance. It shows what mortality would be if cancer were completely cured as are, for example, contagious diseases, that is to say, if mortality after the cure was the same as for those who did not suffer the disease, or if neither

Table 3.4. Probabilities of dying, males (over the corresponding age interval), all causes and cancer only, 2000, France.

	Probabilities of death	
Age groups	All causes	Tumors
0–1	0.0049	0.0000
1–4	0.0011	0.0001
5–14	0.0016	0.0003
15–24	0.0092	0.0006
25–34	0.0123	0.0010
35–44	0.0245	0.0055
45–54	0.0556	0.0231
55–64	0.1128	0.0561
65–74	0.2447	0.1137
75–84	0.4808	0.1804
85–94	0.8514	0.2823
≥95	0.9849	0.3182

the treatment nor the disease had any life-threatening aftereffects. If we calculate life expectancy in this table omitting mortality from cancer and compare it with life expectancy in the general life table for mortality from all causes, we can deduce the average number of years gained and, symmetrically, the average number of years lost due to cancer. Table 3.4 shows such a calculation conducted for mortality in France.

These probabilities are used to calculate the survivors in the life table for all causes of death and in that for causes excluding tumors. The life expectancy obtained is 75.3 years in the first and 80.00 years in the second. The gain in life expectancy of 4.7 years is not as large as might be imagined, even though tumors are responsible for more than one in five deaths. As a comparison, the difference between male and female life expectancy in France in 2000 was 7.8 years, that is, nearly twice the gain that would be achieved if all cancers were cured without any aftereffects. Since men face a mortality risk (probability) higher than that for women at all ages, we might liken being of male sex to a disease that is twice as serious as cancer.

Calculation of gains in life expectancy is one of the oldest techniques in demography. Bernoulli used it in 1760 in his debate with d'Alembert to prove that inoculation, an early form of smallpox vaccination, was worthwhile despite the short-term risk of dying. Bernoulli calculated life expectancy without the risk of dying from smallpox but with that from inoculation and showed it to be three years longer than life expectancy with the risk of smallpox and thus without inoculation.

The opposing argument presented by d'Alembert was subtler than the caricatured version of it given by his critics. He contended that the child's death in the month following impregnation with infected material was a much greater loss for its parents to bear than death many years later when the child had reached adulthood, even though the latter was a higher risk. Expressed differently, years of life gained in the remote future were worth substantially less than years lost immediately. Two vantage points were in conflict here. One was that of the state, for which the calculation was made in a given year by finding the total for each generation, the gains at older ages compensating easily for the children lost through inoculation. The other was that of the parent who attached more importance to events the closer they were in time, preferring years of life saved immediately over years of life gained at a much later age. D'Alembert attributed to the years gained a value that decreased with age, whereas for Bernoulli all years were of equal value. The difference between these two positions can be compared with a difference in the discount rate attached to the value of extra years of life in the future. Bernoulli assumed a discount rate of zero, while calculation shows that d'Alembert's position becomes correct with a discount rate above 8%, that is, when one year is reckoned to be worth 8% more than the next year or, in terms of annuities, that the interest rate is 8%. The individual vantage point of d'Alembert is longitudinal and comparable with that of a funded pension system, while the vantage point of the state adopted by Bernoulli is analogous to that of a pay-as-you-go system.

Bernoulli's success was reinforced by progress in inoculation, followed shortly by Jenner's introduction of vaccination that practically eliminated deaths at the time of incision. But it was also part of the broader framework of utilitarianism. The sacrifice of some individuals was compensated by the advantage for others. The amount of pain experienced by some could be summed and subtracted from the amount of pleasure derived by others. D'Alembert's calculation remained individualist. Only the individual, in the depths of his or her own heart and mind, was qualified to make the trade-offs between pleasure and pain. Simple demographic calculations were already central to issues that pertained not directly to politics but to political philosophy.

3.6   Double Censoring

The lifelines considered so far all shared the same starting point, an age or a date, before ending one after the other through death or exit. But their number may also increase through the arrival of new members or by immigration. It can also happen that the observation period cuts only one or several segments of the lifelines and leaves unobserved the events occurring on the remainder of the lifeline. In these conditions, the lifelines may start not at the initial time or age but at some date after a certain length of time has elapsed. They are left censored. Thereafter, they may or may not be right censored. Four types of lines thus coexist: double-censored, left-censored, right-censored, and complete lines. Under the assumption of independence between censoring and the process—mortality or fertility—being studied, the age-specific fertility and mortality functions can be estimated as before. The intuitive

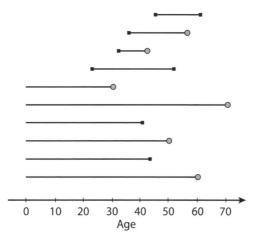

Figure 3.3. Example of double-censored mortality data. Light circles represent deaths and dark squares represent censorings or exits from observation. Lines arranged in order of age at first event.

method works in the same way as for right censoring. All the intervals situated between two censorings, either left or right, are considered separately. Over these intervals, all the lifelines are complete and the probabilities of dying and the fertility rates can be calculated by the conventional method of dividing the number of events studied by the number of lifelines. Since no event of the kind considered occurs on a censoring,[2] the fertility rates are simply chained to obtain the fertility curve and to calculate the survivors and deaths for the life table.

In figure 3.3 and table 3.5 we give an example of a life table calculated from double-censored data.

It can be shown that the intuitive method of estimation is consistent. In the case of fertility, a term $G(t_1, 100)$ is added to the formula used for right censoring. $K(t_1)$ corresponds to the effect of left censoring after t_1 under the independence assumption that in this case is stated as: fertility before the censoring is the same as that observed if there is no censoring

$$K(t_1) = \frac{1}{P(t_1)} \left(B(t_1, 50) + \sum_i K(t_i) + G(t_1, 100) + \sum_j K(t_1) \right).$$

The demonstration follows the same principle as for right censoring, examining the three possible events (left censoring, right censoring, birth).

---

[2] If two events occur on the same date, this can only result from rounding up. By increasing precision the two dates can always be separated, even if the interval between them is very short (for example, twins are never born on the same date but a few minutes or more apart). Hence it is pointless extending the demonstrations to the case where several events occur simultaneously. In this way mathematical complications are avoided.

Table 3.5.   Life-table calculation with double censoring.

Age (C, censoring)	Number present before death	Deaths	Probabilities of dying	Life-table survivors	Life-table deaths
25(C)	6	0	0	1000	0
33	7	1	$\frac{1}{7}$	857	143
35(C)	6	0	0	857	0
39(C)	7	0	0	857	0
44(C)	8	0	0	857	0
46	7	1	$\frac{1}{7}$	735	122
47(C)	6	0	0	735	0
49(C)	5	0	0	735	0
54	6	1	$\frac{1}{6}$	612	0
56(C)	5	0	0	612	0
61	4	1	$\frac{1}{4}$	459	153
65	3	1	$\frac{1}{3}$	306	153
66(C)	2	0	0	306	0
76	1	1	1	0	306

In this case the formula expressing the independence of births and deaths is written

$$K(t) = \frac{1}{N}\left(B(0,t) + \sum_i (K(t) - K(t_i)) + \sum_j K(t_j) \right),$$

where the sum $\sum_j K(t_j)$ represents the effect on cumulative fertility at t of all the left censorings numbering $G(t)$ up to age t. The values of $K(t)$ are found using the same principle as in the case of right censoring. The two sums are expressed relative to the other parameters:

$$\frac{1}{N + G(t)}\left(-\sum_i K(t_i) + \sum_j (t_j) \right) = \frac{B(0,t)}{N + G(t)} - K(t)\left(1 - \frac{C(t)}{N + G(t)} \right).$$

When the age goes past the date of a birth, $K(t)$ increases by exactly

$$\frac{1}{N + G(t) - C(t)}$$

by the same reasoning as in the case of right censoring N is replaced by $N = G(t)$.

When the age goes past the date of a right censoring, final completed fertility (number of children ever born) is unchanged, again using the same reasoning as in the case of right censorings.

When the age goes past the date of a left censoring, $G(t)$ increases by one unit and the sum $\sum_j K(t_j)$ increases by $K(t_2)$, all other quantities remaining unchanged. Writing the value of the two sums just before the censoring and at t_2, we have

$$\sum_i K(t_i) + \sum_j K(t_j) = B(0,t) - K(t_2)(N + G(t) + 1 - C(t)) - K(t_2)$$

$$= B(0,t) - K(t)(N + G(t) - C(t)),$$

which simplifies to

$$K(t_2) = K(t).$$

Cumulative fertility at t is thus the sum of the "jumps" occasioned by each birth observed before t:

$$K(t) = \sum_i \frac{1}{N + G(t_i) - C(t_i)} \quad \text{with } t_i < t.$$

The same reasoning applies in the case of mortality, where in addition maximum likelihood estimation gives the same result.

Introducing left censoring is less obvious an exercise than right censoring. If a left censoring occurs at t_i prior to t, the independence assumption implies that this appearance at t_i is what remains of a number of lines $1/S(t_i)$ that appeared at the initial point in time, since at t_i there remain only $S(t_i) \times 1/S(t_i) = 1$ if the mortality of those who experience the left censoring is the same as the mortality of those who do not. The equation expressing the consistency of the survival function is then

$$S(t)$$
$$= 1 - \left(D(0,t) + \sum_i \left(1 - \frac{S(t)}{S(t_i)}\right) + \sum_j \left(\frac{1}{S(t_j)} - 1\right) \right) \Big/ \left(N + \sum_j \frac{1}{S(t_j)}\right)$$
$$= 1 - \left(D(0,t) + C(t) - G(t) - \sum_i \frac{S(t)}{S(t_i)} + \sum_j \frac{1}{S(t_j)} \Big/ \left(N + \sum_j \frac{1}{S(t_j)}\right) \right).$$

Notwithstanding the slightly daunting length of the formula, $S(t)$ or more precisely the probabilities of dying are obtained by the same method as for simple right censoring.

In the vicinity of a death, the reasoning is the same as before. We find $-\sum S(t)/S(t_i)$, which does not change as long as the interval is not censored.

We replace N by $N + \sum_j 1/S(t_j)$ and $D(0,t) + C(t)$ by $D(0,t) + C(t) - G(t)$. The formulas are then identical, which leads to

$$q(t,t_1) = \frac{1}{N - D(0,t) - C(t) + G(t)}.$$

In the vicinity of a right-censored observation, the same substitutions are performed and the formulas also become identical and so we also have

$$S(t) = S(t_1).$$

In the vicinity of a left-censored observation, the expression can be written as before, using the first sum, $\sum_i 1/S(t_i)$:

$$\sum_i \frac{1}{S(t_i)} = \left(1 - \frac{1}{S(t)}\right)\left(N + \sum_j \frac{1}{S(t_j)}\right)$$
$$- \left(D(0,t) + C(t) - G(t) + \sum_j \frac{1}{S(t_j)}\right).$$

At t_1, just after the censoring, the sum $\sum_j 1/S(t_j)$ increases by $1/S(t_1)$, and $G(t)$ increases by one unit. Thus we have

$$\left(1 - \frac{1}{S(t)}\right)\left(N + \sum_j \frac{1}{S(t_j)}\right) + \frac{1}{S(t)}\left(D(0,t) + C(t) - G(t) + \sum_j \frac{1}{S(t_j)}\right)$$
$$= \left(1 - \frac{1}{S(t_1)}\right)\left(N + \sum_j \frac{1}{S(t_j)} + \frac{1}{S(t_1)}\right)$$
$$+ \frac{1}{S(t_1)}\left(D(0,t) + C(t) - G(t) - 1 + \sum_j \frac{1}{S(t_j)} + \frac{1}{S(t_1)}\right).$$

Simplifying, we get

$$\left(\frac{1}{S(t_1)} - \frac{1}{S(t)}\right)\left(N + \sum_j \frac{1}{S(t_j)}\right) - \frac{1}{S(t_1)}\left(1 - \frac{1}{S(t_1)}\right)$$
$$= \left(D(0,t) + C(t) - G(t) + \sum_j \frac{1}{S(t_j)}\right)\left(\frac{1}{S(t_1)} - \frac{1}{S(t)}\right)$$
$$+ \frac{1}{S(t_1)}\left(\frac{1}{S(t_1)} - 1\right),$$

then

$$\left(\frac{1}{S(t_1)} - \frac{1}{S(t)}\right)\left(N + \sum_j \frac{1}{S(t_j)}\right)$$
$$= \left(D(0,t) + C(t) - G(t) + \sum_j \frac{1}{S(t_j)}\right)\left(\frac{1}{S(t_1)} - \frac{1}{S(t)}\right),$$

hence

$$S(t) = S(t_1).$$

The full life table is thus built up using the probabilities of dying from either side of the observed deaths:

$$q(t,t_1) = \frac{1}{N - D(0,t) - C(t) + G(t)}.$$

Outside of these infinitely small intervals the probabilities of dying are nil because the survival function does not vary on either side of the points of censoring.

Particular attention is given to double censoring because in the next chapter it will provide the means to relate period (or cross-sectional) analysis and longitudinal analysis, that is, the tracking of a single group through time and the observation at a single point in time or over a short period of a set of groups each at a different stage in its trajectory. This is a fundamental operation in demography, but also a fragile technique that requires a perfect understanding of the multiple ramifications of the double-censoring technique.

3.7 Grouped Data

Up to this point it has been assumed that the individual data of the lifelines are available, even if some are censored. But demography often works with data that are more crude, composed of events aggregated and counted by periods of time, age groups, or durations. The lifelines can then never be recovered. This does not make such data worthless. At the limits of the temporal subdivisions they use, these data can supply values as exact as those that would be obtained from the lifelines. Between these limits, on the other hand, the only solution is to make interpolations. One of the chief difficulties arises from interpolating with censored data. The demographic literature contains numerous empirical methods for dealing with this problem, according to the type of source and the data. Deciding on their degree of validity is often difficult. It seems to us that the best means of judging them—and in particular of replacing them when they are unsatisfactory—is to get back to the underlying elementary processes, and hence to interpolate on the lifelines. For behind the aggregates lie individual lifelines, and these alone. These must be reconstituted or, less ambitiously, be imagined behind the often simple classificatory scheme of the aggregate data. Between them and the statistics of events or situations there is no mystery, no black box that can derive regularities or laws from individual data. If these exist it is already at the level of individuals. The problem of the transition from lifelines to statistical aggregates is an administrative problem. If data of a particular kind have been collected, it is for reasons of state policy. We may wish to question these reasons, but we may also take the view that a small section of reality has been revealed and try to work back to the lifelines that have been swept up indistinctly in the data-gathering exercise.

To achieve this requires postulating laws for the distribution of events between the interval limits, and thus the use of parametric methods. The two main cases will be examined here, those of renewable and nonrenewable events, illustrated by fertility and mortality. On the face of it the question is quite simple: the total number of events between two ages or durations is known, as is the total number of exits from observation, thanks to continuous registration or a census, for example.

Begin with the case of fertility disturbed (interrupted) by mortality. Assume that the number of births B and the number of female deaths D over a period of duration

T are known between two ages. We also know the total population present $P(0)$ at the start of the period. How can we deduce fertility ϕ between these two ages, with no mortality as was done earlier by means of estimations of the censored lifelines? Whatever the approach employed, an assumption is needed regarding the distribution of deaths and births within the interval under consideration. More exactly, a continuous process must be assumed in the course of which these births and deaths occur. The most obvious assumptions seem to be those of a fertility and a mortality risk that are constant over the interval and of independence between the two. Let μ and ϕ be the instantaneous probability and rate of mortality and fertility constant during the whole period. The number of survivors $P(t)$ can be calculated at any time t:

$$P(t) = P(0)e^{-\mu t}$$

and from it is deduced the number of deaths over the period T situated between times 0 and T:

$$D = P(0)(1 - e^{-\mu T}).$$

The number of births is deduced from $P(x)$ and ϕ:

$$B = \phi \int_0^T P(u)\,du$$
$$= (\phi/\mu)P(0)(1 - e^{-\mu T}).$$

With the two equations giving D and B, it is possible to ascertain μ and ϕ:

$$\mu = -\frac{\log(1 - D/P(0))}{T} \quad \text{and} \quad \phi = \frac{\mu B}{D},$$

or the more symmetric

$$\frac{\phi}{\mu} = \frac{B}{D}.$$

This exact formula should always be used when no alternative hypothesis is available for the instantaneous fertility and mortality behavior, but an approximation is often preferred since it saves having to change to logarithmic notation.

With a limited expansion of the logarithmic function, we obtain

$$\phi = \frac{B}{D}\left(\frac{D}{P(0)} + \frac{1}{2}\left(\frac{D}{P(0)}\right)^2\right)\frac{1}{T} = \frac{B}{P(0)}\left(1 + 0.5\frac{D}{P(0)}\right)\frac{1}{T}.$$

An alternative procedure is more widely used because it is more direct. It starts from the formula

$$B = \phi \int_0^T P(u)\,du$$

from which is found ϕ

$$\phi = B \Big/ \int_0^T P(u)\,du,$$

which means that the fertility rate is equal to the births divided by the mean population size over the observation period and by the length of the interval. This mean population size is approximated by one half of the sum of the populations at the limits of the selected interval (0 and T here):

$$0.5(P(0) + P(T)),$$

whence

$$\phi = \frac{B}{T(P(0) + P(T))}.$$

The simplicity of this formula explains why it is frequently used. In this case we speak simply of the *fertility rate* and not of the *instantaneous rate*, even though it is the assumption of a constant instantaneous rate over the period under study that leads to this result. By extension, demographers tend to apply the term *rate* to any empirical situation in which a set of events over a period is related to the one half of the numbers present at the start and end of the period.

When two nonrenewable events are competing, for example, two causes of mortality, or mortality and first marriage or emigration, the formulas become

$$D_1 = (\mu_1/(\mu_1 + \mu_2))P(0)(1 - e^{\mu_1 + \mu_2 T}),$$
$$D_2 = (\mu_2/(\mu_1 + \mu_2))P(0)(1 - e^{\mu_1 + \mu_2 T}),$$

where μ_1 and μ_2 designate the two probabilities being sought and D_1 and D_2 the two numbers of deaths (or of deaths and first marriages or emigrations). The exact solution is

$$\mu_1 = \frac{D_1}{P(0)}\left(-\log\left(1 - \frac{D_1 + D_2}{P(0)}\right)\right),$$
$$\mu_2 = \frac{D_2}{P(0)}\left(-\log\left(1 - \frac{D_1 + D_2}{P(0)}\right)\right).$$

A limited expansion gives the approximation

$$\mu_1 = \frac{D_1}{P(0)}\left(1 + \frac{D_1 + D_2}{2P(0)}\right)$$

but the mean population reasoning can also be used, of which the approximation then gives

$$\mu_1 = \frac{D_1/P(0)}{1 - (D_1 + D_2)/2P(0)}.$$

3.8 Method and Critique of Estimation by the Principle of Indifference

A different explanation is often proposed for the formula of interference between fertility and mortality. We start from the fertility rate f and the probability of dying

q. For the two events to occur independently of each other, a proportion $f(1-q)$ of the women in the group will have to bear a child and survive, a proportion fq bear a child and die, a proportion $(1-f)q$ do not bear a child and die, and finally a proportion $(1-f)(1-q)$ experience neither event. The decisive category is that which is to experience both events: if the anticipated birth occurs before the anticipated death, it will be observed, otherwise the death will prevent it occurring. The principle of indifference states that in the case where both events occur, by symmetry, each is as likely to precede the other, so that they share half of the cases and that the births in these circumstances are in a proportion of $fq/2$. In all there will be $f(1-q) + fq/2$ births B, that is,

$$P(0)(f(1-q) + fq/2) = P(0)f(1-q/2) = B.$$

Therefore, $f = (B/P(0))/(1-q/2)$, which is the formula obtained above by two other reasonings. Why not make do with this simple general level reasoning instead of imagining a behavior for each woman at each point in time? Because the principle of indifference reasoning, however attractive it may be, is false, and it is by accident that a result similar to the theoretical approximation is obtained.

Assume that the distribution of births with no mortality at age x over the interval being considered is $B(x)$ and that of deaths $D(x)$. For an interval 0, 1, the numbers of births preceding and following the deaths at age x are respectively

$$\int_0^x B(u)\,du \quad \text{and} \quad \int_x^1 B(u)\,du.$$

For the number of births before and after the death to be equal over the entire interval, we must have

$$\int_0^1 \left(\int_0^x B(u)\,du \right) D(x)\,dx = \int_0^1 \left(\int_x^1 B(u)\,du \right) D(x)\,dx.$$

In general this condition is not respected when an a priori assumption is made about the unknown distribution of the births and deaths over the interval. The assumption usually made is that the instantaneous rates of fertility and mortality are constant over the interval considered. In this case $B(x) = \phi$ and $D(x) = \mu e^{-\mu}$. The two members of the previous relation are then written

$$\int_0^1 \left(\int_0^x \phi\,du \right) \mu e^{-\mu x}\,dx = \int_0^1 \left(\int_x^1 \phi\,du \right) \mu e^{-\mu x}\,dx$$

or, integrating,

$$\int_0^1 \phi \mu x e^{-\mu x}\,dx = \int_0^1 \phi(1-x)\mu e^{-\mu x}\,dx,$$

that is,

$$\int_0^1 \phi(2x-1)\mu e^{-\mu x}\,dx = 0,$$

which integrates to $\phi(\mu + 2)e^{-\mu} + \phi(\mu - 2) = 0$. This equation for μ is verified only when $\mu = 0$ and is therefore false in all cases where mortality is nonzero, which invalidates the reasoning based on the principle of indifference. Thus it is by some sort of fluke that the formula based on the principle of indifference coincided with the approximate formulas in the case of a renewable event combined with a nonrenewable event.

The search for a macrolevel processing of aggregate data to obtain from them rates and probabilities with no disturbance is futile and should be abandoned since it leads to errors of reasoning of which an example has just been given. We cannot escape making the transition to the microscopic level formed by lifelines, either by using individual observations or by making an assumption about microscopic behavior such as that of a constant fertility function or instantaneous mortality probability during the period considered. Just as in physics it is impossible to do without the fact that all matter is composed of atoms that account for all of its properties, so in demography it must be remembered that all populations are made up of individuals and hence of lifelines. Regularities in macrolevel behavior derive from characteristic and frequently simple microscopic (or individual) behavior, whether of atoms in physics or of lifelines in demography.

3.9 Estimating Rates in the Case of Censoring

Where the nonparametric Kaplan and Meier estimation required an extremely detailed demonstration, so the parametric case in which fertility is assumed constant over a given age interval is simple. Estimation by the maximum likelihood method is in fact identical to that performed in the case of mortality. The probability of observing p births over the period t_i is $\phi^p e^{-\phi t_i}$. The maximum likelihood equation thus again includes the sum of the times t_i and the number of deaths n is replaced by the number of births, the sum therefore of all the p. This differs from the case of mortality in that the lifelines observed are not terminated by an event. The events (births) are spread along the lifeline at the time they occur. A serious objection arises from the fact that the birth dates of successive children are not independent. This point is discussed below in the appendix (section 3.10.1.2).

When the individual observations are not available and all we know is the number of events—the deaths D and the births B—between two ages, rates must be used as in the case of mortality, since an assumption is made about their value between two ages, in general a constant ϕ for fertility and μ for mortality. Thus we can reconstitute the distribution of the durations of observation which have the value 1 in the case that death has not occurred (in the proportion $e^{-\mu}$) and that where it has interrupted observation (in the proportion $1 - e^{-\mu}$), where the mean, m, stands at

$$\left(\int_0^1 x e^{-\mu x} \right) \Big/ \left(\int_0^1 e^{-\mu x} \right).$$

As was shown in chapter 1, the rate is generally equal to the number of events (B births) divided by P (the number of persons observed) and by the mean duration of each observation ($e^{-\mu} + (1 - e^{-\mu})m$):

$$\phi = \frac{B}{(e^{-\mu} + (1 - e^{-\mu})m)P}.$$

Replacing m by the value found for it in chapter 1, the formula becomes

$$\phi = \frac{B}{e^{-\mu} + (1 - e^{-\mu})(1/\mu - e^{-\mu}/(1 - e^{-\mu}))P}$$

$$= \frac{B}{(e^{-\mu} + (1 - e^{-\mu})/\mu - e^{-\mu})P}$$

$$= \frac{B}{((1 - e^{-\mu})/\mu)P}.$$

However, because the instantaneous mortality probability is μ over the entire interval, we have

$$D = P(1 - e^{-\mu}).$$

Substituting into the expression for the fertility rate gives

$$\phi = \frac{B}{D/\mu} = B\frac{\mu}{D}.$$

These last two relations are the same as those that defined ϕ and μ in the direct calculation performed in the section on aggregate data. Thus the rates again have the property of convergence: the instantaneous rates converge on the probabilities. This time, however, in contrast to the demonstration in chapter 1, convergence becomes equality purely and simply, because we are no longer working on observed data but directly on the probability function postulated for the occurrence of events.

The above demonstration has been concerned with the case of right censoring. What happens when there is double censoring? The same thing, since we make the assumption that the instantaneous probabilities of entry and exit are constant over each interval. If, for example, E persons enter during the interval, L leave before the end of the interval, and D die, replacing the deaths D by $D + E - L$ is not formally different. The probability μ no longer attaches to mortality but to all entries and exits of whatever kind.

The use of approximations presented as rules or as miracle formulas should be discouraged since they tend to obscure the logical spirit that informs the approach and the estimation. By stating explicitly the assumption made about the behavior of individuals whose exact life history is not available and by applying general rules for the calculation of rates and probabilities, we obtain the result directly and know how and why it has been obtained.

3.10 Appendix

3.10.1 Maximum Likelihood Estimation in the Case of Simple and Double Censoring

3.10.1.1 Estimation of Mortality from Simply Censored Data

The probability of death i occurring at t_i is the product of the probabilities of it not occurring before t_i, that is, $S(t_i)$, by the probability of it occurring at exactly t_i, that is, $q(t_i)$. By definition this product is the probability of death d_i at i in the table to be built. If right censoring occurs at t_j, the probability for the lifeline concerned is the probability of dying after t_j, therefore the sum of the deaths d_i is such that $t_i > t_j$. The sample likelihood or probability is the product of the probabilities of each lifeline since we make the assumption that they are independent. It is written

$$L = \left(\prod_i d_i \right) \left(\prod_{i:ti>tj} \left(\sum_{ti>tj} d_i \right) \right).$$

The first product is extended to all the observed deaths i, and the second product to all the censorings j. The maximum likelihood is found by equating to zero the partial derivatives of L at d_i, under the condition that $\sum d_i = 1$, which introduces a Lagrange multiplier λ. For any reasonable value of d_i, the partial derivative equation is written

$$\frac{1}{d_i} + \sum_j \left(1 \Big/ \sum_{ti>tj} d_i \right) + \lambda = 0.$$

The sum is that of the inverses of the sums of the deaths for the censorings that occur before death i. In fact, each denominator is simply the survivors $S(t_j)$ from censoring j, therefore from the first death following j, that is,

$$\frac{1}{d_i} + \sum_j \frac{1}{S(t_j)} + \lambda = 0.$$

This system of equations appears on the face of it fairly complicated, but it can be solved easily in a way similar to that used to demonstrate the consistency of the estimations. Assume that two deaths i and $i + 1$ follow each other without any censoring occurring between t_i and t_{i+1}. The sum present in the equation is the same for both. Subtracting both their equations yields

$$1/d_i - 1/d_{i+1} = 0,$$

therefore $d_i = d_{i+1}$.

The other case is that where 1 or more generally k censorings occur between the deaths i and $i + 1$. The sum for death $i + 1$ is different by the k fractions corresponding to the k censorings. They are all equal to $1/S(t_{i+1})$ since death $i + 1$

is the first after these censorings. If we again subtract the two equations of the derivatives at d_i and d_{i+1}, we obtain

$$1/d_i - 1/d_{i+1} = k/S_{i+1}$$

setting $S_{i+1} = S(t_{i+1})$.

In the life table we have $d_i = S_i q_i$ and $d_{i+1} = S_{i+1} q_{i+1}$. Substituting into the previous equation and simplifying by S_{i+1}, we obtain

$$S_{i+1}/S_i q_i - 1/q_{i+1} = k.$$

Yet by definition $S_{i+1} = (1 - q_i)S_i$. Substituting, we have

$$1/q_i - 1 - 1/q_{i+1} = k,$$

that is,

$$1/q_i - 1/q_{i+1} = k + 1.$$

The formula is also valid for $k = 0$, that is, when no censoring intervenes. The probability corresponding to the death at the highest age has the value unity. From this basis all the probabilities can then be calculated from one to the next. By recurrence we see that they are equal to the inverse of the number of lifelines reaching the age considered, which was the result obtained by the intuitive method and by the consistency method.

3.10.1.2   Estimation of Mortality from Double-Censored Data

If there is a left censoring, the probability of a subsequent death at i will be $d_i / \sum d_j$, where the sum is extended to all the deaths occurring after the censoring since the probability of not observing a death before the ith is now S_i/S_j, where S_j denotes survivorship from the first death that follows the censoring. In the case of a doubly censored lifeline, for the same reason, the probability will be written $\sum_i d_i / \sum_j d_j = S(t_1)/S(t_2)$, where t_1 and t_2 are the ages at the first and second censorings. The numerator is the probability of dying after the second censoring, therefore the sum of the deaths occurring subsequently or survivorship from the first death that follows the censoring.

The likelihood function L will contain the product of all these terms, and the partial derivatives of the logarithm of L at d_i are calculated in a similar way:

$$\frac{1}{d_i} + \sum \left(1 \Big/ \sum_i d_i\right) - \sum \left(1 \Big/ \sum_j d_j\right) + \lambda = 0.$$

The first sum corresponds to the right censorings that precede death i, and the second to the left censorings. This system is solved in exactly the same way as the previous one, distinguishing the intervals over which only one type of event occurs. In the case of deaths that follow each other directly the result is unchanged. In the case where the two deaths are separated by k right censorings and m left censorings, the same reasoning gives

$$\frac{1}{d_i} - \frac{1}{d_{i+1}} = \frac{k - m}{S_{i+1}},$$

whence is found in the same way

$$\frac{1}{q_i} - \frac{1}{q_{i+1}} = k - m + 1.$$

Once again, by recurrence, the probability is the inverse of the number of lifelines present at the time of the death considered.

3.10.1.3 Maximum Likelihood in the Case of Fertility

It may be wondered why the maximum likelihood method was not used for estimation in the case of fertility and more generally in the case of renewable events such as migration or marriage. The reason lies "upstream" from these calculations and involves another type of independence that is not generally verified, the independence of successive events. As an example take a set of lifelines punctuated by births. For each birth i there corresponds the instantaneous fertility rate f_1. It might be thought that the probability for a given lifeline with, for example, one birth at j and one at k would be written

$$(1 - f_1)(1 - f_2) \cdots (1 - f_{j-1}) f_j (1 - f_{j+1})$$
$$\cdots (1 - f_{k-1}) f_k (1 - f_{k+1}) \cdots (1 - f_n),$$

which would be to consider the successive intervals between observed births as independent. With a sample of fairly large size, the births to different women will occur over a short period of time, and because of the length of pregnancy and the nonsusceptible period they cannot occur to the same woman. There is short-term dependence. This is not the most troublesome, as we saw when applying the Poisson model. The absence of independence arises chiefly as a result of fertility regulation by marriage, contraception, and abortion, which includes decisions based on birth order. If, for example, all women stop family formation after the second child, the previous product would stop at f_k. To be able to postulate the independence of births after an interval of a few years—so as to weaken the effect of the nonsusceptible period—all the parity progression ratios would have to be the same, including those governing the birth of the first child. In reality, for reasons of biology (sterility) and social conventions (traditional disapproval of the childless couple) the progression ratio of parity 1 is always different from the following ones. In the Poisson model used in chapter 2, the probability of having a first child at age x was $F(x)$, while for a second child and subsequent children it was only $k f(x)$. We can, however, overcome this difficulty by introducing the parity progression ratios directly into the estimation. The probability of a lifeline counting n births will be the product of the parity progression ratios from a_0 to a_{n-1} and of the complement of the nth a_n. Thus we lose the cases where the birth despite being possible has not occurred (due to waiting too long or to acquired sterility), but we saw that their probability was very low. We can then complete the product of the parity progression ratios by the product indicated earlier of the fertility rates, which are "natural" rates, and of their complements. Applying maximum likelihood for such a model would give empirically calculated ratios for the estimation of parity progression ratios, while for the estimation of fertility rates it would give rates analogous to natural rates that are quite simply equal to the inverse of the number of lifelines containing at least one subsequent birth. By means of this artifice we could get closer to the results obtained for mortality. The censorings would have their equivalent in the dates of entry into the fertility process (union) and exit (union breakdown or permanent sterility) assuming these are known, which in the latter case (permanent sterility) is difficult.

Finally, it may be noted that direct estimation of the parameters for the microsimulation model of fertility would in fact be impossible because they are interrelated. Thus the formula giving a good approximation of natural fertility shows that fertilities with different parameters nonetheless give the same result (relatively strong correlation between the estimators). From the start, therefore, the difference between processes of renewable and nonrenewable events is bound up with questions of independence in probability.

4

Period and Cohort Approaches

The tools developed thus far have enabled us to describe entry (fertility) and exit (mortality) phenomena and to measure them despite the presence of interference (censoring). But these tools cannot be used to interpret what is happening at the present time or to anticipate the future course of change. The observation periods they require are very long. Before a life table can be calculated for a group of people born in the same year—i.e., of a single generation or birth cohort—we must wait at least 100 years for almost all the individuals to have died. Similarly, the final completed fertility of a female cohort cannot be known until all the women have crossed the age 50 limit. Because of these long waiting periods, longitudinal methods based on lifelines have been used chiefly in historical studies of demographic regimes. Given their data requirements (parish registers, vital registration records), such studies are limited to the early modern and modern periods. Methods using lifelines are also employed in the case of fairly short durations of observation in epidemiology, particularly for comparing the effects of different treatments and medicines, and, in economics, notably for analyzing episodes of unemployment. I now go on to show that if we wish to determine current trends in fertility and mortality, the techniques for handling censored observations must be pushed to their extremes. For this purpose I introduce a useful graphic device, the Lexis plane (or diagram), with which we can display sets of lifelines and give a visual representation of the operations they are subjected to.

4.1   The Lexis Plane

The lifelines shown in the figures in the previous chapters were stacked in no particular order. The vertical dimension of the diagram was neglected and only the horizontal was used to express the durations by the dates or ages at which events occurred. The late-nineteenth-century German statistician Lexis (1875) had the idea of using both dimensions of the plane by displaying calendar time along the horizontal axis and age along the vertical axis. Since years of age and calendar years proceed at the same pace, an individual's lifeline moves forward both through time and by age. Because the unit of increase is the same for both (individuals age one

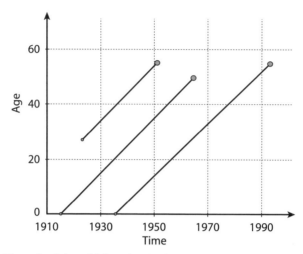

Figure 4.1. Example of three lifelines in a Lexis plane. The *x*-axis represents time and the *y*-axis age. The light circles indicate deaths and the black point an exit from observation.

year at a time), it can be represented by a 45° line or by a parallel line to the bisector of the axes. This is illustrated in figure 4.1, where the first lifeline represents a person who enters observation in 1923 at age 27 and who dies in 1952 at age 56 and the second line corresponds to a person born in 1913 who dies in 1962 (i.e. at age 49 or 50). The third line is perhaps of most interest for the subject of the present chapter. It corresponds to a person born in 1935 and who was still alive in 1993, the date at which the figure was produced. In this case right censoring occurs when the present point in time is passed.

Up to this point, the individuals in the groups studied all had a common starting date, generally an initial defining event such as being born in the same year or undergoing the same course of medical treatment. The individual lifelines for such groups form a bundle of segments angled at 45°. Some of these are easy to characterize, for example, those pertaining to a single birth cohort. This is because the lifelines of the persons born in the same year are all situated inside the 45° corridor whose base is formed by that year on the time axis. This is illustrated by figure 4.2, where all the lifelines correspond to persons born in the same year, and thus between 1 January in two consecutive years.

The Lexis plane is well suited for representing most demographic phenomena. Thus, with the set of lifelines that cut the vertical line at time *t* in figure 4.3 we can immediately construct the age pyramid at this date. The number of individuals of a given age or in a given age group is the number of lifelines that cross the vertical at *t* between the two limits of the age group (since the vertical axis represents age). Once we have the population sizes by age, it is easy to construct the corresponding age pyramid, which is simply the histogram of this age distribution. Here it is drawn opposite to the Lexis plan on the same figure, since by convention the histogram

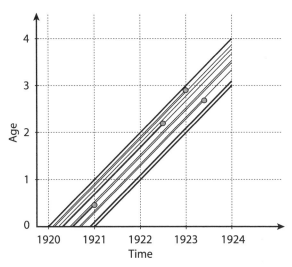

Figure 4.2. Set of lifelines for members of the same cohort, born in 1920. The light circles represent deaths and the two bold lines mark the bounds within which the lifelines of this 1920 birth cohort are situated.

is represented with age in the vertical direction. The objection may be made that half the pyramid is missing, but in the present case the sex of the individuals whose lifelines are represented is not specified. If sex were taken into account, we would have lifelines of two types: male and female. Drawing the histograms by age for these two groups and arranging them symmetrically in relation to the vertical (age), we would obtain the familiar age–sex population pyramid.

The Lexis plane is also particularly suited for representing series of events, and thus aggregate statistics, since all we have to do is count the events occurring in given age groups and over given time intervals, that is, the points situated inside certain regions delineated on the Lexis plane. Three types of regions or cells can be defined depending on age and time. They are shown in figure 4.4 by (a), (b), and (c). In the parallelogram on the left we count the events (births, deaths, migratory moves) occurring to a given cohort between two given dates, in this example between 1 January 1990 and 1 January 1991. In the lower parallelogram, the events are counted for a cohort between two given ages, in this case all the deaths occurring between ages 26 and 27. Lastly, in the square at the top of figure 4.4, the count is of the events occurring over a given period to a given age group (instead of to a given cohort). When the lifelines are omitted and we display just the parallelograms, squares, or their constituent triangles, the resulting figure is known as a Lexis diagram.

It is immediately apparent that double classification by age and date introduces a problem in the form of a time lag between the three descriptors: age, period, cohort. In the first parallelogram, fixing the year of the cohort and the year of observation leaves us with two possible years of age. Similarly, in the second parallelogram, fixing the cohort year and the year of age gives two possible years of observation.

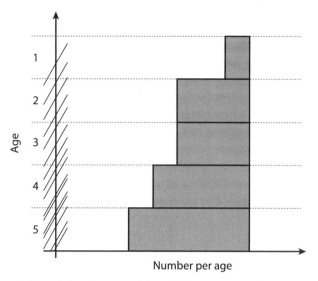

Figure 4.3. Age pyramid (on right) constructed from the
lifelines observed at a given point in time (the y-axis).

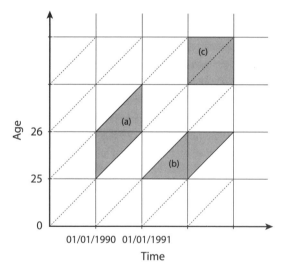

Figure 4.4. Three types of regions on the Lexis diagram,
depending on the definition by age and date of the counted events.

Finally, when the year of age and the date are fixed, as in the square, two cohorts are
involved. In other words, it is not enough to have two of the three terms to be able
to pass from one system of classification to the other. We need data that give what
is called a *double classification* of the annual events, by age and by year of birth, so
as to know the content of each of the two triangles that compose the quadrilaterals
in figure 4.4. This is rarely the case with aggregated statistics. When the double

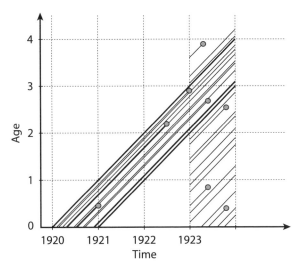

Figure 4.5. Lexis plane showing the difference between cohort observation (diagonal corridor) and period observation (vertical corridor).

classification is not available, a preliminary stage involves reconstructing it from the parallelograms or squares that are available. As we shall see, this does not mean that we can dispense with the lifelines, nor that the triangles are the elementary figures from which the changes by age and by year can be reconstructed.

With the configurations of the Lexis plane thus identified, we can address the problem of period (cross-sectional) observation and, more specifically, its formal characterization in this framework. The question is summed up in stark simplicity in figure 4.5. This shows the events occurring to one cohort, that is, in the cells of a one-year-wide path or "corridor" angled at 45°. Thanks to the techniques developed in the three previous chapters, we know how to characterize formally the age distribution of the phenomenon being considered, entries, exits, and combinations of both. By contrast, the vertical column of figure 4.5 contains the events observed during the most recent year known. Each cell thus corresponds to one or more different cohorts. How can we bring order to this column, organize the events into an intelligible structure, and then summarize them so as to interpret the trends that they indicate? The question could be disregarded by treating demography as a historical science based on results from longitudinal analyses performed once each group being studied has completed its trajectory. Comparative analyses would be conducted on life expectancies in cohorts born up to the start of the twentieth century, for example, or on the final completed fertility of women born before 1955. But demography excites interest much more for what it can say about the present, and indeed the future, than about the past. The discipline is expected to develop instruments that can make sense of the most recent data, that is, period data. With this in mind, an ingenious mechanism has been developed for converting period to

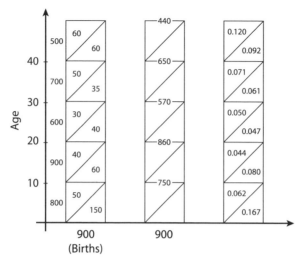

Figure 4.6.   Three stages in calculation of mortality risks from the Lexis diagram triangles. 1. Period deaths and numbers. 2. Reconstitution of cohort sizes at interval ages. 3. Probabilities from the triangles calculated by dividing the number of deaths by the number entering.

cohort observations, thus making the full range of longitudinal methods available for analysis of current conditions. To evaluate accurately the risks associated with this exercise, it will be presented from two angles. The first uses the Lexis diagram, the second uses a particular censoring of the lifelines that allows the validity of the operation to be discussed in terms we are becoming familiar with, notably independence between the observation procedure and the events.

4.2   The Fictitious or "Synthetic" Cohort

The procedure of interest to us involves a fictitious or hypothetical cohort, generally called in English a "synthetic cohort." To understand the procedure, we start from a period observation of the population, and thus from a column on which the triangles of the double classification are shown (the first column of figure 4.6). The procedure will be illustrated using the example of mortality. Inside each triangle we have indicated the number of deaths that occur there, that is, which appear on the section of the lifelines located within the triangle considered. On the left edge of the column are noted the number of lifelines that cross each segment, which is thus the age distribution at the point in time given by the left-side vertical, while at the bottom are shown the number of births, thus the lifelines entering the column. We make the assumption that observation is complete and that there are no disturbing phenomena such as emigration or immigration (we shall see later how to take these into account). The number of lifelines that cross each horizontal line in the column is then calculated by simple subtraction. Their number is equal to the number on the vertical edge of

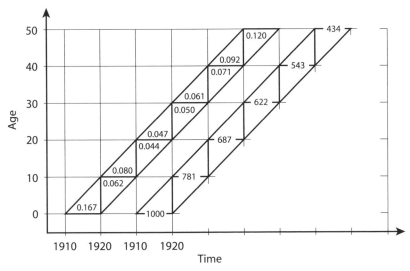

Figure 4.7. The triangles from figure 4.6 are kept at the same height and arranged in the diagonal corridor that characterizes a cohort. The probabilities are then used to obtain the life-table survivors (second diagonal column).

the same triangle minus the number of deaths in the triangle through which the lines in question pass. Having determined the numbers on the horizontal lines, i.e., at each change of age, the numbers on the right-hand edge of the vertical can then be calculated, again by simple subtraction from the number in the corresponding triangles. These results are presented in the second column of figure 4.6.

We can now say that after passing through a triangle the number of lifelines is reduced by a proportion q, which is the ratio between the number of events and the number of lifelines that enter the triangle. This proportion is like a mortality risk but is not one, because the different lifelines do not have identical duration times in the triangle. The values of the proportions q are written in the triangles of the third column of figure 4.6. Let us now separate all the triangles—cutting them out with scissors, for example—and reassemble them while keeping them at their height (and hence their age) as before, which has the effect of inverting those on the same level two by two and reinstating the horizontal sides between them (figure 4.7). By this trick we obtain the 45° corridor identical to that of a cohort. Since each individual triangle is characterized by a particular rate of loss q, it is unchanged during this rearrangement and we record it on the left-hand corridor in figure 4.7. Thus we know the transition coefficient $1 - q$ from each triangle in this "imagined" cohort, and thus between each horizontal line and each vertical line and between each vertical and each horizontal. Applying these coefficients successively to the numbers reached, and taking the actual account at the base of the corridor as the radix, a life table is built up in which the survivors at successive ages appear on the horizontal segments, and the deaths, by subtraction, in the triangles. The entire

84

4. *Period and Cohort Approaches*

Table 4.1. From period to cohort (mortality).

Age (years)	Number in age groups	Deaths (triangles)	Numbers on horizontal line	Transition coefficients	Survivors	Deaths
0			900		1000	
		150		0.167		
	800					219
10			750		781	
		60		0.080		
	900					94
		40		0.044		
20			860		687	
		40		0.047		
	600					65
		30		0.050		
30			570		622	
		35		0.061		
	700					79
		50		0.071		
40			650		543	
		60		0.092		
	500					109
		60		0.120		
50			440		434	

operation can be performed by simple calculation of a life table (table 4.1), but its logic emerges more clearly in the diagram. Indicated in the table are the numbers in the initial age groups, then the numbers in both kinds of triangle. In the third column are calculated the numbers on the horizontal segments. The fifth column contains the transition coefficients $1 - q$ of all the triangles. By treating them as life-table survival probabilities, we can derive the survivors at each exact age (sixth column) and the deaths in the table.

Whereas comparing even one line with the next line was difficult in the tabulation of the initial data, changing to a cohort perspective makes possible an overall interpretation. Working from age-specific deaths in cohorts of unequal sizes, we have constructed an authentic life table whose descriptive properties can be used to calculate life expectancy, for example, or the mean length of life, the age at which the number of persons alive equals the number dead. This is the principle used in the construction of all recent life tables, and the life expectancies (at birth or at a given age) all pertain to a particular year also (for example, life expectancy in country X or Y in 2000 or in 1950, as published in national and international statistical yearbooks). This usage is so common that when reference is made to life expectancy, the label "period" is systematically taken for granted, while, in contrast, when the mortality of a cohort is being studied we specify that it is a cohort life table. What was originally the source of the procedure has become a rare modality. This shows the importance of the technique involved and the need to justify it.

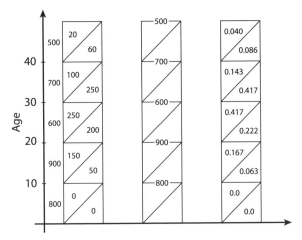

Figure 4.8. Three stages in the calculation of birth probabilities from the triangles of the Lexis diagram. 1. Period births and numbers. 2. Cohort size recopied to the defining ages. 3. Calculation of the probabilities from the triangles by dividing the number of births by the number entering.

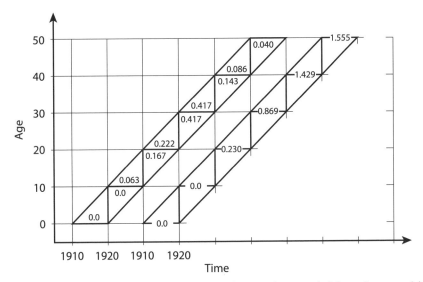

Figure 4.9. The triangles from figure 4.8 are kept at the same height and arranged in the diagonal corridor that characterizes a cohort. The probabilities are used to construct cumulative fertility at each interval age (second diagonal corridor).

The procedure is identical in the case of fertility (still under the assumption of no censoring), except that the size of the cohort remains unchanged throughout and that instead of combining the transition coefficients by the life-table principle we add them together to obtain cumulative fertility at each age and final completed fertility. In figures 4.8 and 4.9 we have repeated the operations performed in figures 4.6

Table 4.2. From period to cohort (fertility).

Age x (years)	Number in age groups	Births (triangles)	Transition coefficients	Cumulative fertility at age x
0		0	0	0
	800			
		0	0	
10				0
		50	0.063	
	900			
		150	0.167	
20				0
		200	0.222	
	600			
		250	0.417	
30				0.869
		250	0.417	
	700			
		100	0.143	
40				1.4299
		60	0.086	
	500			
		20	0.040	
50				1.555

and 4.7 to demonstrate the similarity of the method and the difference between the two situations. In table 4.2, we indicate the fertility calculation that corresponds to figures 4.8 and 4.9, as we did for table 2.1.

In this case, completed fertility obtained in the fictitious cohort (1.555) is called a *period index* as a reminder that the result is obtained from period data. However, this index is measured in number of children, thus doing little to deter its assimilation to a completed fertility (total number of children ever born). Because mortality is an example of processing a nonrenewable event and fertility that of a renewable event, the schema can be applied to any type of event occurring on a lifeline, notably to immigration and emigration, but also to first marriage, divorce, departure by children from the parental home, and similar events.

So far it has been assumed that the double classification of demographic events is available. In practice this is rarely the case. Civil registration statistics normally indicate simply the number of events occurring in the year by the age of those who experienced them. This corresponds to the third case in the Lexis diagram in figure 4.4. Two cohorts are thus mixed together and the procedure outlined above cannot be applied without further elaboration.

4.3   In the Absence of Double Classification

We will demonstrate the method using the case of mortality. That of fertility can be obtained by mechanical deduction. If all we have is the sum of the events occurring at each age over one year, this must be split into two sums corresponding to the two triangles on the Lexis diagram: those who experienced the event before their birthday and those who experienced it after their birthday. We make a simple assumption of equality of the coefficients q in each of the two triangles. We then have to determine the horizontal numbers, that is, on the birthday lines. Since we know the first of them, the births, the first coefficient can be determined:

$$q_1(B + P_1) = E_1,$$

where E_i denotes the number of events in the ith square (thus at age i), P the initial number at age i (on the left-hand vertical), B the number of births, and q the coefficient we want to find. Having determined the first coefficient, we can calculate the number on the second horizontal line A_2, when the first birthday is passed:

$$A_2 = (1 - q_1)P_1.$$

Thus we find ourselves in the same situation with the second square as with the first, since we now know the number at the base A_2 and on the left side B_2. We thus have an equation of the same form as that for the first coefficient with which to determine the second:

$$q_2(A_2 + P_2) = E_2$$

and so on up to the last age.

The same principle can be applied to determine period fertility from the events in the squares. In the case of mortality, because infant mortality is higher in the first days and weeks after birth, the assumption is not that the coefficient is the same for both triangles, but that the one at the base has a coefficient k times higher (depending on the level of mortality, k is set at 2 or 3). This does not alter the principle but merely modifies the starting value of the recurrence. These finer points are often neglected, the events in the square being instead simply divided into two equal parts for each of the two triangles. Such corner cutting is justified, however, since the main source of uncertainty lies not in this division but in the processing of missing data, that is, of censoring, as we will see in the appendix (section 4.7.1).

The generality of the procedure must raise questions over the legitimacy of its constituent operations. What significance attaches to the two-by-two repositioning of the triangles in the Lexis diagram? What is the validity of assimilating the passage through a triangle, from one side of the right angle to the other, to a probability? What, finally, is the validity of the assimilation to a cohort (itself termed *fictitious* or synthetic), under the pretext that the cohort form emerges out of the given manipulations? In this context, it is the nature of the probabilities in the triangles that appears the most questionable. We prefer the neutral term *coefficient*. It is scarcely accurate to speak of individual risks when lifelines that cut the triangle adjacent to its right angle are present only for an instant, whereas those that run close to the hypotenuse are present for virtually the entire period. Thus the coefficient depends on the distribution of the lifelines over a period and is not comparable with an individual risk.

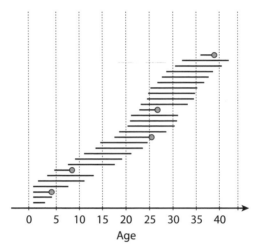

Figure 4.10.   Segments of lifelines corresponding to a ten-year period observation.

It is an empirical coefficient that by its nature looks inadequate for use in a life table or a fertility function. A first step toward clarification of the argument will be to circumvent this coefficient by finding an alternative way to construct cohort measures from period observations.

4.4   Double-Period Censoring

Leave the Lexis diagram and go back to where we started, with lifelines flowing across the Lexis plane. A period observation is composed of all the line segments situated between two vertical lines corresponding to the start and end of observation, for example, from 1 January in one year to 1 January in the next, or between two censuses. In figure 4.5 we saw how the lifelines and their observed segments are displayed. Period observations are thus quite simply double-censored data of the kind studied in the last chapter. In terms of their nature, they do not represent a new phenomenon but provide an extreme example of the familiar censoring phenomenon. Indeed, they can be represented, as we did in previous chapters, by horizontal segments juxtaposed in no particular order (figure 4.10). In figure 4.10 we see all forms of censoring: left censoring, right censoring, double censoring with or without events. The procedure for finding the fertility function or life table that corresponds to these data was specified in the last chapter. For this, however, segments of lifelines are required, whereas in the majority of situations, general statistics supply only breakdowns of events by age and the age structure at a given time in the observation period. Yet we know that these counts and aggregate data are not primary or "raw" information but are derived from counting the more elementary data that are the segments of lifelines. We should therefore attempt to reconstitute these lifelines by making simple assumptions such as linear distribution or distribution according to a fixed seasonal schedules both for events and for age groups. Methods employed at the macrolevel invariably reflect such assumptions and it is as well to formulate them clearly in terms of individual lifelines. For example, it is tempting to replace the assumption of linear distribution within age groups—which creates discontinuities between groups—by a more powerful method of interpolation, for example one using splines. Since these techniques belong to mathematical statistics rather than to demography the discussion appears in an appendix (section 4.7.1).

Presenting the period approach by means of censorings is valuable not only for its greater generality compared with that using the triangles of the Lexis diagram in the previous section. Above all it allows us to discuss the conditions of application in this specific case, and in particular the condition of independence.

4.5 Independence of Period Data

Prima facie, the method used for the censorings meets all the requirements for independence. The fact of cutting the lines on 1 January or on the exact date of a census has no connection with the distribution of the events over the lifetime. Similarly, in the opposite direction, the events are not affected by the cutoff operated by the two dates used. Their occurrence is neither impeded nor hastened by the choice of observation dates. Viewed thus, period data are just a special case of observation from longitudinal data, the only kind appropriate for describing life histories.

If, however, we go back to the definition of independence in the probabilistic sense, the independence assumption appears a good deal less solid. It signifies that for an individual observed between ages x and $x + T$ (where T denotes the annual, quinquennial, or intercensal observation interval) the probability of dying or of giving birth will be identical X years later to that observed directly for individuals of ages between $x + X$ and $x + X = T$. In other words, the mortality probabilities or the fertility rates at a given age are assumed to remain constant over the coming years, for as long as the youngest individual in the period observation has not reached the highest ages, which is in 100 years for a life table and in 35 years for a fertility function (which extends from ages 15 to 50). Such an assumption looks highly unrealistic when we consider the large fluctuations in fertility and mortality over the last fifty years and even earlier. It is not illogical, however. There is, it seems, nothing to prevent fertility and mortality from suddenly becoming fixed at their current values. This, however, is an illusion fostered by the mode of measurement which obscures the dynamics of the lifelines. These unfold according to certain initial orientations that by continuing will influence the unfolding of future events, and thus the aggregate data. To assume that age-specific rates and probabilities of events can become set at their current value denies the dynamic and thus often irreversible character of the trends initiated by the lifelines, notably the timing factors that dictate the unfolding of events like successive births. Almost certain therefore is that the independence assumption is not valid for the processing of censorings and that consequently the change from period to cohort is incorrect.

It could be thought, however, that future variations will balance out on average, that some probabilities or rates are overestimated while others are underestimated. This is not the case. When mortality rises in a given year, almost all the probabilities rise together. And when fertility falls in a given year, almost all the rates move in the same direction. This is understandable since the short-term factors that operate on fertility and mortality affect large age groups if not all ages. If there is a war, more young men will die than in years of peacetime, but so too, in a lesser proportion, will civilians of all ages, either directly through the damage arising from the conflict or indirectly through the change in their living conditions. This finds expression in dependence of a statistical kind. When we compare two adjacent years, the variations in the probabilities and age-specific rates are as a rule strongly correlated. From cohort to cohort, by contrast, the age-by-age differences in the tables and longitudinal functions are, if not statistically independent, only weakly correlated, since the short-term fluctuations are time lagged relative to the age difference between the two cohorts. It would therefore be dangerous to interpret period data in the same way as cohort data. Thus the actual objective of transforming periods to cohorts can itself be criticized. Variations in life expectancies and especially in final completed fertility calculated on period bases are overstated due to the tendency for all the rates and probabilities to move in the same direction. To explain variations in period indices we must once again go back to the lifelines and think through how they are modified by short-term fluctuations. This will form the subject of the next chapter.

4.6   Period Indices

One of the justifications for the *fictitious* or synthetic cohort is that it allows use of longitudinal indices to characterize the situation at a particular point in time. We can speak of period life expectancy and period fertility to differentiate them from the equivalent longitudinal measures based on cohort experience. A statistical argument is frequently advanced to overcome objections to the assumption of constant values for rates and probabilities up to the extinction of all the cohorts involved. The actual numbers of deaths or births do not accurately represent mortality and fertility because they depend on age composition. If the age groups containing young adults are large, more children will be born than would be expected on the basis of fertility, and if elderly people form a large proportion of the population, there will be more deaths. The total period fertility rate and the period life expectancy cut out the effect of the structure of the age pyramid. Because of how they are structured they correspond to a population in which all age groups are of the same size at birth. They allow us to compare fertility and mortality in different populations from which the effect of their age structure has been eliminated. The reference sometimes made to the *standard population method* is intended to make clear this replacement of the age structure by a standard structure.

Two objections can be made. First, why choose such and such standard population structure rather than another for weighting the number of events observed at each age? When used in economics, the standard structure chosen is usually the average structure or the structure of a specified period, i.e., with empirical values as reference. Had there been no difference in structure, all the groups would have the average structure. For populations, however, the structure chosen is not empirical but is given a priori. There is no reason why the populations studied should all have age groups of the same size at birth. The reference is not a standard structure but the longitudinal life history of a cohort. The second objection concerns the actual idea of using a single criterion to summarize a set of rates or probabilities pertaining to different cohorts. To do so implies that there exists a character common to all the fertility rates or all the mortality probabilities, which we attempt to isolate by reducing the local fluctuations inherent to the particular rates and probabilities. This is in fact what all index numbers aim to do. For example, the consumer price index that measures inflation represents a "household's shopping basket," that is, a household expenditure that is more stable than the price of each item individually. Similarly, the CAC40 index of the Paris Bourse (stock exchange) is designed to track the value of an average share portfolio over and beyond the frequently large fluctuations that affect particular shares from day to day. Behind the price index there is the household's shopping basket, and behind the CAC40 there is the portfolio of an average investor. Behind the total period fertility index or sum of age-specific fertility rates, therefore, necessarily stands an object that can only be completed fertility, while behind the combination of mortality probabilities must stand life expectancy, and thus a mean number of years to live. A seemingly real quantity by its name, but one which is unreal or fictitious compared with the reality of the household's shopping basket or the investor's share portfolio. At best it is an object realized in the future. The contents of the shopping basket can be ascertained through expenditure surveys, and share portfolios are also monitored. But the average number of children per woman will not be known until much later, and life expectancy not until later still. There is nothing wrong with making projections of course, but they must not be confused with the current reality. The total period fertility rate and the period life expectancy are long-term projections, and are based on questionable assumptions that, as we have noted, take no account of lifeline dynamics. They are projections too because they reflect the nature of demography, itself heavily conditioned by long-term projection and shaped for this purpose, as we shall see in part II. This is why we must now estimate the value of such projections, not by measuring their past success—which is mediocre—but by examining how such and such a behavior of the lifelines induces such and such a variation or trend in the indices—in other words, by performing thought experiments on the indices. This will be the subject of the next two chapters.

4.7 Appendix

4.7.1 Estimation of Synthetic Cohorts Using Incomplete Aggregate Data

When the data are not sufficiently detailed, the methods of this chapter can still be applied on condition that we estimate what is missing. This is done by making assumptions about the behavior of the lifelines, in general those of constant rates and instantaneous probabilities and of linear distribution of lifelines within a cohort. Here we give a few of the most common examples. The first concerns what to do when we do not have the double classification of observations, but, as is most commonly the case, merely a simple distribution of the events by age over the year of observation, corresponding therefore to squares on the Lexis diagram. The crudest method involves allocating the events equally between the two triangles that form the square, but this disregards all individual behavior. A more refined procedure takes into account the sizes, P_1 and P_2, of the two cohorts that cross the square of the observations and assumes that their lifelines are subject to constant risks or probabilities while passing through the square. The numbers of events d_1 and d_2 in the two triangles of the square are then proportional to the respective populations, which gives

$$d_1 = D\frac{P_1}{P_1 + P_2} \quad \text{and} \quad d_2 = D\frac{P_2}{P_1 + P_2}.$$

Another assumption is rarely verified, that of the absence of entries and exits by individuals during the period and thus of no censorings other than those operated by the limits of the observation or, in the case of fertility, by death. A good method involves using the age distribution of events for the year before and for the year after determination of the age pyramid. We start by separating the events into the triangles using the methods indicated above. Then the sum of the triangles for the same cohort is divided directly into the number in the corresponding age group, which is a good approximation of the number at mid period. We thus have an estimate of the instantaneous fertility or morality rate, as shown in the last chapter. This is the estimate sought for the annual fertility rate and, for mortality, the instantaneous rate μ is converted to an annual probability Q by

$$Q = 1 - e^{-\mu}.$$

5
Interpreting Period Variations in Fertility

Cross-sectional or period analysis seeks to capture changes in demographic behavior as soon as they become apparent, without waiting for their effect on the cohorts involved to be played out in full. Thus a rise or fall in the total period fertility index appears to suggest that completed fertility rate in the cohorts of reproductive age is going to rise or fall relative to the trajectory they had begun to follow. Likewise, changes in period life expectancy are interpreted as a rise or fall in the life expectancy of the persons currently in the population. In this way demographic phenomena are treated rather like driving a car. The course initially taken is changed with a flick of the steering wheel, then it's straight ahead again until the next change of direction. But instead of imagining that the driver behaves thus to take the best route for reaching a destination that he knows from the outset, in the case of demography each new direction is assumed to indicate a new destination. Such a view is not entirely incorrect. Longitudinal surveys on couples' projects concerning family formation show that initial plans are often modified in the course of lifetimes. But while a cohort may not realize the plan it initially gave itself, nor does it swing abruptly from one goal to another. Rather it adapts the family-building process to the difficulties and opportunities it encounters, using the various means of fertility regulation at its disposal: age at union formation, methods of contraception, availability of induced abortion, sterilization, length of breastfeeding. These fertility-regulating practices, which were described in chapter 2, in turn condition both the volume and the timing of births. The general indices that summarize this process—final completed fertility, period indices, and mean ages of mothers at childbearing, which were also defined and described in chapter 2—can be calculated when it is complete.

Since direct observation of the behavior, intentions, and strategies of couples in respect of family formation is difficult if not impossible, these are normally reconstructed from the movements in the general indices. If the period index falls, we conclude that couples are doing more to limit the number of their children; if the mean age of mothers at childbearing falls, we infer that families are being formed earlier. In both cases we may be seriously mistaken. As we shall see, the period index can fall because childbearing is occurring later, without any reduction in the number of children when the cohort fertility is complete. Similarly, a fall in the mean age of mothers at maternity can result solely from a reduction in family size without any shift in the timing of births. These difficulties arise because this interpretation reverses the true direction of the process, attempting to derive causes from their consequences. The system of interrelationships between them is actually too complex to permit any simple and direct inferences to be made. Each event affects those that follow on, creating conditions of general interdependence. We will show this first of all by using schematic examples that cannot be taken very far on account of the multiplication of interactions. The only satisfactory way of studying the mechanism as a whole is to restore the correct direction of the process by using microsimulation techniques. With these we assume the causes, calculate the consequences, and select as the most plausible the simplest configuration of causes that gives the result closest to the observations. This very general technique will be presented in the analysis of a concrete example that has given rise to conflicting interpretations: the decline of fertility in France (1965–85) following the baby boom.

5.1   First Examples of Change in Reproductive Behavior

Take a population in which the successive birth cohorts are of equal size and the lifelines equally spaced on the Lexis plane. Assume that each woman gives birth to exactly one child when she reaches the age of 20.5 years. Then, at time t_0 (1 January 1992 in figure 5.1), one half of the women abruptly modify their behavior and postpone this birth by one year (i.e., to age 21.5 years). Examples are given in figure 5.1, where, on the lifelines, the births occur regularly up to 1992, while after that date the birth continues to occur at 20.5 years on one half of the lifelines and is delayed to 21.5 years on the other half. Using the vertical lines drawn at 1 January in each year the events can be counted year by year. Beneath the diagram we have transcribed the fertility rates in the triangles (number of events in the triangle divided by the number of lifelines passing through the triangle), the period fertility index (sum of the fertility rates for a given year), and the mean age of the mothers when they give birth.

The small delay of one year affecting only half the women has a large impact on the course of fertility. During one year the period index is halved, then it goes back to its initial value. But at the end of this episode, the fertility function has changed. Whereas previously the age-specific fertility rates were all zero—except the rate for 19–20 years, which was 1—the rate for 19–20 years and that for 20–21 years now stand at 0.5. If we relied solely on the changes in the period index, we would infer from these variations that during a single year the fertility of the women had been halved, hence that their intended number of children had been halved, and that they then swung back to their original plan the following year. On its own the period index cannot take account of the shift in timing or, as demographers call it, in *tempo*. We also need to look at the mean age at childbearing, which, one year after the change in behavior, shoots up by half a year. A precise relationship between

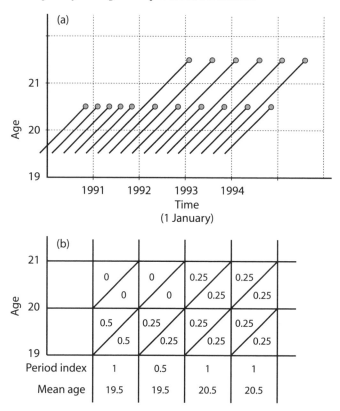

Figure 5.1. Examples of a change in timing. (From 1 January 1992, one in two women delays having her child by one year. The corresponding triangles of the Lexis diagram and the cross-sectional indices are shown below the diagram.)

these numbers will shortly become apparent. We note here that the reduction in the number of births over one year is equal to the completed fertility rate multiplied by the mean delay and by the number of women. If, on the contrary, age at childbearing had remained unchanged but half the women had decided not to have a child, we would see the Lexis plane of figure 5.2 and the fertility rates, period indices, and mean ages indicated below it. During the first year of the changed behavior it is impossible to distinguish the two trends. Only in year two, when fertility returns to its initial level and mean age at childbearing rises, does the first model diverge from the second. At this point we can speak of delay and a timing effect in the former case and of a fertility reduction in the latter.

To make the situation more complex, the change in behavior may occur not at a given point in time but across an entire cohort. Attitudes toward childbearing remain unchanged in the oldest cohorts and are modified from a certain cohort onward. Such a situation is represented in figure 5.3. The earlier cohorts of women all had a child at age 19.5 years and a second one at 21.5 years. From the cohort that reaches age

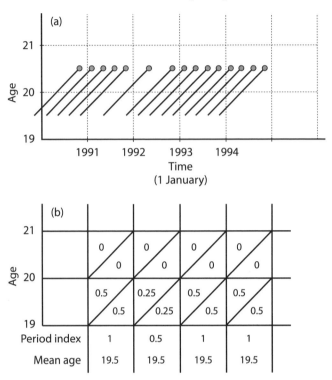

Figure 5.2.   Examples of a change in intensity. (In 1992, half the women have no child. The corresponding triangles of the Lexis diagram and the cross-sectional indices are shown below the diagram.)

18 in 1990, the women have one child only and at 20.5 years. As was done for the previous diagrams, we have counted the events each year and calculated the fertility rates in the triangles, the period index, and the mean age of the mothers at the birth of their children. The result is confused to say the least. The period index falls gradually, but the mean age at childbearing rises before returning to its initial value. An overall assessment cannot be made until the third year after the change, when the cohort that changed has already completed its fertility. There is nothing to prevent reproductive behavior from being modified again in the fourth year, in which case the stabilization of the third year is illusory and impossible to detect.

The conclusion from these first experiences is disappointing. Even with a biography as simplified as the succession of births along the lifeline, changes in behavior are not directly reflected by changes in the cross-sectional indices. Quite the opposite is true. Is the oversimplicity of the examples responsible for this unrealistic outcome? To find out we must get closer to real-life situations by taking into account successive births and considering gradual variations in behavior instead of the abrupt movements in the previous models.

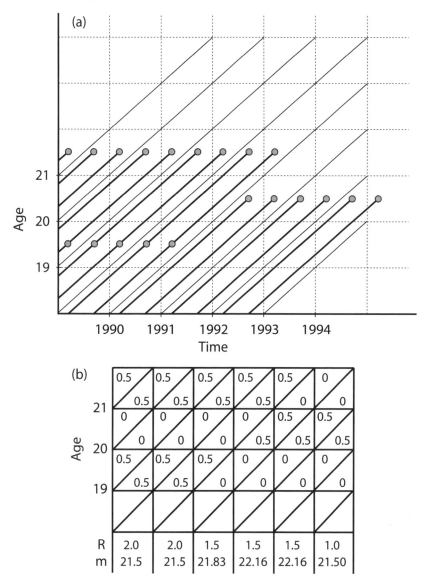

Figure 5.3. Examples of a longitudinal change in behavior. (From 1 January 1990, women who previously had two children have only one. The corresponding triangles of the Lexis diagram and the cross-sectional indices are shown below the diagram.)

5.2 The Logic of Changes in Tempo

Let U be the delay in age at childbearing from time t_0. If we draw the lifelines from this delay (figure 5.4), all the events are shifted backward by a translation of length U on each axis, along the lifelines angled at 45°. During the period extending from

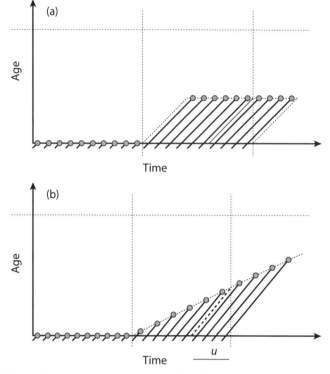

Figure 5.4. Reduction in the period fertility index through a delay u
in age at childbearing: (a) instant increase; (b) linear increase.

t_0 to $t_0 + U$, the lifelines contain no births and so the period index over this interval
of time is zero, then the births come back in their usual number. The relative decline
ΔR in the period index between t_0 and $t_0 + 1$ is thus proportional to U. This is also
the rise in mean age at childbearing Δm. Hence,

$$\Delta m = U \frac{\Delta R}{R}.$$

This simple relationship only applies after the fact, when the effects of the change
in behavior have stabilized.[1]

In reality, the variations are neither this abrupt nor as limited in time. Trends in
mean age at childbearing are fairly smooth with few sharp changes of direction. To
study fertility in the interval between two changes, assume that, from t_0 onward,
the delay in age at childbearing increases steadily over time. Simplify by letting
$t_0 = 0$. A birth that should occur at t is postponed by an interval of time ut, where
u denotes the annual increase in the delay. By assuming constant cohort sizes, we

---

[1] Norman Ryder (1964) was the first to bring the conceptual basis of cohort analysis to the forefront
in demography. In recent years his analysis has been enlarged and systematized by John Bongaarts and
Griffith Feeney (1998).

get the result established already. The births that should have occurred at t are postponed to $t + tu$. All the births that were to have occurred between the time of the change 0 and time 1 are thus spread out between 0 and $t + ut$. The lifelines for such a situation are shown in figure 5.4(b) along with the schema that summarizes the distribution of the births between 0 and $t + ut$. Hence the births observed in the interval represent only the proportion $t/(t + ut)$ of what they would have been in the absence of change. The period index is thus reduced by a ratio of $1/(1 + u)$. As soon as age at childbearing starts to rise, it immediately drops to $1/(1 + u)$ of its value and stays at that level for as long as the mean age continues to rise by an annual amount u. This abrupt movement in the period index is not intuitively obvious. Moreover, it is by no means insignificant. For example, a steady rise in age at childbearing of 2 months per year—like that observed in Western Europe over the last thirty years—automatically causes the period index to fall to $1/(1 + \frac{1}{6}) = 86\%$ of the value of the completed fertility rate that has remained unchanged. In these conditions a completed fertility rate of 2.1 children per woman on average gives a period fertility index of $2.1 \times 0.86 = 1.80$ children per woman. In fact, ignoring slight fluctuations, 2.1 and 1.8 are the values observed in France over the last thirty years for these two indices.

The reasoning can be extended to any variation that delays or brings forward the events being studied. For as we can verify in figure 5.4, in the year under consideration the number of births is equal to their number between the two lines running at 45° through the intersection point of the births' curve (or the changes in timing) with the vertical lines representing the dates t and $t+1$. If cohort membership is constant and equally distributed, the number of births is thus proportional to the difference between these two 45° lines, or, alternatively, as we see directly to $1 + r(t) - r(t + 1)$ if $r(t)$ denotes the age at which the event occurs at time t. Changing from age-specific fertility rates to instantaneous rates, this difference becomes a derivative and we can write that the instantaneous fertility rate $\phi(t)$ varies relatively as $1 - \partial r(t)/\partial t$:

$$\frac{\partial \phi(t)}{\partial t} = \left(1 - \frac{\partial r(t)}{\partial t}\right)\phi(t).$$

The reasoning assumes the delay $r(t)$ is homogeneous, the same for all the lifelines. This is logical since if the delay were variable, the age-specific fertility function would be increasingly dispersed (i.e., its variance would increase) due to the coexistence of women with a large delay and those with a small one. The age-specific fertility functions observed in Western Europe at different times since 1960 exhibit no such dispersion but instead a systematic shift along the age axis, as is seen in figure 5.5 that represents the age-specific fertility rates in 1977 and 1987 for France. The two curves are practically superimposed except for a shift in the mean age of childbearing of around one and a half years (see Le Bras 1997).

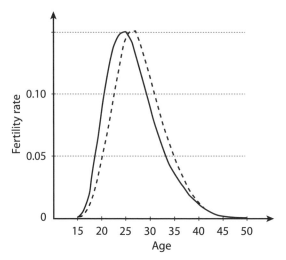

Figure 5.5. Age-specific fertility rates observed
in France, 1977 (solid line) and 1987 (broken line).

The simple relations that have just been established are only valid under the assumption that the delay affects all births, i.e., if all birth intervals grow by the proportion $1/(1 + u)$. All that is involved here is a "stretching out" of time, which explains the simplicity of the formulas obtained. In reality, however, it seems likely that only the first birth is postponed and that subsequent births then follow on at the usual intervals. It is therefore no longer possible to establish simple relations between the changes in the period index and in the mean age of childbearing. In the case of delayed fertility, it is likely that first births are delayed and birth intervals necessarily lengthened, but not in the same proportions. Indeed, mismatches between trends in interval length and in age at first birth may explain the secondary fluctuations in the period index observed in Europe on several occasions since 1974, as we will show later. The only way to measure the impact of such changes and the extent to which they are consistent with observed aggregate data is by microsimulation of lifelines as set out and applied in chapter 2. Working from simple hypotheses about behavioral changes, we reconstruct the lifelines and use them to infer the movement in the main indices, setting the parameter values to get as close as possible to the annual statistics (age-specific fertility rates and their associated summary measures, the period index, completed fertility rate, and mean ages at childbearing).

5.3   Principle of a Fertility Simulation (France 1955–87)

This period has been chosen because of major changes in family-building behavior that were translated into large variations in the fertility indices. In France, after oscillating around 2.7 children per woman between 1946 and 1964, the period index fell rapidly between 1965 and 1976, since when it has stabilized at around 1.8 children per woman. Age at first birth has also undergone a remarkable change. After falling by roughly two months every three years since the end of World War II, it stabilized around 1964 and then, from 1973, quite suddenly began to rise by two months per year. At the same time, completed fertility rate—which reached 2.6 children for the cohorts born between 1925 and 1935—began to fall toward 2.1, the level around which the more recent cohorts born after 1950 are situated. Taken together these changes have often been presented as a fall in fertility to below the cohort replacement level, without any explanation being given for the persistent disparity between final family size (2.1 children per woman) and the period index (1.8). In the previous section we saw that this disparity corresponded to the delay in family building. Simultaneously, however, there was a reduction in final completed fertility. How can we determine the respective contribution of these two changes, and explain, by reference to simple types of behavior, the trends in the different fertility indices? This is where a simulation becomes necessary.[2]

It will be conducted in several stages. First, we will define the stable regimes at the start and end of the transition, and thus determine the parameters that governed final completed fertility for the cohorts born in the middle of the interwar period and for those born after 1955. Then, working from the oldest cohort (1905) up to the most recent (born in 1975), over a total of 840 months, we simulate the reproductive life, month after month, of 100 000 women each month. The first cohorts will follow exactly the process associated with the initial cohort; then we will introduce the bringing forward of events from 1946, their stabilization, and finally the steady delaying of them from 1973. From 1965, the parameters of fertility intensity, hence the parity progression ratio (the probability of going on to have another birth after one of a given order or "parity") will also begin to vary and ten years later will have reached the value corresponding to the final regime.

5.4 Reconstitution of the Fertility Processes at the Start and End of the Transition

The behavior corresponding to a final completed fertility of 2.6 children is simulated by using the microsimulation fertility model developed in chapter 2, for which we have adjusted the parameters to the observations made on the 1931 cohort. To do this we have the following elements: final completed fertility (2.6 children per woman), completed fertility by birth orders 1 to 3 and birth orders 4 and over (average number of children of the birth order considered per woman in this cohort indicated in table 5.1). We also assume that the age-specific fertility rates are those of the permanent regime observed in 1965 when the fertility decline had not yet started.

---

[2] For further details on this reconstitution by simulation, see Le Bras (1993).

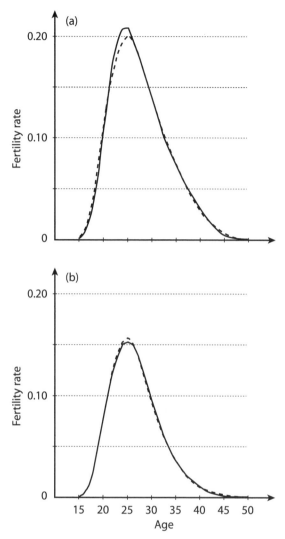

Figure 5.6. Age-specific fertility rates (fertility functions) simulated (unbroken lines) and observed for the permanent regime of the (a) 1931 and (b) 1956 cohorts (broken lines).

They are rescaled to a total of 2.6 so as to neutralize the shifts in timing (figure 5.6(a)). Finally, from the family survey conducted following the 1975 census, we know the average intervals between successive births by completed family size for the women of the 1901–30 cohorts (figure 5.7(a)).

The aim is to specify a microsimulation model with the minimum number of control parameters. Given the fertility conditions prevailing before 1960, that is, before the widespread introduction of modern means of contraception (intrauterine device or pill), the assumption is made that all women entering a union wanted one

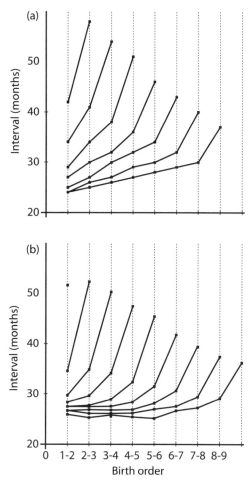

Figure 5.7. (a) Mean lengths of successive birth intervals ranked by final family size (total children ever born) observed for women in the 1901–30 cohorts. (b) Mean lengths of successive birth intervals classed by final family size (total children ever born) obtained with the model simulating the fertility of the 1931 cohort.

child—as indicated by the average first-order fertility of 0.876—and that after each birth, from the first onward, a fixed proportion q of the women wanted a further child, another proportion q_1 wanted no additional children but used contraceptive techniques of low effectiveness (E), and that the remainder, a proportion $1 - q - q_1$, avoided having an additional child by using 100% effective means (abortion, abstinence). Finally, a proportion r of the women who previously used inefficient means switched to using completely efficient means after an unwanted birth (including induced abortion). The numerical estimates of the parameters q, q_1, and r were made by using a simple model where only numbers of births are counted, independently of intervals and ages, hence by comparing just the final completed fertility

Table 5.1. Comparison of final completed fertility by birth order observed
for the 1931 cohort and simulated by the initial model of 2.6 children.

Birth order	1	2	3	≥ 4
1931 cohort	0.876	0.701	0.443	0.596
Simulation	0.862	0.690	0.454	0.564

by birth order. The intervals were fitted by varying the efficiency, E, of the delaying
contraception. The mean age at childbearing was fitted by simple translation. The
values $q = 0.6$, $q_1 = 0.22$, $r = 0.666$, and $E = 90\%$ allow a precise reconstitution
of the various distributions observed as can be verified from figure 5.6(a) and from
table 5.1. The agreement is even excellent for final fertility by birth order, which is
logical since it played a central role in the estimation, but the network of birth intervals (figure 5.7(b)), whose configuration was varied by using a single parameter,
effectiveness, is also well reconstituted. The age-specific fertility rates are themselves fairly close to those observed for 1965. Account must also be taken of the
fact that the distribution of age at couple formation, constructed from that of ages at
first marriage, is hypothetical. The surveys on unwanted births conducted by Jean
Sutter in 1960 provide an indirect but important argument in favor of this reconstitution of initial fertility. From questioning mothers following a birth he found that
20% of them declared not having wanted another child (in addition, 15% would
have preferred a longer interval from the last birth). 20% of 2.6 equals 0.5 children
unwanted. If efficiency is assumed to be 100% instead of the 90% postulated, the
microsimulation indicates that final completed fertility falls by 0.5 children to stand
at 2.1 children.

It would be tempting to conclude that the transition from fertility with traditional
controls to recent fertility with modern means of contraception boils down to this
increased effectiveness of the means of regulation. But that would be a mistaken
simplification. The distribution of births by order (based on mean final completed
fertility by birth order) in modern fertility (1956 cohort) is not the same as that
obtained when effectiveness is increased. Modern means of contraception have
transformed the family-building process, enabling it to be planned with precision.
Thus was established the two-child family model, which signifies a probability of
growth (parity progression ratio) that is high after first births and low after second
and higher-order births, rather than the constant growth probability of 0.6 from the
first child onward of the previous model. Family formation in the 1930s occurred
in a context of greater uncertainty over final completed fertility than is the case
nowadays. If you were aiming for a two-child family, best not be in too much of a
hurry, since with the low efficiency of contraceptive techniques the chances were
that you would conceive additional children. At a deeper level, the two-child family
was largely meaningless as a model since it could not be aimed at with accuracy.

Table 5.2. Comparison of final completed fertility by birth order observed for the 1956 cohort and simulated by the initial model of 2.1 children.

Birth order	1	2	3	≥4
1931 cohort	0.887	0.695	0.306	0.183
Simulation	0.896	0.699	0.311	0.183

Ideas about family size were therefore different, which means that the difference between the two models cannot be reduced to the variation in efficiency alone.

This new family-building behavior must be incorporated to estimate the parameters of the fertility process in the cohorts with access to modern means of contraception. We did this in the same way as for the traditional process. We started from the hypothesis that the parity progression ratio, p, of rank 1 (the probability of having a second child) was high, and that beyond this the probability q of having an additional child was low and constant. We assumed that traditional contraception of limited effectiveness was no longer practiced. We also took into account the fact that modern contraception does sometimes fail and we set its effectiveness at 99.5%. Estimation of the parameters gave the results $p = 0.77$ and $q = 0.42$. The reconstitution of fertility by birth order using these values (table 5.2) is excellent, which is logical as we have seen, but that by age-specific fertility rates is also good (in figure 5.6(b) we compare the result from the simulation with the fertility rates observed in 1985, rescaled to sum to 2.1). Finally, the network of intervals is different from the first model and is consistent with observations made in recent population groups. The intervals are practically constant for a given final family size, except for the last that increases considerably.

5.5 The Transition between the Two Models of Fertility

Simulation of timing changes uses the method put forward at the start of the chapter. From 1946 to 1964, age at union formation fell by 1/15th of a month per month, then stabilized and, from 1974, rose by 1/5.5th of a month per month, equivalent to just over two months per year. These values correspond to the shifts observed for age at first birth. What this means in practice is that an event that should have occurred at t for a woman of age x is postponed to $t + R(t)$ at age $x + R(t)$ when $R(t)$ is the value of the delay at t. A slight difficulty arises here since, at $t + R(t)$, the observed delay will be $R(t)$ and the delay in the events that should have occurred at this time will be $R(t + R(t))$. If we observe a steady delay R of 2 months per year, the delay that occurs will in fact be larger and equal to $R/(1 - R)$, or one fifth of a year instead of one sixth. It will also be noted that all the events are pushed back and not just the initial event, formation of the union. In other words, the delay affects all births regardless of their order (parity) and thus lengthens the birth intervals. This is a strong assumption, which we shall return to later.

The simulation of the reduction in the intensity of fertility is the simplest to model. We performed linear interpolation on all the parameters of the fertility model from those of the initial model in 1965 up to the final model in 1975. The traditional model with a final completed fertility of 2.6 children prevails up to 1965, and from 1975 everyone adopts the modern model. A more complicated transition could be imagined, for example, using a logistic curve or S-shaped curve that represents the continuities more accurately. Here too, however, our choice is guided by the imperative of simplicity. As long as a procedure that is more realistic but more complicated and dependent on more parameters does not give a substantially better fit, the simpler procedure should be preferred.

5.6   Reconstitution of Fertility Change, 1955–87: Two Experiments

We begin by examining what the end result would be if only one of the two changes in fertility—timing or intensity—took place. Assume therefore that final completed fertility alone changed and that age at union formation remained constant from the 1905 cohort to the 1975 cohort. Using microsimulation the birth dates of more than 10 million children and the ages of their mothers can be determined to the day. From this information we derive the age-specific fertility rates for each year, and then their related summary measures, the annual fertility indices, mean ages at birth for each year, and, by following the cohorts, the completed fertility rates. Parts (a)–(c) of figure 5.8 compare the results of the simulation (dotted lines) with the observed values for these three indices during the period studied 1955–87, and for the last three cohorts born between 1924 and 1953 for which final completed fertility is known.[3]

The results from this first experiment are disappointing. The reduction in the period index is considerably underestimated. It starts from a lower level than that of 1964 and stabilizes at a significantly higher level than that in the years after 1975. Similarly, the trend in mean age at birth (calculated on the period fertility rates, i.e., for each calendar year) does not correspond to that observed. Although age at union formation is held constant, mean age at birth falls since it is lower in the modern 2.1 children model than in the traditional 2.6 children model. This is because there are fewer births beyond order three and because shorter intervals due to unwanted births corresponding to unreliable contraception are far less frequent. Only the cohort trend is well reconstituted, which is logical since the initial and final levels in the observation and in the model are identical. The pace, however, is slightly slower. Counterintuitively, this signifies that the changes in behavior preceded and

---

[3] The fourth diagram compares the simulated mean age at childbearing and that observed in the cohorts and is not shown here, since it supplies no additional information and is seldom if ever included.

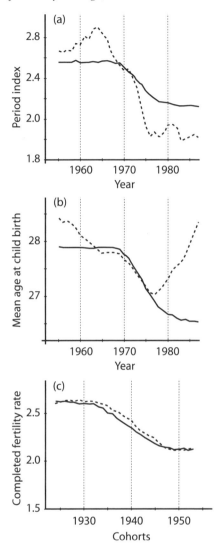

Figure 5.8. (a) Period fertility index observed in France, 1954–87 (dotted line), and reconstituted by microsimulation under the assumption of a transition in final completed fertility from 2.6 to 2.1 children. (b) Mean age at birth (cross-sectional) observed in France, 1954–87 (dotted line), and reconstituted by microsimulation under the assumption of a transition in final completed fertility from 2.6 to 2.1 children. (c) Final completed fertility observed in France for the 1924–53 cohorts (dotted line), and reconstituted by microsimulation under the assumption of a transition in final completed fertility from 2.6 to 2.1 children.

even anticipated on access to modern means of contraception, whereas the oldest cohorts might have been expected to continue using unreliable methods. The fear of unwanted births and the shortcomings of the traditional methods were sufficiently real for the modern means to be adopted without hesitation.

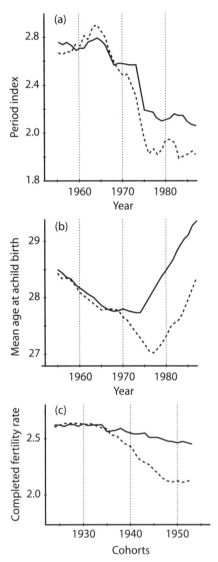

Figure 5.9. (a) Period fertility index, France, 1954–87, observed (dotted line) and reconstituted by microsimulation under the assumption that only the timing of births (age at childbearing) changes over time. (b) Mean age at childbearing (cross-sectional), France, 1954–87,
observed (dotted line) and reconstituted by microsimulation under the assumption that only
the timing of births (age at childbearing) changes over time. (c) Final completed fertility,
France, cohorts 1954–87, observed (dotted line) and reconstituted by microsimulation under
the assumption that only the timing of births (age at childbearing) changes over time.

Assume now that final completed fertility remains at 2.6 children on average per
woman from the 1931 cohort up to the present and that the only changes result from
shifts forward or backward in the timing of births of the kind described earlier. The

trend in the period fertility index and that in mean age at birth (cross-sectional) are represented in figure 5.9. Once again, the trends in the indicators do not match those actually observed. The period indicator mirrors almost exactly the hypotheses selected for the trend in age at couple formation. If it behaves in a highly simplified fashion this is because the hypotheses chosen were simple. The same is true of the mean age at childbearing, for which the trend does not correspond to that observed since it lacks the fall caused by the change of fertility model. We note nonetheless that the period index is highly sensitive to shifts in timing, falling from 2.75 to 2.1 children per woman on average, even though final completed fertility remains practically constant (the slight reduction being due to permanent sterility which becomes more important as age at childbearing rises). A shift backward or forward by a single month over the year is all that is required for the fertility indicator to fall or rise by over 8%. This extreme sensitivity removes much of the interest from the period index. It is more useful for tracking shifts in the timing of fertility than changes in its intensity or in its final completed size.

5.7 Reconstitution Combining the Change in Final Completed Fertility and in Timing

We now combine the two previous developments, the change in the fertility model with the changes in timing. We obtain the three graphs of figure 5.10 for the trend in the period index, the mean age at childbearing, and total number of children ever born. This time the fit is precise. For the period index, all that is missing is the peak around 1965 and the slight hump in 1980–82. For mean age at childbearing and final completed fertility, there appears no significant difference between the simulated and observed results. The same quality of fit is seen in the accuracy of the annual age-specific distributions of fertility.

Can we explain the two remaining discrepancies observed for the period index? It is tempting to see this as an accident of timing and thus to modify the hypothesis of a wholesale shift of all the events, by distinguishing the time of couple formation from that of the first birth and this from subsequent births. The assumption can in fact be made that when modern means of contraception became available in the early 1960s but before they were made legal by the Neuwirth law in 1967, French couples anticipated their legalization and started to use them. This would have the effect of reducing the interval between couple formation and the first birth, whence an apparent increase in the period index. Likewise, in 1980, after five years during which events were delayed, the intervals between successive births then lengthened. Once later age at couple formation was established on a virtually permanent and stable basis, and as a function of the new preference for a two-child family, it is likely that birth intervals reverted to their usual lengths in high-parity families. As can be seen in figure 5.11, which shows the period fertility indices for birth orders

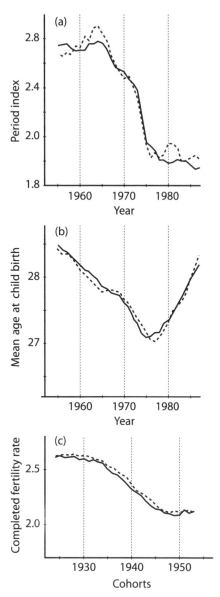

Figure 5.10. (a) Period fertility index, France, 1954–87, observed (dotted line) and reconstituted by microsimulation under the assumption of a change in timing and in final completed fertility (combination of changes represented in figures 5.8 and 5.9). (b) Mean age at childbearing (cross-sectional), France, 1954–87, observed (dotted line) and reconstituted by microsimulation under the assumption of a change in timing and in final completed fertility (combination of changes represented in figures 5.8 and 5.9). (c) Final completed fertility, France, cohorts 1924–53, observed (dotted line) and reconstituted by microsimulation under the assumption of a change in timing and in final completed fertility (combination of changes represented in figures 5.8 and 5.9).

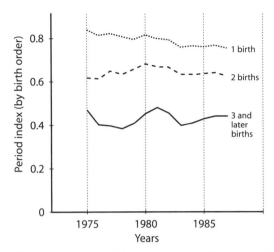

Figure 5.11. Period index by birth order, observed in France, 1975–89.

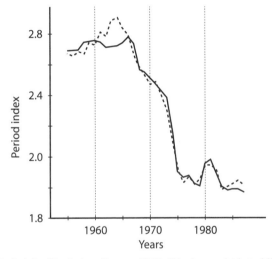

Figure 5.12. Period fertility index, France, 1954–87, observed (dotted line) and reconstituted by microsimulation on the assumptions of figure 5.10 and birth intervals that return to their initial value from 1979.

one, two, and three and higher, the temporary rise in the period index is produced only by children of birth order three and over and owes little or nothing to children of birth orders one and two. This point was in fact noted at the time and, somewhat hastily, was attributed to the "*million Giscard*" named after the French President who, hoping to raise fertility, introduced a special welfare benefit to be paid for third and subsequent births. The effectiveness of such benefits is doubtful. The same increase was observed at the same time in neighboring countries, in particular in Germany, where no measure of this kind had been introduced.

It is likely that after increasing the intervals between successive births, couples reverted to intervals similar to those of the stable regime. This change in behavior is very simple to simulate. All we need do is set up the model so that from 1978 only first and second order births are delayed while subsequent births then occur at their normal pace.[4] In figure 5.12 we see that this extra condition exactly accounts for the temporary fertility increase of the early 1980s. Had the supplementary information on fertility changes by birth order not been available, the hypothesis adopted would have been weaker but it would not have been tautological since there was nothing to suggest that this return to normal applied to all births of order three or above reconstitutes the observed movement. Only 50% or 70% of families would have been concerned, and not all as was actually the case.

5.8   Rules of Interpretation

The last example illustrates the flexibility of simulation and shows how it can be used to verify or invalidate reasoning of the "if . . . , then . . . " kind linking behavioral assumptions to numerical results suitable for comparison with actual observations. Fertility cannot be reduced to one or other summary index. It forms a dynamic system. The only way causes and behavior can be linked to observations and outcomes is by operationalizing this system, and for this simulation is required, since the processes involved are too complex to be reduced to explicit mathematical formulas or functions. Our reason for developing the foregoing simulation in considerable detail was to show an important change in the rules of interpretation. Statisticians and demographers usually infer causes directly from results. They interpret a rise or fall in the period index in longitudinal terms of final completed fertility and speak of a rise or fall in fertility. Such and such an index may certainly rise or fall, but what this signifies depends on a large number of intermediate behavioral factors, including contraceptive effectiveness, parity progression ratios, and variations in age at couple formation, in age when birth is sought, and in desired intervals between births. For a cause of the observed changes to be accepted, it is not enough to invoke the evidence of variations in such or such index. We must test that the change in behavior in question does indeed produce the observed events. The simulation of the new behavior and its transition must therefore be performed on the basis of the previous behavior. Let us make no mistake: without such a simulation an explanation cannot be accepted. If we subsequently wish to contradict the results of a simulation, another, more convincing simulation must be proposed, one that achieves greater precision with the same number of parameters, for example, or gives a better account of observations and indicators overlooked by the simulation being criticized. Mutatis mutandis, the situation is comparable with that classic episode in the

---

[4] To avoid too sharp a discontinuity, this change has been spread over two years, thus 24 months from June 1977 to June 1979.

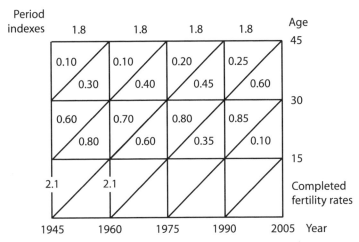

Figure 5.13. Example of a fertility change in which final completed fertility is continuously 2.1 and the period index is continuously 1.8 children. Final completed fertility is thus not the weighted mean of the period indices experienced by the cohort.

history of science, the battle between the Ptolemaic and Copernican models during the period 1550–1650. Merely asserting heliocentrism or the virtues of uniform circular trajectories was not enough; they had to be related to planetary observations and to mechanisms (for example, retrocession or retrograde motion). No inviolable rule exists for comparing the two models (prior to Kepler they were equivalent in precision). But a minimum rule to observe is as follows: against one model we set another model, not arguments of self-evidence.

5.9 Replacement of Generations

What has just been said applies especially to the incorrect but widely used notion of "replacement" level of fertility. The term represents an attempt to determine if, at the current value of age-specific fertility and mortality rates, the population will increase or decrease. It can be answered by computing how many births result on average from a given birth. If fertility and mortality are constant across generations, the answer is in theory known: one female birth is replaced on average by 0.488 times the sum of the age-specific fertility rates multiplied by the probabilities of survival at this age (0.488 is the proportion of female births for one birth of either sex). By summing the fertility rates, we deduce how many births are needed on average to replace one female birth. For the populations of today's developed countries, the value is between 2.07 and 2.1 children per woman, which is why the figure of 2.1 has become so popular as a "threshold of generations' replacement." As is made explicit when accompanied by the term *generation* (cohort), the replacement level is a longitudinal concept. However, it has been wrongly used for making judgments about cross-sectional indices. Thus, the fall in period fertility indices to below 2.1 was interpreted in France as a fall to sub-replacement level. That this is mistaken can be shown by using a simple example (figure 5.13) in which the generations ensure their replacement at the 2.1 level even though the period index they experience throughout their reproductive life is always 1.8.[5] In conditions of varying timing (tempo) and intensity (volume) of fertility, it is impossible to "freeze" the dynamics of the overall process and describe it at a particular point in time by means of a concept like the replacement level. More fundamentally, a comparison between fertility indices and a replacement level mixes up individual characteristics, such as fertility, with collective or population-level characteristics such as population growth rates. In part II of this book we will see that modern demography has been constructed by establishing a bridge between the two levels, of individuals and populations. But this bridge is fragile, and in the case of the replacement level concept, being structurally unsound, it is doomed to collapse.

5.10   Appendix

5.10.1   Method of Microsimulation of Fertility with Variation of Control Parameters over Time

Here we give the means for repeating and modifying the general microsimulations from the previous sections.

   Each simulated lifetime is started (born) at exact time t (a monthly cohort is formed by distributing t randomly over the month considered). An advance-delay function $f(t)$ is defined for any t. The first random choice is that of the exact age at marriage, z. It is drawn randomly from the distribution of age-specific marriage rates, $n(z)$. At $t + z$, the delay is $r = f(t + z)$. Marriage is postponed to age $x = z + r$ and to time $t_1 = t + x$. Simulation of fertility begins from x. The state changes occur month by month, according to the method described in chapter 2. Age and date are treated as rounded values (number of months) of x and t. After each month, the real time and age are updated in the same way as for marriage by adding to the time and the age the exact change backward or forward $f(t + 1) - f(t)$. Thus the progression is by two processes simultaneously, one continuous with time and age, the other discrete and inhomogeneous Markovian with the monthly changes.

   The Markovian states are denoted (a, C, T, n), where a stands for age in months, C the three possible states for contraception—no method used (C_1), traditional method used (C_2), modern method used (C_3)—T the start of the nonsusceptible period (two positions A and V depending on whether there is a birth or a spontaneous abortion, and position 0 for outside the nonsusceptible period) and n the number of children

---

[5] This example is discussed at greater length in Le Bras (2000a,b, pp. 91–99).

Table 5.3. Distributions of the simulation parameters
(Fec., fecundability; NS, nonsterile; NM, never-married).

Age	Fec.	% NS	% NM	Age	Fec.	% NS	% NM
15	0.150	0.983	0.975	33	0.235	0.863	0.090
16	0.160	0.981	0.920	34	0.230	0.846	0.082
17	0.170	0.979	0.850	35	0.225	0.827	0.076
18	0.180	0.976	0.780	36	0.215	0.805	0.072
19	0.200	0.973	0.695	37	0.200	0.781	0.069
20	0.220	0.970	0.600	38	0.185	0.754	0.066
21	0.240	0.986	0.500	39	0.170	0.724	0.063
22	0.250	0.962	0.420	40	0.155	0.689	0.060
23	0.250	0.957	0.360	41	0.135	0.651	0.058
24	0.250	0.952	0.310	42	0.115	0.607	0.056
25	0.250	0.946	0.267	43	0.095	0.559	0.054
26	0.250	0.939	0.230	44	0.075	0.504	0.052
27	0.250	0.932	0.198	45	0.055	0.443	0.051
28	0.250	0.924	0.171	46	0.035	0.373	0.050
29	0.250	0.914	0.148	47	0.015	0.296	0.050
30	0.250	0.904	0.129	48	0.005	0.208	0.050
31	0.245	0.891	0.113	49	0.000	0.110	0.050
32	0.240	0.878	0.100				

already born. The transition formulas are

$$(a, C_i, 0, n) \to (a + 9, C_i, V, n) \quad \text{with probability } \phi(C_i, a)(1 - g(a))$$
$$\to (a + 1, C_i, A, n) \quad \text{with probability } \phi(C_i, a)g(a)$$
$$\to (a + 1, C_i, 0, n) \quad \text{with probability } 1 - \phi(C_i, a),$$
$$(a, C_i, V, 0) \to (a + v, C_i, 0, 1),$$

where v is the random nonsusceptible period following live birth.
For $n > 0$:

$$(a, C_1, V, n) \to (a + v, C_1, 0, n + 1) \quad \text{with probability } 1 - q - q_t,$$
$$(a, C_1, V, n) \to (a + v, C_2, 0, n + 1) \quad \text{with probability } q$$
$$\text{(efficient contraception),}$$

$$(a, C_1, V, n) \to (a + v, C_3, 0, n + 1) \quad \text{with probability } q_t$$
$$\text{(inefficient contraception),}$$

$$(a, C_3, V, n) \to (a + v, C_2, 0, n + 1) \quad \text{with probability } 1 - r,$$
$$(a, C_3, V, n) \to (a + v, C_3, 0, n + 1) \quad \text{with probability } r,$$
$$(a, C_2, V, n) \to (a + v, C_2, 0, n + 1).$$

For any value of n:

$$(a, C_i, A, n) \rightarrow (a + u, C_i, 0, n),$$

where u is the random nonsusceptible period following intrauterine mortality.

In addition, every month, irrespective of the state, the risk of permanent sterility has the probability $st(a)$. If it occurs, construction of the family lifeline is terminated.

The distributions of nonsusceptible periods were given in chapter 2. The probability of spontaneous abortion $g(a)$ is taken as equal to 0.25 irrespective of age. The functions of fecundability with modern contraception $\phi(C_2, a)$ and with traditional contraception $\phi(C_3, a)$ are equal to the biological function of fecundability $\phi(C_1, a)$ multiplied by, respectively, 0.005 and 0.1, the complements of the contraceptive efficiencies. Lastly, the proportions of never-married and nonsterile women and natural fecundability by age in years are given in table 5.3.[6]

---

[6] The monthly values used in the model are obtained by linear interpolation on these annual values.

6

Timing Changes and Period Mortality

A change in timing (tempo) does not exert the same influence on cross-sectional mortality measures, life expectancy in particular, as on the period fertility index.[1] The period index measures an intensity that varies with the pace of the delay or advance, while in a life table the intensity of the phenomenon is always equal to 1 since everyone dies eventually. Does this mean that changes in tempo have no effect on the measurement of mortality? John Bongaarts and Griffith Feeney recently showed that delays (or advances) in the timing of mortality modified period life expectancy.[2] They calculated that, with the current improvement in mortality conditions, life expectancy was overestimated by 2.4 years in France and by 1.6 years in the United States and Sweden. After reviewing the principle of their calculations, we show that the notion of delay does not apply to mortality in the same way as to fertility or marriage. We construct a general model that represents the true nature of mortality processes more accurately. The results obtained show that the discrepancy found by Bongaarts and Feeney probably does not exist. Stated succinctly, in the case of fertility, delays are a cause, while in that of mortality they are a consequence.

6.1 Mortality Decline Envisaged as a Delaying of Deaths

On the example of fertility, assume that from 1 January of year t all deaths are suddenly delayed by a fraction u of that year.[3] Following this on the Lexis diagram, the half plane to the right of vertical t undergoes a 45° translation by the vector (u, u). No deaths occur between t and $t + u$, then deaths reappear in their former number, at ages increased by u. The instant period life expectancy is infinite during the period with no deaths and becomes equal to its former life value raised by u thereafter.

Although the change appeared only at t and the delay persists thereafter, period life expectancy calculated between t and $t + u$ is not a good estimate of cohort life

---

[1] The text for this chapter appeared in a slightly different form in Le Bras (2005).

[2] This approach was introduced in Bongaarts and Feeney (1998, 2003). For a full discussion of their claims, see Wachter (2005) or Goldstein (2006).

[3] We deal with the case of a delay since it corresponds to the actual trend in mortality, but the reasoning is the same for an advance.

expectancy under the new conditions, even though these are stabilized from time t. The same discrepancy is observed if the delay is assumed to increase over time. In this case, the start of the delay is set at $t = 0$, and the delay in the mean age at death observed at t is called $f(t)$.[4] Denote by $s(x,t)$ the survival function at time t and age x, and $S(x)$ the survival function in the initial period. We have

$$s(x,t) = S(x + t - f(t) - t) = S(x - f(t)).$$

The deaths after time $t - f(t)$, and thus after age $x - f(t)$, have not yet occurred due to the delay $f(t)$. By simple derivation we deduce the density of deaths $d(x,t)\,dt$ between t and $t + dt$, and the age-specific instantaneous mortality rate $q(x,t)$, which is also called the force of mortality or the hazard rate (it equals the limit of the probability of dying between ages x and $x + n$ divided by the length of the age interval n as n goes to zero expressed as a function of time t, that is, a function of the period life table applying at time t):

$$\begin{aligned}
d(x,t)\,dt = d(x,t)\,dx &= s(x,t) - s(x + dt, t + dt)\\
&= S(x - f(t)) - S(x + dt - f(t + dt))\\
&= S(x - f(t)) - S(x - f(t)) - (1 - f'(t))S'(x - f(t))\,dt,\\
d(x,t) &= (1 - f'(t))D(x - f(t)),
\end{aligned}$$

and, consequently,

$$q(x,t) = (1 - f'(t))\mu(x - f(t)),$$

where $\mu(x)$ denotes the force of mortality before the initial time.

A simple case is that of a linear change in the delay at rate α for which we thus have $f(t) = \alpha t$ and

$$d(x,t) = (1 - \alpha)D(x - \alpha t).$$

The same relationship holds for the forces of mortality. From them we derive the relationship between the survivors in the period life table $s(x,t)$ and those of the initial table:

$$s(x,t) = (S(x - \alpha t))^{1-\alpha}.$$

Period life expectancy, which is the primitive of the survival function, is then written

$$\begin{aligned}
e(t) &= \int_0^\omega S(x,t)\,dx = \int_0^\omega (S(x - \alpha t))^{1-\alpha}\,dx\\
&= \int_0^\omega (S(x))^{1-\alpha}\,dx + \alpha t.
\end{aligned}$$

---

[4] $f(t)$ is the delay that ends, not starts, at t. Bongaarts and Feeney use it because it corresponds to the delay noted for the mean age of the deaths standardized at t, but its use makes the demonstration artificial since it is conducted from the present to the past. In an appendix (section 6.8.3) we show how to conduct the reasoning with the delays $g(t)$ starting at t, thus from the past toward the future, which clarifies the relationship between $f(t)$ and $g(t)$ and more importantly explains why $f(t)$ cannot exceed unity, which is prima facie strange.

Table 6.1.

Delay per year (%)	Overestimation of life expectancy
5	0.44
10	0.86
15	1.26
20	1.65
25	2.02

If the delay is stabilized immediately after t, longitudinal life expectancy becomes

$$E(t) = \int_0^\omega (S(x)) \, dx + \alpha t.$$

Calculation of $e(t)$ overstates the life expectancy that would be observed if the conditions stabilized, and the faster the delay increases, the greater the overestimation. For the life table for French males in 2000, and depending on the value of α (the delays begin only at age 35), the overestimation would be as in table 6.1 (see Beaumel et al. 2003).

With a rate of 25% we have a value close to that obtained by Bongaarts and Feeney. This is logical since the observed rate of increase in life expectancy in France is around one quarter (three months) per year, i.e., a quarter of a percent each year.

It is not necessary to develop the mathematical formulas to calculate the consequences of this. The delay $f(t)$ introduces a continuous deformation to the Lexis diagram. At t, the deaths over an interval Δt, which can be as small as wanted, are $d(x - h(t))(1 - h(t)/t)\Delta t$; the survivors are $S(x - h(t))$; and the corresponding life table will have, as survivorship function,

$$S(x,t) = S(x - h(t))^{\beta(t)} \quad \text{with } \beta(t) = 1 - h(t)/t.$$

6.2 Mortality Decline as an Elimination of Causes of Death

The process can, however, be construed other than as delays or advances of deaths by analyzing more precisely the mechanism of mortality decline and increase. If we compare the present breakdown of causes of death with statistics for historical populations, for example, the earliest of these, the table published under the name of Graunt and Petty in 1661, we see that many causes have disappeared (e.g., smallpox) or become unimportant (e.g., infectious illness, appendicitis, abscesses). The elimination or reduction of specific causes does not follow the same schema as their short-term postponement, for two reasons. First, it does not involve all of those who are to die, only those who have caught the disease that is now curable; second, the additional survival time after the cure is long on average and uncertainly determined.

Start with a simple case. At time t_0, a treatment is discovered that eliminates overnight a specified cause of death. Under the assumption that the treatment has, from t_0, no aftereffects, so that the cured will live as long as those who never catch the disease, all the survivors are subjected to the risks of the life table that excludes this cause of death. If no other cause of death is subsequently cured, mortality and in particular life expectancy are constant. The temporary increase in life expectancy seen in the case of delayed death is not observed in this case. From the change in the mortality regime, period mortality becomes equal to that of the cohorts subject to the new regime. No correction of the kind proposed by Bongaarts and Feeney is required. Period and even instantaneous measures of mortality accurately reflect current and even instantaneous conditions of cohort mortality. The reason for this warrants explanation.

6.3   Elimination of a Cause of Death: A More Detailed Account

The cure postpones the death of the sufferers to a later date and thus introduces a delay into the timing of mortality. But a delay can take more than one form. In the Bongaarts and Feeney model (referred to here as the *delay* model or method), the shift in the timing of death affects everyone uniformly and is independent of age. In the case of the elimination of a cause of death (which I call the *elimination* model or method), the delay concerns only those who were going to die from that particular cause and it does vary with age. More precisely, let (S, μ, D), (S_1, μ_1, D_1), (S_2, μ_2, D_2) denote the survivors, probabilities (forces of mortality), and deaths, for, respectively, (i) before discovery of the treatment for the cause, (ii) that cause only, and (iii) all other causes, that is, after time t_0. Thus we have the very simple relationships:

$$\mu_1(x) + \mu_2(x) = \mu(x) \quad \text{and} \quad S(x) = S_1(x)S_2(x).$$

Before $t = 0$, the population is exposed to the mortality of the first life table. At time $t_0 = 0$, those who are assumed to die at age x represent a proportion $\mu(x)\,dx$. Of these, $\mu_2(x)\,dx$ actually die from a cause other than the one that is now curable, and $\mu_1(x)\,dx$ are saved and from age x are exposed to the mortality distribution without the cause being considered. Thus for a delay u we have a probability density $k(u) = D_2(x+u)/S_2(x)$. Under the no-aftereffects assumption, this density of the delays is the same as that for persons who have not caught the disease in question. From this we can obtain the total deaths observed at t, $d(x, t)$ taking into account all the delays ending at t and adding in the deaths that have not been postponed (corresponding to the remaining causes of death):

$$d(x,t) = \int_0^t \frac{S(x-u)\mu_1(x)D_2(x)}{S_2(x-u)}\,du + \mu_2(x)S(x). \qquad (6.1)$$

In the same way, the survivors $s(x, t)$ include those who have survived all causes of death and those who have been cured of the eliminated cause and are still alive, thus in the proportion

$$s(x,t) = S(x) + \int_0^t \frac{S(x-u))\mu_1(x-u)S_2(x)}{S_2(x-u)} \, du. \qquad (6.2)$$

We can quickly verify (see the appendix (section 6.8.1)) that the force of mortality $q(x,t) = d(x,t)/s(x,t)$ is constant and independent of t from when $t > 0$ and that we have exactly $q(x,t) = \mu_2(x)$. The forces of mortality are thus constant after the change at $t = 0$ and immediately take their value in the final table.

The case of a sudden change in mortality regime is conceivable. But it was used in the case of fixed delays primarily to introduce the more general situation where delays change over time. This has an equivalent in the situation discussed here of the elimination of certain causes of death. We postulate simply that the cause being considered is eliminated gradually in n stages occurring at intervals T/n, each accounting for $1/n$ of the cured cause of mortality $\mu_1(x)$. Over each period T/n, the same reasoning used above for the single cause can be used, since period mortality instantly becomes equal to cohort mortality. By the same reasoning we also see that there is no need to assume linearity of change since the adjustment is instantaneous and the intensity of the eliminated cause can vary over time, as too can its age pattern. Here then we have a general model.

6.4 A Numerical Example of Both Methods (Delays and Elimination of Causes)

As the above is slightly abstract, let us compare the two methods using a single example. Start with a mortality function over five years where survivors from 0 to 5 years are $\{100, 60, 30, 10, 0, 0\}$, and assume to begin with that mortality is delayed by six months at $t = 0$ (Bongaarts and Feeney refer to a "survival pill" taken by everyone that prevents deaths for six months). By assumption deaths are distributed linearly over the whole age group, so only half the deaths are observed during the first year following $t = 0$ (fourth column of table 6.2). From the following year, deaths occur in the same number as before the pill was introduced at $t = 0$, but shifted to six months later (all new entrants, i.e., children born afterwards, are also assumed to take the pill, delaying their death by six months). By subtracting the deaths from the survivors in each cohort, year-on-year, table 6.2 can be extended for as long as we want. But this is not necessary since as of year two the situation stabilizes for deaths as well as for survivors and mortality probabilities. The number of deaths goes back to what it was before $t = 0$ but life expectancy is extended by six months. If we draw the survival functions, deaths and mortality probabilities for the year preceding the change and the two years following it (table 6.2), a shift or constant delay of six months is seen to appear between the first and third years (and the subsequent years that are identical). But the second year is very different, for the

Table 6.2. Example of a delay in mortality.

	Survivors (Sur) and deaths (D)										Quotients			
Time	−1		0		1		2		3		−1–0	0–1	1–2	2–3
Age	Sur	D	Sur	D	Sur	D	Sur	D	Sur	D				
0	100		100		100		100		100					
		40		20		20		20		20	0.4	0.2	0.2	0.2
1	60		60		80		80		80					
		30		15		35		35		35	0.5	0.25	0.44	0.44
2	30		30		45		45		45					
		20		10		25		25		25	0.67	0.33	0.56	0.56
3	10		10		20		20		20					
		10		5		15		15		15	1.0	0.5	0.75	0.75
4	0		0		5		5		5					
		0		0		5		5		5			1.0	1.0
Deaths (total)	100		50		100		100		100					
Life expectancy	1.5		2.5		2.0		2.0		2.0					

Table 6.3. Quotients of the life table before and after the removal of a cause.

Age x	Final table $Q_2(x)$	Mortality cause removed $Q_1(x)$	Initial table $Q(x)$
0–1	0.2	0.25	0.4
1–2	0.4375	0.11	0.5
2–3	0.5556	0.25	0.67
3–4	0.75	1.0	1.0
4–5	1.0		

number of deaths is substantially lower and the mortality probabilities increase half as quickly. All this is easily explained by the assumptions made about the delay. As a consequence, the total number of deaths in the second year is half that observed in the other years, and the life expectancy calculated from the probabilities is substantially higher than before or after.

Now take the same initial and final life tables (survivors of column 1 and of column 9 of table 6.2) but assume a different story by which mortality is suddenly reduced at time $t = 0$, the difference between the two life tables thus resulting from the removal of a cause of death. For that cause, the quotients of mortality Q_1 are such that $1 - Q_2(x) = (1 - Q_1(x))(1 - Q(x))$, which gives table 6.3.

With this different assumption of a cause removed instead of a delay imposed, the equivalent of table 6.2 becomes table 6.4. Each year after $t = 0$, and at each age,

Table 6.4. Distribution of survivors by age at elimination of the cause of death.

Starting age	Survival time (years)				Total surviving the eliminated cause
	1	2	3	4	
0–1	8.75	6.25	3.75	1.25	20
1–2	2.08	1.25	0.42		3.75
2–3	2.50	0.83			3.33
3–4	2.5				2.5

Table 6.5. Example of removal of a cause of death.

	Survivors (Sur) and deaths (D)												Quotients			
Time	−1		1		2		3		4		5		−1–0	0–1	1–2	2–3
Age	Sur	D	Sur	D	Sur	D	Sur	D	Sur	D	Sur	D				
0	100		100		100		100		100		100					
		40		20		20		20		20		20	0.4	0.2	0.2	0.2
1	60		60		80		80		80		80					
		30		26.25		35		35		35		35	0.5	0.25	0.44	0.44
2	30		30		33.75		45		45		45					
		20		16.67		18.75		25		25		25	0.67	0.56	0.56	0.56
3	10		10		13.33		20		20		20					
		10		7.5		10		11.25		15		15	1.0	0.75	0.75	0.75
4	0		0		2.5		3.33		5		5					
		0		0		2.5		3.33		3.75		5			1.0	1.0
Deaths (total)	100		70.42		86.25		94.58		98.75		100					
Life expectancy	1.5		2.0		2.0		2.0		2.0		2.0					

the survivors of the initial table are distributed in three groups: those who die from a cause in the final table, those who would have died from the eliminated cause, and those who would have survived anyway. The computation is easy because the survival of the second group is like that of the third, i.e., it follows the final table. Thus, of the 40 deaths at 0–1 years in the initial table, 20 in fact die as given by the quotient of the final table, and 20 survive according to the final table, i.e., are distributed like the deaths in the final table between ages 2 and 5. Similarly, of the 30 in the initial table who were to die between ages 1 and 2, 13.2 die and 3.75 survive as defined by the final table, i.e., are distributed like the deaths in the final table between 3 and 5 years, which means using the quotients of the first column of table 6.3 that 8.75 die between ages 1 and 2, 6.25 between ages 2 and 3, 3.75 between ages 3 and 4, and 1.25 between ages 4 and 5. The survival times of those cured of the eliminated cause at each age are distributed as shown in table 6.4.

With this distribution of the delays we can now compute year after year the successive annual totals of deaths and survivors as we did for the previous case of a delay of constant duration. We obtain table 6.5, which is similar to table 6.2. The number of deaths is calculated from table 6.4 using the delays ending at the date and age under consideration. Thus the 11.25 deaths for the period 3–4 at age 3 in completed years result from 7.5 immediate deaths (due to a cause other than that eliminated), 2.5 deaths after being hit by the removed cause 1 year before (starting age 2–3 and survival time 1 in table 6.4), and 1.25 deaths after being hit 2 years before (starting age 1–2 and survival time 2 in table 6.4).

We see in table 6.5 that the quotients and expectations of life reach directly and immediately their value in the second or final table where the given cause is removed. However, deaths and survivors rejoin the structure of the final table only after four periods, which is the length of the greatest delay after being hit by the removed cause of mortality. The overall structure displayed by table 6.5 is more general than that of table 6.2: no proportionality hypothesis is further required.

6.5 Specifying the Reference Mortality

Bongaarts and Feeney contrast a measure of life expectancy calculated, first, from the survival function (of which it is exactly the integral), second, from the standardized distribution of deaths (of which it is the mean age at death) with a survival function calculated from the mortality probabilities. In the real world, public statisticians almost invariably compute period life tables from the observed probabilities. It is practically impossible to work on survivors by cohort, due to the severe distortion of results for the oldest cohorts caused by migration. The purpose of a cross-sectional life table is not to describe conditions long ago but to provide an indicator of current mortality trends. Conventionally, the justification for cross-sectional calculations rests on the "fictitious cohort": if all the observed mortality values were "frozen" at their current levels, the cross-sectional table would exactly represent the longitudinal table.

This pseudo-empirical definition is of little practical use. We can achieve greater precision. It is not the observed values, which are empirical results, that should be "frozen," but the behavioral factors that govern them. A good cross-sectional life table, therefore, is exactly the longitudinal table that would be obtained if all the behavioral factors affecting survival conditions—specifically delays in mortality and elimination of causes of death—suddenly became constant at their current levels. In the example comparing the two methods, these longitudinal tables were generated gradually because the behavioral factors became constant from time 0. Following some erratic values, the last columns of tables 6.2 and 6.4 gave the survivors of the longitudinal table made constant after $t = 0$. What is in question, therefore, is not the comparison between the calculation by probabilities and by survivors—which arises neither empirically or theoretically—but the validity of cross-sectional tables for describing longitudinal trends, that is, the future experience of groups of individuals, or, at least, the orientation of this future experience at a given point in time.

In table 6.4 we see that the mortality probabilities (quotients) adjust instantly and so too therefore do the life expectancies in the life table computed from them. The deaths and survivors, on the other hand, reach the structure of the final table only after four periods, which is the length of the longest delay. We see that this second table presents a much more general structure than the first. The probabilities for the second table can take any value (though smaller than those of the first and those for the eliminated cause also). No proportionality assumption is needed here.

Compared with the notion of a fictitious cohort, the freezing of behavior at a given point in time is relatively clear in meaning. But there are nevertheless some aspects that require further explanation. From this point of view, the two methods already differ in the simple case of the sudden one-time change at $t = 0$. In the elimination method illustrated in table 6.4, we do not convert the cross-sectional observations to longitudinal observations but wait for the full effect of the behavioral factors becoming constant to be felt and for the table to stabilize. The longitudinal table does not exist empirically but is the result of applying a model, in this case the elimination of a cause of death. The question being answered is, What will future mortality be in the absence of this cause? In the delay model, stabilization is faster, since it occurs as of year one. In both models, however, the longitudinal life table cannot be defined empirically during the stabilization period. This is a process that converges more or less quickly.

The case of a gradual or continuous change is more problematic. In the elimination model, the final life table probabilities are reached immediately through instantaneous adjustment. But in the case of a delay $f(t)$, with delays or advances varying over time t, which behavioral factors, and thus which delays must be frozen, those starting at t or those ending at t? The first solution is the most rational, but the duration of the shift starting at t is unknown and cannot be determined until it ends by calculating the mean age at death. Between the two possibilities the difference is large, as can be shown by a small calculation. When $f(t)$ grows steadily (linearly) from time 0 at a pace α, the last delay observed at t comes from the period $t - \alpha t$. The delay starting at t then has the value $\alpha t / (1 - \alpha)$ (see the appendix (section 6.8.3)). The delay ending at t equals αt. When behavior is frozen at t, the difference d should therefore again increase by $d = \alpha t / (1 - \alpha) - \alpha t$, or $\alpha^2 t / (1 - \alpha)$. With a rate of growth of 25% and $t = 30$, which are the conditions currently prevailing in Western Europe, we get $d = 2.5$ years. It is amusing to note that this is the same value that Bongaarts and Feeney obtain for their correction, which is thus attributable entirely to the fact of considering the expected behavior at t and not that observed at $t - f(t)$. Compared with the elimination-of-causes method, the delay method presents the weakness of not permitting an empirical definition of behavior at time t, and nor therefore construction of a fictitious cohort table. If a correction is required, what it is made in relation to must first be defined, and this reference is what is wanted instead of the observed pattern.

6.6   Unifying the Viewpoints: The Repartition Function of the Deaths

The difference between the two methods arises from the way the delays are handled. By formulating the problem in more general terms, it will be seen that we are dealing with two particular cases that possess remarkable and even unique properties. To do this, call $\lambda(x - u, v)$ the proportion of deaths expected at age x that were delayed by duration v at $t - u$, and let $\theta(x)$ be those that actually occurred. Counting all the deaths, delayed or not, at t and of age x, gives us the density of deaths[5]:

$$d(x,t) = \int_0^t S(x - u)\lambda(x - u, u)\, du + \theta(x)S(x). \tag{6.3}$$

Similarly, the survivors at t and of age x are those whose delay is not yet finished or who have not yet appeared among the possible deaths:

$$s(x,t) = S(x) + \int_0^t S(x - u)\left(\int_u^\omega \lambda(x - u, v)\, dv \right) du. \tag{6.4}$$

The two methods can be rewritten as follows.
   The elimination-of-causes-of-death method:

$$\lambda(x, v) = (\mu(x) - \theta(x))D_2(x + v)/S_2(x), \quad \theta(x) = \mu_2(x).$$

The delay method:

$$\lambda(x, v) = \delta(v - T)\mu(x),$$

where δ is the Dirac function and T the delay, $\theta(x) = 0$.
   Each of these two examples for the choice of a distribution of delays has a special property. The elimination-of-causes-of-mortality method is the only decomposable repartition for which the age-specific mortality probabilities are immediately identical to the final probabilities of the life table without the eliminated cause. The delay method assumes a fixed delay $f(t)$ common to everyone. The demonstrations of these properties are given in the appendix (sections 6.8.2 and 6.8.3). The first property constitutes a serious reason for using cross-sectional mortality values to derive longitudinal values. It justifies their use, which is not the case for the period fertility index compared with final completed fertility. The fictitious cohort method that is

---

[5] The formulas could be simplified by using Lebesgue integrals instead of Riemann integrals, which would allow everything to be placed under the integral sign. But we consider it preferable to remain in touch with the actual process, distinguishing between those who benefit from a delay and those who die immediately.

highly sensitive to tempo changes when used on fertility appears on the contrary adapted for use on mortality.

The delay method, on the other hand, is fairly restrictive. In the appendix (section 6.8.3), we show that it in fact assumes that all the deaths expected at $t - f(t)$ are delayed by $f(t)$ exactly and thus occur at t. At t, the observed functions for survival, deaths, and force of mortality are shifted by amount $f(t)$. It is not a priori obvious that the delay method is based on a uniform and constant delay of duration $f(t)$ at $t - f(t)$. The method's authors recall that the assumption of proportionality in the force of mortality at t results in the shift in the life table functions of $f(t)$ at t. But this shift in turn necessarily assumes that all deaths at $t - f(t)$ be postponed by exactly t. To illustrate just how restrictive this condition is for the definition of behavioral change, look again at the example given at the outset of a sudden, one-time and uniform delay T at $t = 0$. Assume instead that a proportion p benefit from the postponement T while $1 - p$ die with no delay. For $t < T$, applying formulas (6.3) and (6.4) gives

$$d(x,t) = (1 - p)\mu(x)S(x)$$
$$= (1 - p)D(x),$$
$$s(x,t) = S(x) + p(S(x - t) - S(x))$$
$$= (1 - p)S(x) + pS(x - t).$$

The result is a force of mortality:

$$q(x,t) = \frac{\mu(x)}{1 + pS(x - t)/((1 - p)S(x))}.$$

Proportionality no longer holds since the denominator varies with age x. When delay T has ended, the postponed deaths are again counted and the force of mortality becomes

$$q(x,t) = \frac{(1 - p)D(x) + pD(x - T)}{(1 - p)S(x) + pS(x - T)}.$$

It can be seen that the shift varies with age due to the varying slope of $S(x)$. So proportionality is also lost when equilibrium has been restored. These remarks can be extended to the case where the delays follow a distribution $h(T)$ (see the appendix (section 6.8.3)). The delay method assumes therefore that the shift of size $f(t)$ applies to all individuals uniformly. This is not very plausible. We now have enough information to compare the two methods, or more exactly to compare their validity.

6.7 The Two Models Compared

The contradiction between the two possible models of mortality change has been clarified. It stemmed from a difference in the distribution of the delays in deaths.

This does not eliminate the difference in the results, since life expectancy is over-estimated (or underestimated) when mortality declines (or increases) in the first model, and not in the second. Which of the two models should we choose? Which is the most plausible when judged from the standpoint not of mathematics but of the real processes of mortality change? The answer is found through a comparison of how risks and delays are handled by each method. As its name suggests, the delay method starts from the shifts that delay mortality and from these infers the risks. The elimination-of-causes method puts the risks first and from them infers the size of the delays. Does mortality change involve changes in delays that transform the risks or changes in risks that modify the delays? This is the central point at issue.

Begin by comparing the two simple cases of a single change at $t = 0$. Is it likely that every death would be pushed back by a few months? This could perhaps be accepted in the case of the extremely old or terminally ill, but the kind of medical care that postpones deaths due, for example, to infections or accidents, leaves life expectancy much as it would have been without the risk, and thus of a large duration. More importantly, it is unreasonable to assume that no single accident will occur during a length of time equivalent to the delay. A murder, an earthquake, a new disease may happen or appear at any time. Someone wanting to avoid a birth during a given period of time can practice contraception or, if this fails, terminate the pregnancy. Shifts in timing play a major role in fertility and nuptiality since they are subject to human control. A wedding day can be postponed; but the date of death, save in the case of suicide, can scarcely be modified by the person at risk—otherwise the vast majority of persons would put off the fatal hour indefinitely.

Another argument concerns the consistency of the longitudinal reference model itself. In this model every death is delayed by a length of time $T = f(t)$, but only once. Examine the detail of the longitudinal mortality process under the assumption of the constant delay T. When a death was to occur according to the risk in the reference table before the change, it is delayed by T. But after this delay, it is not delayed again at the point when it is supposed to occur. There is no second chance of delaying death. Thus the population is split into two groups: those whose date of death is already programmed, and those who are not yet threatened. Life expectancy differs substantially between these two groups. Difficulties of this kind do not arise with the elimination-of-causes model. After the cause in question has been removed, mortality is the same for everyone and corresponds to the new table calculated without this cause. The reasoning applies in the same manner in the area of risks, and the delays are computed afterwards. In the delays model, by contrast, the risks of the new table are calculated from the delays. If we broaden the perspective and take a very long-term view of mortality—from the time of Cro-Magnon, for instance—mortality reduction in the delays model operates through the addition of many small delays that are identical for everyone. Differentiating individuals is not possible since hazard plays no part, and if it did its result would have to be Gaussian in form.

The elimination-of-causes model is more realistic. It describes well the process of long-term mortality decline through the elimination or attenuation of causes of death. From the standpoint of the demographer it also fits in well with the analysis of mortality by causes and with the calculation of multiple decrement life tables under the hypothesis of independence of causes. In sum, mortality is a multiplicative rather than additive process. It could be argued that both methods are possible by saying that they represent the two faces of the same reality, but this is incorrect. The risks can be calculated from the delays (with the notation used before):

$$\mu_2(x) = \mu(x) - \mu_1(x) = \mu(x - T),$$
$$\mu_1(x) = \mu(x) - \mu(x - T).$$

If $\mu(x)$ follows a Gompertz curve of the form $\mu(x) = Ae^{rx}$, $\mu_1(x)$ and $\mu_2(x)$ also follow a Gompertz curve with the same slope but shifted toward the older ages:

$$\mu_1(x) = A(1 - e^{-eT}).$$

This property could be seen as an argument in favor of the delay method, since, for ages over 30, this does describe the current situation in developed countries. But the same result is obtained by postulating the elimination of a cause of death whose probability varies exponentially with age at the same rate r. Many causes of death present this profile. In addition, other $\mu_1(x)$ profiles are possible, which have no equivalent in terms of given delays, nor of the proportionality rule. In sum, the balance is clearly in favor of the elimination-of-causes method:

- Life expectancy following a postponed death at age x is more likely to be close to life expectancy at age x than to a low value of a few months.

- In reality, this life expectancy probably varies substantially with age, falling as age increases, whereas in the first model it is held constant.

- In the delay method, the reference remains the initial life table, whereas in the elimination method it disappears and the new table established by elimination of the cured cause immediately becomes the reference.

- The longitudinal model corresponding to elimination of a cause is more coherent than that in which a delay T is added to each death. In the former case, the new table is simulated on the basis of the initial one and excluding any death from the eliminated cause, however many times the person is affected by this cause of mortality. In the second case, we have to differentiate between those who have benefited once from the delay and will not benefit from it again, and those who have not yet benefited from it and will be able to benefit from it. This creates a distinction between two subgroups with sharply contrasted mortality, the first subject to the original table, the second to a short additional survival time, T.

Table 6.6. Mortality rates by age in August 2003 in France during the heat wave compared with the average annual mortality rates of the three former years.

Age group	Heat wave mortality rate (per million)		Mortality rates of the three former years (per hundred thousand)	
	Men	Women	Men	Women
60–64	115	50	65	27
65–69	244	138	99	41
70–74	396	281	149	69
75–79	786	673	226	122
80–84	1901	1 923	356	227
85–89	2759	2 821	528	400
90–94	5702	6 696	712	620
95+	9900	12 431	809	780

However, we have examined primarily the textbook example of a single change and not that of a continuous change. Could the delay model have the advantage in the latter case? All the previous remarks still apply, and one more is added, concerning the longitudinal reference table that we showed to be poorly defined. The delays cannot be assumed to have stabilized since the period $t - f(t)$, and we are unable to say how they have evolved. This problem does not arise with the elimination-of-causes method, since at any point in time it equates to the longitudinal reference table.

The preceding discussion does not mean that all mortality change is of the elimination-of-causes kind. This is true only for the long term. But in the short term there are numerous sources of fluctuations, such as seasonal variations in temperature and rainfall or influenza epidemics. These may advance or delay deaths by a few months, but on average, because they oscillate, their influence over the medium term is insignificant. The judgment of a Solomon might be to take the delay method for the short term, and the elimination-of-causes method for the long term. But the proportionality rule is not generally satisfied over the short term. Influenza, periods of extremely high or low temperatures, can be fatal for the very young and very old. A good recent example of this is provided by the mortality from the heat wave in France in August 2003. The age-specific mortality rates observed at this time are reported in table 6.6. It can be seen that they increase much faster than the general mortality probabilities.

The best way of handling seasonal accidents in fact remains the multiple-decrement life table. With it can be calculated the fraction of life expectancy that has been abruptly lost in the accident, since by definition this is not a new and lasting change in longitudinal survival conditions. Contrary, therefore, to the judgment of

Solomon (or that of an inhabitant of Normandy) proposed above, the elimination-of-causes method remains the most pertinent and, as a final advantage, necessitates no correction.

6.8 Appendix

6.8.1 Calculation of Deaths and Survivors of Age x for Elimination of a Cause of Mortality at the Origin

The calculation allows us to show that the ratio of deaths to survivors (force of mortality) at age x is independent of t and thus that the period life table adjusts instantly to the new longitudinal table minus the eliminated cause. From the distribution of delays in the risks model, we obtain the deaths in the life table without the treated cause.

The distribution of delays u in $t = 0$ at age x was seen to be $u = 0$ in $\mu_2(x)$ cases and $f(u) = D_2(x+u)/S_2(x)$ in $\mu_1(x)$ cases. In the opposite direction, deaths in a cohort at age x can be calculated from the delays ending at age x:

$$
\begin{aligned}
s(x,t) &= S(x) + \int_0^t \frac{S(x-u))\mu_1(x-u)S_2(x)}{S_2(x-u)}\, du \\
&= S(x) + \int_0^t S_1(x-u)\mu_1(x-u)S_2(x)\, du \\
&= S(x) + \int_0^t S_1(x-u)\mu_1(x-u)S_2(x)\, du \\
&= S(x) + S_2(x) \int_0^t -S_1'(x-u)\, du \\
&= \begin{cases} S(x) + S_2(x)(S_1(x-t) - S_1(x)) = S_2(x)S_1(x-t) & \text{if } t < x, \\ S(x) + S_2(x)(1 - S_1(x)) = S_2(x) & \text{if } t > x. \end{cases}
\end{aligned}
$$

The force of mortality $q(x,t) = d(x,t)/s(x,t)$ is

$$
q(x,t) = \begin{cases} D_2(x)\dfrac{S_1(x-t)}{S_2(x)S_1(x-t)} = \dfrac{D_2(x)}{S_2(x)} & \text{if } t < x, \\[2ex] \dfrac{D_2(x)}{S_2(x)} & \text{if } t > x. \end{cases}
$$

Therefore, for any $t > 0$, the force of mortality at age x is the force of mortality $\mu_2(x)$ of the final life table, the one that no longer contains the eliminated cause.

6.8.2 Properties of the Two Methods

Let (S, D, μ) be the life table of reference, $d(x,t)$ the density of deaths at age x, at time t after the change, $s(x,t)$ the survivors, and $\lambda(x - u, u)$ the probability that a death expected at $t - u$ at age $x - u$ will be delayed by u. Summing all the deaths that occur at t at age x after observation of the delays, we have

$$d(x,t) = \int_0^t S(x - u)\lambda(x - u, u)\, du + \theta(x)S(x),\qquad (6.5)$$

$$s(x,t) = S(x) + \int_0^t S(x - u)\left(\int_u^\omega \lambda(x - u, v)\, dv\right) du.\qquad (6.6)$$

Finally, let the sum of the probabilities of death and of postponement at x, for any $t > 0$, be the instantaneous probability $\mu(x)$:

$$\int_0^\omega \lambda(x + u, u)\, du + \theta(x) = \mu(x).\qquad (6.7)$$

As examples, the function λ takes the following forms:

(i) $\lambda(x, v) = (\mu(x) - \theta(x))D_2(x + v)/S_2(x)$ in the case of the elimination of a cause of mortality. (S_2, D_2, μ_2) denotes the table derived from the reference table by eliminating the cause under consideration.

(ii) $\lambda(x, v) = \mu(x) f(v)$ in the case of a distribution of the delays v independent of age and with the probability distribution $f(v)$.

We will show that the method of an eliminated cause of mortality is the only decomposable one in which the mortality probability observed at age x does not vary once the change has occurred, and that, in this case, $\theta(x) = \mu_2(x)$.

Define

$$\phi(x) = d(x,t)/s(s,t).$$

The derivative in t of the second member must be nil for any value of $t > 0$, and, using the formulas for the deaths and survivors, is written

$$\frac{\partial d(x,t)}{\partial t} s(x,t) = d(x,t)\frac{\partial s(x,t)}{\partial t},$$

$$S(x - t)\lambda(x - t, t)s(x,t) = d(x,t)S(t - x)\left(\int_t^\omega \lambda(x - t, v)\, dv\right),$$

that is,

$$\lambda(x - t, t)s(x,t) = d(x,t)\left(\int_t^\omega \lambda(x - t, v)\, dv\right),$$

$$\lambda(x - t, t) = \phi(x)\left(\int_t^\omega \lambda(x - t, v)\, dv\right).\qquad (6.8)$$

Substitute $\lambda(x - t, t)$ in formula (6.3) giving the deaths to get

$$d(x,t) = \phi(x)\int_0^t S(x - u)\left(\int_u^\infty \lambda(x - u, v)\, dv\right) du + \theta(x)S(x)$$

$$= \phi(x)(S(x,t) - S(x)) + \theta(x)S(x)\quad \text{because of (6.4)}$$

$$= d(x,t) + S(x)(\theta(x) - \phi(x)).$$

Therefore,

$$\phi(x) = \theta(x),$$

whence

$$\lambda(x - t, t) = \theta(x)\left(\int_t^\omega \lambda(x - t, v)\, dv\right). \tag{6.9}$$

Assume now that the delay function is decomposable:

$$\lambda(x - t, t) = A(x - t)B(x).$$

Substituting into (6.9), we have

$$A(x - t)B(x) = \theta(x)\int_t^\omega A(x - t)B(x + v - t)\, dv,$$

$$B(x) = \theta(x)\int_t^\omega B(x + v - t)\, dv$$

$$= \theta(x)\int_x^\omega B(u)\, du.$$

The last formula is that of a life table, and more specifically the life table (S_2, μ_2, D_2), encountered earlier in the case of the elimination of a cause of mortality. We have

$$B(x) = D_2(x),$$

$$S_2(x) = \int_x^\omega B(u)\, du = \int_x^\omega B_2(u)\, du,$$

$$\mu_2(x) = \theta(x).$$

It remains for us to find the possible values of $A(x - t)$. For this, we take equation (6.7), which becomes

$$\int_0^\omega D_2(x + u)A(x)\, du + \mu_2(x) = \mu(x),$$

$$A(x)\int_x^\omega D_2(v)\, dv = \mu(x) - \mu_2(x),$$

$$A(x)S_2(x) = \mu(x) - \mu_2(x),$$

$$A(x) = (\mu(x) - \mu_2(x))/S_2(x).$$

Since $\mu_1(x) = \mu(x) - \mu_2(x)$, $A(x) = \mu_1(x)/S_2(x)$.
   We can now give the expression for $\lambda(x - t, t)$:

$$\lambda(x - t, t) = A(x - t)B(x)$$

$$= D_2(x)\mu_1(x - t)/S_2(x - t).$$

This is exactly the expression obtained with an instantaneous elimination at $t = 0$ of a cause of mortality described by the life table (S_1, μ_1, D_1). The model of the elimination of a cause of mortality is thus the only decomposable model for which the mortality probability observed immediately takes its current longitudinal value and is therefore independent of the time elapsed since the change.

In the case of a distribution of delays independent of age, $\lambda(x - t, t)$ is written

$$\lambda(x - t, t) = \mu(x - t)g(t).$$

Substituting this expression in formula (6.9) giving the equality for the longitudinal and cross-sectional tables after the change, we have

$$\mu(x - t)g(t) = \phi(x)\left(\int_t^\omega \mu(x - t)g(v)\,dv \right),$$

$$g(t) = \phi(x) \int_t^\omega g(v)\,dv.$$

This imposes $\phi(x) = k$ (a constant) and $g(t) = Ce^{kt}$.

Substituting in equations (6.3) and (6.4) giving the deaths $d(x, t)$ and the survivors $s(x, t)$, we get a contradiction since their ratio depends on t:

$$d(x, t)/s(x, t) = k(s(x, t) - S(x))/s(x, t)$$

6.8.3   Fixed and Variable Delays

First, look again at the evaluation of the deaths and forces of mortality from the value of the delays $g(0)$ counted from their beginning θ (and not $f(t)$ at their end at t). Let θ be the starting time of the delay that ends at t. We have $t = \theta + g(0) = 0 + f(t)$. Take an interval $\Delta\theta$ after θ. The delay beginning at $\theta + \Delta\theta$ ends at $t_1 = \theta + \Delta\theta + g(\theta + \Delta\theta)$, which is equivalent to $\theta + \Delta\theta + g(\theta) + g'(\theta)\Delta\theta$. The interval Δt between t and t_1 is therefore

$$\Delta t = (1 + g'(\theta))\Delta\theta.$$

At the end point at t, the density of delayed deaths is thus at the ratio $1/(1 + g'(\theta))$ with the density of the delayed deaths at the start at θ. What happens now to the increase in the delay at arrival? Between t and t_1, delay $f(t)$ grows by $g'(\theta)\Delta\theta$. Its derivative is thus

$$f'(t) = \frac{g'(\theta)\Delta\theta}{\Delta t} = \frac{g'(\theta)\Delta\theta}{(1 + g'(\theta))\Delta\theta} = \frac{g'(\theta)}{1 + g'(\theta)}.$$

Here we have the relationship for the deaths in the case of a delay:

$$d(x, t) = (1 - f'(t))D(x - f(t)) = \frac{D(x - g(\theta))}{1 + g'(\theta)}.$$

By the previous formula, we have

$$1 - f'(t) = 1 - \frac{g'(\theta)}{1 + g'(\theta)} = \frac{1}{1 + g'(\theta)}.$$

The formula from the start and not from the end is needed to write the case where delay u varies according to a law of probability $k(u)\,du$. Let us show that the proportionality assumption then no longer holds and that Bongaarts and Feeney are therefore operating from the hypothesis of a fixed delay according to age at time t. Begin with the simple case of a sudden change at time $t = 0$. In this case the deaths $d(x,t)$ at age x will be

$$d(x,t) = \int_0^t k(u)D(x-u)\,du \tag{6.10}$$

and the survivors $s(x,t)$ will be

$$s(x,t) = S(x) + \int_0^t G(u)D(x-u)\,du, \tag{6.11}$$

where

$$K(u) = \int_u^\omega k(v)\,dv. \tag{6.12}$$

For the proportionality assumption to be met requires that

$$d(x,t) = p(t)D(x-l(t)). \tag{6.13}$$

Integrating over the entire age range of the formulas of the deaths (6.10) and (6.13), we obtain

$$\int_0^t k(u)\,du \int_{-\infty}^\omega D(x-u)\,dx = p(t) \int_{-\infty}^\omega D(x-l(t))\,dx,$$

so, because of (6.12),

$$1 - K(t) = p(t).$$

Under these conditions we obtain

$$D(x-l(t)) = \int_0^t \frac{k(u)}{1-K(t)} D(x-u)\,du,$$

where $k(u)/(1-K(t))$ is a probability distribution over $\{0,t\}$, the distribution of deaths at each age should be a weighted mean of itself with a constant shift, which is a priori impossible given that the distributions of delays, $k(u)$, and of deaths, $D(x)$, are not related.

If, in the simplest case, the proportionality property is lost when a single delay is replaced by a distribution of possible delays, this is also the case a fortiori when the delay varies over time. In adopting the proportionality assumption, therefore, Bongaarts and Feeney make a very strong—and, as we have seen, questionable—assumption of an identical delay $g(\theta)$ for all the persons who were to die at θ.

Part II

Populations

7

Forecasts, Projections, and Prospects

Before the twentieth century no relationship could be established between the behavior of individuals subject to probabilities of dying and reproducing, i.e., experiencing a set of mortality and fertility distributions, on the one hand, and, on the other, the behavior of populations as defined by increase and decrease in numbers and by age distributions. By the eighteenth century, measurement of mortality and calculation of life expectancy were already in wide use. The average number of children per couple was another topic that captured attention early on, as Deparcieux's book (1746) and a long chapter in Malthus's *Essay* make clear. At a different scale, evaluations of population-doubling times and of the proportions of different age groups first appeared in works of political arithmetic during the second half of the eighteenth century.

But the relationship between these two kinds of facts, those at the individual and population scales, was not established formally until the 1920s. It had of course been clear since time immemorial that high mortality reduced the growth of a population and that high fertility would increase it. But no one was able to go beyond this empirical truth and specify the relationship between the exact rate of population growth on the one hand and the quantitative measures of mortality and fertility on the other. Efforts to bridge this gap had not been lacking. Indeed, the earliest works of demography contain attempts to link the vantage points of the total population and of the individuals composing it. In their *Natural and Political Observations* (1661), Graunt and Petty constructed the first life table and went on to try to compute population growth on the basis of the average number of children per couple. In 1760, Euler established a relationship between population growth and mortality on the one hand, and age distribution on the other, though he accorded no role to couples' progeny size. Malthus in turn tackled the question but the formulas he produced were muddled, incorrect, or unsound. This upshot of this situation was the coexistence of two demographies. One studied the four major behavioral factors of mortality, fertility, nuptiality, and migration; the other focused on populations, particularly their growth and age structure. The inability to connect the two viewpoints helps to explain why demography had difficulty emerging as a scientific discipline. In the course of the nineteenth century, official statistical services collected ever more plentiful data of increasing precision, assembling an immense stock of information for the study of individual behavior and populations. Yet the gulf between the two scales remained. Thus, for example, it was impossible to say by how much the rate of population growth would rise if life expectancy gained a few years or if couples had on average 0.1 or 0.5 additional children.

The solution to this problem would come from the convergence of two preoccupations. Firstly, that of the biologists, who in developing the evolutionary approach directed their attention to animal populations (justly so given Darwin's acknowledged debt to Malthus); and, secondly, that of government statisticians who came under pressure from politicians to predict the consequences of the fertility decline that spread rapidly across all of Europe in the late nineteenth century. Population forecasting, when allied with the natural or biological science perspective on human populations, would provide the unifying framework from which modern demography emerged between 1910 and 1930. Save in points of detail, the method developed at that time is the one used for population forecasts today. Population "projections" or "prospects"—as this forecasting is labeled to emphasize its hypothetical character—make up the hard core of the discipline, its central paradigm that guarantees coherence between individual behavior and aggregate population processes. It is with the population forecasting model, the component method as it is currently called, that we must therefore start in order to understand population dynamics and, more generally, the existence of demography.

7.1   The Laws of Population

Forecasting of the most rudimentary kind was already present in William Petty's *Essays of Political Arithmetic*. This involved calculating the amount of time required for the population to double in size. In a famous calculation, Petty uses it to reconstitute the population of the earth's globe since Adam "according to the prediction of the Scriptures." Noting that in his day the population of the world doubled every 1200 years, he forecasts that the end of the world will come about after the next six doublings, when there will be two humans for every acre of cultivable land.[1] A few years later, Vauban (1933) projected the future population of Canada by assuming a doubling every 25 years as of 1700, which as luck had it, came out exactly in 1975 (and not in 1950 or in 2000). Predicting a constant doubling time is equivalent to predicting a geometrical or exponential population growth, and thus to assuming a fixed annual rate of growth. This was the assumption that Malthus vigorously opposed for the first time in his *Essay* of 1798. As is well-known, he argued that over the average population, growth would not be exponential but linear (arithmetic) due to the tendency of the means of substance to expand more slowly. The idea that

---

[1] On the basis of the 320 million that Petty attributes to his own period, this corresponds to 20 billion. The calculation is reasonable when compared with the current level of world population and the outlook for the near future (Petty 1683).

the population developed according to a "law" became popular, bringing with it all the ambiguity of this term that denotes both a mathematical formula and a logical relationship.

In his *Essai de physique sociale* published in 1835, Quetelet gave a good example of the problem that would confront the future discipline of demography. The first volume, containing 240 of the 560 pages of the whole book, is in fact a treatise on demography. It is divided into two parts, one devoted to mortality and fertility, the other to the population, but without any link between them. Because he has no means of articulating population growth, age distribution, and levels of fertility and mortality, Quetelet (1835, p. 250) is reduced to postulating a "law of population" that he states thus:

> Population tends to grow by geometric progression.
>
> The resistance or sum of obstacles to its development is, other things being equal, like the square of the speed at which the population is tending to grow.

In this we can recognize a mixture of Malthus and the laws of friction in mechanics. Continuing with the mechanical analogy, if force represents the second derivative and speed the first derivative of the population, Quetelet's formulation can be expressed as a simple differential equation for the population P with constants r for the exponential rate of growth and b for the friction:

$$P'' = rP' - b(P')^2.$$

Making $U = P'$, we have the differential equation for a logistic function whose solution is written

$$P' = \frac{rKe^{rt}}{1 + bKe^{rt}}.$$

Quetelet thought that his function led to a limit, which is incorrect, since it is not the population but the derivative of the population that tends to a limit.[2] It is possible that Quetelet himself had a doubt, for he asked his pupil Verhulst (1845) to study the question. The latter presented the problem differently, dropping the reference to the laws of friction. He assumed that population growth occurred at a constant rate reduced by a factor proportional to the size attained, i.e.,

$$P' = rP - bP^2.$$

---

[2] Since the numerator is the derivative of the denominator, integration of P' is immediate:

$$P = P(0) + \log \frac{1 + bKe^{rt}}{1 + bK}.$$

When time t is large, population P tends to an asymptote:

$$P = P(0) + \frac{1}{b} \log \frac{bK}{1 + bK} + rt.$$

In other words, we again have the Malthusian model in which growth is governed by the linear development of resources.

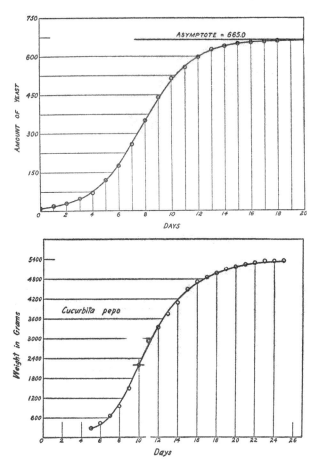

Figure 7.1. Growth and stabilization in a population of yeast cells and in the weight of a pumpkin, fitted by the logistic. Original figure from Pearl's book.

This is exactly the formulation of the logistic function or S-shaped curve, and thus of the path followed by a population tending to a limit that is reached when $P' = 0$, that is, for $P = r/b$. The work of Verhulst made no impact at the time. Seventy-five years later, however, the logistic function or "law" was brought back onto the agenda for forecasting population trends.

7.2   Raymond Pearl and the Logistic Law

The ending of World War I did not halt the fertility decline that had begun across most of Western Europe and North America in the late nineteenth century. There was a catching up of the births that had been delayed by the war, but from 1921 the decline resumed as strongly as before. The by now unmistakable downward

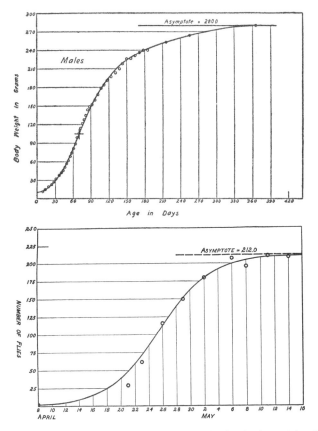

Figure 7.1. *Continued.* Growth and stabilization in the weight of
a rat and in a population of fruit flies, fitted by the logistic.

movement was perceived differently on the two sides of the Atlantic. In Europe
the question began to be asked of how many births were necessary to avoid a fall
in population. Less concern was expressed in the United States, where population
growth depended heavily on immigration. Raymond Pearl, who founded the Office
of Population Research at Princeton and was the first president of the International
Union for the Scientific Study of Population, attributed the fertility decline to a
general homeostatic mechanism characteristic of all living organisms. In his great
work *The Biology of Population Growth*, Pearl (1925) showed that a logistic law
led all biological populations to stabilize around an equilibrium size. This idea
of an equilibrium in the living world was later taken up by the ecologist Edgar
Odum (1971), who used it to develop the concept of carrying capacity, which is still
frequently invoked in connection with sustainable development.[3]

---

[3] For an account of these influences, see Le Bras (1984).

Pearl proceeded in a systematic manner, fitting a logistic curve first to unicellular colonies in culture (yeasts), then to clusters of simple cell structures (tadpole tails in metamorphosis, growth of pumpkins). Continuing with higher organisms (rats), he showed that their weight increase, which was proportional to cell numbers, also followed a logistic law. Next he considered populations of organisms, *Drosophila* (fruit flies), on which he performed laboratory experiments over several years. He demonstrated that the number of these flies in a jar grows according to a logistic law whose parameters vary with the size of the jar and the type of fruit fly but which led inevitably to a stable equilibrium. In figure 7.1 we display the curves fitted by Pearl for these populations. His logistic laws are the result not of a theoretical hypothesis, as they were for Quetelet and Verhulst, but of a biometric adjustment.[4] The logistic law acquired a generality for the organic world comparable with that of Newton's law of universal gravitation for matter in general.

Armed with these results, Pearl turned his attention from populations of fruit flies in bottles to the human populations of particular nations. From figure 7.2 we see that he obtained good fits for many countries: United States, Sweden, and France. But whereas for nonhuman organisms he could always continue observation until equilibrium was reached, his data pertaining to nations are necessarily interrupted at the point of their collection. Compared with the logistic curves for animal populations, therefore, those for human populations have a very different status. They project the population under consideration into the future—a distant future, for Pearl's diagrams continue up to 2100. The most arresting curve is that in figure 7.3 for world population. We see that it was to grow from 1.62 billion people in 1920 to a maximum ceiling figure of 2.026 billion around 2100.

Since world population in 2005 largely exceeded 6.3 billion inhabitants, it might be thought that the size of the forecasting error explains why Pearl's method was abandoned. But that is a bad explanation. In his major study of prophecies, Norman Cohn (1957) showed that their failure did not discredit the prophets, quite the reverse. Besides, a few years later equally large errors were obtained with the component method. The discrediting of the logistic model for forecasting purposes is attributable rather to Pearl's ideological isolation among demographers and, even more so, to the possibility offered by the component method of linking together the parameters of fertility, mortality, and growth and thus of unifying demography.

Pearl certainly occupied a special intellectual position. Far from being reductionist, it was that of a liberal and humanist. Throughout the interwar period he battled almost singlehandedly against the eugenicists, led by figures as prestigious as Ronald Fisher and Corrado Gini, who maintained that the fall in fertility was due to loss of vigor and miscegenation among the European races. Pearl, by contrast, defended the idea—which nowadays appears obvious—that fertility decline

---

[4] On several occasions, indeed, he uses an exponential with a polynomial higher than first order, not a linear function.

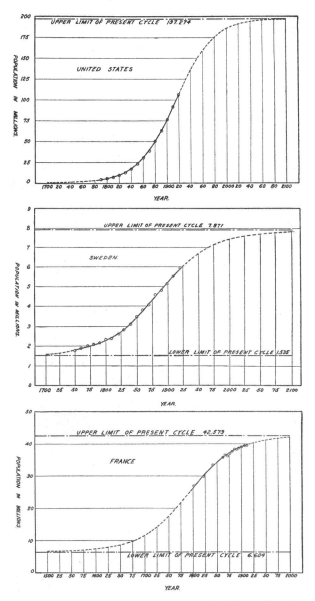

Figure 7.2. Population growth in the United States, Sweden, and France, fitted by a logistic. Original figure from Pearl's book.

resulted from contraception and abortion, i.e., from deliberate choices. His own conception of human freedom probably explains why he was drawn to the logistic law. If individuals alone decide how many children they will produce, how can an explosion or extinction of the population be avoided? There had to be an equivalent in demography of the "invisible hand" in economics, i.e., a regulatory mechanism

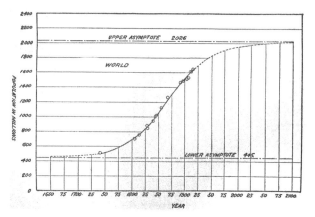

Figure 7.3.   Growth of world population, fitted
by a logistic. Original figure from Pearl's book.

that coexists with freedom of choice. Freedom was no more threatened by the logistic law embedded deep in the living world than it was by the law of gravity or the circulation of blood. The logistic law provided the indispensable safeguard without which individual freedom could lead to catastrophe. Yet it was literally "inhuman," situated far from what made man's humanity, preserved in the most enduringly biological part of his being. This also explains why Pearl found it too in the fruit flies that are so remote from man and that he described as even more rudimentary than they are in reality, likening them to projectiles crashing around at random in the bottle. Pearl adopted a position diametrically opposed to that of the social Darwinists, who assigned little importance to individual freedom and a preponderant role instead to race and heredity. Pearl's conception of biology was egalitarian. From the lowliest unicellular organism up to man—all were subject to the same law. The biology of the social Darwinists (not to be confused with neo-Darwinists, who speak of the differential survival of entities) was differentialist in outlook. Nations and social classes differed fundamentally in their qualities and in their reproductive capacities. Hence there was little likelihood that the universalism of the logistic law would appeal to Pearl's colleagues. Indeed, he found followers only among urban planners who applied the idea of a logistic saturation at the level of the city.

7.3   The Beginnings of the Component Method

The second reason for Pearl's failure lay with the technique itself. The relationship between fertility, mortality, and population size was no more present in his logistic law than it had been in the work of his predecessors. What was the point of achieving highly refined observation of mortality, family size, and age structures if one still did not know how these data were interrelated? The decline of fertility in Europe raised for the first time the question of continued population growth. Between 1925 and 1928, a number of statisticians—Bowley (1924) in Great Britain, Sauvy (1928) in France, and Oly (1924) in the Netherlands—almost simultaneously conceived the idea of dividing their countries' populations into subgroups by age and projecting forward one year at a time, each one, independently of the others. The change in the total population over time was then obtained simply by summing the numbers in each age group. Concretely, they made the assumption that the population was not subject to immigration. From one year to the next, each age group moves forward by a step of one year and is diminished by the number of deaths. Whether mortality remained constant or changed over time, the number of deaths was obtained by applying the mortality probability at that age to the number present before making the one-year step. The idea was not particularly original. Bowley probably came across it in an article written by his teacher, the economist Edwin Cannan, in 1895. The same principle was also used, albeit in a theoretical framework, in the earlier work of Euler in 1760.

With the method of sliding forward the population one year at a time, however, it is not possible to calculate the size of the first age group—i.e., of persons under age one—whose members, by definition, were not present the previous year but were born during the course of the year. This was not a problem since the level of births that would be needed to bring about a given change in the total population was precisely what the three statisticians wanted to study. They proceeded by making an assumption about births in future years and then took this first age group defined by the births in the year and "aged" it forward like the others. The movement of population change was still not related to the number of children per couple, only to the overall number of births. The trend in the number of births was given a priori without reference to the population that produced them.

7.4 Alfred Lotka and Stable Populations

In 1924, at almost exactly the same time as these early attempts, Alfred Lotka published his *Elements of Physical Biology*, a fundamental work in which he introduced a strict relationship between births and populations. This book brought together in more systematic way a number of articles that Lotka had published on the subject since 1907, while also developing from the work by Euler (1760). Like Pearl, whose researches with the logistic curve he discussed at length, Lotka constructed a theory for all living creatures; but unlike Pearl's his was a theory of reproduction, not of population growth. Lotka postulated that mothers of a certain age had a fixed probability, related only to their age, of giving birth to a female child during the period under consideration. In other words, the age-specific female fertility rates, $f(x)$, depended only on age, x. Lotka was not concerned with population projections but with the application of mathematics to biology.[5] Indeed, he worked in continuous-age notation rather than in discrete intervals. By associating his fertility assumption with a life table that is constant over time, he established two important results that form the core of stable-population theory. A population subject to constant mortality and fertility conditions over time tends to grow exponentially and its age distribution tends to become constant. The growth rate, called the *intrinsic growth rate* (or the *intrinsic rate of natural increase*), is determined uniquely by the life table and the age-specific fertility function.

Lotka's work went unnoticed by most statisticians (Pearl mentions it in his bibliography but not in the text of his book). The statisticians were concerned with a situation of declining fertility, whereas Lotka dealt with constant fertility. Moreover, the considerations guiding them were not so much scientific as political. At the intersection of these two positions, however, Robert Kuczynski published in 1928 *The Balance of Births and Deaths* in which he unified the preoccupations of the statisticians and the mathematicians. Since the former were looking for the conditions that the birth rate must meet to prevent population from decreasing, and since the latter could define a long-term rate of population growth (the intrinsic rate to which the population converges in stable conditions), it was therefore possible to say which combinations of fertility and mortality—observed or anticipated—lead eventually to population increase or decrease. As we shall see in the next chapter, stable-population theory supplies this result in a very simple form. The equilibrium point at which the intrinsic growth rate has a value of zero is such that

$$\int_{15}^{50} S(x) f(x) \, dx = 1,$$

where $S(x)$ is the survival function with radix 1. The integral is over the entire childbearing age interval (from 15 to 50 years). It can also be expressed in discrete numerical terms. At zero growth, the products of the age-specific female fertility rates at age x and the survivors at this age must sum to unity. If the sum falls below 1, the population tends to decrease; conversely, if it exceeds 1, the population tends to grow.

With this remarkable result, it was no longer necessary to make projections under the assumption of a constant mortality and birth rate: the existing data gave the answer immediately. But the introduction of fertility rates simultaneously opened the possibility of making projections under an assumption of variable fertility. Thus it was that the following years saw projections using mortality probabilities and variable fertility rates conducted by leading statisticians in the developed countries: Sauvy in France in 1931 (who referred in a footnote to Lotka's stable-population theory, which he had not mentioned in 1928), Corrado Gini and Bruno de Finetti

---

[5] Indeed, when his book was republished in 1956 he changed the title to *Elements of Mathematical Biology*.

in Italy, Enid Charles in England, Wassili Stroumiline in the USSR, and Friedrich Burgdörfer in Germany.[6]

7.5 The Unification of Demography

The component method does not directly attempt to forecast population change but instead requires that forecasts first be made of change in fertility and mortality behavior. In so doing it provides the justification for studying fertility and mortality and for using the corresponding indices, and thus for work that had long been performed by national statistical institutes. The four elements—life tables, age-specific fertility functions, population growth, and age pyramids or distributions—were henceforth parts of a coherent whole. This represents a substantial advantage. The variations in fertility and mortality can be quantitatively related to those in the age distribution and rate of growth. This, for example, was how Sauvy elaborated his theory of demographic aging, by demonstrating that for modern populations, fertility variations have far more influence than mortality variations on the growth rate, and thus on the shape of the age pyramid, notably the proportions of young people and the elderly.

The unification of concepts and methods was obtained at a price. This was not perceived immediately but has been given prominence by recent developments. The future population that forms the object of the forecast is estimated from the most recent data, and thus from cross-sectional distributions. No allowance is made, therefore, for the extreme sensitivity of these to changes in timing. The latter were not perceived in the 1930s for two reasons. First, changes in the intensity of fertility greatly exceeded those in its timing, whereas after 1945 they became comparable in magnitude. Second, following Lotka's model, fertility behavior becomes a biological characteristic of the woman and even of the age of the woman. The unit of observation for fertility had formerly been the couple, but this now disappeared and with it the effect of marriage and of union dissolution. Last, migration is disregarded. Lotka reasoned at the level of biological species and thus had no reason to restrict his analysis to a geographical group; but at the level of nations it is unrealistic not to take migration into account. However, it was not included in any of the forecasts made in the interwar period. The last major population projection from this time—carried out by the demographers of Princeton in 1944 for a commission from the League of Nations (Notestein et al. 1944)—was conducted with migration omitted.[7] Here we see emerging a general logic of present-day demography. Its coherence was achieved at the expense of two phenomena that we will consider in part III: migration and nuptiality.

---

[6] Glass (1936) contains an excellent analysis of these works.

[7] For a comparison of these and the previous projections with the actual evolution of the population, see Le Bras (1984, 1994, chapter 12).

7.6   The Mechanism of Component Projection

The defects mentioned above are not irremediable. Once the principle of projecting forward year by year and age by age is accepted, it can be—and in the more recent forecasts has been—adapted and generalized without calling into question the logic of the method itself. We will demonstrate this for the simplest case—projections during the interwar period—and for the most complicated—modern multiregional projections.

In the simple case, we denote by $q(t, x)$ the probability of dying at age x, where t is the year and $f(x, t)$ the female fertility rate in year t at age x. The number of females at each age in the following year $P(t + 1, x)$ can be determined by the following relations:

$$P(t + 1, x) = P(t, x - 1)(1 - q(t, x - 1)) \quad \text{for } x > 0,$$

$$P(t + 1, 0) = (1 - q(t, 0)) \sum_{y=15}^{50} P(t, y) f(t, y) \quad \text{for } x = 1$$

$$\text{(0–1 year age group).}$$

The procedure can be illustrated by means of a Lexis diagram (figure 7.4). Going from one year to the next is equivalent to calculating the population flowing across the vertical line one year on from that representing the initial population. The mortality probabilities represent the probability of dying for any individual crossing the parallelogram whose two vertical sides represent the age group x at t and the age group $x + 1$ at $t + 1$. This is not the conventional probability over a single age group, which would be the probability of dying between exact ages x and $x + 1$, to which correspond two horizontal lines on the Lexis diagram. For this reason the probabilities used in the projection may reasonably be called *projective probabilities*. As a first approximation, these probabilities $q(t, x)$ are the mean of the two probabilities of the life table from age x to age $x + 1$ and of age $x + 1$ and $x + 2$.[8]

The same formulas are used for the male age distribution as for the female, except that of the first age group, for which the female births are multiplied by the sex ratio of male to female births (usually 1.05). It would lead to contradictions to attempt to introduce male fertility rates in a symmetric fashion since this ratio would then depend on the assumptions made regarding the male and female fertility rates and the size of the age groups of the fathers and mothers. There would be no reason for it to come out at 1.05, which is the value observed in all the developed countries, or

---

[8] The first projective probability is different since it corresponds to a triangle on the Lexis diagram. It translates the impact of mortality in the early months. To determine it, it is useful to know the monthly distribution of deaths under age 1, to derive the probability for any birth during the year of reaching 1 January. The complement of this probability relative to infant mortality will be used to determine the projective probability of the following age group of 1–2 years so as to be coherent with the life table used.

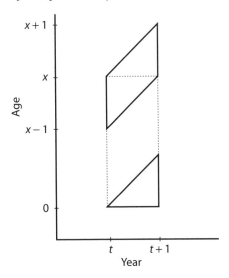

Figure 7.4. Lexis diagram for the definition and calculation of projective probabilities.

at some slightly different value that is fixed by a sex preference as in certain Asian countries.

Migration can be incorporated in this forecasting scheme simply by adding the amount of net migration to each age and sex for each year. Denoting by $M(t, x)$ the count of women of age x at t entering in the course of year t, the recurrence relations are written

$$P(t + 1, x + 1) = P(t, x)(1 - q(t, x)) + M(x, t) \quad \text{for } x > 1,$$

$$P(t + 1, 1) = (1 - q(t, 0)) \sum_{x=15}^{50} P(t, x) f(t, x) + M(t, 1) \quad \text{for } x = 1$$
$$\text{(0–1 year age group).}$$

The difficulty lies not in the increased complexity of the formulas but in the practicalities of determining the net migration $M(t, x)$ and above all of forecasting its subsequent evolution, since migration exhibits nothing like the same regularities by age and over time as fertility and mortality. The usual solution is to take a model age pattern of migration balances, i.e., a time-invariant distribution by age groups, and multiply it by the total predicted balance that can vary over time.

From 1970 onward *multiregional* projection models in which several populations are considered simultaneously made their appearance. These postulate that the migratory movements $M_{i,j}(t, x)$ from region i to region j at age x are proportional to the initial number $P_i(t, x)$ in i at age x:

$$M_{i,j}(t, x) = p_{i,j}(t, x) P_i(t, x).$$

To get from age group x to age group $x + 1$ of region j between time t and time $t + 1$, all we need do is sum the immigration $M_{i,j}(t, x)$ from the other regions, deduct the emigration $M_{j,i}(t, x)$ toward the other regions i, and allow for mortality, i.e., using summations at i:

$$P_j(t + 1, x + 1) = P_j(t, x)(1 - q_j(t, x)) - \sum_i p_{j,i}(t, x) + \sum_i p_{i,j}(t, x) P_i(t, x).$$

In this form, all the age groups $x + 1$ at $t + 1$ are linear combinations of the age groups x at t. If the coefficients $p_{j,i}(t, x)$ and the probabilities of dying $q_j(t, x)$ are both independent of time t, the previous linear combination has constant terms over time. In this case it is easily amenable to matrix calculation.

In reality, this formulation—which enjoyed a degree of success precisely because it could be handled by matrix calculation—is still not very effective. As we shall show in part III, migratory flows are in general proportional to the populations at both origin and destination, not just at the origin.

7.7   Implementing Population Projections: An Example

Component projection adds an extra stage to forecasting the future size and age structure of the population. Determining the future population level begins with forecasting the change in mortality, fertility, and migration, the individual constituent items or components—hence the method's name—that are then assembled. The problem of forecasting is not solved, therefore, merely pushed back a step. On the issue of how to project change in the components, there is no general rule. Two main techniques are used. The first is statistical and involves the use of standard extrapolation techniques to extend the trend in mortality and fertility indices observed to date. This is of limited value, however, since projections over long time horizons can generate unreasonable values for life expectation and children ever born. The second technique involves selecting a stable final state for mortality, fertility, and migration, and interpolating between the present and the selected horizon. Because of the high degree of uncertainty over this final state, it is usual to retain several scenarios described as *high*, *medium*, and *low assumptions*. One can also combine several assumptions regarding fertility, mortality, and migration levels. The variants are useful for highlighting the wide range of the changes after ten or so years. We give an example with the projections made in 1975 to forecast the population of France over the following hundred years (see Le Bras and Tapinos 1979).

Two assumptions were retained for life expectancy with the horizon of 2075: no increase and an increase from 72 to 76 years. The annual probabilities of dying were estimated by interpolation using principal components.

For fertility, four values were chosen for the number of children ever born (1.4, 1.8, 2.1, and 2.6) which covered the range of period fertility indices observed at that time in Western Europe. Fertility was projected from its 1975 level to that of 2075 by interpolation using a logistic curve.

Table 7.1. Total population (millions) of France, forecast for 1975–2075 on four fertility assumptions.

Year	Fertility index (in 2075)			
	1, 4	1, 8	2, 1	2, 6
1975	52, 7	52, 7	52, 7	52, 7
1980	53, 3	53, 4	53, 4	53, 5
1985	53, 7	54, 1	54, 4	54, 9
1990	53, 7	54, 7	55, 4	56, 6
1995	53, 5	55, 2	56, 5	58, 5
2000	53, 1	55, 4	57, 4	60, 4
2025	46, 9	53, 5	59, 9	70, 5
2050	35, 3	47, 0	59, 7	84, 5
2075	25, 0	40, 6	59, 8	101, 1

Two migration assumptions were included: zero net migration at all ages and a positive balance of 50 000 persons per year distributed by age using a fixed model pattern.

Outcomes for the 16 possible combinations ($2 \times 2 \times 4$) of the assumptions were calculated. The evolution of the total population from 1975 to 2075 under these different assumptions is given in table 7.1. We verify that after a few decades the range of sizes becomes very large and that after a hundred years the extreme populations differ by a factor of four, which robs the exercise of all practical interest. It may be objected that the extreme assumptions of 1.4 and 2.6 children per woman are responsible for the large discrepancy observed at the end point, but the median assumptions also diverge quite quickly. Nathan Keyfitz (1981) has evaluated the degree of error in past population forecasts and shown it to be between +0.5% and −0.5% per year for the total population, corresponding to a spread of a factor of three between the extremes after one hundred years. This is roughly the discrepancy between the 2 billion predicted by Pearl in 1925 and today's figure of 6.3 billion, and the discrepancy of 1–2 for the French population forecast by Sauvy for the period 1930–80 (29 million instead of 56 million).

Choosing an example of forecasting that is thirty years old also makes it possible to measure the errors of diagnosis in the assumptions. Contrary to a widely held view, it was not over fertility levels or migratory movements that the greatest inaccuracies arose, since the actual evolution was situated more or less within their range of values. The error concerned rather the timing of events. Completely underestimated in 1975 was the rapid reduction in mortality observed down to the present, and so also was the substantial rise in mean age at childbearing. Unavoidably, the projection assumptions reflect the spirit of the era in which they are framed. To them are transmitted its hopes and fears. For example, the assumption of zero net migration was akin to wishful thinking and corresponded to the policy of strict immigration controls introduced in 1975, while the fertility assumption of 2.6 children reflected pro-natalist nostalgia for the baby boom.

These considerations tending to limit use of projections have not prevented the introduction of new refinements, including stochastic projections, and use of microsimulation and thus lifelines for projections. Such developments are natural if projection is considered not as a forecasting exercise but as a technique for illustrating the current trends in the components. Like any crude extrapolation, projection does not say what will happen—Sauvy used to say "Prévoir pour ne pas voir," which translates as "Foresee so as not to see"—but what might happen if the current trend continued. Projection represents existing conditions in a way that makes their meaning clearer. What is meant by life expectancy of 40 years combined with fertility of 5 children per woman and emigration of 1% per year? A projection made using these parameters shows that the population subject over time to these parameters will slowly decrease while the proportion of young people under 15 will stabilize at the relatively low level of 25%.

These conditions make more understandable the choice of the component method in preference to direct methods of projection such as Pearl's logistic law. Projection provides a showcase for the components, making them visible and intelligible and demonstrating their irresistible influence. It justifies the longstanding preoccupations of statistical services with cross-sectional measurement of mortality and fertility and with the associated summary indices, period life expectancy, and the period fertility index. Demographers indeed emphasize the mechanical rather than predictive character of the exercise, going so far as to advocate use of the term *prospect* instead of *projection*. This also explains the modest amount of space given to projections in treatises on demography. Their real aim, paradoxically, is not to make predictions but to strengthen the tools of demography, *its* components.

7.8   Retroprojections

This attitude also explains the use of projection in the reconstitution of change in past populations. Two methods exist. One involves going backwards from the present to the past by reversing the projection relations. This is the inverse projection technique, which has to be used with caution owing to the instability of the results.[9] We shall see shortly when studying convergence toward stable populations how discrepancies due to error or imprecision can snowball. Logically, moreover, when convergence is observed in one direction through time there is divergence in the opposite direction.

---

[9] There are many ways of applying projection methods to the past, depending on the available data. Examples can be found in Wrigley and Schofield (1981), with a method devised by Jim Oeppen, and in Ronald Lee's (2004) recent application of a one-parameter family of model life tables in conjunction with time series of total numbers of population, births, and deaths. The backward method using generalized inverse matrices was developed by Nathan Keyfitz (1978, pp. 348–52).

More valuable and more widely used is retroprojection. This involves starting from a date in the past and making the projection forward to a more recent date, even to the present. On the face of it this technique is not of interest since the present population and its age structure are known. Besides, it is no longer necessary to project the components because they have been observed. Therein, however, lies the utility of retroprojection: it helps to fill gaps in the data. Thus when recording of migratory movements is defective but births and deaths are known precisely, comparison of two censuses gives by differencing the volume and age structure of migrations over the intercensal period. This is done by going from the population by sex and by age at the first census and projecting it forward to the second using the probabilities of dying and fertility rates for the intervening years (which can be calculated when the breakdown by age of deaths and the age of mothers at the birth of their children is available). Comparing the projected number with the observed number at each age in the second census gives as a difference item the share of migratory movements or the migration contribution at each age. This is not exactly net migration at these ages—since some migrants will have died during the period— but the share of the present population that is attributable to net migration. In other words, it is the surplus or deficit in the population relative to what the population would have become if net migration had remained zero at each age or, more crudely, if there had been no migration.

The method can be generalized for evaluating the demographic contribution over long periods and for components other than migration. Thus the OECD asked the question of what the contribution from migration had been since World War II in each age group one generation later, i.e., in 1982. Figure 7.5 gives the result for several developed countries for which the retroprojection has been conducted. The size of the migratory contribution or deficit is indicated for each age-sex group. It is seen that migration played an important role in several age groups in these countries. The migratory contribution must not be confused with the proportion of the population of foreign origin. The exact definition of the migratory contribution is the difference between what the population would have been without and with migration. The effect of migration on probabilities of mortality and fertility rates is open to discussion though it is known to be small. It can also be argued that society would have been different and that migration has had an effect on the nuptiality, fertility, and mortality of persons present in the population at the start, but it is doubtful that this effect has been large for there is no example of it from the past. These issues have been examined in the framework of counterfactual history, of the kind practiced notably by Robert Fogel (e.g., how the U.S. economy would have developed if the railroads had not been built or if slavery had been abolished earlier or later). The concept of foreign-origin population, on the other hand, belongs not to demography but to policy and moreover to politics. Thus the migratory contribution includes returning colonial settlers but not foreigners present at the start of the period. Furthermore, the size of the foreign-origin population is actually impossible to determine statistically,

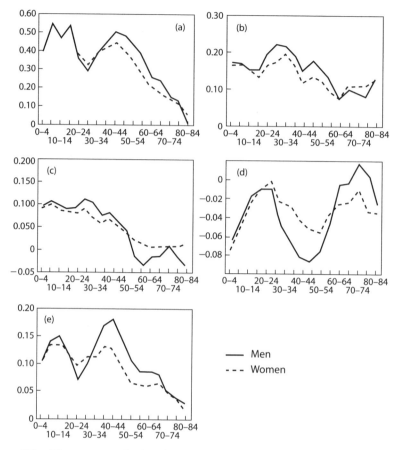

Figure 7.5. Migratory contribution since 1945 at each age in 1980–85, as a proportion of total age group (surplus or deficit relative to the population level if net migration had been zero at each age since 1945). (a) Australia (1981); (b) Germany (1984); (c) Belgium (1981); (d) Italy (1982); (e) France (1982).

partly for reasons related to observation but also for theoretical reasons since some children are born with one parent of foreign origin and the other of French origin. The demographic contribution counts up the different contributions in the aggregate with no possibility of separating them. It is coherent in the same way that the component method is coherent. In contrast, attempts to isolate individual elements and enumerate a foreign-origin population lead either to a dead end or to making a large number of assumptions most of which cannot be verified.

7.9   The Demographic Feedback Loop

By way of conclusion the essential aspect of the theoretical change that occurred between 1925 and 1930 must again be emphasized.

The introduction of the age-specific female fertility rate has the effect of creating a feedback loop in the model of demographic projection. Population numbers in the most distant future are henceforth linked to those in the present by a chain of cohorts. Instead of being predicted independently, births are calculated from the numbers of mothers at the different childbearing ages. Since those numbers are themselves a consequence of the action of mortality on the number of mothers at their birth, x years ago for those of age x, births are indirectly linked to the births that precede them, however far into the future or back into the past we look. Thus the sequence of annual births sustains itself indefinitely. It behaves as feedback loops do in systems theory, and like them it follows a path leading either to extinction (negative feedback) or to explosion (positive feedback). This mechanism is often referred to as *population renewal*, and mathematical techniques exist for handling it, notably renewal theory. We shall encounter these in the next chapter with stable-population theory and its extensions, which provide a formal framework for the component projection method and more generally for population dynamics, of which it is a founding illustration.

8

Stable Populations and Weak Ergodicity

The relationship between population size, mortality, fertility, age structure, and, in some cases, migration is based on a general property that can be expressed in the following simple terms. All elements of the population being linearly interdependent, they tend toward a structure that is independent of conditions in the past. This property is expressed mathematically by the weak ergodicity (convergence) of matrices that are nonnegative and indecomposable. In a certain form these matrices represent the transition from the age distribution in one period to that in the next; when the coefficients of this form are constant over time a stable population is achieved. We will first give a proof of the most general proposition and then, via successive specifications, come to stable populations. An additional reason for proceeding thus is that the most general proposition can be demonstrated using high-school mathematics—a "shopkeeper's arithmetic" to use another of Graunt's phrases.[1]

8.1   Weak Ergodicity of Nonnegative Matrices

Consider a sequence of matrices $A^{(n)}$ all of whose elements are strictly positive and finite and suppose that the elements are bounded below by a fixed strictly positive quantity b and bounded above by another quantity B. The general element of the nth matrix is denoted $a_{ij}^{(n)}$. Let there be two initial vectors $X^{(0)}$ and $Y^{(0)}$ with nonnegative elements with at least one element of each vector being strictly positive. Multiplying both vectors by the first matrix $A^{(1)}$ causes all the components of the resulting vectors $X^{(1)}$ and $Y^{(1)}$ ($X^{(1)} = A^{(1)}X^{(0)}$ and $Y^{(1)} = A^{(1)}Y^{(0)}$) to become positive. The ratios of the homologous components of the two vectors ($x_i^{(1)}/y_i^{(1)}$) are thus situated between a minimum and a maximum, m_1 and M_1. By repeated multiplication by the successive matrices of the sequence, we will show that the difference between m_1 and M_1 reduces geometrically and thus that the ratio of the components of the two vectors tends toward a fixed value, signifying that the two vectors become proportional.

---

[1] Norton (1928) was the first to prove weak ergodicity in a paper related to population genetics. Alvaro Lopez (1961) later applied weak ergodicity to population theory. Demonstrations were subsequently given in Le Bras (1977) and Feichtinger (1979).

To do this we establish the following simple lemma. When a sequence of r values z_i of minimum m and maximum M, hence contained in an interval $(M - m)$, is weighted by a set of weights p_{ij}, such that each is bounded below by c, the result Z_i lies in an interval of length $(M - m)(1 - rc)$. It is sufficient to subtract c from each weight by writing

$$\max(Z_i) - \min(Z_i)$$

$$= \max\left(\sum_j p_{ij} z_j\right) - rc \sum_j z_j - \left(\min\left(\sum_j p_{ij} z_j\right) - rc \sum_j z_j\right).$$

Now

$$\max\left(\sum_j p_{ij} z_j\right) - rc \sum_j z_j = \max\left(\sum_j z_j(p_i - c)\right) < M \sum_j(p_{ij} - c)$$

$$= M(1 - rc)$$

since $\sum_j p_{ij} = 1$ by assumption.

Similarly,

$$\min\left(\sum_j p_{ij} z_j\right) - rc \sum_j z_j = \min\left(\sum_j z_j(p_{ij} - c)\right) > m \sum_j(p_{ij} - c)$$

$$= m(1 - rc),$$

whence a fortiori

$$\max(Z_i) - \min(Z_i) < M(1 - rc) - m(1 - rc) = (M - m)(1 - rc).$$

Return now to the matrices $A^{(n)}$ and the vectors $X^{(n)}$ and $Y^{(y)}$ and express the ratio of the ith components of X and Y at the following step $n + 1$:

$$\frac{x_i^{(n+1)}}{y_i^{(n+1)}} = \left(\sum_j a_{ij}^{(n)} x_j^{(n)}\right) \Big/ \left(\sum_j a_{ij}^{(n)} y_j^{(n)}\right)$$

$$= \left(\sum_j a_{ij}^{(n)} y_j^{(n)} \frac{x_j^{(n)}}{y_j^{(n)}}\right) \Big/ \left(\sum_j a_{ij}^{(n)} y_j^{(n)}\right).$$

Simplify the notation by writing

$$\pi_j = a_{ij}^{(n)} y_j^{(n)} \Big/ \left(\sum_k a_{ik}^{(n)} y_k^{(n)}\right) \quad \text{and} \quad z_j = \frac{x_j^{(n)}}{y_j^{(n)}}.$$

It can immediately be seen that $\sum_j \pi_j = 1$ and the previous equation is written

$$\frac{x_i^{(n+1)}}{y_i^{(n+1)}} = \sum_j \pi_j z_j.$$

Given the positive bounds b and B between which the matrix coefficients $a_{ij}^{(n)}$ are by assumption all situated, we have

$$y_i^{(n)} = \sum_j a_{ij}^{(n-1)} y_j^{(n-1)} < B\left(\sum_j y_j^{(n-1)}\right),$$

$$y_i^{(n)} = \sum_j a_{ij}^{(n-1)} y_j^{(n-1)} > b\left(\sum_j y_j^{(n-1)}\right).$$

Hence,

$$\pi_j = a_{ij}^{(n)} y_j^{(n)} \Big/ \left(\sum_j a_{ij}^{(n)} y_j^{(n)}\right) > \frac{b^2}{rB^2}.$$

Making $c = b^2/(rB^2)$, we have exactly the conditions of the lemma and we can write that

$$\max\left(\frac{x_i^{(n+1)}}{y_i^{(n+1)}}\right) - \min\left(\frac{x_i^{(n+1)}}{y_i^{(n+1)}}\right) < \left(1 - \frac{b^2}{B^2}\right)\left(\max\left(\frac{x_i^{(n)}}{y_i^{(n)}}\right) - \min\left(\frac{x_i^{(n)}}{y_i^{(n)}}\right)\right).$$

The only departure from the lemma is that the minima and maxima b and B must be taken over all the coefficients of matrix $A^{(n)}$ and not simply over one row. But this alters only the bounds—which are thus further apart at the start—not the reasoning itself. After each multiplication by a matrix A for which the only condition is that all its entries have a value between b and B, the range confining the ratios of the components of X to those of Y in the same place i reduces by $(1 - b^2/B^2)$. As announced, the minimum and maximum converge by geometrical series toward a single value and, ultimately, become infinitely close and hence the vectors approach proportionality. One of the immediate consequences of this result is that the product $D^{(i)}$ of the matrices $A^{(i)}$ from the first to the nth tends toward a singular matrix such that

$$d_{ij}^{(n)} = u_i v_j.$$

Because any initial vector $X^{(0)}$ tends as a result of the multiplications toward a vector $Z^{(n)}$ that is independent of it, we can write

$$z_i = \sum_j d_{ij}^{(n)} x_j^{(0)}.$$

If we take initial vectors with successively the single nonzero component j when j varies from 1 to r, the previous equation reduces to

$$z_i = d_{ij}^{(n)} x_j^{(0)}.$$

z_i is defined to a factor k that depends on the component j chosen, and hence is written k_j, which gives the result announced if we choose $x_j^{(0)} = 1$:

$$u_i = z_i \quad \text{and} \quad v_j = k_j.$$

The term u_i thus takes the structure of the vector $Z^{(n)}$. The term v_j is of interest. It expresses the share of the final vector that is imputable to the initial component j, that is to say, its potentiality. We shall see shortly that it can in fact be considered as the growth "potential" of a population. Weak ergodicity is bound up with a condition on the matrices $D^{(i)}$ called primitivity, exploited in the next section. It expresses the tendency to "forget" the past. The structure of vector $Z^{(i)}$ no longer depends on the initial vector $X^{(0)}$ but only on the successive matrices. This forgetting of the past is not immediate but gradual, hence the use of the term convergence.

8.2 Projection Using Components and Matrices

What is the connection between the previous calculation and demographic projection? We shall establish this in two stages. First, by associating a matrix with population projection, then, as the elements of this matrix are not all strictly positive but include many zeros, by showing that after a finite number of stages the matrix product corresponding to the successive forward steps of the projection is a strictly positive matrix.

According to the previous chapter, the projection equations for a closed population (without migrations) are

$$P(t+1, x+1) = P(t,x)(1 - q(t,x)) \quad \text{for } x > 1,$$
$$P(t+1, 1) = (1 - q(t,0)) \sum_y P(t,y) f(t,y) \quad \text{for } x = 1$$

(age group 0–1 year).

Changing notation, we again have the matrices $A^{(n)}$ of the previous section. Let

$$n = t, \quad j = x \text{ (age-group order)}, \quad x_j^{(n)} = P(t,x).$$

With the new notation the equations are written

$$x_{j+1}^{(n+1)} = a_{j+1,j}^{(n)} x_j^{(n)} \quad \text{with } a_{j+1,j}^{(n)} = 1 - q(t,x)$$

and

$$x_1^{(n+1)} = \sum_j a_{1,j}^{(n)} x_j^{(n)} \quad \text{with } a_{1,j}^{(n)} = (1 - q(t,0)) f(x,t).$$

In this formulation the age distribution at time $n+1$ is obtained from the age distribution at the previous time through matrix multiplication. We see that the matrix $A^{(n)}$ has the following form: the elements in the top row corresponding to the ages where fertility is positive have the value of the product of the fertility rate by the survivorship ratio from birth to the end of the first age group. The following rows have a single nonzero element, which is that at place j for the row $j+1$ and that contains the prospective survival probability from age group j to age group $j + 1$. In matrix formulation the transition from one period to the next is thus written as[2]

$$X^{(n+1)} = A^{(n)} X^{(n)}.$$

Unfortunately, the weak ergodic property cannot be applied to this relation as many entries in matrix $A^{(n)}$ are zero.

The product of several consecutive matrices, however, has fewer zero entries. Indeed, we shall show that the matrix resulting from r multiplications, hence the product of r consecutive matrices, has strictly positive elements throughout. We do this by using the property of strong connectivity. The matrix $A^{(n)}$ with r rows and columns is represented visually by a graph with r points (vertices). If the element $a_{ij}^{(n-1)}$ is strictly positive, we draw an arc from i to j. If on the graph obtained we can go from any point to any other point by a succession of arcs, the graph is strongly connected. Consequently, from a certain value N, there will be at least one path of N arcs from every point to every other point. If we draw the graph obtained for the product of two successive matrices, the nonempty cells will correspond to the presence of at least one path of two arcs between the two points i and j corresponding to the cell numbers. Matrices for which the graph is strongly connected are said to be *indecomposable*. This property is essential for weak ergodicity. If a matrix is indecomposable, there is a value N such that the product of N or more consecutive matrices is a strictly positive matrix. Collecting the successive matrices into N groups and replacing them by their products, we get back to the strictly positive matrix product, and so the weak ergodic property is verified.

If the matrices representing the projection of an age distribution from one time to the next are indecomposable, weak ergodicity will apply to the demographic projection. The graph corresponding to the projection matrix is easy to draw (figure 8.1). The points represent the age groups. The points marking the childbearing ages are connected to the first age group (nonzero coefficients of the first row of the matrix) and in addition each group is connected to the next by an arc corresponding to survival from one age to the next (element j of row $j + 1$ containing the prospective survival probability. It is seen immediately that the graph is strongly connected since we can go from any point to any other point either by going directly from age group to age group or by going back through the first age group. If r_1 and r_2 denote the minimum and maximum age groups of childbearing for the projection matrices of all the periods, $r_1 + r_2$ is the number N from which there is always at least one path from every point to every other point on the associated graph. To go from s_1 to s_2, the last path is counted from the birth and contains s_2 arcs. The remaining $N - s_2$ arcs are occupied by a simple age-by-age progression if that is possible or else by again going through the first cell. For example, if there are one-year age groups, 15

---

[2] Leslie introduced matrix notation in 1945. For this reason the projection matrix is often called the "Leslie matrix."

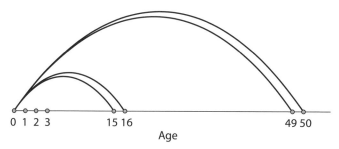

Figure 8.1. Representation of nonzero coefficients of the transition matrix from one period to the next, verifying that the graph is strongly connected—a finite path leads from every vertex to every other vertex—and nonperiodic, and hence that the Perron–Frobenius theorem applies to the matrix.

and 50 years are usually chosen as the minimum and maximum childbearing ages. Hence $N = 65$. To go from age 38 to age 22 in 65 steps we must first go from 38 to 1 in $65 - 22 = 43$ steps. We go there directly and then return in 43. Another possibility is to go first from 38 to 48, go through 1, and return there in 33.

Because the product matrix of the N successive projection matrices is strictly positive, it is subject to weak ergodicity. The weak ergodic result can now be stated in demographic terms.

A population subject in each period of time (generally one year) to changing mortality (but such that survivorship from one age to the next is nonzero) and fertility (but such that the fertility rate is never zero between age groups r_1 and r_2) tends to have an age distribution independent of its initial distribution. It is therefore determined exclusively by the fertility and mortality conditions to which it has been exposed. The contribution of each initial age group tends to become a constant proportion of each age group in the final population and is distributed as the age distribution of the final population. Similarly, the rate of growth from one period to the next tends to be no longer influenced by the initial age structure.[3]

8.3 Stable Populations

A particularly interesting case is that in which fertility rates and survival probabilities are independent of time. The projection matrices from one period to the next are

---

[3] We have disregarded the cyclical case in which the graph of the matrix is strongly connected but where all the cycles are multiples of a certain time period T. In this case, zeros remain and weak ergodicity does not apply exactly. But this is a textbook case, one ruled out by the fact that fertility is positive over an age interval and hence at the earliest of the ages, thereby excluding cycles.

We have also limited the age distribution to the last fertile age. If we had included ages beyond the last fertile age, the graph would have been connected but not strongly connected. We would not, going from the points representing the age groups after the last fertile ages, be able to reach the points representing the younger age groups. But as they are reached from these age groups all the paths in the opposite direction exist. Their number can thus be calculated afterwards (with the survival probabilities). Introducing them is not therefore problematic, but stopping at the last fertile age simplifies the demonstration.

then all identical, which allows a particularly simple formulation of the stable state Z. For very large n, we have

$$Z = A^n X^{(0)}.$$

The n of matrix A is no longer enclosed in parentheses since, with all the projection matrices being identical to A, their product n times is A raised to the nth power. The relationship can be written differently

$$Z = A^{n-1}(A X^{(0)})$$

and, multiplying both parts by A, we have

$$AZ = A^n(A X^{(0)}).$$

Now, by virtue of weak ergodicity, the two vectors (age distributions) $X^{(0)}$ and $A X^{(0)}$ lead to practically the same age structure after a large number of periods, n. Therefore,

$$AZ = \lambda Z.$$

Put differently, the limiting age structure is an eigenvector of matrix A. Specifically, it is the eigenvector whose eigenvalue has the largest modulus by the Perron–Frobenius theorem: any nonnegative, indecomposable matrix has a unique positive eigenvalue. This has the largest modulus, and the corresponding eigenvector is positive. Z is called the *stable age structure* since it is the limiting value toward which the age distribution tends, irrespective of the initial structure. λ is the ratio of the population at one time to that at the previous time. Hence it is equal to the growth rate plus 1. We call $\lambda - 1$ the intrinsic growth rate. It is "intrinsic" because it is entirely determined by the mortality and fertility conditions.

Substituting these results in the projection formulas, we determine the composition of the age distribution exactly and obtain a simple equation for λ:

$$\lambda z(x+1) = z(x)(1 - q(x)) \quad \text{for } x > 1,$$
$$\lambda z(1) = (1 - q(0)) \sum_y z(y) f(y) \quad \text{for } x = 1.$$

Applying the first relation age by age (or line by line in the A matrix), we can express all the age groups as a function of the first one:

$$z(x) = \lambda^{-x+1} \prod_{y=1}^{x} (1 - q(y)) z(1) = \lambda^{-x+1} \frac{S(x)}{S(1)} z(1),$$

where S denotes survival at age x in the prospective life table. Substituting these values in the second relation, we obtain an equation for λ:

$$\lambda z(1) = (1 - q(0)) \sum_x f(x) \lambda^{-x+1} \frac{S(x)}{S(1)} z(1).$$

As $S(1) = 1 - q(0)$ and the first age group $z(1)$ is a factor in both sides of the equation, this simplifies to

$$1 = \sum_x S(x)f(x)\lambda^{-x}.$$

Because x is always positive, the second term is a decreasing function of λ. Therefore, it goes through value 1 only once and the equation has a single positive solution, as predicted by the Perron–Frobenius theorem.[4] Finally, the expression of $z(x)$ can be simplified by reducing the value for the first age group to $1 - q(0)$, which gives

$$z(x) = \lambda^{-x+1}S(x).$$

Because the stable population has a growth rate of $\lambda - 1$, each age group grows as a geometric progression with common ratio λ.

Besides their theoretical interest, stable populations have three practical applications that have ensured their usefulness in demographic analysis. First, their age distributions approximate closely to many real distributions, notably those for developing countries prior to the fertility transition and for historical populations. Second, they are very useful in demographic models to illustrate the effects of population growth on various parameters, the proportion of young or retired people, for example. And third they can be used for estimating incomplete data and for adjusting flawed data in the same way as with inverse projections. Plausible conjectures can thus be made about mortality and fertility levels in a population that is thought to be subject to a stable regime—for example, a Neolithic population known from the skeletal remains in its burial grounds—but on which actual information is scarce.

8.4 Stationary Populations

The stationary population occupies a special place among the different types of stable population. It is the stable case where growth is zero, thus where $\lambda = 1$. The stable-population formulas are further simplified. The age distribution is equal to the survivorship function, since in the stable formula, when $\lambda = 1$, we have

$$z(x) = S(x).$$

The formula for calculating λ becomes

$$1 = \sum_x S(x)f(x).$$

Since $f(x)$ designates female fertility, we again have the condition imposed on the net rate of reproduction to ensure that the population just replaces itself. Total population size remains constant and is equal to the annual number of births multiplied by

---

[4] The equation for λ is also the characteristic equation of matrix A with which the eigenvalue spectrum can be determined.

life expectancy (e_0). For if B designates total births per period, then total population size must be

$$P = B \sum_x S(x) = B e_0.$$

From this we also derive the birth and death rates, b and d:

$$d = b = B/P = 1/e_0.$$

Like stable populations, stationary populations are used for modeling purposes and for estimating demographic parameters. One of the most famous applications dates from when concern with demographic matters first emerged. In 1693, Edmund Halley, after observing the number of deaths by age over successive years in the German town of Breslau, formulated the hypothesis that its population was stationary and thus that the deaths observed were proportional to deaths in a life table, thus enabling him to compute the first life table based on observed data.

8.5   Migration and Multiregional Projection

Multiregional projections (Le Bras 1971; Rogers 1975) are subject to weak ergodicity because the age groups in the different population groups or regions considered are linearly interrelated. However, the regions must all be strongly connected by migratory movements. This is verified by constructing a graph on which each region is represented by a point. When there is migration at a given age from one region to another, an arrow is drawn between the two regions. If the graph obtained is strongly connected, the group of regions respects weak ergodicity.

This condition is almost always verified since migratory movements systematically produce countermovements of return migration (this being one of the "laws of migration" formulated by Ernst Ravenstein, the pioneer of migration studies).

Such projections are rarely actually carried out, and to this extent the stable model is of less interest in multiregional projections. Convergence occurs in it much more slowly than with a single population since the fluctuations have a stepped impact. Thus, if the regions are "chained"—i.e., if migration usually occurs from one region to its neighbor and from there to the next region—the fluctuations are transmitted at an interval of one generation, which increases their duration.

The multiregional model is of theoretical interest for the insight it provides into the interaction of differential fertility and mortality with social mobility. Assume the population of a country is divided into three social classes: the poor, with high mortality and fertility, the middle class, with low fertility and mortality, and the upper class, with medium fertility and low mortality. If we know the probabilities for the transition from one class to another, and thus the age-specific rates of social mobility, we can calculate the growth of the population as a whole and determine the stable age distributions of the three social classes.

Table 8.1.

Classes	% of population	Fertility	Children	%
Lower	70	2.5	175	77.8
Middle	20	1.5	30	13.3
Upper	10	2	20	8.9

In fact, for migration, as for social mobility, single age-group models—or generational models, since the population is organized as a succession of generations—are more commonly used because we seek to solve the problem from the other direction. Determine what level of migration would maintain equilibrium between the regions, or determine what share of social mobility is structural, this term being taken to mean the mobility needed to keep the social classes in the same proportions. The nature of the problem can be illustrated with a simplified example. Assume that net fertility is 2.5 among the poor, 1.5 in the middle class, and 2 for the wealthy. If there is no social mobility, from one generation to the next, the size of each class will evolve as in table 8.1.

If social promotion occurs only by entry into the class immediately above, it can be seen that for the percentages of the previous generation to be restored, 1.1% of the population must go from the middle class to the upper class, which represents an 11% renewal for the upper class and social promotion for $1.1/13.3 = 8.3\%$ of the children in the first generation of the middle class. The middle class is reduced both by fertility and by this promotion into the upper class, and its remaining children account for only 12.2% of the population. For it to recover the proportion it had in the previous generation, 7.8% of the population must rise from the lower class. These 7.8% signify a renewal of nearly 40% for the middle class but a social promotion for only 10% of working-class children. Of course, overall upward movement may be greater as a result of rising living standards and skill levels in society, but this does not do away with structural mobility that remains a large component in total mobility. Thus, if the percentages of the three classes one generation later are 55, 30, and 15%, mobility into the upper class results essentially from social progress (1.1% structural and 5% progress-related), but the structural element remains important for the promotion of children from the lower class (7.8% for 17.8%, or almost half). It can be seen that such models are bound to remain schematic. They are a source of reflection on social dynamics rather than a tool for their precise measurement.

8.6 The Renewal Equation

Matrix notation in the case of the projection model is fairly clumsy. It is used to apply known theorems and to work with a general formulation. But projection can be reduced to the renewal equation for a single variable, $B(t)$, the number of births in period t. By successively replacing the number for one age by that for the previous age, in the previous year, we can still write

$$P(t,x) = B(t-x) \prod_{y=1}^{x} (1 - q(t-y,y)) = B(t-x)S(t,x),$$

where $S(t,x)$ designates prospective survivorship probability in a cohort born in $t-x$.[5] The equation for the first age group then becomes

$$B(t) = \sum_{x} f(t,x)S(t,x)B(t-x).$$

The births from the successive periods form a recurrence sequence. This formulation, called the *birth renewal equation*, is equivalent to and simpler than the matrix formulation, but is less amenable to demonstration. Armed with the renewal equation we can revert to a matrix notation that is simpler than the original notation by applying the usual method for handling recurrence sequences. Consider a vector B^t whose components β are the births from previous years in order, where β denotes the highest age at childbearing. B^t is obtained from B^{t-1} by a transition matrix with ones in the subdiagonal since $B^{t-1} = B^{t-1}_{i-1}$ and a first row given by the coefficients $f(t,i)S(t,i)$ of the renewal equation, coefficients sometimes referred to as *maternity rates*:

$$B^t_1 = \sum_{i} f(t,i)S(t,i)B^{t-1}_i.$$

8.7   Convergence of the Fertility Model

In part I it was seen that the model for simulating fertility could be expressed by an equation giving the proportion of women who were fertile at age t (in months), C_i, as a function of this proportion at the earlier ages:

$$C_i = C_{t-1}(1-\phi_{t-1}) + \sum_{i} C_{t-i}\phi_{t-i}(1-a)\mathrm{TV}_i + \sum_{i} C_{t-i}\phi_{t-i}a\mathrm{TA}_i.$$

By grouping the terms of the two sums as factors of the same C_{t-i}, we get a renewal equation for C_t:

$$C_i = C_{t-1}(1-\phi_{t-1}) + \sum_{i} C_{t-i}(\phi_{t-i}(1-a)\mathrm{TV}_i + \phi_{t-i}a\mathrm{TA}_i).$$

Since all the coefficients can be bounded below, and at least two of them are in positions prime to each other, weak ergodicity applies. Hence we can say that C_i tends to be independent of the initial conditions. This is an important result since it means

---

[5] It may be recalled that this perspective implies counting the cohort lifelines that cross exact year t represented by a vertical line in the Lexis plane, whereas the exact age is represented by a horizontal line.

that as age increases, fertility becomes more independent of the age distribution at the start of the reproductive span. The fertility rates obtained (natural fertility) thus depend only on the intrinsic values of the model's parameters (nonsusceptible period and fecundability).[6]

In chapter 2 we gave a parameter-based approximation of C_i. It was obtained by assuming that the coefficients of the renewal equation remained constant from t, and thus that the population of the C_i became stable and even—because the sum of the coefficients was unity—stationary. The result of the approximation is correct because the coefficients vary slowly over time. More generally, in this case we speak of a *quasistable* population. This is of primarily practical interest, for showing the variability of natural fertility relative to that of the nonsusceptible period and fecundability, as well as for estimating missing data or correcting unreliable information.

8.8 Weak Ergodicity: The Continuous Version

In the previous example, a time period of one month was the obvious choice because the menstrual cycle approximates to the calendar month. When working with the more general case of populations, however, no one time period is preferable to any other. The projection may proceed by annual steps but just as well by monthly or quinquennial steps. As was the case for fertility rates and mortality probabilities, one way to dispense with the measurement unit and allow comparison of the coefficients is by postulating the continuity of the phenomenon. This should be understood not in the strict sense—which would presume an infinite population—but in the probabilistic sense. During the infinitesimal period of time dt, the probability of one birth is $B(t) \, dt$ and the probability of several births simultaneously is made as small as we please by a suitable choice of dt. For a mother of age x at t, in the following period of time dx the probability of surviving is $S(t, x)$ and that of having a female birth $f(t, x) \, dx$. We can write

$$B(t) = \int S(t, x) f(t, x) B(t - x) \, dx.$$

In order to extend the weak ergodic result to this function $B(t)$, a serious difficulty must be overcome. Matrix calculation can no longer be used because the dimension of the matrices involved would have to be of the cardinality of the continuum. It might be thought that continuity could be approximated by dividing time into smaller and smaller units, but a difficulty arises here. Some coefficients of the transition matrix can—and in fact do—become smaller than the minimum fixed in advance. Indeed, a partitioning can always be found such that the coefficient is less than any given

---

[6] This is true in the absence of permanent sterility. The latter is reintroduced by multiplying the fertility rates obtained by the proportion of women not permanently sterile at the age considered.

fixed value. The proportion of the coefficients this affects is very small, but the weak ergodic demonstration considers all the coefficients and hence is no longer valid. Solving the problem directly in continuous notation is not simple.[7] A demonstration can be given, however, based on the principle of the matrix demonstration used to establish weak ergodicity at the beginning of the chapter.

Assume that a certain number of coefficients $a_{ij}^{(n-1)}$ are less than the minimum b and that they all lie in a given number p of columns of the matrix $A^{(n-1)}$, which are the same for any value of n. We denote by the letters u_j the z_j of the first lemma which are in the columns where the lower bounding is verified, and by v_j the others for which the lower bounding is not valid for at least one matrix A^n. In the recurrence formula giving the maximum and minimum deviation of the z_j, subtraction need be performed only for the u_j, which gives

$$\max(Z_i) - \min(Z_i) = \max\left(\sum_j p_{ij}u_j + \sum_j p_{ij}v_j\right) - rc\sum_j v_j$$
$$- \left(\min\left(\sum_j p_{ij}u_j + \sum_j p_{ij}v_j\right) - rc\sum_j v_j\right).$$

Forming groups in the same way as in the initial demonstration, we arrive at

$$\max\left(\sum_j p_{ij}u_j + \sum_j p_{ij}v_j\right) - rc\sum_j v_j$$
$$= \max\left(\sum_j u_j(p_i - c)\right) + \max\left(\sum_j p_{ij}v_j\right)$$
$$< M\sum_j (p_{ij} - c) + M\sum_j p_{ij}$$
$$= M(1 - (r - p)c).$$

By the same reasoning we end up with

$$\max\left(\sum_j p_{ij}u_j + \sum_j p_{ij}v_j\right) - rc\sum_j v_j > m(1 - (r - p)c).$$

The decrease in the difference between maximum and minimum thus becomes

$$\max(Z_i) - \min(Z_i) < M(1 - (r - p)c) - m(1 - (r - p)c)$$
$$= (M - m)(1 - (r - p)c).$$

This formula is remarkable since it indicates that convergence continues to occur even when very few columns have coefficients all higher than b.

---

[7] For a demonstration of this, see Le Bras (1977). An early, incomplete demonstration appears in Lopez (1961).

The second stage of the demonstration involves showing that the coefficients $p_{ij} = a_{ij}^{(n)} y_j^{(n)}/(\sum_j a_{ij}^{(n)} y_j^{(n)})$ are bounded below when a proportion of the $a_{ij}^{(n)}$ is. When the lower bound b held for all the coefficients $a_{ij}^{(n)}$, the upper bound and lower bound were written

$$y_i^{(n)} = \sum_j a_{ij}^{(n-1)} y_j^{(n-1)} < B\left(\sum_j y_j^{(n-1)}\right),$$

$$y_i^{(n)} = \sum_j a_{ij}^{(n-1)} y_j^{(n-1)} > b\left(\sum_j y_j^{(n-1)}\right).$$

In the new conditions of lower bound, and using the same u_j and v_j notation, they become

$$y_i^{(n)} = \sum_j a_{ij}^{(n-1)} u_j + \sum_j a_{ij}^{(n-1)} v_j < B\left(\sum_j u_j + \sum_j v_j\right),$$

$$y_i^{(n)} = \sum_j a_{ij}^{(n-1)} u_j^{(n-1)} + \sum_j a_{ij}^{(n-1)} v_j > b \sum_j u_j + \sum_j a_{ij}^{(n-1)} v_j > b \sum_j u_j,$$

and thus, in the case of the columns for which lower bounding by b is verified,

$$p_{ij} = a_{ij}^{(n)} y_j^{(n)} \bigg/ \left(\sum_j a_{ij}^{(n)} y_j^{(n)}\right) > \frac{b}{B}\left(b \sum_j u_j\right) \bigg/ \left(rB\left(\sum_j u_j + \sum_j v_j\right)\right)$$

$$= \frac{b^2}{rB^2}\left(\left(\sum_j u_j\right) \bigg/ \left(\sum_j u_j + \sum_j v_j\right)\right).$$

The difference between the initial case of weak ergodicity and this new formula comes from the presence of the second factor in parentheses. This has to be lower bounded. To do this a further expansion of the u_j and v_j by means of matrices must be made. Naming U_j and T_j the sums of the coefficients of the $y_j^{(n-2)}$ from this decomposition for the columns lower bounded by b, and for all the columns, respectively, we lower bound the numerator by $b(r-p)b$ and upper bound the denominator by rB:

$$\left(\sum_j u_j\right) \bigg/ \left(\sum_j u_j + \sum_j v_j\right) = \left(\sum_j U_j y_j^{(n-2)}\right) \bigg/ \left(\sum_j T_j y_j^{(n-2)}\right)$$

$$> \frac{b(r-p)}{rB}.$$

Substituting into the lower bounding formula of p_{ij}, yields finally

$$p_{ij} > \frac{(r-p)b^3}{r^2 B^3}.$$

The recurrence formula for the difference between the maximum and minimum bounds of $x_i^{(n+1)}/y_i^{(n+1)}$ becomes

$$\max\left(\frac{x_i^{(n+1)}}{y_i^{(n+1)}}\right) - \min\left(\frac{x_i^{(n+1)}}{y_i^{(n+1)}}\right)$$

$$< \frac{1-(r-p)^2b^3}{r^2B^3}\left(\max\left(\frac{x_i^{(n)}}{y_i^{(n)}}\right) - \min\left(\frac{x_i^{(n)}}{y_i^{(n)}}\right)\right).$$

Weak ergodicity is thus certain even though the lower bounding of the difference from one step to the next is much smaller. With this formula we can consider the continuous case. However fine the division into age groups, dx, a fixed interval of length L can be drawn such that $S(t,x)f(t,x) > b$. If B designates the (finite) maximum of $S(t,x)f(t,x)$, the ratio b/B is finite and tends toward a constant as the division gets smaller. Similarly, L tends toward a constant for a fixed b. So we have $r - p = L/dx$, and by proportionality, $r = \beta/dx$, hence $(r-p)/p = L/\beta$. Thus, the lower bound of the recurrence relation for the zone in which the ratios $x_i^{(n)}/y_i^{(n)}$ are confined tends toward a fixed value. The transition to continuity is thus assured. With this last and slightly laborious demonstration, the demographic model achieves coherence. Each particular case of projection, with its particular temporal division, can now be handled by reference to the more general continuous case of which it will be a partial expression.

8.9   Overlapping Generations

The connection between the renewal equation and the matrix approach is problematic because of our inability to imagine in simple terms how the indecomposable matrix ends up strictly positive—i.e., with strictly positive coefficients throughout—from a matrix containing numerous zeros. It is helpful to give the form of this matrix for a simple case. Take a female population divided into ten-year age groups. Assume that childbearing is zero in the first two age groups and equal to a constant ϕ in the next three. We write the transition matrix for going from one ten-year period to the next by allocating the top row to the oldest age group and then progressing toward the younger age groups. We obtain the first five rows of table 8.2. To multiply this matrix by itself we multiply the last row by each column and we move the other rows down a row. The square of the matrix is thus represented by rows 2 to 6. To cube the matrix we apply the same principle again, and so on. The columns represent the initial vector and thus in order the age groups corresponding to the births of year 4 to year 0 in decreasing order. It is seen that we have to wait until period twelve for the matrix for the transition from the births at 0–4 years to the births at 8–12 years to become strictly positive. It remains so thereafter. By way of example, the births of decade twelve (i.e., the last row of the matrix) are written as a function of those

Table 8.2. Projection of a population element (only the first age group is nonzero). Age groups are on the same row, and successive rows correspond to successive periods.

	Bases				
Periods	4	3	2	1	0
1	0	0	0	1	0
2	0	0	1	0	0
3	0	1	0	0	0
4	1	0	0	0	0
5	0	0	ϕ	ϕ	ϕ
6	0	ϕ	ϕ	ϕ	0
7	ϕ	ϕ	ϕ	0	0
8	ϕ	ϕ	ϕ^2	ϕ^2	ϕ^2
9	ϕ	ϕ^2	$2\phi^2$	$2\phi^2$	ϕ^2
10	ϕ^2	$2\phi^2$	$3\phi^2$	$2\phi^2$	ϕ^2
11	$2\phi^2$	$3\phi^2$	$\phi^3 + 2\phi^2$	$\phi^3 + \phi^2$	ϕ^3
12	$3\phi^2$	$\phi^3 + 2\phi^2$	$3\phi^3 + \phi^2$	$3\phi^3$	$2\phi^3$

Table 8.3. Distribution of the members of a single generation (row) by their birth period (column) from a population element.

	Generations					
Decades	1	2	3	4	5	6
0	1					
1	0	ϕ				
2	0	ϕ				
3	0	ϕ	ϕ^2			
4	0	0	$2\phi^2$			
5	0	0	$3\phi^2$	ϕ^3		
6	0	0	$2\phi^2$	$3\phi^3$		
7	0	0	ϕ^2	$6\phi^3$	ϕ^4	
8	0	0	0	$7\phi^3$	$4\phi^4$	
9	0	0	0	$6\phi^3$	$10\phi^2$	ϕ^5

of the base, the decades 0 to 4:

$$B(12) = 3\phi^2 B(4) + (\phi^3 + 2\phi^2)B(3) + (3\phi^3 + \phi^2)B(2) + 3\phi^3 B(1) + 2\phi^3 B(0).$$

This way of proceeding is rather unnatural compared with that based on iterating the renewal function generation by generation. For a person of the first generation (decade 0), table 8.3 shows the births of successive generations in the decade in which they occur.

The sum of the rows again gives us the total number of births from the initial generation (1 in decade 0). If we represent the births over time for each generation and for the whole, we see that the distribution of births over time for a given generation tends toward a normal (Laplace–Gaussian) distribution, which is a direct consequence of the central limit theorem. Any birth date in the nth generation is the sum of $n - 1$ mother–daughter age differences independent of each other and distributed by age in proportion to the maternity function. This is the condition for application of the central limit theorem when n is large. If μ designates the mean age at childbearing and σ its standard deviation, the births of the nth generation at time t after the birth of the initial population element are thus distributed by an exponential of $-(t - n\mu)^2/(2n\sigma^2)$. By virtue of the properties of the population, we also know that the sum of births for all generations combined tends to grow exponentially over time. The sum of the terms from the normal distributions corresponding to the successive generations is thus equivalent to a simple exponential. This is neither obvious nor simple to demonstrate and this illustrates the difference between the matrix and successive generation representations. Unlike the age groups used in the matrix proof of convergence, the generations tend increasingly to overlap, with the result that individuals from several different generations are born during the same decade and thus belong to the same ten-year cohort. When we work on an aggregate of successive generations we are manipulating an abstraction since the persons involved may live at very different periods of time. Thus in the example presented in table 8.3 the fifth generation that starts at decade nine lasts for eleven decades, up to the start of decade 20 therefore. Models using successive generations are of course much simpler than those working on periods and cohorts, but they very quickly lose all historical meaning. For this reason they are more often used for animal than for human populations, or just for the transition from one generation to the next, as in the case of structural social mobility.

8.10   Branching Processes

Successive generations play an important role in the estimation of probabilities of population extinction. In the case of small human groups—say, people with the same family name—the action of chance may result in an empty generation, thereby putting a stop to renewal. This question generated interest in the late nineteenth century when it looked as if the great noble families were dying out through a lack of descendants. Galton and later Lotka worked on this topic and laid the foundations for the study of the branching process, also known as the *Galton–Watson–Bienaymé process*, after Watson, who gave the first mathematical solution. Branching processes were also used in population genetics, following that field's adoption of the evolutionary theoretical framework formulated by Ronald Fisher in the 1930s, for the study of genera and species diversification (George Udney Yule) and for the study of rare genes.

In the context of demography, the branching process can be likened to parity progression ratios (growth probabilities) in that it describes the variability in the number of descendants to an individual. We assume that each member of the population can give birth to i offspring according to a probability distribution $p(i)$ and that the process repeats for the descendants and from generation to generation. In the case of the family names studied by Galton in England, i denoted the number of male offspring, the only ones to inherit the name or title. When q is the probability of extinction from one person (no matter the number of generations for this event to be reached), the probability of extinction from n persons will be q^n since the number of children each has is independent of how many the others have. Write the probability of extinction when passing from one generation to the next. By definition it is q for the one person in the first generation. In the second generation it will be the sum of the separate probabilities of extinction for the n descendants multiplied by their probability of extinction, hence the sum of the $p(n)q^n$, whence the simple equation for determining q:

$$q = \sum p(n)q^n.$$

In probability theory, the second term is the *characteristic function g* of the probability distribution p. The probability of extinction q is thus equal to the characteristic function for this value: $g(q) = q$.

Branching processes are also used in theoretical physics to model cascades of particles. Accordingly, they have been studied in depth. One major result to emerge concerns their instability. In the long run they evolve either toward zero or toward infinity. The probability of them remaining indefinitely in predetermined limits is zero. If the mean number m of descendants (derivative of $g(s)$ for $s = 0$) is less than or equal to 1, extinction is unavoidable (and the equation for q no longer has any real solution situated between 0 and 1). With Z_n denoting the size (random) of the nth generation, the variable Z_n/m^n is almost certain to converge to a fixed distribution usually denoted W. By the recurrence formula, the expected value of Z_n is that of Z_{n-1} multiplied by m. If the time interval between generations is μ years, the growth rate is such that

$$e^{n\mu r} = m^n,$$

hence, as a first approximation, $1 + r = m^{1/\mu}$. This formula is often used for a rapid calculation of the intrinsic growth rate of the population. m is in fact the net reproduction rate and μ the mean age of mothers at childbearing. The more general branching processes studied by Harris, in particular, make the assumption that the interval between generations is not μ but y, a random variable subject to a probability distribution $f(y)$ independent of the number of descendants n and of the generation considered. The difference thus becomes slight with respect to stable populations. The stable population represents the average evolution of a branching process with variable intervals. When the number of individuals is small, it does not capture the effects of chance, in particular, the risk of extinction although this enters into the calculation of the mean m. The point can be illustrated with a schematic example. Assume a process in which everyone has 2 offspring in 60% of cases and none in the remaining 40%. Hence, $p(0) = 0.4$, $p(1) = 0$, and $p(2) = 0.6$. The equation for the probability of extinction q is written

$$q = 0.4 + 0.6q^2 \quad \text{for which the solution different to 1 is } q = \tfrac{2}{3}.$$

Start from a population of three persons (at length, therefore, this population has a probability of dying out of $(\tfrac{2}{3})^3 = 0.296$). On average, after one generation it will contain 3.6 persons, since $m = 2 \times 0.6 = 1.2$, but with a probability of 0.064 it will die out and thus no longer enter into the calculation of the growth rate. In the cases where the population survives to the first generation, the average number of persons is then $3.6/(1 - 0.064) = 3.85$, an increase of 28% and not of 20% that stable-population theory obtains by reasoning on averages. When the calculation is continued to the second generation the average number of persons obtained is 4.32 for stable populations and 4.92 for populations actually surviving and whose proportion has fallen to 0.878. Average growth over the two periods, instead of 20%, remains at 27%. It declines slowly in the following generations, due to the greater number of cases in which the population has increased considerably, and faces a low risk of extinction (it falls from 29.6% for the initial population of 3 persons to 0.8% for one of 12 persons).

   Demography rarely busies itself with populations of three persons. Consequently, the risk of inconsistency between branching processes and stable populations does not represent a danger. It is a sign rather that stable populations and branching processes are constructed for different realities. Branching processes nearly always start out from a small number of individuals, though they may come to large numbers through a series of cascades, such as those in atomic reactors. Also, they are applied to natural phenomena whose laws do not change over time. For human populations, by contrast, our interest from the start of this book has been with the measurement, modeling, and understanding of change—change in timing in part I and, in the present chapter, change in the probabilities of childbearing for which weak ergodicity had to be established. The next chapter will in turn focus on the fluctuations that occur in many demographic phenomena.

   Demography is a social and historical science. As such it is concerned with change in human societies. Specifying the conditions of equilibrium and stability can be a way of bringing out the characteristics of change. A good example of this is the study that Peter Laslett and Kenneth Wachter conducted on the extinction of descent lines in the English baronetcies (Wachter and Laslett 1978). The branching process provided the authors with a benchmark measure with which to show that the rate of extinction was not what would be expected from the workings of chance.

This set them on the track of other mechanisms—adoption, in particular—that not only distorted the workings of chance but were intended to offset its effects. Atoms and particles do not possess the property of intelligence—at least not according to contemporary physics. Hence they respond blindly to mechanisms that can only be disrupted by chance whose action is equally blind. Humans, but also animals, have the ability to anticipate and rectify the consequences of determinism, often indeed by establishing other mechanisms, thereby leaving the way open for feedback models, of which the next chapter will give several examples.

9

Equilibrium and Fluctuations

The final state toward which populations with weak or strong ergodicity tend is of interest only if it is reached quickly, that is to say, if convergence is rapid. Now convergence is in fact fairly slow—typically of the order of a few generations rather than a few years—with the result that in many situations there are more problems associated with the fluctuations than with the relatively distant equilibrium state.[1] This does not mean that the theory from the previous chapter, and the stable-population model in particular, is an irrelevance, for it can also be used to estimate the amplitude and periodicity of the fluctuations and the time that they take to die out. We will see that the characteristics of the fluctuation are just as much a part of the stable-population equation as is the intrinsic growth rate. So an approximate value can be found for the period of fluctuation and for the speed of convergence. With it we will explain a number of situations in which large fluctuations occur. The first is a textbook example—to be exact an illustration of a logical but absurd result—in which total control of fertility is used to hold population size constant. More concrete cases follow: fluctuations in the progression of teaching careers after erratic recruitment to the profession, and settlement by a sedentary population in which strong aging induces a long-term fluctuation with implications for educational and health infrastructures. These different models show how populations react to scarcity of a factor and in this respect are close to economics, which is often defined as the science of scarce resources. For this reason they form a link to the economic-demographic models considered in the following two chapters.

9.1   Approximations of Fluctuations

In the matrix version of stable populations with a finite number of age groups n, any vector, and hence any population, can be represented as a weighted sum of all the eigenvectors. By virtue of spectral decomposition of matrices, the transformed vector is obtained by multiplying the coefficient of each eigenvector by the corresponding eigenvalue. After t stages, hence after t projection intervals, the population vector

---

[1] The study of demographic fluctuations is laid out in Keyfitz (1978) and Le Bras (1983).

P will be written

$$P^{(t)} = \sum_1^n \lambda_i^t k_i V_i,$$

where λ_i and V_i represent the eigenvalues and eigenvectors and k_i the coefficients (coordinates) of the initial population $P^{(0)}$ in the canonical basis formed by the eigenvectors. If the eigenvalues are arranged by increasing order of modulus, after a long period of time only the first term is important. Hence for any stable population we know that this first term is equal to the annual intrinsic growth factor raised to a power. If approximation of the population is taken a degree further, the second eigenvector and the second eigenvalue are selected. It is known that the latter is complex and has the third eigenvalue as its conjugate. This pair of roots must be associated in order to estimate the difference between the actual population and the stable population it is converging toward. The two imaginary parts cancel out and the population in the second approximation is written

$$P^{(t)} = \lambda_1^t k_1 V_1 + \lambda_2^t k_2 V_2 \cos(\gamma t),$$

where all the terms are real. In the case of the continuous formulation we have the same expression, the powers of the λ_i being replaced by exponentials whose growth rates are the real and complex roots r of the integral equation

$$1 = \int_0^\varpi f(x) e^{-rx} \, dx.$$

Taking known functions for $f(x)$, such as a constant function or a gamma density, we can in practice calculate the roots r of the equation and hence find the one with the highest modulus after the intrinsic rate of growth. Whichever function is selected, within the limits of what is reasonable, we find that the first complex root has a constant γ of cosine close to $2\pi/\mu$, where μ designates the mean age at childbearing. In the general case, therefore, this value can be used to carry out a limited development to obtain a more precise approximation of the period of the fluctuations and the exponent of their damping by writing the two conditions[2]

$$1 = \int_0^\varpi f(x) e^{-\delta x} \cos(\gamma x) \, dx,$$

$$0 = \int_0^\varpi f(x) e^{-\delta x} \sin(\gamma x) \, dx,$$

where the complex root r is written $r = \delta + i\gamma$.
  We obtain the following values:

$$\delta = r_1 - \frac{2\pi^2 \sigma^2}{\mu^3} + \left(\frac{2\pi}{\mu}\right)^4 \left(\frac{5\sigma^6}{8\mu^3} - \frac{\sigma^2 \mu_3}{3\mu_2} + \frac{\mu_4 - \sigma^4}{24\mu}\right),$$

$$\gamma = \frac{2\pi}{\mu} - \left(\frac{2\pi}{\mu}\right)^3 \left(\frac{\sigma^4}{2\mu^2} - \frac{\mu_3}{6\mu}\right).$$

---

[2] The approximations are established in Le Bras (1969).

σ^2 designates the variance of the maternity function and μ_3 and μ_4 its third and fourth moments about the origin. The approximation obtained by selecting just the first term of the development is already good and is sufficient for distinguishing slow and rapid convergences (depending on the size of the term δ and the speed of the fluctuation γ, close therefore to $2\pi/\mu$). In fact, the speed of the convergence is judged by reference to the intrinsic rate r_1, which is the root with the largest modulus of the integral equation. Hence it is the second term $-2\pi^2\sigma^2/\mu^3$ that characterizes the convergence. As was to be expected, it is proportional to the variance, thus to the dispersion of the ages at childbearing. With these two values $2\pi/\mu$ and $-2\pi^2\sigma^2/\mu^3$ it will now be possible to characterize any fluctuations around stability or stationarity in the age distribution.

9.2 A Zero Growth Rate for Mexico from 2000

In 1970, a proposal made by General William Draper, at that time U.S. representative at the UN Population Commission, that Mexico would experience a zero growth rate from 2000 onward, received a literal treatment from demographers Jean Bourgeois-Pichat and Si Ahmed Taleb (1970). Starting from 1970, they projected the Mexican population forward to 2000 by increasing its life expectancy to 74 years—a correct anticipation—and steadily reducing fertility until equilibrium with deaths was reached in 2000. They then continued the projection while holding the population size constant, i.e., through making births equal deaths by applying a multiplier of fertility rates that was determined each year by this condition. On the assumption that fertility varied in the same way at all ages according to an $f(x)$ schedule, its level, R, was easily inferred for each year since 1960. From 2000 they had exactly

$$D(t) = B(t) = R \int_0^{\varpi} f(x) P(t, x)\, dx,$$

where $D(t)$ is the density of deaths at time t, $B(t)$ the births, and $P(t, x)$ the density of females of age x at t, thus

$$R = D(t) \bigg/ \left(\int_0^{\varpi} f(x) P(t, x)\, dx \right).$$

Figure 9.1 reproduces the curve of variation in R between 1960 and 2050 as calculated by Bourgeois-Pichat. In order to hold the population constant, fertility had to vary very considerably, falling from 6 children per woman in 1960 to 0.5 in 1990, rebounding to 4 children per woman by 2040 and then starting to fall again, caught in a yo-yo movement. The repercussions of this huge oscillation were visible in the age pyramids, which took on shapes never before observed.

The amplitude of the period and the slowness of the damping of these oscillations are simple to explain. As of 2000, mortality being constant and with a life expectancy

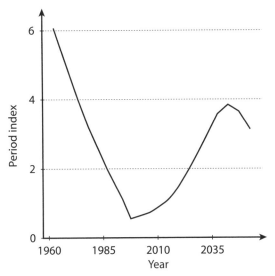

Figure 9.1. Variation in total period fertility (TFR) needed to keep the Mexican population at a constant level from 2000. (Based on Bourgeois-Pichat and Taleb (1970).)

of 74 years, deaths can be determined from the age distribution

$$D(t) = \int_0^{\varpi} q(x) P(t, x) \, dx.$$

In a situation of constant mortality, $P(t, x) = S(x) B(t - x)$, where $S(x)$ designates the proportion of survivors at age x. In addition, by assumption, the births $B(t)$ are equal to the deaths. Substituting into the integral equation, we find

$$B(t) = \int_0^{\varpi} q(x) S(x) B(t - x) \, dx = \int_0^{\varpi} D(x) B(t - x) \, dx.$$

Thus the function inside the integral is not equal to the product of fertility by survivorship, or maternity function, as is generally the case, but to the function $D(x)$ representing the life-table deaths. The quantity corresponding to the mean age at childbearing is the life expectancy at birth, since by definition this is the mean age at death. In the case of Mexico, life expectancy was 74 and the variance in the curve of deaths was quite small ($\sigma = 17$). With the formulas given in the previous section we can infer the approximate value of the speed of convergence $\delta = -2\pi^2 \sigma^2 / \mu^3 = -0.010$. These figures show that it takes 70 years for the amplitude of the fluctuation to diminish by half. The period of the fluctuation is very long because it is close to the life expectancy, 74 years. By comparison, Mexican fertility in 2000 had a mean age of 30 years and a standard deviation of 9 years. Hence the fluctuations in it take around 40 years to halve in size ($\delta = -0.017$) when the approximate formula is applied.

This demonstration of a logical but absurd outcome by Bourgeois-Pichat and Taleb is a good example of the aberrations produced by a reversal of causality.

The rate of population growth is the consequence of the difference between the levels of mortality and fertility; it is not autonomous but depends on these two independent variables. By reversing the causality, fertility becomes the consequence of an independent growth rate. The time path it follows, like the causality it obeys, is at odds with the empirically realistic order.

9.3 The Hidden Constraint of Stable Populations: Stable Equivalent Populations

The preceding argument does not represent an isolated oddity; on the contrary, it indicates a general rule. The demonstration can in fact be reversed. If we start out from the renewal equation, we will end up at a constraint. The fact that the function in the renewal equation of the preceding paragraph contains the distribution of deaths by age instead of the fertility by age is unimportant. Any function that is positive over an interval of time and bounded will do the job, notably the net maternity function $m(x) = S(x)f(x)$, which is the product of the survivorship function and the fertility function $f(x)$. The renewal equation is written

$$B(t) = \int_0^\varpi f(x)S(x)B(t-x)\,\mathrm{d}x = \int_0^\varpi m(x)B(t-x)\,\mathrm{d}x.$$

When $\int_0^\varpi m(x)\,\mathrm{d}x = 1$, the constraint

$$\int_0^\varpi M(x)B(t-x)\,\mathrm{d}x = K \quad \text{with } M(x) = \int_0^x m(y)\,\mathrm{d}y,$$

hence, $M'(x) = -m(x)$, where K is a constant, is satisfied from the start of the projection.

This property can be demonstrated directly by integrating the renewal equation by parts:

$$B(t) = \int_0^\varpi m(x)B(t-x)\,\mathrm{d}x$$

$$= [-M(x)B(t-x)]_0^\varpi + \int_0^\varpi M(x)\frac{\partial B(t-x)}{\partial x}\,\mathrm{d}x.$$

Now, $\partial B(t-x)/\partial x = -\partial B(t-x)/\partial t$, hence,

$$\int_0^\varpi M(x)\frac{\partial B(t-x)}{\partial x}\,\mathrm{d}x = -\int_0^\varpi M(x)\frac{\partial B(t-x)}{\partial t}\,\mathrm{d}x$$

$$= \frac{\partial}{\partial t}\left(\int_0^\varpi M(x)B(t-x)\,\mathrm{d}x\right).$$

Replacing the terms of the right-hand side, we have

$$B(t) = [B(t) - 0] - \frac{\partial}{\partial t}\left(\int_0^{\varpi} M(x)B(t-x)\,dx\right),$$

$$\frac{\partial}{\partial t}\left(\int_0^{\varpi} M(x)B(t-x)\,dx\right) = 0,$$

$$\int_0^{\varpi} M(x)B(t-x)\,dx = K.$$

The constraint $\int_0^{\varpi} m(x)\,dx = 1$ is removed by multiplying both sides of both equations by e^{rt}:

$$B(t)e^{rtg} = \int_0^{\varpi} m(x)e^{rx}B(t-x)e^{r(t-x)}\,dx,$$

$$\int_0^{\varpi} M(x)e^{rx}B(t-x)e^{r(t-x)}\,dx = Ke^{rt}.$$

The first equation is that for a stable population $B_1(t) = B(t)e^{rt}$, with a net maternity function $m_1(x)$ given by $m_1(x) = m(x)e^{rx}$, and intrinsic growth rate r determined in accordance with the definition of $m_1(x)$ by the condition $\int_0^{\varpi} m_1(x)e^{rx} = 1$.

In the second equation, we see that the function $M_1(x)$ such that

$$\int_0^{\varpi} M_1(x)B_1(t-x)\,dx = Ke^{rt}$$

is written

$$M_1(x) = M(x)e^{rx} = e^{rx}\int_x^{\varpi} m(u)\,du = e^{rx}\int_x^{\varpi} m_1(u)e^{-ru}\,du.$$

The function $M_1(x)$ is independent of the initial population and is fixed once we know the maternity function $m_1(x)$. If we think about it, this is a quite remarkable result. Once a population is subject to fertility and mortality that are invariable over time—but that vary with age—a linear combination of the initial population with fixed coefficients immediately begins to grow at the intrinsic rate r directly without any convergence or fluctuations. How, concretely, should these coefficients, or more specifically the function $M_1(x)$, be understood? Assume that at the initial time there is a single age group of size $P(x)$ at age x and of zero size at all other ages. The constant K of the hidden constraint is determined by setting its equation at the initial time:

$$P(x)M_1(x) = Ke^{r\cdot 0} = K.$$

After a long time t, the offspring of this initial element converge toward a stable population in which the births at time t evolve as an exponential of the intrinsic rate r:

$$B(t) = B(0)e^{rt}.$$

Substituting this value into the equation for the constraint,

$$\int_0^{\varpi} M(x)B(0)e^{r(t-x)}\,dx = Ke^{rt} = P(x)M_1(x)e^{rt}.$$

A person aged x at the initial time thus contributes in proportion to $M_1(x)$ to the final stable population. It is for this reason that $M_1(x)$ is sometimes referred to as the *stable equivalent population*. Paul Vincent (1945) introduced a similar concept with "population growth potentials."

If we reason on a population divided into a finite number of age groups instead of a continuous density, matrix notation offers an elegant way of obtaining the same result. The multipliers $M_1(x)$ become the components of the leading eigenvector of the transpose of the projection matrix. We can easily verify from the equation for this vector that it has the same structure as $M_1(x)$. The hidden constraint is then written simply in matrix notation with the vector of the age groups in the nth period, $P^{(n)}$, the projection matrix M, the conjugated eigenvector V, and the first eigenvalue, λ:

$$VP^{(n)} = V(M^n P^{(0)}) = V(M^n)P^{(0)} = \lambda^n VP(0) = K\lambda^n.$$

The constraint has a very simple explanation in terms of contribution to the limiting population. This contribution cannot change over time by the very definition of the growth potential that it represents.

9.4   Fluctuation in the Size of a Professional Population

Recruitment into professions that require training and specialization can be subject to large fluctuations. This case has been studied for teachers and medical practitioners, in particular (see Henry 1971, 1972). Consider the example of secondary school teachers. They are recruited between ages 20 and 40 and remain in teaching until retirement, which they take between ages 60 and 65. A certain—in reality small—number of them will leave teaching for another occupation before retirement. Others will die while economically active. If, as is the case in many developed countries, the total number of teachers remains constant, recruitment will be a function of the exits for the three reasons given above. If we know the age distribution of the teachers at time t, the age-specific probabilities of exit for the three causes combined, and the distribution by age of new entrants, a population projection can be performed to predict the age pyramid in subsequent years (total population size is constant by assumption) and the number of new recruits. Before any projection is made, however, large fluctuations can also be predicted by calculating with approximate formulas the first complex roots of the renewal function associated with the projection.

As an example, such a calculation has been performed for the French teaching corps since 1975. In table 9.1 we indicate by five-year age groups the age distribution at entry, the survivorship function for membership in the profession, and the age

Table 9.1. Entries and exits from the French teaching corps.

Age u (years)	Entries $\phi(u)$	Survivorship $S(u)/S(20)$	Pyramid $P(t, y)$ at start	Renewal function — Duration y (years)	$\phi(y)$
20–24	0.23	1.0	25	0–4	0.007
25–29	0.44	0.995	230	5–9	0.008
30–34	0.19	0.989	210	10–14	0.013
35–39	0.14	0.981	176	15–19	0.018
40–44	0	0.970	117	20–24	0.087
45–49	0	0.955	85	25–29	0.172
50–54	0	0.931	89	30–34	0.300
55–59	0	0.897	42	35–39	0.297
60–64	0	0.420	26	40–44	0.098

pyramid in 1975. These elements are all that is needed to calculate the renewal function shown in the last column. The process can in fact be written in continuous notation by setting up two equations. The first expresses the equality of the entries (actual or intended) and of the exits, each age group x of size $P(t, x)$ losing a proportion $q(x)$ of its members, for all causes combined:

$$E(t) = \int_0^{\varpi} q(x)P(t, x)\, dx.$$

The second equation says that membership of the age group x at t, $P(x, t)$ is made up of those who entered y years ago and numbering $E(t - y)\phi(x - y)$, where $\phi(u)$ designates the proportion of entrants of age u, and who have continued in teaching since this date, hence in a proportion $S(x)/S(x - y)$:

$$P(t, x) = \int_0^{\varpi} E(t - y)\phi(x - y)\frac{S(x)}{S(x - y)}\, dy.$$

Replacing $P(t, x)$ in the first equation by its value in the second, and reversing the order of the integration variables, we get

$$E(t) = \int_0^{\varpi} q(x)\left[\int_0^x E(t - y)\phi(x - y)\frac{S(x)}{S(x - y)}\, dy\right] dx$$

$$= \int_0^{\varpi} E(t - y)\left[\int_0^y q(x)\phi(x - y)\frac{S(x)}{S(x - y)}\, dx\right] dy$$

and setting $\psi(y) = \int_0^y q(x)\phi(x - y)S(x)/S(x - y)\, dx$,

$$E(t) = \int_0^{\varpi} E(t - y)\psi(y)\, dy.$$

In figure 9.2 we represent the total entries over a period of 150 years from the start, and in figure 9.3 the age pyramids at the start and at 25-year intervals. The number of

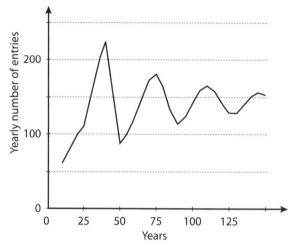

Figure 9.2. Annual recruitment of secondary school teachers over 150 years, satisfying the objective of constant numbers despite a destabilized initial pyramid.

entries fluctuates widely and over a long period of time, producing large variations in the age distribution. The massive recruitment of secondary school teachers in the 1960s and 1970s is reflected in the youthful profile of the initial pyramid. Twenty-five years later, however, the pyramid's young elements have got old, and the low level of recruitment has further aged the pyramid. The subsequent pyramids show little improvement. Although the oscillations diminish slightly, they remain irregular and variable, with an alternation of large and small cohorts.

This description is confirmed by applying the approximations established at the start of the chapter. The statistical indicators for the renewal equation are

$$\mu = 34.8, \qquad \sigma^2 = 50.4,$$

so the period is around 35 years, which corresponds to the value observed in the diagram. The real part of the first complex root is $r_1 = -2\pi^2\sigma^2/\mu^3 = -0.024$. This negative number seems to indicate a fairly rapid damping, but as the period is shorter than in the Mexican case, the reduction in amplitude from one period to the next—equal to the exponential of $r_1\mu$—is of similar size. It is 0.48 in the Mexican case and 0.43 in that of teacher recruitment. Curiously, these are lower values than those for the damping in the Mexican population (0.60). Thus the size of the fluctuations is primarily related not to the slowness of the damping but, in the case of the teachers, to the amplitude of the initial disturbance, i.e., the wave of recruitment in the 1960s, and, in the case of Mexico, to the sharp fall in fertility between 1960 and 2000.

Can the effects of a disturbance in the age pyramid resulting from several years of excessive or insufficient recruitment be corrected? The most certain method is to recruit each year exactly the number of persons that corresponds to the stationary

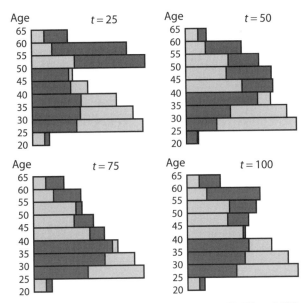

Figure 9.3.   Age pyramids of teaching corps, 25, 50, 75, and 100 years
after the start of the simulation (initial age pyramid in gray).

equilibrium. But in this case the total number present is no longer fixed. It rises
and then falls if recruitment in previous years has been too high, and vice versa
in the opposite case. In figure 9.4 we have represented the result of this policy in
terms of the total number of persons employed, for a final total equal to that in the
initial pyramid (broken line) and 15% smaller (solid line). The overshoot is large
in the early years. With a target of a stable membership of 1000 persons, equal to
the initial population, the total climbs to a maximum of 1220 persons twenty years
later; equilibrium is reached after a further twenty years since beyond this point
all the cohorts present have a constant size of intake. We see that policies can be
envisaged in which the aim of ultimate stability is combined with a variable intake,
as a function of the number of exits, in order to select an optimal policy with respect
to a given criterion, in an intermediary position between the two extreme cases
depicted in figures 9.2 and 9.4.

In reality, the fluctuations were reduced and masked during the years of expansion
in another way: through continuously increasing total membership. Consider what
happens when membership grows at the instantaneous rates r:

$$\int_0^{\varpi} P(t, x)\, dx = K e^{rt}.$$

The level of entries must then equal that of exits increased by a constant proportion
of the total number (which is equivalent to differentiating the equation for the total

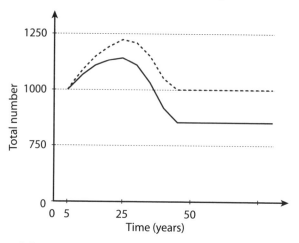

Figure 9.4.   Evolution over 75 years in teacher numbers when annual recruitment is fixed to restore the initial number (broken line) or 15% smaller.

population):

$$E(t) = \int_0^{\varpi} q(x)P(t, x)\,\mathrm{d}x + r \int_0^{\varpi} P(t, x)\,\mathrm{d}x = \int_0^{\varpi} (q(x) + r)P(t, x)\,\mathrm{d}x.$$

The renewal equation is the same as that for the previous case, replacing $q(x)$ by $(q(x) + r)$, hence writing

$$\psi(y) = \int_y^{\varpi} (q(x) + r)\phi(x - y)\frac{S(x)}{S(x - y)}\,\mathrm{d}x$$

$$= \int_y^{\varpi} (D(x) + rS(x))\phi(x - y)\frac{1}{S(x - y)}\,\mathrm{d}x,$$

$$E(t) = \int_0^{\varpi} E(t - y)\psi(y)\,\mathrm{d}y.$$

As $\psi(y)$ is no longer stationary but growing at rate r, the fluctuations depend on the first two complex roots of $\psi(y)e^{-ry}$. In table 9.2 we calculate this function when the population size in the previous model was not stationary but increasing by 1 and 2% a year.

Convergence is much faster under these new conditions. With a rate of growth in population size of 1% a year, the real part of the first pair of complex roots is lagged relative to r, by -0.086 and -0.152 respectively. This reduces the amplitude of the fluctuations in one period (i.e., in 30–33 years) to 0.08 and 0.02 of their value, corresponding to a rapid convergence. The disparities in recruitment relative to the stable situation are quickly corrected. When total numbers decrease, by contrast the fluctuations gain in size. Indeed, a point is reached where they stop being damped and start to grow. Without realizing it we leave the framework of stable-population theory since one of its main conditions—that the renewal function be positive—is violated.

Table 9.2. Renewal function for the teaching corps,
with a continuous increase in total numbers.

Duration y (years)	Renewal function $\psi(y)$	
	Growth: $r = 1\%$	$r = 2\%$
0–4	0.054	0.096
5–9	0.053	0.087
10–14	0.054	0.082
15–19	0.055	0.081
20–24	0.107	0.117
25–29	0.160	0.152
30–34	0.238	0.188
35–39	0.214	0.153
40–44	0.065	0.044

The term $q(x) + r$ in the formula can in fact become negative when the growth rate r is negative, which in turn influences the function $\psi(y)$. In reality, in this case the problem becomes indeterminate since a course of action must be selected for the situation where the number leaving is smaller than the anticipated decrease. Negative entries are nonsensical and hence unacceptable. Either recruitment is halted—but then total numbers no longer decrease at a constant rate—or else exits must be imposed in addition to those determined by the survivorship function $S(x)$—but then we have to define the criterion on which to decide these exits.

Historically, this question has not been of great importance owing to the expansion of the membership of the professions in question. But it could become important in the context of the population decline that has begun in several countries. From a theoretical viewpoint, this leads on to models that are more unstable, of which the Easterlin and Samuelson models will shortly provide us with other examples. Before then we will consider a case very similar to that of professions with fixed memberships: population growth in new neighborhoods or new towns.

9.5 Populating a New Neighborhood and Modeling the Household Life Cycle

When a new neighborhood is constructed, migrants move in to settle. They have the age distribution observed for migration in general, with a preponderance of children and young adults aged 25–40 and, conversely, few adolescents and elderly people. Change in this initial population occurs through members moving away or dying. To begin with the turnover may be relatively fast, since the inhabitants are young and therefore mobile. Gradually, however, unless out-migration is at relatively high levels, the population stays put for life and is renewed primarily through replacement of those who die. Analysis is complicated by the fact that dwellings are occupied not by single individuals but by households. The death of one member of a household is not a sufficient condition for a departure. There is a range of possibilities, running from departure at the first death in the household to departure at the death of the last surviving member, not counting changes in household composition, for example, through remarriage.

Once these modalities have been defined, however, the replacement process remains of fundamentally the same kind as in the case of the professions studied above. We have an initial population grouped by age—the first arrivals—and a joint distribution of departures through out-migration and death. These departures represent the places that become available. They are filled by other arrivals according to the same age composition as the former. The only difficulty is over determining the joint distribution of those leaving and those dying. Because the population is organized as households, the mortality and out-migration probabilities cannot be used directly. A model of the household life cycle must be constructed. Such is the multiplicity of possible configurations that no general solution currently exists. Theoretically, it would require knowing the evolution from one period to the next of any group of n persons, each characterized by age. If attention is limited to households of fewer than 8 persons and to 20 five-year age groups, we end up with 20^8 configurations, a number that constitutes a challenge to computing capacity, let alone to statistical observation. Any formalization of the household life cycle thus assumes choosing from among this vast number of configurations and from among the possibilities (probabilities) of transition from one configuration to another during the reference period. An example will allow the difficulty of the question to be judged despite the extreme simplification involved.

For the developed countries, where the vast majority of households are of the nuclear form, we need consider only the adults who occupy the dwelling, either alone or in couples. To obtain the age structure of the total population, an age distribution of children (some perhaps of adult age) is associated with the adults according to their age. This leaves three types of household, comprising a woman on her own, a man on his own, and a couple—and this for each age. In order to limit the number of categories, it is assumed that the women in couples are always two years younger than the men (the current average age gap). Between ages 20 and 100 there are sixteen five-year age groups, so we have to consider $16 \times 3 = 48$ different situations. Further difficulties arise over the probabilities of transition between situations. For households comprising one adult only, the proportion remaining in their dwelling from one age to the next is given by $(1 - q(x))(1 - p_o(x))$, where $q(x)$ is the mortality function for their sex and $p_o(x)$ is the probability of out-migrating. For couples the situation is more complicated. They remain present if neither partner dies, if they continue to live as a couple, and if they do not migrate. Let us assume that this probability is known by observation (which is far from simple). There remain the cases of couple dissolution. We disregard the (rare) cases where both members die at the same time. What we have to determine, therefore, is the probability of one member staying on in the dwelling. This may be high in the case of divorce but low in the case of widowhood. Designate by $H(x)$, $F(x)$, $C(x)$ the numbers of single persons, men and women, and couples of age x (that of the male member of the couple). We thus have the following relations:

$$
\begin{aligned}
H_{n+1}(x+1) = {} & H_n(x)(1 - q_H(x))(1 - p_o(x)) \\
& + C_n(x)(d(x)(1 - q_H(x))(1 - q_F(x))(1 - p_m(x)) \\
& + q_F(x)(1 - q_H(x))(1 - d(x))(1 - p_c(x))), \\
F_{n+1}(x+1) = {} & F_n(x)(1 - q_F(x))(1 - p_o(x)) \\
& + C_n(x)(d(x)(1 - q_H(x))(1 - q_F(x))(1 - p_w(x)) \\
& + q_H(x)(1 - q_F(x))(1 - d(x))(1 - p_d(x))), \\
C_{n+1}(x+1) = {} & C_n(x)(1 - d(x))(1 - q_H(x))(1 - q_F(x))(1 - p_o(x)).
\end{aligned}
$$

The interpretation of the transition probabilities is as follows:

- $d(x)$: probability of divorce;
- $p_o(x)$: probability of out-migrating when household situation is unchanged;
- $p_m(x)$ and $p_w(x)$: probability of out-migrating after divorce for the man and for the woman (the sum exceeds 1 because only one dwelling is available for both members of the couple, the one they occupy);
- $p_c(x)$ and $p_d(x)$: probability of out-migrating after widowhood for the survivor, man and woman, respectively;
- $q_H(x)$ and $q_F(x)$: male and female probabilities of dying at age x.

Entries, for their part, whose volume is defined by the sum of exits, are distributed by age and household situation according to a distribution $f(i, x)$, in which i has three modalities: men alone, women alone, and couples.

9.6 Mathematical Model, Projection, or Microsimulation

Even a simple case like this leads to a high degree of complexity in the formulas and uncertainty over the values for the distributions used. Three options are available. Once all the coefficients have been determined, a projection can be made by applying the formulas period-by-period. This method is often referred to as *macrosimulation*, since it replicates what are considered to be the relationships between population-level or macroscopic categories. The model can also be solved mathematically, like the previous ones, for the relations linking the numbers in the various categories from one period to the next are all linear. This is seen from the formulas given earlier for those that concern survival in a state and also for those that concern the new arrivals since these are fixed proportions $f(i, x)$ of the total exits, i.e., of a linear combination of the numbers present in the last period. Replacing the number of arrivals by its formula as a function of the number in the preceding period, we obtain a transition matrix. Its characteristic equation corresponds to the renewal function for this population. By calculating the first two complex eigenvalues, we can determine its period and the speed of its damping. Before giving an example of this—if only to show the difficulty of the task—a few words are in order concerning the third, and most tempting, of the possible methods. Because transition probabilities are postulated, we can start out from a set of individuals distributed as in the initial population but where each one is individualized. Then, each is subjected to the probabilities of the various events that he or she may experience (divorce, migration, widowhood, death) and, after a suitable number of periods n, the individuals are sorted by the selected categories of age and household situation. With this method we see more clearly that what is important in simulation of the household life cycle is the set of transition rules postulated. True to the logic of systems, variations in the transition rules are considered to have more influence on the result than variations in the values taken by the distributions (at least within the limits of what is plausible).

However appealing microsimulation methods are, partly because they are easy to implement using computers (as has been experimented in several previous chapters), the mathematical method remains of value since it alone yields results that have a degree of generality. With it we can examine the influence of changes in coefficients or the rules for distribution into categories, whereas countless microsimulations are needed to obtain inferences of this kind. Advocates of microsimulation emphasize the possibility of estimating the variability of results in relatively small populations like those of a new neighborhood, once broken down by age and household type. No general rule for deciding between macro- and microsimulation can be established since everything depends on the complexity (usually considerable) of the life-cycle model postulated, on the quality of the data available to run it, and on whether the type of result expected is theoretical, for establishing general relations, or practical, for projecting the future of a particular neighborhood.

9.7   An Example of a New Neighborhood's Population

Make a further small simplification to the previous model by assuming that only couples will move in as first arrivals and as replacements. Assume also that unions are stable ($d(x) = 0$) and will be dissolved only by the death of one of the spouses. Select two extreme cases: that where the surviving partner moves out of the dwelling and that where he or she stays in it. Hence the calculation can be made with only four distributions: male and female mortality, age-specific migration probabilities, and the initial population. These four distributions (observed in France in 2000) are indicated in table 9.3. (A concrete example of a new neighborhood's population is in Le Bras and Chesnais (1976).)

Table 9.3. Age distribution of the parameters required
for household projection (mortality probabilities).

Age group x	Men $q_H(x)$	Women $q_F(x)$	Out-migration $p_o(x)$	Population
20–24	0.005	0.002	0.090	72.228
25–29	0.006	0.002	0.150	193.286
30–34	0.006	0.003	0.200	217.701
35–39	0.009	0.004	0.140	137.335
40–44	0.015	0.007	0.100	137.335
45–49	0.023	0.013	0.070	88.505
50–54	0.033	0.011	0.050	72.228
55–59	0.046	0.019	0.040	48.830
60–64	0.067	0.027	0.030	24.415
65–69	0.102	0.042	0.020	8.138
70–74	0.153	0.070	0.020	0.000
75–79	0.230	0.124	0.010	0.000
80–84	0.362	0.232	0.010	0.000
85–89	0.531	0.409	0.010	0.000
90–94	0.753	0.622	0.010	0.000
95–99	1.000	1.000	0.010	0.000

Given the assumptions made, the migration coefficients $p_o(x)$ at age x are not dependent upon marital status:

$$H_{n+1}(x+1) = H_n(x)(1 - q_H(x))(1 - e(x))$$
$$+ \lambda C_n(x)q_F(x)(1 - q_H(x))(1 - e(x)) + f_H(x+1)E_n,$$
$$F_{n+1}(x+1) = F_n(x)(1 - q_F(x))(1 - e(x))$$
$$+ \lambda C_n(x)q_H(x)(1 - q_F(x))(1 - e(x)) + f_F(x+1)E_n,$$
$$C_{n+1}(x+1) = C_n(x)(1 - q_H(x))(1 - q_F(x))(1 - e(x)) + f_C(x+1)E_n.$$

λ takes the value 1 when all widows and widowers remain living in their dwelling and 0 when they move out following the death of their spouse. So as to know the value of the total exits E_n (and hence of entries) between time n and time $n+1$, we write the relations in abbreviated form, which makes the linearity more apparent:

$$H_{n+1}(x+1) = (1 - \alpha(x))H_n(x) + \beta(x)C_n(x) + f_H(x+1)E_n,$$
$$F_{n+1}(x+1) = (1 - \gamma(x))F_n(x) + \delta(x)C_n(x) + f_F(x+1)E_n,$$
$$C_{n+1}(x+1) = (1 - \zeta(x))C_n(x) + f_C(x+1)E_n.$$

Since the sum of the numbers in the different categories is constant and the sum of the $f_i(x+1)$ is 1, for it is a distribution, we derive from it the number of dwellings that become vacant E_n:

$$E_n = \sum_x (\zeta(x) - \lambda\beta(x) - \lambda\delta(x))C_n(x) + \sum_x (\alpha(x)H_n(x) + \gamma(x)F_n(x)).$$

Table 9.4.   Renewal functions for the four types of
life cycle and the characteristics of their convergence.

Age	Out-migration at:		No out-migration at:	
	widowhood	death	widowhood	death
0–4	0.145	0.125	0.022	0.000
5–9	0.121	0.097	0.030	0.001
10–14	0.095	0.067	0.041	0.003
15–19	0.081	0.047	0.056	0.007
20–24	0.077	0.041	0.072	0.016
25–29	0.078	0.046	0.087	0.032
30–34	0.078	0.057	0.101	0.053
35–39	0.077	0.069	0.112	0.077
40–44	0.072	0.079	0.117	0.101
45–49	0.063	0.084	0.115	0.123
50–54	0.051	0.089	0.103	0.149
55–59	0.035	0.079	0.078	0.153
60–64	0.019	0.069	0.046	0.155
65–69	0.007	0.040	0.018	0.100
70–74	0.001	0.011	0.003	0.030
75–79	0.000	0.000	0.000	0.000
80–84	0.000	0.000	0.000	0.000
85–89	0.000	0.000	0.000	0.000
90–94	0.000	0.000	0.000	0.000
95–99	0.000	0.000	0.000	0.000
Mean	28.138	36.209	40.355	53.900
Variance	63.486	91.390	49.210	30.898
r	0.056	0.038	0.015	0.004
$E_n + T/E_n$	0.205	0.253	0.551	0.811

Iterative replacement of $C_n(x)$, $H_n(x)$, and $F_n(x)$ by their values at time $n-1$ gives
us the renewal equation for E_n since, at each backward step, only one previous E_n
is left. The substitutions can also be made on the general projection matrix for
the $C_n(x)$, $H_n(x)$, and $F_n(x)$ as a function of their equivalents one period earlier.
Whichever technique is used, we arrive at a renewal equation

$$E_n = \sum_i \Psi_i E_{n-i},$$

where the Ψ_i are entirely a function of the parameters. We have calculated this
function by recurrence for the example corresponding to the data in table 9.3 for four
cases: out-migration/no out-migration, combined with departure following the first
or last death in the couple. The four corresponding renewal functions are indicated
in table 9.4. The renewal function is found by using a shortcut. In the case where
the dwelling is not retained by the widows and widowers, we note that those who

arrived y periods earlier numbering E_{n-y} are distributed by age according to the coefficients $f_C(x)$. At $n - 1$ there remain

$$E_{n-y} \sum_x f_C(x) \frac{S(x + y)}{S(x)},$$

$S(x)$ being the survivorship function constructed from the exit probabilities (by death and out-migration) $\zeta(x)$. Those exiting the population during the last period are a proportion $\zeta(x + y)$ at age $x + y$. Hence we have

$$E_n = \sum_x f_C(x) \left(\sum_y E_{n-y} \zeta(x + y) \frac{S(x + y)}{S(x)} \right).$$

In the case where the widows and widowers move out of their dwelling only at death, a general procedure for this type of problem is used. The E_{n-y} are observed up to their exit. The sum of the exits is E_n. In this particular case, four kinds of exit are possible: by migration (at least one member of the couple is surviving), by death of the man (when the death occurs before migration, there is no migration at all, of course), by death of the woman (same reason), and finally by death of both simultaneously. The probabilities for each of these four, denoted $U_{i,x,y}$, are for the entries in $n - y$ at age x and the exits at n, hence for the coefficient of E_{n-y} in the equation giving E_n:

$$U_{1,x,y} = \frac{S_E(x + y - 1)}{S_E(x)} f_C(x)$$
$$\times \left(1 - \frac{S_M(x + y - 1)}{S_M(x)}\right)\left(1 - \frac{S_F(x + y - 1)}{S_F(x)}\right) e(x + y - 1),$$

$$U_{2,x,y} = \frac{S_E(x + y)}{S_E(x)} f_C(x)$$
$$\times \left(1 - \frac{S_F(x + y - 1)}{S_F(x)}\right) \frac{S_M(x + y - 1)}{S_M(x)} q_H(x + y - 1),$$

$$U_{3,x,y} = \frac{S_E(x + y)}{S_E(x)} f_C(x)$$
$$\times \left(1 - \frac{S_M(x + y - 1)}{S_M(x)}\right) \frac{S_F(x + y - 1)}{S_F(x)} q_F(x + y - 1),$$

$$U_{4,x,y} = \frac{S_E(x + y)}{S_E(x)} f_C(x)$$
$$\times \frac{S_F(x + y - 1)}{S_F(x)} \frac{S_M(x + y - 1)}{S_M(x)} q_H(x + y - 1) q_F(x + y - 1).$$

The coefficient $\psi(y)$ of E_{n-y} in the renewal equation is the sum of the $U_{i,x,y}$ extended to all the values of i and x:

$$\psi(y) = \sum_x \sum_i U_{i,x,y}.$$

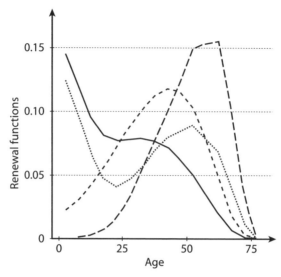

Figure 9.5. Renewal functions for the household population of a new neighborhood under two hypotheses on out-migration (with or without) and two hypotheses on behavior after widowhood (survivor stays or moves). Spaced dots and dashes, staying after widowhood; unbroken and dotted, no out-migration.

In table 9.4 we show the values of $\psi(y)$ for the four cases of migration/no migration coupled with widows and widowers staying in the dwelling or moving after the first death. Figure 9.5 displays these four distributions corresponding to the four hypotheses selected. We note that the modalities of out-migration and of staying in the same place of residence after widowhood have a considerable effect on convergence and fluctuations, since the four distributions differ clearly from each other.

The four bottom rows of the table report the characteristics of the four distributions: mean, variance, real part of the first pair of complex roots, and proportion of reduction in amplitude of the fluctuation after one period (which is close to the expected value of the renewal function). Curves describing entries over 100 years in each of the four cases are plotted in figure 9.6. The fluctuations are clearly related to the dynamics of residential occupation. Depending on the case, the fluctuations either damp rapidly or continue over 100 years with a long period. The differences between the four cases are well represented by the values taken by the first complex root of the characteristic renewal equation.

The object of discussion for this book is not housing policies but the demographic methods and models capable of illuminating them. In this respect, the model of household and housing life cycle developed above raises serious questions. A mathematical modeling approach has been possible only at the cost of major simplifications: all women are two years younger than their husbands, all new arrivals are couples, there is no divorce, separation, or remarriage, there are no complex households (one or several adults, an elderly parent for instance, in addition to the couple

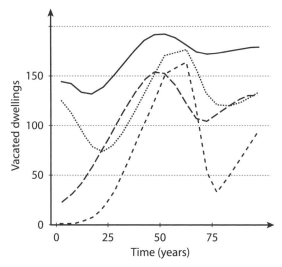

Figure 9.6. Numbers of new arrivals over 100 years under the four
hypotheses in figure 9.5 (same commentary as for the hypotheses).

or the single person who occupies the dwelling), the age distribution of entries is
invariable, the out-migration probabilities are independent of family situation and
duration of residence, and so on. In constructing a model amenable to mathematical treatment and whose parameters (such as migration rates and the distribution
of households) can be known with sufficient precision, we have drastically simplified reality. More seriously, a normative vision has been imposed, under which
only certain configurations or outcomes are permitted. The population of a new
neighborhood is generally much more heterogeneous, and the changes in situations
much more varied, than in the preceding model. But taking account of this would
require using a household life-cycle model that was both realistic and precise, and
at present no such model exists. There remains the possibility of measuring the
differential impact of particular practices, in this case the level of out-migration
and the continued residence by widows and widowers, which were seen to have an
important influence on the renewal and age pyramids of the inhabitants.

In the introduction to this book reservations about family and household demography were expressed. The present discussion has shown those reservations to be
founded. But the criticism does not apply only to household life-cycle modeling.
The same difficulties over rule specification and data availability, and often the same
simplifications, are found in most approaches that project forward several population categories using transitions probabilities between categories. This was the case
in recent years with the ill-starred attempts to classify residents of France according
to their "ethnic origin." Faced with the impossibility of finding reliable data and
of specifying rules that describe the situation, many excessive simplifications were
made (see Le Bras 1998).

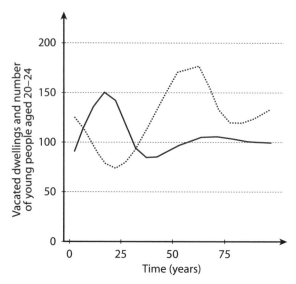

Figure 9.7. Comparison of young people aged 20–24, children of inhabitants (solid line), and vacant dwellings among those made vacant by out-migration and by departure of surviving partner (corresponding to the solid lines in figures 9.5 and 9.6).

9.8 Out-Migrants and Immigrants

Notwithstanding these criticisms, the forecasting model for the population of a new neighborhood serves as an introduction to economic models of population change. For this we note that the immigrants who fill the places made vacant through mortality and out-migration come from neighborhoods that have a demographic trajectory of their own. There is no certainty that they will be able to supply immigrants distributed according to the age structure postulated in table 9.3. Indeed, to take an extreme case, if the neighborhood was isolated on a remote island, the only possible source of immigrants would be the children of the inhabitants. Now their age distribution is generally quite different from that of new arrivals. This can be shown by calculating how many of these children reach the 20–24 age group in each five-year period[3] and by comparing their number with that of dwellings becoming vacant in the same period, as represented in figure 9.6. Figure 9.7 compares the evolution of these two quantities over the first one hundred years in the new neighborhood's existence (under the system of rules where out-migration and a departure occur at the death of the first member of the couple). The two curves are completely out of phase.

---

[3] The number of offspring entering the 20–24 age group is obtained by multiplying the number of women aged x by the fertility rate pertaining during the period between 20 and 24 years earlier. For the calculation we used the quinquennial fertility rates for 2000 in France (Beaumel et al. 2003, p. 27), transformed into maternity rates (multiplied by 0.488 and by female survivorship up to the age considered), and we rescaled them so that the maternity function was that for a stationary population.

To begin with, the children of the inhabitants reach adult age (20 years) in increasing numbers whereas the number of dwellings available over each period decreases. The new neighborhood is unable to house the offspring of the first arrivals. After twenty years the movement is reversed, and thirty years after construction of the neighborhood, the available dwellings outnumber the adult children and continue to do so thereafter, which is logical because there is substantial out-migration. When equilibrium is reached, the number of children reaching adulthood is roughly equal to that of dwellings made vacant through a death, since the population is roughly stationary (though not exactly, since some in-migrants enter at relatively high ages).

The foregoing discussion shows that the different components of the population are mutually interdependent. A neighborhood cannot be considered on its own. In the next chapter we will see how this interdependence is at the origin of economic theories of population, beginning with Malthus's famous *Essay* published in 1798. The discussion also pinpoints a curious phenomenon. In a population that is stabilized at its stationary age distribution, there may nonetheless exist sectors such as new neighborhoods, where the age pyramid remains subject to large oscillations that must therefore be compensated for by fluctuations in the opposite direction in older neighborhoods. Because dwellings do not last forever—in some countries, such as Japan, their length of life is actually planned for—the housing life cycle interferes with that of households, leading to mismatches between supply and demand. Young people may adapt to this imbalance by putting off or bringing forward their departure from the parental home. But this is not enough to check the rises and falls in price, of which recent decades have seen many examples across the world.

10
Economics and Population

An economic interpretation can be given for the constrained models explored in the previous chapter. The fluctuations and equilibria observed in the membership of a profession or the population of a new neighborhood originate in a limitation on resources. The emergence of demographic fluctuations has been of interest to economists, who have often had difficulty explaining satisfactorily the long cycles in economic activity and the shorter business cycle. A number of models have been developed in economics and economic history. We will begin from a historical perspective, with the self-regulating (or homeostatic) model, which prefigures the models of Samuelson and Easterlin and, less expectedly, leads on to Malthus.

The study of fluctuations is not the only point of contact between economics and demography. Economic theorizing at both macro and micro levels has long integrated population size and demographic behavior into theoretical and econometric models. We will see that the macroscopic treatment of population in economics proves disappointing, despite the many issues raised by the interaction between economic growth and population growth. By contrast, microeconomic models of the family—in particular those of Gary Becker and his colleagues at Chicago, and the life-cycle models initiated by Modigliani's article (Modigliani and Ando 1963)—open valuable perspectives, notably on the questions of retirement pensions and future fertility trends.

Combining the demographic and economic angles is difficult. The two disciplines do not proceed from the same principles since they are not based on a single conception of man. One postulates a *homo demographicus* subject to precisely constructed probabilities, the other a *homo economicus* intent on maximizing his utility. Each discipline has a tendency to adopt a naive and narrow conception of the other and to assimilate it in this incomplete form. Demographers view economics primarily in terms of work and labor market participation, while economists often equate demography with the growth rate of the total population. But when each discipline eschews its naive vision of the other, common spheres of interest emerge. For economics this means incorporating age groups and the stable-population model into life-cycle theories, while for demography it means explaining fertility levels by reference to the trade-off between the quality and quantity of children and the full costs of raising them. With the issues of retirement pensions and population aging it is even a vast field for common study that opens up, on condition that each discipline avoids caricaturing the other's approach.

10.1 The Self-Regulating Model of Historical Populations

This model was borrowed from ethology. While studying sparrow colonies, Moffat (1903) noticed how the couples divided up a coppice where they built their nests. Those that had not occupied a territory were forced to live on the periphery of the wood where they were unable to build nests or even form couples. Living in this more exposed area, they were more likely than the others to fall victim to predators. When they ventured into the wood, the owners of territories drove them out again. In his great work on the spatial distribution of animals, Wynne-Edwards (1962) took up Moffat's observations and put them into systematic form. By this distribution of population, the sparrows were able to avoid both the overpopulation that would have disrupted their group and the underpopulation that would have allowed another species to move into their ecological niche. In the event of a major crisis—an epidemic or a failure of food supply—the territory left vacant by a couple that had died was taken over by sparrows formerly confined to the peripheral zone. The crisis enabled them to form a couple and obtain a territory. Except in the event of an intense crisis that would have wiped out this pool of potential couples, a continuous occupation of the territory was thus guaranteed. Emmanuel Le Roy Ladurie became interested in this model when working on the peasantry of the southern French province of Languedoc, for when transposed to human populations it supplied a mechanism capable of explaining "immobile history," in particular, the long stagnation of the French population between the thirteenth and eighteenth centuries.[1] The parallel was made more tempting by the fact that a customary right of families to stay on their land existed in southern France. Did Moffat base his description of sparrows on how he thought human societies functioned? It is possible, and if so he was not the first. Marx had queried whether Darwin was portraying animal species and not rather the competitive capitalist entrepreneurs of Victorian Britain.

Moffat's model is directly transposable to a society of small peasant proprietors if it is assumed that the household structures remain of the nucleated (one couple only) or stem form (the couple plus an adult descendant who may be married and who will inherit the holding). The noninheriting offspring who do not marry a female heir find themselves without a territory, comparable in this respect to the sparrows on the edge of the wood. Unable to set up a household of their own, these peasants often moved to a neighboring town and found work as servants, traders, or artisans,

---

[1] The epidemics of plagues, the famines, and the wars occasioned great human losses but societies were organized to limit these great human losses. They developed an internal mechanism of control for this purpose.

striving to amass a sum of money to purchase a holding that had no heir or that the heir did not wish to keep. This was the occasion they waited for to marry and to set up their own household, the two terms incidentally often being synonymous.

This description has strong similarities with the population dynamics of new neighborhoods examined in the last chapter. Assume that there is a fixed number, N, of holdings, each held by one couple. When the couple is dissolved, its place is taken by another formed from among young people who were as yet not established. It may be assumed that a queue is created by age order and that the holding thus freed goes to the oldest in the queue. The peasant landholders are therefore the N oldest married persons. Knowing the population of couples (for example, by age of the husband and assuming, as in the case of new neighborhoods, a fixed age gap between spouses), we can determine the youngest couple that has already set up on its own (the age of the husband is $\Omega(t)$ at time t). Assuming that births occurred essentially within marriage—as was the case in preindustrial Europe—and knowing the age distributions of female fertility $f(x)$ and female mortality, the population can be projected forward from one period to the next. In fact (in continuous notion) the density of births $P(0, t)$ at time t will be equal to

$$P(0,t) = \int_{\Omega(t)}^{\varpi} f(x) P(x,t) \, dx. \tag{10.1}$$

Since the survivorship of couples at the woman's age x is $S(x)$ independently of time t, we also have

$$P(x,t) = S(x) P(0, t - x).$$

Finally, at each point in time, $\Omega(t)$ is determined by the fact that the number of couples where the woman is older than x is N:

$$\int_{\Omega(t)}^{\varpi} P(x,t) \, dx = \int_{\Omega(t)}^{\varpi} S(x) P(0, t - x) \, dx = N. \tag{10.2}$$

This last equation determines $\Omega(t)$. There is a simple stationary solution such that

$$\Omega(t) = \Xi \quad \text{and} \quad P(0,t) = P_0.$$

It is determined by

$$1 = \int_{\Xi}^{\varpi} f(x) S(x) \, dx \quad \text{and} \quad P_0 \int_{\Omega(t)}^{\varpi} S(x) \, dx = N.$$

To verify that the self-regulating model has the qualities claimed for it, a comparison must be made with other models not featuring small landowners or a neutralization of young adults. Three simple models of equilibrium are possible. In the first, infant mortality keeps fertility equivalent to a net rate of reproduction of unity. This is Malthus's positive check. The age structure in this case is that of the stationary population. In the second model, emigration by young people occurs before marriage, in such a way that population numbers stay constant. The age pyramid comprises two stationary sections, since the age groups after the out-migration are smaller on account of the departures. In the third case, migration (or mortality) affects all ages equally and the population has a stable age structure corresponding to the mortality functions $f(x)$ and $S(x)$. The behavior of these three models after a crisis can be compared with that of the self-regulating model. Assume that a fraction of the population suddenly dies out in proportions unrelated to age. Under the self-regulating model, the places made vacant will be occupied by younger elements, which has the effect of raising fertility and facilitating a fairly rapid recovery. Curiously, however, recovery is even faster in the other three models, assuming no losses through out-migration and infant mortality for as long as the upper limit to population growth has not been reached again. This can be verified by simulation of the four models.

The virtues of the self-regulating model have perhaps been overstated then. True, it ensures continuity in the occupation of a territory despite a large fall in population size. But it does not speed up recovery following a crisis, in spite of the reservoir of unmarried young generations. More curiously—though this was foreshadowed in the last chapter—it may generate larger fluctuations than the other models. This becomes apparent when we seek to establish the speed and even the presence of convergence to equilibrium. We do this by differentiating the two equations for the self-regulating model in the neighborhood of equilibrium by setting

$$\Omega(t) = \delta(t) + \varXi \quad \text{and} \quad P(0, t) = P_0 + \epsilon(x).$$

Differentiating the equations gives

$$\int_\varXi^\infty f(x) S(x) \epsilon(t - x) \, dx + \delta(t) S(\varXi) f(\varXi) = \epsilon(t),$$

$$\delta(t) S(\varXi) + \int_\varXi^\infty S(x) \epsilon(t - x) \, dx = 0,$$

replacing $\delta(t) S(\varXi)$ by its value in the second equation, the first takes the form of a renewal equation:

$$\epsilon(t) = \int_\varXi^\infty (f(x) - f(\varXi)) S(x) \epsilon(t - x) \, dx.$$

The function $(f(x) - f(\varXi)) S(x)$ is not always positive or zero, so renewal theory does not apply. Convergence of $\epsilon(t)$ to zero is obvious for as long as the integral of the modulus of $(f(x) - f(\varXi)) S(x)$ is below unity. Above this there is convergence up to some value A such that $\int_\varXi^\infty |(f(x) - f(\varXi))| S(x) \epsilon(t - x) \, dx < A > 1$. At A, the solution becomes periodic and beyond A, $\epsilon(t)$ diverges with long and progressively larger oscillations around zero. In this case it is no longer correct to consider only differential behavior in the neighborhood of equilibrium.

Simulation of the exact behavior of $P(0, t)$ by projection gives the following curious result. We still have a region of convergence and a region of divergence, but sandwiched between them is a fairly large region of periodic fluctuations. In

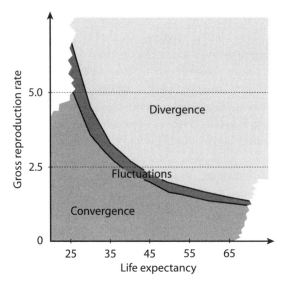

Figure 10.1. Population trajectories in the self-regulating
model by levels of mortality and fertility.

figure 10.1 we have shown the location of the three regions on a plane where the
two axes represent life expectancy and the gross rate of reproduction. The region
of fluctuations expands inversely to life expectancy. At the low life expectancy of
25 years, the zone of divergence is pushed toward fertility values that exceed the
largest observed (gross rate of reproduction of 7 female children, or an average of
14 children per woman). As life expectancy rises, the interval of fluctuations and the
threshold of divergence get lower: the gross rates of reproduction are 3.6 and 4.5 for
a life expectancy of 30 years, 1.90 and 2.30 for a life expectancy of 45 years, and
1.40 and 1.60 for a life expectancy of 60 years. In the high-mortality demographic
systems of the past, therefore, the self-regulating model fulfills its role. But in the
modern period the rise in life expectancy transforms the model's advantage into a
disadvantage. The rapid return to equilibrium often generates explosive fluctuations.
A qualitative explanation of the mechanism runs as follows: at low levels of mortality,
the crisis establishes a large generation of young couples to replace the dead and
who, as they get older, retain their territories to ages where reproduction is low or
nonexistent, thus causing a shortfall of births and further recruitment when they in
turn die out.

10.2   The Easterlin and Samuelson Models

In 1975, Richard Easterlin identified in fertility variations a remarkable illustration
of his theory of economic motivations. His general argument was that changes in
behavior are influenced by the relationship between individuals' aspirations and

the resources they can mobilize to realize them. Now, in respect of fertility, while most couples aspire to have children, they do not always immediately dispose of the resources for rearing them, or to be more precise the resources that they consider necessary by comparison with couples' normal practice. The realization of their desire for children will thus depend on their "relative affluence." Members of small birth cohorts enter the labor market without difficulty and have the resources to found a family early on; members of large birth cohorts, by contrast, experience keen competition and lower incomes, and thus delay having children. Easterlin proposed to measure the slower rise in living standards by the ratio of the male population aged 35–64 to that aged 15–34. According to the author, the focus was on men because—this was the 1970s—the male is the principal breadwinner of the family. If his wages are too low, his wife takes a job to supplement them, and thus postpones having children.

Easterlin tested his hypothesis by comparing trends in period fertility and in the ratio of older to younger adults. In figure 10.2, where the two curves for the period 1946–75 are superimposed, we see that the agreement is excellent. The correlation coefficient between the two series is 0.81. The linking of the two indices permits a comparison between aspirations (fertility) and the resources for their realization (the ratio of age group sizes as a measure of the chances of obtaining a satisfactory standard of living). But it also implies two other important facts. First, that the period fertility index gives a tolerably adequate measure of the timing changes— delaying or bringing forward of childbearing—implied by the behavioral model. A change in the intensity of fertility, and thus in final family size, will only come about if the possibilities for realizing aspirations are never achieved, but the effect then concerns the mature population and not the young couples. The second fact implied is a comparison of children and parents. The cohort aged 15–34 can on average be taken as the offspring of that aged 35–64. This gives a precise meaning to the notion of relative affluence. Children compare their own standard of living relative to that of their parents when they had them, that is, they compare their present level with that in their childhood. This consideration was of importance for testing the theory at the microeconomic level, but the results were disappointing.

Shortly after Easterlin developed his model, it was used by Samuelson to demonstrate a remarkable consequence—the existence of "Easterlin cycles" with the potential to lead to chronic demographic instability. Samuelson simplifies the movement of the population by combining young adults and mature adults into single age groups, of thirty years, for example, with the younger comprising those aged 0–29 and the mature aged 30–59. Thus the size of the next group of young adults thirty years later depends on the fertility and mortality of the two groups. Samuelson postulates constant mortality over time. Fertility is fixed for the older group (30–59 years) but depends on the ratio of the two age group sizes for the younger group: low if the young are numerous relative to the mature, high if not. Using standard

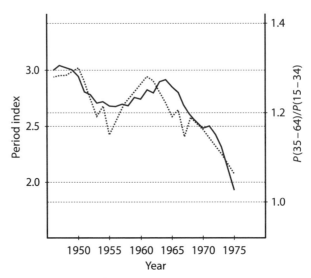

Figure 10.2.   Comparison of the period fertility index (solid line) and the ratio of the mature and young adult populations (dotted line), 1946–75, France.

notation, we can write the projection equations for such a population

$$P(t,0) = S(1)P(t,1)f(t,1) + S(2)P(t,2)f(t,2),$$

where $P(t,i)$ is the population of the ith age group at time t, $S(i)$ is the survivorship at entry into the ith age group,[2] $f(t,i)$ is the fertility of the ith age group at time t, and $N(t) = P(t,0)$ is the size of first cohort, that of children born in period t.

Samuelson's hypotheses are expressed as follows:

$$P(t,i) = S(i)N(t-i),$$
$$f(t,2) = f_2,$$
$$f(t,1) = f(N(t-1)/N(t-2)),$$

which gives the renewal equation:

$$N(t) = f(t,1) = f(N(t-1)/N(t-2))N(t-1) + f_2 N(t-2).$$

The condition expressing Easterlin's model reduces to

$$\partial f(u)/\partial u = f'(u) < 0.$$

This equation can be solved as a geometric sequence with common ratio $\lambda = 1 + r$, r denoting the growth rate:

$$\lambda^2 = \lambda f(\lambda) + f_2.$$

---

[2] Because a projection is being made, survivorship is expressed here in projective form. Thus it is counted from one year to the next in a given cohort, not from one age to the next.

In general there is a positive solution λ for this equation. To find out if it is stable we can differentiate in its neighborhood as we did for the self-regulating model. Setting

$$N(t) = \lambda^t (1 + \epsilon(t)),$$

we obtain

$$\epsilon(t) = (f(\lambda)/\lambda + f'(\lambda))\epsilon(t-1) + (f_2/\lambda^2 + f'(\lambda))\epsilon(t-2).$$

We find a case analogous to that of the differentiation of the self-regulating model, with possibly negative coefficients in the renewal function. If the derivative of f is sufficiently strongly negative at λ, the equilibrium becomes unstable. As there are only two age groups, Samuelson adopted a more ingenious approach, one more commonly used by economists, in the form of a first-order recurrence. He examined the ratio $R(t) = N(t)/N(t-1)$ of births in one period to those in the previous period. The projection equation becomes

$$N(t)/N(t-1) = f(N(t-1)/N(t-2)) + f_2 N(t-2)/N(t-1),$$
$$R(t) = f(R(t-1)) + f_2/R(t-1).$$

At equilibrium, the equation at $R(t)$ is that for λ but differentiation is facilitated by putting

$$R(t) = \lambda + \eta(t),$$

we arrive at

$$\eta(t) = f'(\lambda)\eta(t-1) - (f_2/\lambda^2)\eta(t-1)$$
$$= (f'(\lambda) - f_2/\lambda^2)\eta(t-1).$$

If $f'(\lambda) - f_2/\lambda^2 < -1$, the equilibrium will be unstable. As $R(t)$ stays strictly positive, the population will oscillate indefinitely, all the while growing at the rate $r = \lambda - 1$. Giving the recurrence at $R(t)$ the form $R(t) = F(R(t-1))$, the jump from one period to the next can be iterated by jumping two periods: $R(t) = F(F(R(t-2)))$. In this form, Samuelson switches to a graphical reasoning[3] to show that two cases can arise. One is a convergence analogous to that of stable populations but with a larger fluctuation that he calls the "Easterlin component." The other is a persistent oscillation when the derivative of f is sufficiently strongly negative to prevent convergence.

Simple examples of fertility functions that exhibit the behavior described by Samuelson can be given by making $f(R) = e^{-cR}$ and $f_2 = 1$. The derivative of $f(R)$ is negative, so f is a decreasing function of R, as the model requires. We verify that, at the value $c = 0.835$, the behavior becomes periodic of period 2. For

---

[3] This is analogous to the cobweb diagram in the theory of demand and supply equilibrium. Starting from some value x on the abscissa, the value for the function on the ordinate is found and is entered on the abscissa using the $45°$ line. The operation is then repeated from this new ordinate.

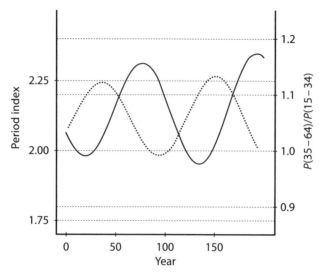

Figure 10.3. Comparison of the period fertility index (solid line) and the ratio of the mature and young adult populations (dotted line) in the self-regulating model.

lower values of c, a stable equilibrium exists. Note that these values are entirely plausible in terms of the fertility rates of each age group. They correspond to net rates of reproduction below 2.

These results are analogous to those obtained earlier with the self-regulating model, but the idea behind Easterlin's model is rather the opposite. In the self-regulating model, the fertility of the younger couples is limited by the relative numerical importance of the older couples. In the present case it is the relative numerical importance of the young that reduces fertility. The trend in the ratio of mature to young adults and in the period fertility index (sum of the age-specific fertility rates) can also be compared in the self-regulating model simulated above. Figure 10.3 shows that when life expectancy is 35 years and the equilibrium age of fertility is 27 years (the case where the fluctuations are self-sustaining), the two curves are no longer superimposed but out of phase. Can the Easterlin model be expressed in terms of individual behavior as was done for the self-regulating model? That is not obvious. The question has in any case become largely meaningless, for the closely superimposed curves that Easterlin observed in 1975 have been replaced by totally divergent curves. This can be seen in figure 10.4, where the series for the ratio of mature to young adults and the period fertility index have been extended up to 2002. The proportion of older couples has increased considerably, but fertility shows practically no recovery. A possible explanation is that the social constraints upon "male breadwinners" in the postwar period have loosened, thereby severing the connection between cohort ratios and fertility and at the same time invalidating the Easterlin model.

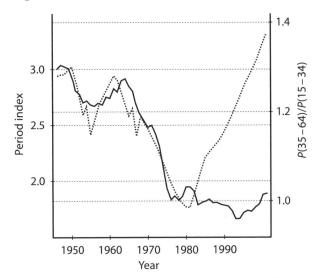

Figure 10.4. Comparison of the period fertility index (solid line) and the ratio of the mature and young adult populations (dotted line), 1946–2002, France (continuation of figure 10.2).

10.3 From Regulation to Chaos

The self-regulating model and the Samuelson model are alike in both having a region of convergence and a region of self-sustained fluctuations. They do not collapse into a more erratic regime that can be termed *chaos*. It was a demographic model, however, that provided the basis for studying one of the earliest chaotic sequences and that was used by Feigenbaum in the article where he demonstrates the existence of a universal scaling constant. In 1973, Robert May published a discrete logistic model corresponding to populations of insects with a one-year life cycle. In this case the population size in one year is derived from that in the previous year using the formula

$$N(t) = rN(t-1)(1 - N(t-1)) = f(N(t-1)).$$

$N(t)$ represents the number in year t as a proportion of the maximum number in the logistic model (hence reduced to unity in the formula).

The two solutions N^*, labeled N_1 and N_2, are

$$N_1 = F(N_1) \quad \text{and} \quad N_2 = rN_2(1 - N_2);$$

hence $N_1 = 0$ and $N_2 = (r-1)/r$.

An equilibrium is stable when $-1 < f'(N^*) < 1$ (this is shown by a limited development around equilibrium by setting $N(t) = N^* + \epsilon(t)$ as we did earlier).

The first equilibrium is stable for $r < 1$. The second is stable between 1 and 3. From $r = 3$ onward, we observe an oscillation analogous to that found by

Samuelson. Iteration of the function f gives a function f_1 such that

$$N(t) = f(f(N(t-2))) = f_1(N(t-2)).$$

These roots are stable (the derivative of f_1 is of less than unit modulus for them). They give the two values between which $N(t)$ oscillates. This solution in turn becomes unstable when r increases and is replaced by a period 4 oscillation whose terms are the additional roots of the iterated f_1 and so on. Feigenbaum showed that the difference between the successive bifurcations decreased in a ratio of 1/4.6692 for a large class of functions f. Very quickly, then, a value of r is attained that exceeds all values of n where a fluctuation of period 2^n appears. At this stage the values exhibit total irregularity, even though this is deterministic and the term chaos is used. Samuelson had therefore discovered the first stage of a more general phenomenon in which the relationship between the successive values of the process loses all significance, so that one variable can no longer be said to have an influence on another. We suspect that certain demographic phenomena pertain to chaos of this kind, which if true would prevent their incorporation into an explanatory model.

10.4   Malthus: Population and Subsistence

Interest in fluctuations is of longstanding, for they were used by Malthus to justify his principle of population. Unlike Easterlin and Samuelson, he studied fluctuations not in their own right but rather to explain how the tension between population growth and the means of subsistence—represented by the famous geometric and arithmetic progressions—was regulated. The functioning of his model will be examined closely, since it provides an introduction to the demographic-economic models that began to be developed in the 1950s. Although the term *Malthusian* is often used incorrectly in the economic literature, from 1798 down to 1950, concern with the relationship between economic development and population growth did not falter, for, surprising as it may seen, Malthus's model is a model of growth.

From the opening chapter of the *Essay*, Malthus (1798, p. 4) lays down the two fundamental principles that he believes govern the course of population movements:

> I think I may fairly make two postulata. First, That food is necessary to the existence of man. Secondly, That the passion between the sexes is necessary and will remain nearly in its present state.

Malthus then proceeds to give a mathematical expression of these two principles: "Population, when unchecked, increases in a geometric ratio. Subsistence increases only in an arithmetical ratio." As we will see shortly, the second of these sentences should, like the first, have been completed with a qualification, namely, when population has exceeded the level of the means of subsistence. The geometric and arithmetic ratios give a description not of the dynamic interaction between population and subsistence, merely of particular phases in it. The relationship is not explained in full until the end of chapter 2 (Malthus 1798, p. 9):

> The way in which these effects are produced seems to be this. We will suppose the means of subsistence in any country just equal to the easy support of its inhabitants. The constant effort toward population, which is found to act even in the most vicious societies, increases the number of people before the means of subsistence are increased. The food therefore which before supported seven millions must now be divided among seven millions and a half or eight millions. The poor consequently must live much worse, and many of them be reduced to severe distress. The number of laborers also being above the proportion of the work in the market, the price of labor must tend toward a decrease, while the price of provisions would at the same time tend to rise. The laborer therefore must work harder to earn the same as he did before. During this season of distress, the discouragements to marriage, and the difficulty of rearing a family are so great that population is at a stand. In the mean time the cheapness of labor, the plenty of laborers, and the necessity of an increased industry amongst them, encourage cultivators to employ more labor upon their land, to turn up fresh soil, and to manure and improve more completely what is already in tillage, till ultimately the means of subsistence become in the same proportion to the population as at the period from which we set out. The situation of the laborer being then again tolerably comfortable, the restraints to population are in some degree loosened, and the same retrograde and progressive movements with respect to happiness are repeated.

The description here is sufficiently precise for it to be translated into present-day terms using diagrams to show the progress of population and of subsistence (converted into the number of persons it can feed under normal conditions). Following the text word by word, we begin with a stage where population increases geometrically (exponentially) and where total subsistence supply is constant (figure 10.5(a)). After the two curves have crossed—i.e., when food supplies become inadequate—the population goes on growing, then stops and remains "at a stand." At this point, the means of subsistence begin to increase arithmetically (linearly) until they reach the level of the stationary population. At the end of this third stage, therefore, we are back to the position at the start of the second, so that the two curves continue to oscillate as stated in Malthus's text.

The text does not have the clarity of mathematical formulas or diagrams and several variant readings can be imagined, but these do not alter the general principle. They merely reposition the two curves, modifying the way in which they overlap. For instance, the assumption may be made that investment in agriculture begins only at the end of stage two once population has come to exceed the means of subsistence (figure 10.5(b)). This would warrant the smooth arithmetic progression in subsistence postulated by Malthus in the first chapter of the *Essay*, in contrast to the alternations of increase and stagnation in population. In both cases, and over the average, the population remains below the level of the means of subsistence (hence with the population curve above the subsistence curve), which eventually forms an obstacle to its survival. What actually happens when the population exceeds

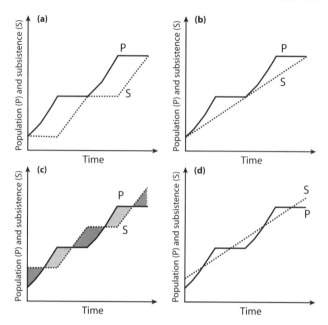

Figure 10.5. Four possible trajectories of subsistence (S) and population (P) corresponding to the model in chapter 2 of Malthus's *Essay*, according to the start point of crisis.

the limit of subsistence? Malthus says that it enters a period of "distress," i.e., it
lives off its reserves, both biological (laborers get leaner) and economic (stocks of
foodstuffs are consumed and livestock slaughtered). Sooner or later these reserves
must be reconstituted; otherwise the laborers will literally die of starvation. The
subsistence curve can be moved upward by imagining stocks being formed and, when
the pressure from population is felt, being reduced (figure 10.5(c): the intermediate
regions have been shaded to show that stock formation and reduction are equal in
volume). Lastly, we can imagine (figure 10.5(d)) that investment starts as soon as
the crisis occurs, as in figure 10.5(b). We then have an uninterrupted linear growth in
subsistence and an oscillation of population above and below the level of the means
of subsistence.[4]

Reconstitution of Malthus's model is difficult because he did not adopt an analytic
approach based on general laws. This is also a prudent position when faced with
a reality whose multiple aspects are not easily summarized. For even if the model
is valid only for one family holding or one hamlet (thirty years later, Von Thünen
also based the description of his famous *"isolierte Staat"* on a single farm), it is a
palpable simplification of a highly diverse peasant civilization. Malthus's caution
was to be forgotten after World War II. Many economists now attempted to formulate

---

[4] The duration of the oscillation remains constant if the maximum population reached at each stage
is a given share of subsistence, for example, 25%, which signifies that well-being falls to 80% of its
equilibrium level.

in mathematical terms the relationship between population and economics with a view to addressing the challenges that the population explosion appeared to pose to economic development.

10.5 Macroscopic Models: Economic Growth and Population Growth

When the scale of Third World population growth—qualified as a "population explosion"—began to be apprehended in the 1950s, the question arose as to whether it represented an obstacle to development. Many eminent economists—Solow, Samuelson, Phelps, Arrow, Boulding—contributed to the debate. They were followed by others with more specialist interests in the field: Peter Nelson, Julian Simon (1977), Robert MacNicoll, and Ronald Lee. Their approaches and contributions can be classified by reference to a two-factor production model in which $Y(t)$, total income in year t, is given by total population $P(t)$ and by capital broadly defined (to include technological progress) $K(t)$:

$$Y(t) = f(P(t), K(t)).$$

Growth of population depends on average income per inhabitant $Y(t)/P(t)$:

$$P'(t)/P(t) = \Phi(Y(t)/P(t)).$$

Growth of capital broadly defined depends on average income and potentially on total population, thereby introducing an effect of increasing returns to scale:

$$K'(t)/K(t) = \Psi(Y(t)/P(t), P(t)).$$

Setting $y(t) = Y(t)/P(t)$ and dropping the indication of time (t) since all the functions are time dependent and all the derivatives are with respect to time, the system of relations becomes

$$y = f(P, K)/P, \qquad P'/P = \Phi(y), \qquad K'/K = \Psi(y, P).$$

The economists deployed great ingenuity over the choice of the exact form of the three functions, f, Φ, and Ψ, for studying the trend in average income. For f, they nearly always selected a Cobb–Douglas function such that

$$Y = f(K, P) = K^\alpha P^{1-\beta},$$

which is used to write the differential equation for the change in income per head:

$$\frac{Y}{P} = K^\alpha P^{-\beta} \frac{y'}{y} = \alpha \frac{K'}{K} - \beta \frac{P'}{P} = \alpha \Psi(y, P) - \beta \Phi(y).$$

The two simplest cases involve setting a constant growth rate r, either for capital or for population. The former case leads to "Malthusian" models and the latter to "Bosrupian" models, these being their accepted names even though they bear little relation to the works of Malthus and Boserup.

10.6 The Malthusian Model

We have $\Psi(y, P) = r$, which results in $y'/y = \alpha r - \beta \Phi(y)$. The change in average income per head—thus with economic progress implied—is directly dependent on the choice of $\Phi(y)$. In fact, the choice of $\Phi(y)$ is all that the model does illustrate. Samuelson and Boulding early on proposed taking an unbounded increasing function for $\Phi(y)$ and selected as an example $\Phi(y) = k \log(y/u)$. This choice was subsequently described as "archetypal" though it might more appropriately be called "amazing" given the extent to which it violates social and historical experience. For what it signifies is that population growth, i.e., the difference between mortality and fertility, is bound to increase without ever reaching a maximum. The consequence of such a hypothesis is a stable equilibrium point with a level of income that can never be exceeded, however rapid the progress represented by the exponential growth of K at rate r, because $\Phi(y)$ will sooner or later exceed the value $\alpha r/k\beta$, which will make y' negative. Hence this equilibrium point y_E is such that $y_E = ue^{\alpha r/\beta k}$. In other words, no amount of technical progress[5] will prevent average income from leveling off at an upper limit. This theoretical result was so favorably received that it was given a name, one still employed in the specialist literature—the *Malthusian trap*, described by Boulding (1955) as a "dismal theorem" since it held out no hope of improvement in the standard of living. The upper limit will be higher when technical progress is faster, but it will be an upper limit nonetheless. Ultimately, therefore, not only will the population grow at a very fast rate, $\alpha r/\beta$, but it will not lead to any economic development. Hence, the population explosion is particularly damaging. In one case only is it halted: that of zero technical progress, for then $y_E = u$, which gives $P'/P = 0$. This prospect is scarcely more appealing, particularly since the maximum living standard, y_E, is below that reached when technical progress occurs.

This extreme outcome can be avoided simply by choosing a slightly more realistic and reasonable $\Phi(y)$. For example, progress in the standard of living clearly leads to a fall in fertility, largely for reasons that will be developed later. In this case $\Phi(y)$ is a decreasing function, and a virtuous circle is initiated where average wealth grows faster as population growth slows and contributes to further reducing its growth rate. Intermediate situations can be imagined in which, initially, income and population growth are positively related because the higher income is used to combat mortality and hence increase the net rate of reproduction with the gross rate (hence fertility) constant. Next, as income continues to increase, fertility falls (here we follow the demographic transition schema in which morality decline precedes fertility decline). Depending on the value of the rate of technical progress, y' can be negative between two values, y_1 and y_2. y_1 will be a point of stable equilibrium and y_2 an unstable one. If the initial average income is higher than y_2, it will grow permanently, but if

---

[5] Denoting by C capital narrowly defined (in the sense of Hicks) and qualifying the rate of technical progress as r, we get the usual formulation of the production function: $Y = K^\alpha P^{1-\beta} e^{rt}$.

situated between y_1 and y_2 it will fall and stabilize at y_1. This conclusion, however, is far less dramatic than that of the Malthusian trap which was unavoidable whatever the level of development, since a higher rate of technical progress will reduce the interval between y_1 and y_2 and from a certain value onward make it vanish, as y' becomes positive over the whole interval.

10.7 The Bosrupian Model: Exogenous Population Growth

In a second class of models, constructed by Solow, Phelps, and Arrow in particular, the assumptions of the Malthusian model are switched around. Population growth is now fixed at a constant rate r, so $\Phi(y) = r$. It is the function $\Psi(y, P)$ giving the growth rate of total capital that must be specified, for this alone governs the evolution of income y, whose derivative is written

$$y'/y = \beta\Psi(y, P) - \alpha r.$$

If $\Psi(y, P)$ is not dependent on P, for example, if the growth of total capital is wholly due to technological progress, the model is the mirror image of the previous one, with $\Psi(y, P)$ in the place of $\Phi(y)$. This model has been labeled "Bosrupian" in reference to Ester Boserup, who in a famous book (Boserup 1965) showed that growth in agricultural output per hectare was the consequence of population increase, i.e., was spurred by necessity. By symmetry with the Malthusian model it is postulated that the lower the average income, the greater the pressure and hence the faster the technological development, thus leading to a similar sort of trap, in which income reaches a maximum (or minimum) at a value $y_E = e^{\alpha r/\beta}$ irrespective of population growth r. This model is also exactly symmetrical to the former by its lack of realism and its disregard for historical and social change in the real world. Boserup's analysis is as little amenable as Malthus's to this kind of oversimplification. Using numerous examples, Boserup demonstrates clearly that, when demographic pressure increases, cultivators respond by intensifying production methods, which signifies longer working times for the same output. Thus, hours of work increase constantly to ensure the same per capita food supply. The hourly product of labor declines while that per unit of land increases. It may also be noted that the transposition of this model to modern agriculture and to industry is largely meaningless.

Subsequent models gave a more precise description of the mechanism of capital formation and technological progress. The best known is that proposed by Solow. In its complete formulation it uses a classic equation for capital renewal through depreciation and saving:

$$C' = sY - aC,$$

where s is the average rate of saving and a is the rate of capital depreciation. With p the rate of technological progress, the Cobb–Douglas equation for production Y

is

$$Y = C^\alpha P^{1-\beta} e^{pt}.$$

Because the population grows exogenously and exponentially at rate r, we can replace $P(t)$ by

$$P(0)e^{rt}Y = P^{1-\beta}(0)C^\alpha e^{pt+r(1-\beta)t}.$$

Substituting this value of Y into the equation for the growth C' of capital, we get

$$C' = sP^{1-\beta}(0)C^\alpha e^{pt+r(1-\beta)t} - aC.$$

We verify that a first integral is an exponential $C = ke^{ut}$ by equalizing the exponents of both terms of the second member:

$$ut = ut\alpha + pt + r(1-\beta)t,$$

that is,

$$u = \frac{p + r(1-\beta)}{1-\alpha}.$$

Y grows at the same pace as capital and population, by definition, at rate r. Consequently, average income rises or falls at the rate v:

$$v = \frac{p + r(1-\beta)}{1-\alpha} - r.$$

Solow began by studying the very simple case in which the production function displays constant returns to scale and where there is no technological progress, i.e., when $\alpha = \beta$ and $p = 0$.

We verify in these conditions that $v = 0$. When there is no technological progress, the population grows exponentially at rate r, but without improving its living standard, which is an even worse outcome than the Malthusian trap. Once sustained technological progress sets in, average income grows linearly at rate v. Growth can also be caused by economies of scale in productivity. In this case, for a fixed capital/labor ratio, population grows faster than both factors, which assumes that

$$\alpha > \beta.$$

Therefore, even in the absence of technological progress, growth in average income will be

$$v = \frac{r(1-\beta)}{1-\alpha} - r = \frac{r(\alpha-\beta)}{1-\alpha} > 0.$$

Several models also introduced a returns-to-scale effect not in capital but in technological progress. Arrow (1962) has it varying with the capital stock, Simon with overall output, while Phelps connects the levels of technology and population by the relation

$$Z'/Z = (P/Z)^\theta.$$

If technological progress e^{pt} is replaced in the Solow model by this new expression, the resolution is equally straightforward, since a first integral of the equation for technological progress Z, where P is replaced by its exponential value $P(0)e^{rt}$ is very simply written as

$$Z = P(0)e^{rt}.$$

We have a particular case of the formulas of the Solow model giving the rate of growth of income v in which $p = r$. Substituting into the formula giving v, we have

$$v = r\left(\frac{1 + 1 - \beta}{1 - \alpha} - 1\right) = \frac{1 + \alpha - \beta}{1 - \alpha}.$$

This quantity is always positive for acceptable values of α and β $(0 < \beta \leq \alpha < 1)$.

Many more new formulations of these models could be produced but it would not make them any more realistic. This is because they start out from a conception of population that is incorrect, both in the simplistic choice of an exponential and in the exogenous assumption, as if neither technological progress nor capital accumulation modified population behavior reduced to its most elementary form. Recent authors have tried to inject a small amount of realism by introducing into Solow-type models a relationship that makes population growth dependent on average income and thus treats population as an endogenous variable, as in the Malthusian model.

10.8 Endogenous Technological Progress and Population Growth

After studying the two unconvincing simplified options, we go back to the initial model formulated thus:

$$y'/y = \alpha \Psi(y, P) - \beta \Phi(y).$$

An approach of this sort is adopted by Niehans (1963), Nelson (1956), and, especially, Ronald Lee (1986), who has produced the most refined syntheses. However, increased generality does not yield the results that were already elusive with the simple models, and since both functions, $\Psi(y, P)$ and $\Phi(y)$, neither of which are susceptible to interpretation in very general terms, must be defined simultaneously, complexity is doubled. Faced with these difficulties, modeling has taken a typological direction and focused on medium- instead of long-run movements. More is known in this case about the initial conditions (level of capital C and of population P) and about changes in the near future (rates of population growth and technological progress, rates of saving and depreciation). It is then possible to determine the regions of evolution toward stable values or, on the contrary, exponential growth, for average incomes. Ronald Lee used this approach to classify the configurations identifiable in recorded history. Clear, however, is that the original objective has been abandoned. There is no longer any question of predicting at an abstract level the results from the interaction between technological progress, capital accumulation, and population increase. But another reason exists for these models being abandoned. The economic and population growth trends for the emerging countries, for the former socialist countries and now for India and China have not revealed a stable relationship between economic growth and population growth. Alfred Sauvy correctly adopted this empirical position in the 1980s as a response to the pessimistic prophecies of the Malthusian models.

If demography is to make a contribution to economic theory, it must not be simplified. On the contrary, it is the subtlest and most refined resources of the field that can cast fresh light on the phenomena where its influence has been neglected. This is particularly the case for the effects of tempo or timing changes studied at the start of this chapter and for the consequences of variations in the age structure that will inform life-cycle theories and the debate over retirement pensions.

10.9   Appendix

10.9.1   Operationalizing the Self-Regulating Model

We have taken as an example a premodern population in which life expectancy is 40 years (the life table is the Ledermann model table for this life expectancy) and marital fertility is equal to the natural fertility in chapter 2 (6.5 children ever born per woman).

We start from the equilibrium regime defined in the body of the text for the four cases. This corresponds to a minimum age at couple formation of 28 years in the self-regulating model; to 20% of the initial population for young people reaching age 15 in the model with out-migration; to an additional infant mortality of 50% in the case of control through mortality; and to a loss of 1% of each age group each year in the out-migration/mortality regime at all ages. Assume a serious crisis that eliminates 20% of the population in a given year and observe the return to equilibrium in each case. The subsequent movement of the population is found simply by projecting it according to the parameters of the four regimes under comparison. The trajectories are quite similar but have different explanations. In the self-regulating model, the vacant holdings will be taken over by unmarried offspring who form couples earlier than they would in ordinary conditions. Age at first birth falls from 28 to 21 years, so the number of births that dropped by 20% in the crisis year climbs back to its usual level almost immediately. Because the population has shrunk, mortality is lower. The difference between deaths and births allows the equilibrium size to be recovered and then exceeded. When the cohorts born after the crisis reach adulthood, the age at couple formation rises again and returns to its equilibrium level. The movement of the other three populations is faster initially for different reasons. In the one controlled by mortality, excess infant mortality disappears, which leads to a strong and—after fifteen years—compensating increase in the number of young cohorts. For the case where equilibrium was formerly maintained through out-migration, young people no longer need to migrate since the upper limit to population has not been reached. They not only stay put but quickly reach the age of childbearing, thus raising fertility. The last case is a combination of the two previous ones, which also leads to a rapid recovery.

11

Life Cycles and Old-Age Pensions

The life-cycle theories that are used for studying human capital and pension systems draw upon demography and economics. From the demographic side they incorporate age distributions and population renewal, and from the economic side they make use of interest rates, activity rates, and productivity rates. A fusion of the two viewpoints is necessary from the outset for defining a rational schedule of lifetime income and expenditure for individuals, which leads on to theories of funded pensions, and also for the purpose of identifying the general equilibria in a population where the balance between the economically active and inactive is at issue. It will be shown that agreement between the individual and the population-level viewpoints—longitudinal and cross-sectional, to employ similar terms—is possible with the *golden rule*, an instrument of reference that ensures coherence between pay-as-you-go and funded pension schemes. But the two viewpoints also converge when we introduce the costs of education and consider children as investments, a position which, via the notion of human capital, leads on to economic theories of the family and in particular that of Gary Becker, who pioneered this approach.

11.1 Equilibrium over the Life Cycle and the Funding Principle

We start by establishing the formulas for an individual's lifetime financial balance sheet, taking into account income $R(x)$ at each age x, expenditure (consumption and saving) $C(x)$ and interest rates $i(t)$ at each date t. The interest rates must be known in order to compare the sums at different times. A sum of money S_1 at date t_1 will be worth S_2 at the later date t_2 since it can be invested at the current rate of interest over the entire period between the two dates. Hence, either

$$S_2 = S_1 \prod_{t=t_1}^{t_2} (1 + i(t))$$

or

$$S_2 = S_1 \exp\left(\int_{t_1}^{t_2} i(t)\, dt \right).$$

The first formula corresponds to an annual calculation of interest, the second to a continuous or instantaneous calculation. With these formulas we obtain the discounted balance $A(z, T)$ of earnings and expenditures up to age z and at time T. Without loss of generality, we will put the origin for time and for age (hence the birth date) at the same point in time, as shown below:

The balance sheet is calculated by adding the differences between earnings and expenditures at each age x, weighted by the effect of interest rates from x to T:

$$A(z, T) = \sum_{x=0}^{z} (R(x) - C(x)) \prod_{t=x}^{T} (1 + i(t))$$

$$= \sum_{x=0}^{z} (R(x) - C(x)) \int_{x}^{T} i(t)\, dt.$$

It is instructive to follow the balance across all ages, so for all values of z when taking $T = z$. An example can be given to show the dominant influence of interest rates. Assume that earnings are zero up to age 12, rising until age 25, constant until age 35, and then falling until reaching zero at age 60 (which was broadly the age-earnings profile of coal miners in early-twentieth-century Europe). Consumption expenditure is assumed constant and corresponds to a living standard close to survival level. In figure 11.1 we have plotted the age schedule of earnings and expenditure, using a different shade of gray for the deficits and surpluses in each year. In figure 11.2 we have calculated the balance $A(z, z)$ corresponding to these levels of income and expenditure at each age z for interest rate values of 0, 3, and 5.5%. Although these rates are relatively modest, the three balances that correspond to them follow radically different paths. With an interest rate of 5.5%, the worker experiences a constant deficit. With 0%, the balance is positive from age 25 and remains so until death at 75 years. With a 3% interest rate, equilibrium is reached later, at age 30; but from age 50 onward, funding is more advantageous than what would have been obtained with a zero interest rate and allows the financing of retirement since the interest from the sums saved is in equilibrium with consumption.

The rate of interest is not the only significant variable. If the consumption level is changed slightly, the shock is clearly visible in the balance. In figure 11.3 we have calculated the lifetime balance for the case of an interest rate of 5.5% when annual consumption is reduced by 4, then by 8%. This moderate change modifies the balance completely. With consumption 4% lower, the balance is now in equilibrium at age 75, while with an 8% reduction in consumption the capital formed is large enough to be able to live off the interest and the capital once working life has ended.

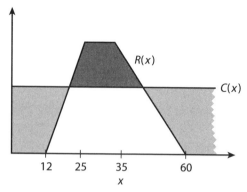

Figure 11.1. Consumption and income of an individual at all ages x (light gray, years when expenditure exceeds earnings; dark gray, years when earnings exceed expenditure).

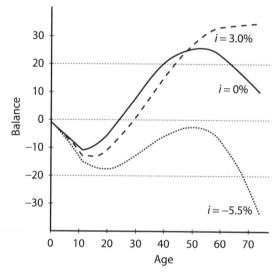

Figure 11.2. Age-specific balance of expenditure and incomes over the sum of previous years, by value of interest rate i.

These balances are meaningful for the external observer but not for the actors involved, whose own existence forms their subject matter. This is because the actors are ignorant of an essential parameter: their age at death. If a person knew that he was going to die at a relatively young age, he would have no interest in reducing his consumption. Conversely, if preparing to live to a great age, he would need to tighten his belt in order to build up capital. The solution to uncertainty of this sort is provided by insurance. If a large enough group of individuals pool their savings, after paying back the costs of their upbringing—a practice known as "*payer sa jeunesse*" in northern France, where young workers used to return their first wages to their parents—the effect is to weight the balance at age u by the probabilities of

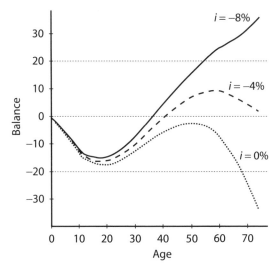

Figure 11.3. Age-specific balance of expenditure and income over all previous ages, for an annual interest rate i of 5.5% when the level of consumption is varied (dotted line, level of figure 11.2; dashed line, 4% lower; solid line, 8% lower).

surviving $S(x)$ at age x:

$$A(z, T) = \sum_{x=0}^{z} S(x)(R(x) - C(x)) \prod_{t=x}^{T}(1 + i(t))$$

$$= \sum_{x=0}^{z} S(x)(R(x) - C(x)) \int_{x}^{T} i(t)\,dt.$$

In order for the system to function, the calculation of the life cycle must be limited to the period of adulthood—individuals being left to incur and repay the costs of upbringing and education that are negotiated mainly within families[1]—which is equivalent to considering ages only from the start of working life. For the system of insurance within the group to be equitable, the sums paid out must ultimately equal those paid in. This is the conventional reasoning of actuarial science. At the ages where earnings exceed expenditure (dark gray in the example in figure 11.1), the surplus $R(x) - C(x)$ corresponds to payments in or contributions at age x, $V(x)$, and at the higher ages where the deficit appears, its opposite, $C(x) - R(x)$ corresponds to payments out or pensions $W(x)$. For the system to be in equilibrium implies that at extinction of the group of contributors, i.e., after the last death at age ϖ, the balance is in equilibrium, that is, zero: $A(\varpi, \varpi) = 0$. Operation along these lines is characteristic of funded pension systems, which are thus merely a variant of life-cycle balances.

---

[1] Exceptions occurred early on, as early as the fourteenth century in Flanders, where insurance contracts were taken out on the survival and dowries of children. In the present day, bank loans for students have brought young people back into the life-cycle balance.

Table 11.1.   Annual contributions over working life
to obtain an annual pension of 1 at retirement.

Interest rate (%)	Life expectancy					
	50	55	60	65	70	75
−1.5	0.41	0.45	0.49	0.53	0.58	0.64
0	0.26	0.28	0.31	0.33	0.36	0.40
1.5	0.16	0.18	0.19	0.21	0.22	0.24
3	0.10	0.11	0.12	0.13	0.14	0.15
4.5	0.06	0.06	0.07	0.08	0.08	0.09

11.2   Funded Pension Systems

In principle, life-cycle balances cannot be calculated until after the last death has occurred. By definition, however, those paying in do so prior to this date. They do not know what interest rates will be subsequently. To ensure that contributions equilibrate with pension payments, a constant interest rate i is set that constitutes a gamble on the future. In this case the equilibrium formula for the balance becomes

$$\sum_{x=20}^{100} S(x)(V(x) - W(x))(1 + i)^{\varpi - x} = 0.$$

In practice, the contributions V are constant from an initial age a to a terminal age b, then pensions are paid from b until ϖ. Here we have taken $\varpi = 100$ years, $a = 20$ years, and $b = 60$ years, but any other values can be chosen. Simplifying by $(1 + i)^{\varpi}$, we can derive the ratio W/V from the previous formula:

$$\frac{W}{V} = \sum_{60}^{100} S(x)(1 + i)^{-x} \Big/ \sum_{20}^{60} S(x)(1 + i)^{-x}.$$

The ratio of payments to contributions, V/W, i.e., the sum of money V that must be paid in to receive a unit W, has been calculated in table 11.1 for various interest-rate and life-expectancy values under the assumption of uninterrupted activity between ages 20 and 60 followed by total inactivity up to the end of life.[2]

Interest rates have a larger effect than mortality. One additional percentage point on interest rates makes more difference than the entire gain in life expectancy from the French Revolution down to 2000. With current real interest rates (allowing for inflation) of around 2% or less, the sums paid out are large, whereas in periods of tight money and higher interest rates they may be very small. Without going into interpretations of economic policy, the scale of the retirement pension problem

---

[2] The life tables are those of the 100 network from Ledermann's model life tables.

is certainly due in part to population aging and increased longevity, but also and primarily to the decline in interest rates.

Another economic consideration is often overlooked. The growth of average earnings means that, if pensioners wish to maintain a relative income comparable with that they are aiming for in present values, they must take into account the rate of earnings growth, thereby offsetting the effect of interest rates by a coefficient that is also cumulative and of similar size. Pensioners seek to receive a pension that is proportional not to their own past annual earnings but to the current earnings of actives in the same occupation as them. So contributions and pensions must also be discounted by the increase in productivity or, from an accounting perspective, in average earnings. The term $(1 + i)$ in the formula must therefore be replaced by $(1 + i)/(1 + e)$, where e is the growth rate of average earnings. If e is higher than i, the ratio drops below 1, which is equivalent to a negative interest rate. This is why we have put a value of -1.5% on the top row of table 11.1, corresponding, for example, to economic growth of 3.5% by volume and a real interest rate of 2%. We see that in such cases contributions can reach very high levels, since, at the life expectancies currently observed in the developed countries, the annual contributions over the working life must be more than half the annual pensions paid out.

At this stage there is still a degree of freedom over the level of contributions and hence of pension payments, since the ratio of income available in retirement, W, to the level available during activity, $R - V$, has not been set. Some people may view their working life as drudgery and give priority to their period of retirement, others may take the opposite view. There is no obvious choice of a rule, a situation translated in neoclassical economics by a collective utility function.

The age pyramid is generally reduced to two subpopulations, the active and the retired, to which correspond two utility functions $u_1(c_1)$ and $u_2(c_2)$, c_1 and c_2 denoting consumption over the two periods. c_1 and c_2 are directly dependent on the contributions and payments: $c_1 = R - V$ and $c_2 = W$ on the assumption that all savings is invested for retirement. V and W are connected by the actuarial equation given above $V/W = \phi(S, e, i) = \phi$ since, at the level of the individual, S, e, and i are fixed, or alternatively $W = \phi/V$. The last unknown, V, is determined by maximizing the general utility, $U(u_1, u_2)$.

The collective utility $U(u_1, u_2)$ is usually expressed by a Cobb–Douglas function in terms of utilities for the two age groups u_1 and u_2:

$$U(u_1, u_2) = (u_1)^\alpha (u_2)^{1-\alpha}.$$

The approach can be illustrated with an example by specifying the utility functions u_1, u_2:

$$u_1(c) = u_2(c) = k \log(c).$$

General utility is then

$$U(u_1, u_2) = (k \log(R - V))^\alpha (k \log(V/\phi))^{1-\alpha}.$$

To maximize U with respect to V, we equate its derivative at V to zero, which gives the condition

$$(1 - \alpha)(R - V) \log(R - V) = \alpha V \log(V/\phi).$$

The left-hand part is a decreasing function of V and the right-hand part an increasing function, hence there is a single solution. The result is not restricted to two age groups. It persists when we consider all the age groups x by assigning a utility function $u(x)$ to each of them. Total utility U can then also be written in a Cobb–Douglas formulation:

$$U(\{u(x)\}) = \prod_x u(x)^{p(x)},$$

where $p(x)$ is a probability distribution ($\sum_x p(x) = 1$).

The value for V that maximizes the utility function U is found by implementing $u(x)$ as a function of R, V, and W and by respecting the constraint ϕ. The result can be interpreted very simply as expressing W as a proportion of net earnings $R-V$. For example, the pension level is 60% of earnings from work. For this reason, pension schemes miss out the stage of economic reasoning and set this proportion directly. In so doing they introduce an important change since the level is the same for everyone whereas the logic of funding is individualistic. There are as many individual values for $W/(R-V)$ as there are individuals. The fact the pension is personal does not alter the actuarial equation ϕ. Instead of counting for one unit, each individual counts for his or her level W. Supplementary pension schemes often operate on this principle.

11.3 Accounting Equilibrium and Pay-As-You-Go (Unfunded) Pension Systems

So far we have adopted the viewpoint of the individual. But there is also the viewpoint of the group that manages the inflows (contributions or payments) and outflows (pensions, allowances, benefits, repayments). It can be assumed to act like the individuals, adjusting the aggregate inflows and outflows by investing at an interest rate i when there is a surplus and borrowing at the same rate when there is a deficit. Its function here is simply to correct for irregularities in the age structure of contributors and fluctuations in mortality by balancing the sums paid in by contributors against those paid out to beneficiaries. This remains possible for small groups, but ultimately, when the state—which by definition is its own insurer—is the guarantor for the system, there is a risk of serious financial imbalance. It seeks to avoid this by ensuring that in any year the pensions paid out equal the contributions received. Such a system is described as unfunded or pay-as-you-go and is summed up by an adage: a year's contributions pay for a year's pension.

If $P(x, t)$ designates the number in age group x at time t, and $a(x, t)$ the proportion in activity at this age, the equilibrium between contributions V and benefits W

is simply written as

$$\sum_{x=15}^{100} VP(x,t)a(x,t) = \sum_{x=15}^{100} WP(x,t)(1 - a(x,t)).$$

As in the case of funding, assume that activity lasts from ages 20 to 60 and then ceases definitively. We can calculate the ratio V/W of the annual payment V to obtain one unit of repayment W, which is also annual. Assume that the population studied has a stable age structure, so that the number at age x is in the form

$$P(x,t) = S(x)/(1 + r)^x = S(x)(1 + r)^{-x},$$

where r denotes the intrinsic growth rate, the equilibrium equation becomes

$$V\left(\sum_{x=15}^{100} a(x,t)S(x)(1 + r)^{-x}\right) = W\left(\sum_{x=15}^{100} (1 - a(x,t))S(x)(1 + r)^{-x}\right).$$

This equation is exactly that obtained in the case of the funded system on condition that we replace the growth rate r by the interest rate i. If, for example, we calculate the values of the V/W ratio for life expectancies ranging from 50 to 75 years and rates of population growth ranging from -1.5% to 4.5%, we obtain exactly table 11.1. It is then tempting to make the same commentary and point out that the variation in the growth rate r has a much bigger influence on the ratio V/W than longevity. This incidentally was the conclusion reached by Alfred Sauvy, who saw it as one of the arguments in favor of population growth. The higher the growth rate r, the lower the contribution of each member of the working population.

The coincidence of the two formulas does not signify that the interest rate and population growth rate are of equal importance, however. In situations of this kind, the size of the variance matters more than the size of the mean. Now, the variations in V/W caused by the demographic structure are small compared with variations in interest rates and in rates of earnings growth. Between 1971 and 2002, the ratio of the population aged over 60 to that aged 20–60 remained within the range 0.33–0.39. If we refer to table 11.1, this signifies that the equivalent for interest rates (with life expectancy varying from 70 to 75 years) is a tiny variation of 0–0.7%. In figure 11.4 we have indicated the interest rates that corresponded to the values of V/W for a known life expectancy, i.e., the stable population with the same mortality that gave the same V/W ratio. The intrinsic growth rate calculated in this way varies between -0.1 and 0.5%, even narrower limits than indicated by table 11.1. On the same diagram we have shown interest rates corrected for inflation (long-term interest rates at 1 January of the year considered minus the rate of growth in retail prices) and the rate of increase in the basic monthly wage over the same period. The erratic movements and temporarily very high and low levels of the two latter quantities contrast sharply with the imperceptible evolution of the growth rate of the stable equivalent population. The diagnosis would of course be very different if the

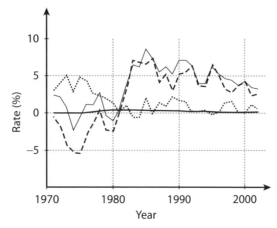

Figure 11.4. Evolution in interest rates corrected for inflation (solid thin line), minimum monthly wage (dotted line), the difference between them (dashed line), and the population growth rate in the stable equivalent population (thick line), 1971–2002, France.

population of France were to grow at 3% a year, but the reality is nowhere near that. Besides, even if fertility tripled, no substantial recovery in the growth rate of the stable equivalent population would be observed for some forty years, this being the time needed to have enough members of contributing age in the new large cohorts.

Because the impact of population growth stays limited, it is in competition with other possible changes. Age at withdrawal from the workforce is not a biological invariant; laws to raise it have been passed in several countries. For instance, if the age of the transition from activity to retirement is moved from 60 to 65 years, the V/W ratio declines substantially, falling from 0.38 in 2002 to 0.28. When calculating such a ratio, the assumption is made that women have the same age-specific activity rates as men. This is not actually the case. If we take into account the fact that female activity currently stands at only 70%, the entry into the labor market of the 30% who are inactive will raise the number of contributors by 15% and will not have an effect on pensions for another thirty years. Allowance must also be made for the possibility that unemployment will come down from high levels. In other words, numerous keys are available with which to modify the V/W ratio that is frequently presented as a demographic inevitability. No key, however, will suffice for unifying the results from funded and pay-as-you-go systems. This is a curious paradox, all the more so since it has a theoretical solution, the *golden rule*.

11.4   Golden Paths, Golden Rule

The contradiction between pay-as-you-go and funded pension schemes arises in a paradoxical way. Assume that each month an individual pays the sum V into a funded scheme in order to receive a pension of amount W_1, calculated on the basis of interest rate i. Assume that his identical twin, who has the same occupation, pays the same sum V into a pay-as-you-go scheme that in retirement will pay him W_2, as a function of the age structure and, for brevity, of the growth rate r of the stable equivalent population. Given that W_1 and W_2 are calculated by using different formulas, there is no reason for them to be identical. Yet how can W_1 be different from W_2 given that the payments V and the economic system are the same in both schemes? Understanding this must be of help in determining the nature of the difference between the two pension systems. The first step toward finding a solution is to note a double aporia. The funded pension model considers only capital. The economy could be functioning with a single individual—like the King of England in Sismondi's (1827) apologue—but this would not make the slightest difference to calculation of V/W. By symmetry, the pay-as-you-go model accords no role to capital or technological progress. It is calculated in exactly the same way in the Bronze Age as in the most advanced contemporary society. The question then is how to give labor a role in the funded model and capital a role in the pay-as-you-go model? The only solution is to construct a macroeconomic model that associates both factors in production. Edmund Phelps (1961) was the first to understand this but, recognizing the enormity of what was implied, he presented it in the form of a fable set in the imaginary kingdom of Solovia run on sound neoclassical lines. His simple and elegant reasoning can be reproduced virtually without modification.

It is assumed that total production $Q(t)$ in year t is obtained by using capital $K(t)$, labor $L(t)$, and technological progress that is assimilated to an augmentation of the labor force. This augmentation is at a constant rate λ and population grows at a constant rate γ. Gross investment $I(t)$ is used to pay for the augmentation of capital $K'(t)$ and its depreciation at the rate δ, that is,

$$I(t) = K'(t) + \delta K(t).$$

Consumption $C(t)$ is what remains of income $Q(t)$ after investment:

$$C(t) = Q(t) - I(t).$$

Assume that the production function $Q(t) = F(K(t), e^{\lambda t} L(t))$ displays constant returns to scale (so is homogeneous of degree 1 for K and L simultaneously). We can write

$$Q(t) = L(0)e^{(\gamma+\lambda)t} F(K(t)/L(0)e^{(\gamma+\lambda)t}, 1) = L(0)e^{(\gamma+\lambda)t} f(k(t)),$$

setting $f(k(t)) = F(K(t)/L(0)e^{(\gamma+\lambda)t}, 1)$, where $k(t)$ denotes average capital per worker or unit of labor.

If $k(t)$ is constant, equal to k', the economy is said to be following a "golden path." In this case, the relations that define the economy simplify to

$$K(t) = k^* L(t) = k^* L(0)e^{(\gamma+\lambda)t} = K(0)e^{(\gamma+\lambda)t}.$$

Because $K(t)$ and $L(t)$ grow at the same rate, this is also true for $Q(t)$, which is a homogeneous function of degree 1 of the two factors. $K'(t)$ also grows at the same constant rate as $K(t)$, hence $I(t)$ and $C(t)$ by virtue of the linear relations that connect them together. In particular, we can write that total consumption $C(t)$ is

$$C(t) = F(K(t), e^{\lambda t} L(t)) - I(t)$$
$$= L(0)e^{(\gamma+\lambda)t} f(k^*) - (\gamma + \lambda + \delta)K(0)e^{(\gamma+\lambda)t}$$
$$= L(0)e^{(\gamma+\lambda)t}(f(k^*) - k^*(\gamma + \lambda + \delta)).$$

All the golden paths corresponding to the possible values of $K'(t)$ are thus homothetic since they are written as the product of an exponential function by a parameter constant over the whole length of the path considered. One of them maximizes consumption at any time t. We find it by deriving $C(t)$ with respect to k^*, which gives

$$0 = \partial C(t)/\partial k^* = f'(k^*) - (\gamma + \lambda + \delta).$$

Now, if we refer to the definition of $F(k^*)$, we straightaway verify that $f'(k^*) = \partial F/\partial K$ or, after rearranging the terms,

$$\partial F/\partial K - \delta = \gamma + \lambda.$$

The neoclassical equilibrium assumption is crucial here since under it the cost of the factors, or their reward, is their marginal efficiency or productivity. $\partial F/\partial K$ is the gross earnings per unit of capital per period and $(\partial F/\partial K - \delta)$ is its net earnings after depreciation, i.e., interest rate i. The golden rule equation takes an extraordinarily simple form

$$i = \gamma + \lambda.$$

This is formulated thus: the interest rate is equal to the rate of population growth plus the rate of economic growth (technological progress or rate of increase in production per worker in the labor force $L(t)$).

The contradiction between the funded and pay-as-you-go schemes is thus resolved. As was predicted, when the missing factor is put back into each of the two systems, their results become identical. If both twins live in Solovia, they will receive the same pension:

$$W_1 = W_2.$$

11.5   Outside the Golden Rule

The golden rule is intellectually satisfying but distinctly less so empirically, for in the real world, as in the example given in figure 11.4, the population growth rate and the interest rate diverge considerably. There are three reasons for this. First, the golden rule is the result of neoclassical thinking in which the price of factors is determined by their marginal productivity. This postulate is sharply disputed by other economic theories—especially that of Sraffa (1960)—which work from the principle that the division of output between rewards to capital and rewards to labor is governed not by the rules of economics but by the balance of political forces. For a Sraffian, therefore, there is no reason why the golden rule should prevail. The second reason for deviations from the golden rule is international. Neoclassical economics suffers from the same defect as stable-population theory: a preference for a closed economy with no links to the outside world. In fact, the interest rate is on the contrary highly sensitive to shifts in the international economy. Hence it cannot be governed by population growth rates, not even in a neoclassical world. The last reason[3] is subtler and has given rise to discussion. If all pensions are run as funded schemes, the total amount in funding represents a significant share of the country's capital and will thus have an influence on the interest rate, this being what brings supply and demand for capital into balance. Whether or not an economy is evolving along an optimal golden path, the volume of capital that funding represents at any given time can be calculated by recalling that each cohort must ensure its own accounting balance. For a person born in $t - y$, the amount invested stands at

$$c(y) = V \int_0^y S(x)a(x)e^{i(y-x)}\,dx - W \int_0^y S(x)(1 - a(x))e^{i(y-x)}\,dx$$
$$= e^{iy} \int_0^y (S(x)(Va(x) - W + Wa(x))e^{-ix})\,dx.$$

To know the total amount invested for all the cohorts $t - y$, we have to multiply the quantity $c(y)$ by the number in the cohort $e^{r(t-y)}$ at birth and sum over all the values of y:

$$C = \int_0^{100} c(y)e^{r(t-y)}\,dy$$
$$= e^{rt} \int_0^{100} c(y)e^{y(i-r)}\left[\int_0^y S(x)(Va(x) - W + Wa(x))e^{-ix}\,dx\right]dy.$$

The formula is complicated but presents the advantage of showing that time enters the first exponential factor only. The capital that secures the funded system thus grows at the same rate as the population. It is also seen that the level of this capital depends on the interest rate. If the funded system absorbed the totality of capital we could write $K(t) = e^{r(t-y)}$. Yet under the neoclassical theory there is no guarantee that the net earnings of capital, $\partial F/\partial K - \delta$, will be the interest rate i. This is not a trivial point. A fully funded system represents several years of national income (as can be verified by calculating the formula with numerical values), varying depending on the proportion of pension income W to the work income (taken as unity in the

---

[3] A fourth difficulty could be added, though it would take us far beyond our present concerns: if the strict definition given by Hicks (1973) in *Capital and Time* is adopted, capital itself is defined as a function of the projected interest rate.

formulas), and the level of the interest rate i and population growth r.[4] A more complete vision of the process is obtained by calculating the rate of variation of the capital at t by its components:

$$\frac{\partial K}{\partial t} = r = i + V \int_0^{100} S(x)a(x)e^{i(t-x)}\,dx - W \int_0^y S(x)(1 - a(x))e^{i(t-x)}\,dx,$$

giving this useful relationship:

$$r - i = V \int_0^{100} S(x)a(x)e^{i(t-x)}\,dx - W \int_0^y S(x)(1 - a(x))e^{i(t-x)}\,dx.$$

When the interest rate is higher than the rate of population growth, total contributions are less than total payouts or pensions. But the financial return from the interest offsets the shortfall and even allows the capital to grow at rate r. Conversely, if the interest rate is lower than population growth, contributions exceed payouts and allow capital to grow faster than from compounded interest. In the latter case, the pay-as-you-go scheme is more advantageous. The capital would grow at the same rate as the interest rate, and contributions V would be lower for the same level of payouts. When the interest rate is high, on the other hand, it is advantageous to switch to the funded principle. But to do this a capital must have already been constituted. It is not in fact possible to switch from a pay-as-you-go system to a funded system unless a capital fund exists. This question has become something of a topical political issue in some developed countries like France, Japan, or Greece with the efforts to build up pension reserve funds, though since the funds must represent several years of national income this is not something that can be done in a short space of time.

11.6   Economize or Breed?

In an aphorism that has remained famous, Jean-Baptiste Say recommended the former course. But for most of human history, it is children who have looked after their aged parents. We can reverse this proposition and say that having children is an insurance against old age. The pay-as-you-go pension system represents an extension of this practice to society at large, spreading out the risk of mortality of offspring that would otherwise leave parents unsupported. A parallel can be made with the spreading of the risk of dying—or rather the risk of surviving for a long time—in the funded system. Under funding, the fact of living to a high age does not exhaust an individual's capital because other contributors will have died relatively young, thus creating a reserve. Similarly with pay-as-you-go the risk of not having any children or of them all dying is offset by the presence of the members of the next generation. It is a remarkable fact that at the aggregate level the children of today's pensioners (the economically inactive aged 50 or over) have broadly the same age

---

[4] The point has been discussed by Keyfitz and Gomez de Leon (1980) and Bourgeois-Pichat (1960).

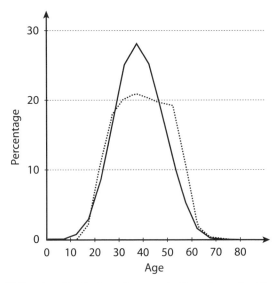

Figure 11.5. Age distribution of economically active males (dotted line) and of the children of retired persons (inactives over 50), France, 1999.

distribution as the current active population, with a similar mean age and a slightly larger dispersion. We verify this in figure 11.5 in which the two distributions are compared. For the economically active the age distribution is that from the 1999 census and for the children it was obtained from age-specific female fertility rates for each year of birth of the pensioners (aged by two years, the average age difference between husband and wife, since we compare the male distributions, where activity is almost 100% between ages 25 and 50, whereas the fertility rates are calculated on the female population).

However, with the ability offered by modern methods of contraception to decide the number of one's children, plus the low mortality of children and adolescents, it becomes difficult to think that the existence of offspring is an entirely random phenomenon. Instead it is reasonable to see the number of children as the result of a microeconomic calculation. One advantage of this approach is that it reintroduces into the calculation the early years of the life cycle that were excluded from the calculation of pensions. During these early years the child represents a cost for its parents. We will start from hypotheses that are simple and thus unrealistic but which open the way to an important, even decisive factor, namely the quality of the child or, alternatively, its human capital.

Start from a model with three ages: childhood, working life, retirement. As before, we will assume that total consumption during working life is c_1 and during retirement c_2. Income over working life will be R. The adult will have the possibility of saving at level S or having n children who are raised at a unit cost of v. In retirement, the individual will derive his income from his savings that he will have invested at interest rate i. So he will dispose of $S(1+i)$ and any children he has will each help him by amount w. Consequently, consumption over the two periods is formalized in the following way:

$$c_1 = R - S - nv \quad \text{and} \quad c_2 = S(1+i) + nw.$$

Assume first that saving is zero and that, in Paul Schulz's blunt expression, children are the capital of the poor. The number of children will be determined by maximizing the total utility function over the two periods $U(c_1, c_2)$. This is equivalent to maximizing the function for n, $U(R - nv, nw)$ hence to seeking in the plane (c_1, c_2) the utility isoquant, $U = k$ tangent to the income line, $c_1 = R - (v/w)c_2$.

If, for example, the formalization of U is a Cobb–Douglas function for c_1 and c_2, this gives

$$U = (c_1)^\alpha (c_2)^{1-\alpha}$$
$$= (R - nv)^\alpha (nw)^{1-\alpha},$$

$$0 = \frac{1}{U}\frac{\partial U}{\partial n}$$
$$= -\frac{v\alpha}{R - nv} + \frac{w(1-\alpha)}{nw},$$

$$0 = -v\alpha n + (R - nv)(1 - \alpha),$$

$$n = (1 - \alpha)\frac{R}{v}.$$

The optimum number of children is thus proportional to parental income and inversely proportional to the cost of raising and educating them. In spite of its simplicity, this result fits empirical observations and fertility theories for premodern populations. The lower the cost of a child, therefore, the higher n. In numerous surveys conducted in Africa, John Caldwell has shown that the cost of a child was low in traditional societies because land was allocated as a function of the size of the families or households and thus did not exercise a limiting role, while from an early age children were used for minding animals or helping their mother in the market, often in place of an adult. This advantage stops with the introduction and continuation of schooling, since the child can no longer be put to use at very young ages. Equally clear to see is that the time preference for the present α reduces the number of children. Note also that the time preference for the present cannot exceed a certain value because the parents' consumption must ensure them the minimum necessary for survival.

We now introduce the possibility of saving, hence of capital accumulation. The utility function becomes

$$U = (R - S - nv)^\alpha (nw + (1 + i)S)^{1-\alpha}.$$

At the maximum, the partial derivatives for n and for S are zero, whence the two equations

$$0 = -\frac{v\alpha}{R - S - nv} + \frac{w(1 - \alpha)}{nw + (1 + i)S},$$

$$0 = -\frac{\alpha}{R - S - nv} + \frac{(1 + i)(1 - \alpha)}{nw + (1 + i)S}.$$

The factor for v in the first equation is the first term of the second equation. Substituting, we have

$$0 = -(1 + i)v + w \quad \text{or, alternatively,} \quad 1 + i = w/v.$$

Because the three quantities are given in advance, this relation is not usually verified. The maximum is thus on the boundaries of the domain, that is, either $S = 0$ if $1 + 1 < w/v$, or, conversely, $n = 0$ if $1 + 1 > w/v$. We can simply speak of the comparative return to saving and education, which leads to choosing either offspring or saving.

11.7 The Return to Education

One curious result of the simple model above is that the number of children does not depend on w, the future transfer, but only on the ratio R/v of total income to the unit cost of educating the child. However, w is an increasing function of v via the costs of education and training. The better the education and training children have received, the more they will earn and the more they can contribute to the transfer w. We write the value U' of the maximum U for a given value of v in the model from the previous section:

$$R - nv = R - R(1 - \alpha)v/v = R\alpha,$$
$$nw = R(1 - \alpha)w/v,$$
$$U^* = (R - nv)^\alpha (nw)^{1-\alpha} = (R\alpha)^\alpha (R(1 - \alpha))^{1-\alpha}(w/v)^{1-\alpha}$$
$$= Rh(\alpha)(w/v)^{1-\alpha},$$

putting $h(\alpha) = \alpha^\alpha(1-\alpha)^{1-\alpha}$. So maximum utility depends on the ratio w/v, which we refer to as the "return" to education. The relationship between this return and the level v of the costs of education is not known exactly but it can be approximated. When the costs are low—because the child is put to work from an early age— the ratio is high, which maintains a high fertility regime (v low and w/v high). With the introduction of a minimum age of mandatory schooling, the cost v rises considerably, w/v decreases and will only start to rise again when the minimum age has been reached. The higher the qualifications required by the economy, the higher the level of educational investment. But a limit will be reached beyond which w/v

starts to fall again. In present-day developed countries, for example, this turning point is located at 4–5 years of third level education. The maximum of w/v fixes the maximum utility. The number of children n is derived from it by using the initial formula. Since the number of children is inversely proportional to v, it falls when the return to education rises.

Although this reasoning is schematic (three age groups, a simple Cobb–Douglas function), it opens lines of inquiry in two promising directions. One is an explanation for technological progress. The other is the solution to one of demography's greatest enigmas, namely the fertility decline in the richest countries and, in all countries, the lower fertility of the most affluent families who a priori are best able to meet the costs of educating a large family. Begin with the first consequence: economic development. If there is a return to education, this is because educated individuals receive a larger income for a larger contribution to the production function. It is common to introduce the educational level of the population, in the form of human capital, into the production function. This linkage between individual behavior and the macroscopic aggregate has the advantage of making fertility, and hence the population growth rate, r, endogenously determined. A general life-cycle model incorporating all these aspects has yet to be developed, but particular models can be postulated since we now possess all the necessary relations. Further development would be to go beyond the scope of the present work whose subject is demography, not economics.

11.8   The Quantity and Quality of Children: Gary Becker's Model

The same conclusions regarding the relationship between fertility and education were arrived at by Gary Becker (1964) from a different and more general direction. His initial postulate was that the parents, or to be more precise, the household could be assigned a collective utility function that is a combination of the utility functions of its members. Within this function he posited an opposition between the "quantity" and "quality" of children. The quality, q, depends on the level and length of education, i.e., on the income that the parents devote to the children, but also on the amount of time or attention they accord to them, thus integrating another of Becker's preoccupations, the time constraint, which he sees as important as that of income. He starts from a very general conception of household utility, which he denotes by $U(n, q, Z)$ in which Z is a single commodity that stands for the total consumption of the parents. By their number and quality, the children increase the utility of the household, and there is no suggestion that their portion be returned when they are grown. The parents can have multiple reasons for wanting children and for investing large amounts of time and education in them, reasons whose common denominator is that of increasing their utility. The income constraint is written

$$nqp_e + Zp_z = R,$$

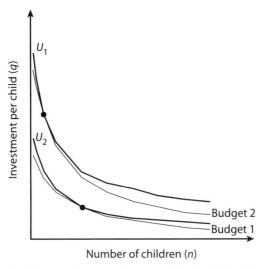

Figure 11.6. Trade-off between the quantity and quality of children: For two values of the budget hyperbola (light line), we have indicated the maximum utility and the corresponding utility curve (heavy line U_1 and U_2). Although the budget is larger in the second case, the optimum number of children (dots) is smaller because the cost of their education (their quality q) is much higher.

where p_e and p_z denote the respective prices of a unit of education and a unit of the general commodity Z. The three partial derivatives of U for Z, n, and q, plus the product of the Lagrange multiplier λ for the above constraint by its respective derivatives are equal to zero when U is maximized. With the three relations and the budget constraint it is usually possible to find the values of n, q, and λ, since there are as many relations as variables.

The general solution is, however, neither assured nor obvious. Becker discusses it by studying budget lines and indifference curves in a plane whose two axes are n and q, the quantity and quality of the children. The indifference curves are of the usual concave form as regards the x-axis, continuous and never intersecting. But the budget lines, instead of being straight, as in microeconomics, are equilateral hyperbola when Z is independent of n and q. We then observe the configuration indicated in figure 11.6 in which a high value of q and a lower one of n correspond to a higher utility. So the increase in income is translated by a fall in the number of children and an increase in their "quality." In 1998 Becker remained confident that with this analysis he had provided "probably the major contribution to the economic analysis of fertility" (Becker 1993, p. 135). Yet the reason why parents believe that the number and quality of children add to their overall satisfaction remains a mystery. In the previous model, which treated the child as an investment, a logic of self-interest was respected, even though it was crude and unappealing (rationalizing child labor, for example). Becker's answer would be that the child is a good, a semi-durable good that is enjoyed by the parents who express a demand for it. Accepting this position limits the interaction between the generations to one direction only, from parents to children, and automatically rules out the idea of national solidarity, as in pay-as-you-go pensions, for example.

Having reached this point, we consider that neither demography nor economics, with all due respect to Becker, have much more to contribute. The issue belongs to the realm of political philosophy. The study of society implies the acceptance of a hierarchy. The social sciences such as demography have developed coherent structures for studying the events and the statistical and legal constructs present in reality. But they also have limited their capacity for general understanding. In all their enterprises they remain tied to the premise of a *homo demographicus* and *economicus* that is crude to say the least. Within particular areas of interest, they produce answers that are remarkable and precise, but they can scarcely venture beyond the boundaries of disciplinary definition. Why are they limited in this way? Because a universal science of man, a truly scientific psychology, does not—and perhaps cannot—exist. Hicks acknowledged that if ever psychology acquired the status of a science, economics would have to undertake a painful revision of its concepts. But psychology is far, very far from achieving such an apotheosis. This disillusioned conclusion is the point of departure for the course taken by demography and economics. Both disciplines concentrate on particular problems, advancing in piecemeal manner, rather than waiting for hypothetical salvation from a universal science of man and society, a position that they believe is occupied ultimately by philosophy.

Part III

Space and Networks

12
The Marriage Market

Up to this point we have considered two extreme cases. That of individuals, each possessing a lifeline, in part I, and that of populations, characterized by age groups and growth processes, in part II. Between these two positions, demography has greater difficulty when formalizing the ties that situate individuals within their networks of kinship and neighborhood. Usual practice is to equate such ties with the events that create them—marriage for the couple tie, migration for that of spatial proximity—and to study the event in the same way as births and deaths. Thus marriage is described for each sex separately as in the mortality model, with unmarried individuals being treated as survivors and marriages as deaths. Nuptiality tables for men and women are constructed independently of each other. The fact of age differences between the spouses is assumed away. Yet these differences are not fixed in a mechanical way by some simple cross-tabulation that links together the male and female nuptiality distributions. The opposite is in fact true. The distributions of male and female ages at marriage are a result obtained by totaling the rows and columns in the joint distribution of partner ages. The matrix of marriage ages contains a concealed system of preferences that brings a demographic dimension to other systems of preference based on, for example, personality traits, wealth, social background, culture, opinions, or geographical proximity.

The system of marital preference is analyzed by using the metaphor of a market, as if suppliers and purchasers, buyers and sellers were being brought into contact. It would be more accurate to speak of a matching or pairing of two subpopulations, but "marriage market" is the established term in the literature on the subject. How this rather particular market operates is one of the issues addressed by the "two-sex model" that exercises demographers from time to time. In what follows we will present several versions of it that account for the observed distributions and show how variations in celibacy levels and in age at marriage of both sexes result from disturbances in the age pyramid caused by wars and crises. We begin with a simple case, the Louis Henry model, and then move on to approach the problem from the angle of the individual "marriage squeeze." We shall see that permanent celibacy is probably the price that must be paid for (relative) freedom over partner choice. Conversely, the universal marriage that is the norm in many societies will be seen to be less simple than it appears. How can a complete pairing off be achieved in a given society? What role do the "structures" of kinship, that the tradition of Lévi-Strauss analyses as marriage rules, play in the pattern of universal marriage? By symmetry, the marriage market with simple systems of preferences as will be proposed here in the framework of the European marriage pattern identified by John Hajnal, raises questions of relevance for all the other systems.

12.1 Marital Attraction

Let there be two closed groups, one of men and one of women, within which all unions have an equal probability. Their frequency in any given period is proportional to the number of single male marriage candidates and to the number of single females:

$$M(t)\,dt = aH(t)\,dt = bF(t)\,dt = k(t)H(t)F(t)\,dt,$$

where $H(t)$ denotes men still single at time t, $F(t)$ the women still single, and $M(t)\,dt$ the number of marriages during the period dt. The coefficient $k(t)$ can be estimated after each marriage, for example, by using the Kaplan and Meier method. When $k(t)$ is constant, we have a fairly simple differential equation for which the solution is a logistic decrease (an S-shaped curve) in the number never-married of each sex:

$$H(t) = H(0) - H(0)F(0)(1 - e^{-k(F(0)-H(0))t})/(F(0) + H(0)e^{-k(F(0)-H(0))t}).$$

In the general case where $K(t)$ varies over time t, its value can be extracted by reversing the previous formula:

$$k(t) = M(t)/(H(t)F(t)).$$

Contrary to the rates and quotients employed in the study of fertility and mortality, $k(t)$ cannot be interpreted directly as a probability. It will be called "coefficient of attraction" or "relative frequency ratio." A simple interpretation is to say that $k(t)$ measures the number of unions actually formed relative to the number of possible unions, i.e., between any bachelor and any spinster, equal to the product of the total number of female candidates by the total number of male candidates. The assumption that all unions are a priori equally possible is known as the panmictic (or random) mating rule. In this case the probability for each individual, $k(t)\,dt$, is very low. A hypothesis this simple is highly implausible. It is in the very nature of marriage that some unions are more desired—and thus more probable—than others. Marriage probably has preferred forms in every setting. It may be strictly regulated when a classificatory system of kinship exists, or be more diffuse in modern societies where differences of age, education, and social background play a role in partner selection. To formalize these preferences, we begin by distinguishing different groups between which the coefficient of attractions can vary. Then we look

Table 12.1.

	H_W	H_B	Proportion never marrying
F_W	63	0	37%
F_B	37	63	0%
Proportion never marrying	0%	37%	

in closer detail by assuming preferences at the level of individuals. We begin with the simplest case where men and women are each divided into two groups between which not all unions are possible, which provides the first example of a "marriage squeeze."[1]

12.2 Social Squeeze on Marriage

We illustrate the phenomenon with a textbook example that we will assume relates to marriage between two groups, blacks and whites in the United States (though any other qualifier yields the same model). Assume that white men (group H_W) marry black (group F_B) or white (group F_W) women, without distinction, but that white women do not marry black men (group H_B). The ties between the groups can be summarized in the following way:

$$H_B \quad \overset{k(t)=a}{\cdots\cdots\cdots} \quad F_B \quad \overset{k(t)=a}{\cdots\cdots\cdots} \quad H_W \quad \overset{k(t)=a}{\cdots\cdots\cdots} \quad F_W.$$

We simulate this model by partitioning time into very short intervals dt during which marriages number $dM_{ij} = aH_i(t)F_j(t)\,dt$, since $H_i(t)$ and $F_j(t)$ can be considered as fixed over the interval dt (i for the man H and j for the woman F denote one of the two characteristics, black and white, also designated by "B" and "W" in the following tables). Starting with 100 persons in each group and simulating the process,[2] we obtain a final result that is stable and independent of the value for attraction a (see table 12.1).

Because men and women are present in equal numbers, all the individuals could in theory have married, but only as in table 12.2.

This second table gives an example of *homogamy*, i.e., of marriage within closed groups, blacks on one side, whites on the other, which is the exact opposite of

---

[1] It is customary to use this bridge term, which signifies the elimination of options for saving an important card, and hence, by extension, the fact of being stuck.

[2] Although the quadratic differential equations that describe this system are very simple, they are not solved by known functions. They are easily programmed, for example, directly on an Excel spreadsheet, simply by writing the populations and marriages in the rows according to the formula and on the next row subtracting the latter from the groups concerned, then reproducing the formula from row to row for as long as is wanted. Writing this program would take an Excel novice under a quarter of an hour, and the values of the attractions, k, and the initial populations of each group could later be changed as desired.

Table 12.2.

	H_W	H_B
F_W	100	0
F_B	0	100

panmictic marriage. This highly schematic example is by itself instructive, showing that panmictic marriage, when confined to certain groups, i.e., when certain ties are prohibited, in this case between white women and black men, operates against rather than in favor of universal marriage. The only possible way to achieve universal marriage then becomes homogamy, i.e., an extension of prohibitions or, what is their obverse, preferences.

In the first example, white men marry white women twice as often as they marry black women, which does not signify a preference since the value of the coefficient of attraction, a, is by definition the same for all groups between which union is possible. The difference in the marriage frequency of white males with black females and with white females arises because white men face competition from black men for black females but not for white females. Besides the levels of celibacy, the distribution of the coefficients of attraction governs the proportions of marriages but it does not reflect them directly. Hence the proportions of marriages observed between the various groups cannot be interpreted independently of the overall system that they form.

The example may appear simplistic, notably because of the dissymmetry in the treatment of white male–black female and black male–white female unions. If there was no prohibition against union between white females and black males as postulated in table 12.1, marriage would again be universal, thereby excluding the possibility of permanent celibacy. This situation might be expected to be the most widespread since it enables one group to avoid being subjected to the other's system of preferences. But in western societies, on the contrary, it is rather the unbalanced pattern that prevails, due to female hypergamy.

Women tend, on average, to marry slightly above their own social origins (the definition of hypergamy). This creates disadvantage on the marriage market at both ends of the social spectrum: for men at the bottom end, because women from their class also marry into a slightly higher class; for women at the top end, because men there also marry women from a slightly lower class. This effect is clearly reflected in celibacy levels by social class. For men these rise as position in the social scale falls while for women the reverse is true. If there were only two social classes, we would have the same pattern as for the blacks and whites, with, instead of white women not marrying black men, higher-class women not marrying lower-class men. But the phenomenon does not depend on the number of classes and is observed equally with three social classes, as is shown by table 12.3 obtained by simulation

Table 12.3.

		Lower class	Middle class	Upper class	Never marrying
			Men		
Women	Lower class	59	41		0%
	Middle class		59	41	0%
	Upper class			59	41%
Never marrying		41%	0%	0%	

Table 12.4.

			Lower class	Middle class	Upper class	Never marrying
				Men		
		Number	400	200	100	
Women	Lower class	400	41			0%
	Middle class	200		59	41	0%
	Upper class	100			59	41%
Never marrying			41%	0%	0%	

of marriages between three social classes (with the panmictic rule retained for all possible marriages).

The proportion never marrying and the differences according to the other partner's social position depend on the constraints introduced by the attractions between groups, and particularly the prohibition against certain unions (i.e., a zero attraction between the classes concerned). If (as is more realistic) the classes are of different sizes, the situation becomes even more complicated, as we see from table 12.4. The proportions of never-marrying females rise due to the fall in the number of men at higher levels of the social scale, whereas celibacy only affects men in the lower, and most numerous, class.

12.3 Dances and Circles

The choice of partner is also limited by the acceptable range of spousal age differences. The two previous examples cannot, however, be extended immediately to age groups, since individuals are not assigned to fixed age groups but change age continuously. The idea of the dance ("*bal*") inspired Louis Henry to conceive a model in which young men and women, on reaching a certain age, progressively enter fixed groups, which he called "marriage circles," in which all unions are of equal probability (i.e., are panmictic) and are formed instantaneously so that only the unmarried of the more numerous sex remain. They then wait for the next batch of the minority sex to arrive in the circle of candidates. Those still unmarried when a given age limit is reached remain permanently single. The model works rather like balancing reservoirs or expansion tanks: when one sex is in oversupply relative to the other it is stocked, and when the stock gets too large it is diverted off into permanent celibacy. In his published example, Henry uses two circles. The female cohorts enter each of these according to a fixed schedule (12% per year at ages 18–22, 2.5% at ages 23–27, 1% at ages 28–32, for the first, and 2.5% at 23–27, 1% at 28–37, in the second). The men enter at the same rate but are three years older. If the women in the first circle are still unmarried at age 33, and the men at age 36, they move into the second circle, which they leave at ages 37 and 40 respectively and become permanently single.

Under a stable regime with male and female cohorts of equal size, all candidates marry immediately. Age at marriage is thus age at entry into the circle, and the age distribution of the marriages is thus exactly the sum of the entries by age into the two circles as detailed above. When one sex is in oversupply in one of the circles, panmictic marriage requires a proportion of the candidates, the same at each age, to remain in the circle and wait for the next year's arrivals of the other sex. Henry uses this mechanism on an example to show that the effects of smaller cohorts (of half the normal size over five years, by analogy with the birth shortfall during World War I) are absorbed through moderate changes in age at marriage. Male celibacy rises to at most 1% in certain cohorts for a short period of time, then returns to zero. Female celibacy remains at zero throughout. Both the concept and the result are important: the circles have the effect of damping fluctuations in numbers. The repercussions of wars and crises on nuptiality are thus neither immediate nor far-reaching as they are on fertility and mortality. However, Henry's behavioral assumptions are unrealistic and the mechanism is partly tautological.

The lack of realism becomes apparent when we calculate the age distributions of marriage for both sexes and the joint distributions of partner ages at marriage. For the former, we saw that they were the same as the entries and were thus fixed a priori. In figure 12.1 we see that they are extremely schematic. The joint distribution of ages at marriage is easily calculated under a stable regime since both circles are panmictic. It is highly implausible (table 12.5) when compared with the usual distributions of marriages by both partner ages (table 12.6 for first marriage in France in 2001). Panmictic marriage leads to almost complete independence of the partner ages (barely moderated by the existence of the two circles that have this as stated objective). Finally, the absence of celibacy under the permanent regime is at odds with the values of around 10% commonly observed in the countries where European

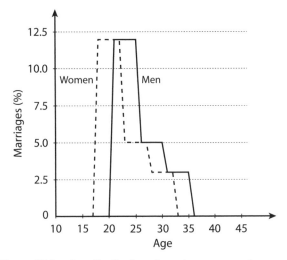

Figure 12.1. Age distribution of marriages, men and women, derived from the parameters of the Henry model.

traditions go back several hundred years. By examining the mechanism more closely it can also be shown that Henry's hypotheses lead to an ad hoc result.

12.4 The Marriage Circles under the Microscope

Begin by combining the two circles into a single one. The simulation conducted under this simplification gives almost exactly the same result as Henry's original simulation, notably for its essential elements—the low level of permanent celibacy in a few male cohorts and the number of male marriage candidates held in reserve at each age. Next, assume that all entries from a given cohort occur at the same age, and examine the effect of a sudden surplus of males of N_1 persons in year $t = 0$ when in every other year, male and female candidates number N. Finally, assume that, as in Henry's circles, the candidates cannot exceed a certain age, which means that they stay in the circle for at most T years. Up to year T, the surplus remains equal to N_1 because, every year, the same number of men and women enter the circle and none exit it. The proportion of marriages among the candidates at each age is $u = N/(N + N_1)$ by virtue of the panmictic rule. Hence after X years, in the cohort that had the surplus of entries, there remain $(N_1 + N)(N/N + N_1)^x$ candidates in reserve and $N(N/(N+N_1))^x$ in the subsequent cohorts. From year $T+1$, successive cohorts reach permanent celibacy, which reduces by the same number the oversupply of male candidates, and hence the ratio u, though its decrease is very slow. If the birth surplus occurs in several consecutive years, the mechanism is the same but the formulas marginally more complicated (see the appendix (section 12.14.1)).

Table 12.5. Joint distribution of ages (years) at marriage,
men (columns) and women (rows), in Henry's marriage circles.

		20					25					30								
	0	0	0	0	0	0	0	0	0	0	0	0	0	0	0	0	0	0	0	0
	0	0	0	0	0	0	0	0	0	0	0	0	0	0	0	0	0	0	0	0
	0	0	0	0	0	0	0	0	0	0	0	0	0	0	0	0	0	0	0	0
20	46	46	46	46	19	19	19	19	19	11	11	11	11	11	0	0	0	0	0	0
	46	46	46	46	19	19	19	19	19	11	11	11	11	11	0	0	0	0	0	0
	46	46	46	46	19	19	19	19	19	11	11	11	11	11	0	0	0	0	0	0
	46	46	46	46	19	19	19	19	19	11	11	11	11	11	0	0	0	0	0	0
25	46	46	46	46	19	19	19	19	19	11	11	11	11	11	0	0	0	0	0	0
	19	19	19	19	8	8	8	8	8	4	4	4	4	4	0	0	0	0	0	0
	19	19	19	19	8	8	8	8	8	4	4	4	4	4	0	0	0	0	0	0
	19	19	19	19	8	8	8	8	8	4	4	4	4	4	0	0	0	0	0	0
	19	19	19	19	8	8	8	8	8	4	4	4	4	4	0	0	0	0	0	0
30	19	19	19	19	8	8	8	8	8	4	4	4	4	4	0	0	0	0	0	0
	11	11	11	11	4	4	4	4	4	2	2	2	2	2	0	0	0	0	0	0
	11	11	11	11	4	4	4	4	4	2	2	2	2	2	0	0	0	0	0	0
	11	11	11	11	4	4	4	4	4	2	2	2	2	2	0	0	0	0	0	0
	11	11	11	11	4	4	4	4	4	2	2	2	2	2	0	0	0	0	0	0
35	11	11	11	11	4	4	4	4	4	2	2	2	2	2	0	0	0	0	0	0
	0	0	0	0	0	0	0	0	0	0	0	0	0	0	0	0	0	0	0	0
	0	0	0	0	0	0	0	0	0	0	0	0	0	0	0	0	0	0	0	0
	0	0	0	0	0	0	0	0	0	0	0	0	0	0	0	0	0	0	0	0

Using Henry's hypothesis of a temporary birth surplus equal to $N_1 = N$ births over 5 years, the ratio u climbs to 5/6 in 5 years for the 5 cohorts concerned and remains at that level up to the age of exit from the circle. During this period, the oversupply of males decreases geometrically with age. It stands at only 16% after 10 years and at 2.6% after 20 years, which are plausible lengths of time to remain a candidate. Because of this, when celibacy after T is low and hence spread over an immense length of time—since u decreases very slowly owing to the small number of single persons who leave the circle—the trend takes us very slowly back to the initial situation. Table 12.7 gives the levels of celibacy by cohort for several values of T.

We have added a column to table 12.7 for a slightly more complex hypothesis of entries evenly spaced over 10 years, hence 10% per year, which is closer to Henry's model. We see that the result presents the same characteristics: permanent celibacy is low and spread over a long period. In fact, 75 years after the first depleted cohort, the stock of single males in the circle still represents the membership of 1.5 cohorts in the case of an exit after 10 years and 3.6 cohorts for an exit after 20 years, whereas by assumption the maximum surplus stood at 5 cohorts. The return to equilibrium is inevitable (we show this in the appendix (section 12.14.1)) but takes a long time.

Celibacy levels will thus be lower, even negligible, the longer the maximum waiting time in the circles. The permanent celibacy that Henry noted is not a structural

Table 12.6. Joint distribution of ages at first marriage, men (columns) and women (rows), France 2001.

	20					25					30					35			
	0	0	0	0	0	0	0	0	0	0	0	0	0	0	0	0	0	0	0
	0	0	0	0	0	0	0	0	0	0	0	0	0	0	0	0	0	0	0
20	1	1	1	0	0	0	0	0	0	0	0	0	0	0	0	0	0	0	0
	3	3	2	1	1	0	0	0	0	0	0	0	0	0	0	0	0	0	0
	4	5	6	4	2	2	1	0	0	0	0	0	0	0	0	0	0	0	0
	4	7	9	10	7	5	3	1	1	0	0	0	0	0	0	0	0	0	0
25	4	7	11	16	19	12	7	4	3	1	0	0	0	0	0	0	0	0	0
	4	7	12	19	25	26	15	9	5	3	1	1	0	0	0	0	0	0	0
	3	6	11	17	26	31	31	18	10	6	3	2	1	0	0	0	0	0	0
	3	5	9	15	24	32	36	33	19	11	5	3	2	1	0	0	0	0	0
	2	4	7	12	19	26	31	34	31	18	10	5	3	1	1	0	0	0	0
30	2	3	6	9	14	20	25	29	30	25	14	8	4	2	1	1	1	0	0
	1	2	4	6	10	13	18	22	24	23	19	10	6	4	2	1	1	0	0
	1	2	3	4	7	9	11	15	16	17	16	12	7	5	2	2	1	1	0
	0	1	2	3	4	6	7	9	12	13	13	11	9	5	3	2	1	1	0
	0	0	1	2	3	3	5	7	9	9	10	9	8	6	4	3	2	1	1
35	0	0	0	1	2	3	3	5	6	7	7	7	6	6	5	3	2	1	1
	0	0	0	1	1	2	2	3	4	4	6	6	6	6	4	4	2	1	1
	0	0	0	0	1	1	2	2	3	3	4	4	4	4	4	3	2	1	
	0	0	0	0	0	1	1	1	2	2	3	3	3	3	3	3	2	2	
	0	0	0	0	0	0	1	1	1	1	2	2	2	3	3	3	2	2	
40	0	0	0	0	0	0	0	1	1	1	1	1	2	2	2	2	2	2	
	0	0	0	0	0	0	0	1	1	1	1	1	1	1	2	2	2	1	
	0	0	0	0	0	0	0	0	0	0	1	0	1	1	1	1	1	1	
	0	0	0	0	0	0	0	0	0	0	0	0	0	0	1	1	1	1	

Table 12.7. Proportions single by cohort following a surplus of births (equal to total births over 5 consecutive years).

Cohorts after the trough	$T = 10$ % single	$T = 20$ % single	Entries spread over 10 years % single
1	6.7	1.1	0.5
2	11.1	1.8	1.4
3	13.7	2.3	2.3
5	14.9	2.6	4.0
10	9.6	1.2	7.2
20	4.4	2.1	4.3
50	1.3	1.3	1.8

result of his model but simply the effect of the oldest entries who stay in the circles for very short lengths of time. This is easily shown by slightly modifying the entry schedule used by Henry. The male entries of 1% between 31 and 40 years in the

Table 12.8. Mean age at marriage after a surplus of births.

Years after surplus	$T = 10$	$T = 20$	Entries spread over 10 years
20	21	21	21
22	21.3	21.3	21.3
25	22.3	22.3	22.3
30	24.5	24.5	24.5
40	23.5	25.8	24.9
60	23.2	25.2	24.2
100	22.6	24.7	23.6

second circle are replaced by entries of 2% between 31 and 35 years, hence twice as numerous and ending 5 years younger for the same total (i.e., a fall in age at entry of 5 years for 5% of the members of a cohort). The effect on the proportion never marrying is dramatic. From a maximum of 1.1%, it falls back to 0.2%. So 80% of the celibacy in the Henry model was caused by the 5% most recent entries.

This gives us a better understanding of how the model operates and shows the basis for the comparison with balancing reservoirs. The surplus of one sex gradually builds up in the circle. If a fluctuation occurs in the opposite direction—as is quickly the case with a trough in birth numbers, since at the end of the trough female candidates will be more numerous relative to the male candidates, who are still coming from the depleted cohorts—the circle empties. Like any balancing reservoir, therefore, it serves to damp transient fluctuations. When the fluctuation is long term and not compensated by the other sex (during sex-selective migration, for example), the surplus of the sex in oversupply eventually attains the maximum duration or maximum age for remaining in the circle and becomes definitively single. The analogy here is with the water in the balancing reservoir finally overflowing its dam and running off toward a diversion canal: permanent celibacy.

The homeostatic role of the circle is translated by a rapid rise in ages at marriage, as Henry noted. In table 12.8 we have indicated the mean ages at marriage in the years (and not in the cohorts) that follow the trough.

This table reveals two tendencies of interest. First, compared with the low values for permanent celibacy, the changes in mean age at marriage are large. The mechanism for stocking in the circles conceived by Henry produces a transfer from intensity to tempo. It allows the proportion single, and hence the intensity of marriage, to hold steady whereas the latter ought to have fallen by 50% if men could not marry until they entered the circle. In return for this, age at marriage rises rapidly. The second tendency is more subtle. Age at marriage rises rapidly to begin with, but thereafter it falls very slowly. In the medium term (and even in the long term since we continued the simulation up to 100 years), the temporary surplus of candidates (over 5 years) has produced a lasting change in the ages at marriage.[3] This raises the question of whether certain large disparities in age at marriage in traditional populations are not attributable to temporary surpluses of men, surpluses caused notably by polygyny or by remarriage among widowers and repudiating husbands and by the prohibitions and difficulties associated with remarriage for widows and repudiated wives.

In summary, the marriage-circles model provides a simple explanation for the spreading out of celibacy over many cohorts following a disturbance in the age pyramid. But it does not inform about the origin of the distributions of age at marriage. This is because it is not based on a realistic matrix of marriage ages and above all, because by assuming zero celibacy under the stable regime it supplies no indication as to the historical origins of permanent celibacy in Europe. Now, there is a strong likelihood that permanent celibacy and its variations are controlled by one and the same mechanism. An alternative formalization must therefore be found.

12.5 The Model of Marriage Squeeze by Age

Return now to the model of marriage between blacks and whites or between three social classes and attempt to transpose it into age group terms. We do this by dividing the population into cohorts, each with a length of p years or months. The assumption is made that men marry women only from their own cohort or from the immediately preceding cohort. The succession of cohorts thus plays the same role as the social classes, the oldest cohort being identified with the top of the social scale. The possible unions between male and female cohorts can be represented in the same way as those between social classes, by a line on which they alternate:

H1 ······ F1 ······ H2 ······ F2 ······ H3

······ F3 ······ H4 ······ F4 ······ H5 ······

Unlike the social classes, however, each cohort is not immediately present on the market but enters it progressively according to a schedule $f(x)$ giving the number of new candidates for marriage at age x. The concern is no longer with estimating celibacy at the end of the chain—the latter is in principle unlimited due to the succession of cohorts—but with understanding how this market reacts to various changes, in particular to the passage of small cohorts (i.e., a fall in male and female numbers), losses due to war (i.e., a sex imbalance), and delayed marriages in times of crisis. As was done in the case of fertility changes, we will put forward a model that is both complete and exact.

Start from successive annual cohorts all containing the same number of men and women, and assume that the marriage candidates enter the market according to an

---

[3] This consequence of a birth surplus had been indicated in Le Bras (1969).

S-shaped curve. Their number increases quite rapidly from age 15, grows linearly at age 20, and then more slowly up to age 25, from which point all are candidates (if not already married).[4] Once the male and female candidates have entered the market, the unions of year t, $M_{i,j}(t)$ between men of age i and women of age j are formed as a function of the coefficients of attraction as in the initial examples:

$$M_{i,j}(t) = k_{i,j}(t)H_i(t)F_j(t).$$

In the stable regime, coefficient $k_{i,j}(t)$ takes a simple form since it can be postulated that it depends only on the age difference between the male and female candidates and that it is constant over time, expressing a deep structure of nuptiality. So we will have

$$k_{i,j}(t) = \phi(i - j).$$

What specifically is the form of the function ϕ? It is reasonable to assume that the attraction is strongest for persons of approximately the same age and then decreases. In fact, the exact form of the function matters little once we know the position of the maximum and the interval over which 90% of marriages occur. The model can then be radically simplified by making ϕ constant over this age interval and zero outside it, which is equivalent to the conditions set between social classes or subpopulations in the initial examples.

There is an important difference, however, between hypergamy and the analysis by age groups. Successive cohorts enter the marriage market. Their initial size changes over time. Now, the coefficient $k_{i,j}$ is sensitive to changes of scale. For example, if the numbers of females and males each double, marriages are quadrupled with a constant coefficient k. In this case, to keep the same coefficient of attraction, and thus the same nuptiality rate, coefficient of attraction must be halved. This difficulty is resolved by a probabilistic formulation based on a simple behavioral scheme: over his or her lifetime, each candidate meets or knows a certain number of people, some of whom are candidates. In order to marry, therefore, the candidate must meet another candidate and be accepted. The probability for a man of age i of meeting a female candidate (and vice versa) is the ratio of the number of candidates met to the total number of persons met $F_j(t)/P_i$, where P_i denotes the set of all the persons the candidate meets. The probability of a marriage p_i is thus the product of this ratio

---

[4] In the numerical applications, we have used the cumulative function for entry to candidacy

Age	Cumulative entries (per thousand)	Age	Cumulative entries (per thousand)
15	30	20	650
16	100	21	790
17	210	22	900
18	350	23	970
19	500	24	1000

but other S-shaped curves give the same results with only minor deviations.

by the probability ψ that a marriage ensues when any two single persons meet:

$$p_i = \psi F_j(t)/P_i.$$

For P_i we can choose the women in the age groups j for which marriage to a man of age i is possible (most of whom are married), hence equal to $\sum P_j^F(t)$, where $P_j^F(t)$ designates the total number of women in age group j. Finally, the number of marriages will be the product of the probability p_i by the number of candidates, $H_i(t)$:

$$M_{i,j}(t) = \psi H_i(t) F_j(t) \Big/ \sum P_j^F(t).$$

The advantage of this formulation is that it is also valid if we reason on the basis of the candidates. We then obtain

$$M_{i,j}(t) = \psi H_i(t) F_j(t) \Big/ \sum P_i^H(t),$$

where $P_i^H(t)$ stands for all adult men, married or not. If we limit this total and that of the women to the marriageable age groups, for example, those between 18 and 50 years, the females are nearly as numerous as the males and the two formulas are equivalent.[5] With this formulation, the model is no longer dependent on scale.

The model has been examined in detail because we will see in the sections that follow that its results are remarkable. With just three parameters (the coefficient of attraction ψ, the difference between the median age at marriage of men and of women, and the age interval over which the panmictic rule holds), it gives a realistic description of the usual nuptiality distributions (age-specific nuptiality rates, marriages by age, proportion never married by age, joint distribution of partner ages at marriage) on both longitudinal and cross-sectional bases. Above all, however, it offers insight into how nuptiality reacts to a variety of demographic accidents (wars, deficits of births, or marriages following a crisis).

12.6   The Age Squeeze and the Distributions

The model was applied to a population in which the male and female cohorts were of equal size. Each year t, new candidates entered the relevant age groups (15–25 years) according to the schedule defined in footnote 4, and were added to the candidates already present (the never married). Next, we calculated the total marriages $M_{i,j}(t)$ according to the panmictic formula given earlier, and then subtracted them from the numbers of candidates in the cohorts concerned. Convergence under the model is rapid and the equilibrium attained is unique. The parameters selected are a 3-year age difference between men and women, a coefficient ψ of 0.333 for one person per cohort, and thus an age interval of 11 years for the men (the women aged from -7 years to $+4$ years relative to them) and likewise for the women (the men

---

[5] In practice we used their geometric mean.

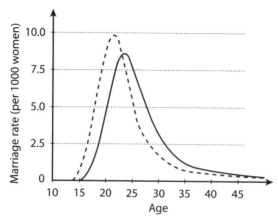

Figure 12.2. Age distribution of marriages of women,
in the marriage market model with age squeeze.

aged from +7 years to −4 years). In figure 12.2 is plotted the age distributions of
male and female marriages that this model of behavior converges toward. Despite
the simplicity of the assumptions used, they are very close to real curves, and the
proportions never married at age 50 (8% for the women, 9% for the men) are well
within the range of observed values.

Table 12.9 gives the number of marriages observed in a given year (or, since the
population is stationary, in a given cohort) by both partner ages. Here again we
are close to actual observations, for instance, from the joint distribution of ages
at marriage in France in 2001 reproduced earlier. Despite the panmictic rule, and
thus equality of the attractions, marriages are more frequent between individuals of
similar age. The numbers fall as we move away from the diagonal. The mean age of
the husband by that of the wife, and vice versa, also vary as in reality, not as fast as the
person's age and starting from higher values and ending at lower values. Thus, at age
20, the women marry a man aged on average 24, the men a woman aged 21.5 years,
but at age 35, the men marry a woman aged on average 30, and the women a man aged
34. A simple operation of the marriage market based on undifferentiated preferences
(though with an age barrier isolating 11 years) has structured the marriage market
as distinctly as is observed in reality, with its differences of intensity by simple or
joint ages of the partners at their marriage.

What happens when the intensity of attraction, ψ, varies? Figure 12.3(a) shows
the age distribution of female marriages for the values 0.2, 0.333, and 0.5. The
corresponding values for the proportions single at age 50 and for the mean age at
marriage fall simultaneously, consistent in this respect with known nuptiality curves,
in which late marriage and high levels of celibacy are almost always combined. This
suggests an interpretation in terms of speed of marriage that is accurately reflected
by the factor of attraction, ψ.

Table 12.9. Ages (years) at marriage,
men (columns) and women (rows), in the squeeze model.

	20						25					30					
	0	0	0	0	0	0	0	0	0	0	0	0	0	0	0	0	0
20	0	0	1	1	0	0	0	0	0	0	0	0	0	0	0	0	0
	0	1	1	2	3	0	0	0	0	0	0	0	0	0	0	0	0
	0	1	2	3	4	5	0	0	0	0	0	0	0	0	0	0	0
	0	1	3	4	6	7	8	0	0	0	0	0	0	0	0	0	0
	1	2	3	5	7	9	10	10	0	0	0	0	0	0	0	0	0
25	1	2	4	6	8	10	11	11	11	0	0	0	0	0	0	0	0
	1	2	4	7	9	11	12	12	11	10	0	0	0	0	0	0	0
	1	2	4	7	9	11	12	12	11	10	8	0	0	0	0	0	0
	0	2	4	6	8	10	11	11	10	9	8	7	0	0	0	0	0
	0	0	3	5	7	8	9	10	9	8	7	6	5	0	0	0	0
30	0	0	0	5	6	7	8	8	8	7	6	5	4	4	0	0	0
	0	0	0	0	5	6	7	7	7	6	5	4	4	3	3	0	0
	0	0	0	0	0	5	6	6	6	5	4	4	3	3	3	2	0
	0	0	0	0	0	0	5	5	5	5	4	3	3	3	2	2	2
	0	0	0	0	0	0	0	5	5	4	3	3	3	2	2	2	2
35	0	0	0	0	0	0	0	0	4	4	3	3	2	2	2	2	2
	0	0	0	0	0	0	0	0	0	3	3	2	2	2	2	2	1
	0	0	0	0	0	0	0	0	0	0	2	2	2	2	2	1	1
	0	0	0	0	0	0	0	0	0	0	0	2	2	2	1	1	1
	0	0	0	0	0	0	0	0	0	0	0	0	2	1	1	1	1

Table 12.10.

ψ	% single at age 50	Mean age at marriage
0.2	17.5	26.6
0.333	8.4	25.1
0.5	5.7	24.0

In the extreme case, for a very strong attraction of 5, ten times stronger than the strongest in the table, celibacy becomes practically nonexistent (less than 0.5%), age at marriage coincides with age at entry to candidacy, but the matrix of marriage ages is concentrated on the ten years of entry to candidacy of both sexes and becomes unresponsive to the age differences of the partners. These are the characteristics of Henry's model. We can also verify that for the case of a birth shortfall, this model of very strong attraction gives the same result as the marriage circles, notably a tiny increase in male celibacy per cohort. Varying the attraction influences the length of waiting time in the state of candidacy, in effect generalizing the marriage-circles model by subjecting all the candidates to a wait hitherto experienced only by the unbalanced cohorts. What was an exceptional situation is transformed into a normal

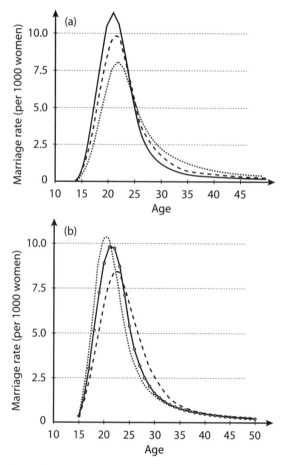

Figure 12.3. (a) Age distribution of marriages of women, in the marriage market model with age squeeze, for three values of nuptial attraction: $\psi = 1$, solid line; $\psi = 0.5$, broken line; $\psi = 0.333$ dotted line. (b) Age distribution of female marriages in the marriage market model with an age squeeze, for three ranges of age differences between potential partners (21 years, unbroken line; 11 years, dashed line; 3 years, dotted line).

one. Note also that permanent celibacy is not unavoidable, as it is in the model with black and white populations, but results from the slowness of the process. After many, many years (hundreds), all would be married under the procedure selected, but long before that happens death has carried them off.

Variations in the boundary of the panmictic group (i.e., of the pool of available partners) also have an important effect on the form of the nuptiality curves, though in a different way to attraction. This can be seen in figure 12.3(b), where we have represented the age distributions of male marriages for three values of the dispersion of the age differences: 21, 11, and 3 years. The configuration of the curves is much the same as is obtained through varying attraction, but the result is paradoxical. It is when the possibilities are greatest, i.e., under panmictic conditions, that marriage is slowest to occur and celibacy is highest, whereas the opposite order might have been expected. Now, the total attraction, i.e., the sum of attractions for all the possible age groups (21, 11, or 3 depending on the case), is the same in all three situations. This phenomenon is interpreted as for the simple cases of hypergamy or for marriage between blacks and whites. When limits exist, the best way of attaining universal marriage is with homogamy, not with panmictic mating, which causes the squeeze situations to multiply. Indeed, ultimately, if the marriages occurred only between persons separated by a given age difference, the male and female cohorts would marry two by two, faster than in a group that was open to all possible competition. In figure 12.3(b) we see clearly that competition is unfavorable when nuptiality begins and then becomes favorable after age 30, since it permits access by the youngest age groups in which the unmarried are still numerous. In the extreme case, marriage can follow kinship rules that severely restrict the number of possible partners and yet still be both universal and early (at puberty) for women, as is the case in many traditional societies. The paradox arises because, in the absence of any model or calculation, it is implicitly and intuitively assumed that panmictic mating increases the probability of meeting potential partners. But a more logical view is that this probability is relatively constant on account of some fixed or mean interaction time corresponding to the courtship period, and therefore that the difference between panmictic mating and the quasi-homogamy observed in the case with three social classes derives not from the number of candidates but from their diversity in terms of age.

12.7 Oversized Cohorts, Nuptiality Crises

Mention has been made of three accidents that impact on nuptiality: a reduction in births during a crisis or war, a shortage of men through wartime losses, and a reduction in marriages due to economic recession, crisis, or war. Each of these cases leads to a disturbance in the marriage market, since those who might otherwise have married a person from the depleted cohort stay single and thus competitors of the unmarried members of the other cohorts, which in their turn are affected, thus modifying the number of candidates and hence the number of marriages between particular birth cohorts. Direct reasoning does not allow us to get even an approximate idea of this long string of reactions. This is a situation that the model handles well, especially since it has few hypotheses and parameters, or in other words, it has the advantage of parsimony.

Start with the case of the wartime deficits that affected the cohorts reaching marriageable age after 1918. We assume that over five years the cohorts of male candidates had lost a quarter of their members, which is quite close to the reality. Figure 12.4 represents the evolution of the proportions single in the male and female cohorts concerned. Under the pressure of candidate numbers, male celibacy declines from 9 to 5% then recovers its initial value twenty years after the lowest value. Logically, the oversized female cohorts contain more single individuals, with a three-year lag, which is the mean difference between the desired ages at marriages of both sexes. Female celibacy climbs to 15%, then falls back fairly slowly. Period celibacy follows broadly the same course, though since what is involved is a short-term accident the notion of fictitious (synthetic) cohort is not very pertinent. Several aspects of this reaction are remarkable and consistent with empirical observations made for this situation. The interdependence of the male and female birth cohorts dissipates the shock over a fairly long (11-year) period in several ways. Thus, the level of female celibacy starts to rise in the first cohorts affected by the crisis and only slowly returns to its initial position. Similarly, a fall in male celibacy is quickly observed. The cohorts are affected, therefore, but less severely than might have been expected on the basis of the 25% reduction in the number of young men. In addition to the shock being spread across several cohorts, we also see that the reduction in male celibacy offsets the rise in female celibacy. If the men married women aged exactly n years less than themselves, female celibacy ought to have risen from 9% to 32% during five cohorts.[6] The spreading across other cohorts and the fall in male celibacy have the effect of keeping female celibacy within the 15% region at its maximum over five years. The number of marriages is also only weakly influenced by the crisis, since it goes from 0.91 (for cohort sizes set to one person) to a minimum of 0.84 from which it recovers almost immediately. The marriage market has attenuated and smoothed the effect of the crisis whose abrupt onset and end are no longer detectable in the nuptiality of the cohorts and still less so in that on a period base. The women adjusted to the shock of the shortage of men by taking longer to marry, but the men did not respond to the pressure of demand by marrying significantly faster.

The second form of crisis has a direct impact on nuptiality. As a result of unfavorable circumstances, the coefficient of attraction, i.e., the probability of forming a couple following an encounter, declines over a certain period of time and then returns to its original value as the crisis recedes. A crisis of this sort has been simulated by assuming that coefficient of attraction is halved for five years. In figure 12.5, we see that the passage of the crisis is marked by an abrupt fall in the number of marriages to one half their usual number, which is logical given that attraction has been halved. What happens next is less obvious. To begin with, the number of marriages recovers quite quickly. After five years, it has already covered nearly half of the distance back to its initial level. Then, with the end of the crisis, it shoots up far above its level in normal years, before falling back steadily to its precrisis position. This scenario closely reproduces the main features of the phenomenon of *recuperation* that has frequently been observed and described in relation to demographic crises.

---

[6] $32\% = 100\% - 0.75\% \times (100\% - 9\%)$.

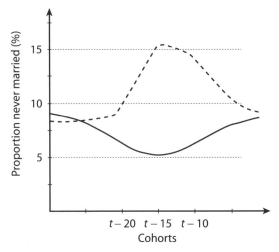

Figure 12.4. Proportion never married by cohort (noted by their date of birth) for the case of wartime losses of young men.

No special assumption is needed to obtain the behavior depicted in figure 12.5. It comes about simply and automatically through the reaction of the marriage market, without the introduction of any additional factor. The behavior of the market can be understood *ex post* in qualitative terms. The fall in attraction was accompanied by an increase in the number unmarried and hence in the number of marriages, at constant coefficient of attraction. When the coefficient of attraction recovers its initial level, it pertains to a larger number of single persons, and so marriages are considerably more numerous than in a normal year. This surplus of single people is gradually reabsorbed, as shown by the return to the usual number of marriages at the end of twenty years.

In a longitudinal perspective, the crisis leaves virtually no trace. At most, the proportion never married increases by a few thousandths in the cohorts that experienced the crisis, particularly those that were already at an advanced stage in their history. Where the passage of the crisis really leaves a trace is on cohort mean ages at marriage, which temporarily rise by slightly more than one year. So the marriage market has absorbed the crisis. When the final balance is calculated, it shows that recuperation is all but complete. On the basis of 94 marriages per year at equilibrium, there is a shortfall of 184 marriages during the five years of the crisis. In the course of the following 25 years, 179 marriages take place in addition to the 94 annual marriages. If we calculate the period indices, however, the picture is confused since they express a temporary change in marital conditions as if it was a permanent change, which refers us back to the discussion of mortality changes. In fact, period mean age at marriage (the equivalent therefore of life expectancy for mortality) varies little because the fall in attraction is felt equally across the birth cohorts of single persons since it is the same for all of them.

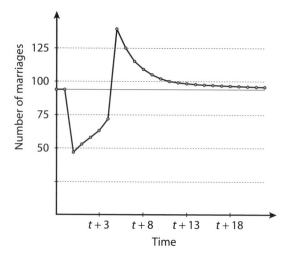

Figure 12.5. Annual number of marriages in the case of a nuptiality crisis (effect of halving the coefficient of attraction in the crisis starting at *t*.

The third type of crisis to be studied is that of a reduction in birth numbers. It is quite different from the first two crises and is less clear to see. It will put us on the track of a microdemographic approach to the marriage market.

12.8   Nuptiality and Undersized Cohorts

Let us again start from an example with which to examine the reaction of the marriage market. We make the assumption that the usual number of births is halved for six years and that the normal situation is then reestablished, which is similar to the fall in birth numbers observed during World War I. The proportions of men and women never married in the cohorts affected by the crisis are displayed in figure 12.6. Although both sexes are affected equally, the associated changes take opposite directions, celibacy levels increasing for one sex while decreasing for the other, and this over nearly thirty cohorts. This case makes considerable demands of the marriage market mechanism. In a first phase, the men who marry younger women face a shortage of candidates. The number of male candidates increases until the smaller male cohorts enter the market, thus gradually reducing the imbalance. When the situation returns to normal, the opposite phenomenon occurs. The female candidates from the large cohorts who depend for partners on the last of the small male cohorts have more difficulty marrying. The proportion unmarried in their ranks rises, then falls back toward its usual value when the larger male cohorts in turn come on to the market. The mean ages at marriage of both sexes follow the same course to a moderate degree since they rise by no more than one year at the point where the proportion unmarried is highest. The most remarkable feature is the dissociation of

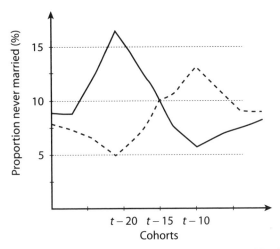

Figure 12.6. Proportion never married by cohort (noted by their date of birth) for the case of a reduction in births over five years.

the two movements. Although the mean age difference observed between partners is 2 years[7], 11 years separate the maxima and minima for men and women.

This behavior is not specific to the example used here. It is also observed for the other marriage markets that feature different spousal age differences (1, 3, and 6 years in figure 12.7, analogous to figure 12.6, for male and female proportions single) or crises of different durations. To understand the reaction of the marriage market, we must consider the numbers of persons available for marriage. In the example under consideration, each male cohort of year t can find brides in the 11 female cohorts running from $t-2$ to $t+8$, regardless of the age at which marriage occurs. Calculating the overall shortfall from these 11 female cohorts when t varies (i.e., for the successive male cohorts), we see that the proportion of single males rises in line with the growing scarcity of female candidates, then falls when their number stabilizes and starts to rise again from the point at which the female shortfall has been reabsorbed, ultimately returning to its original level. The scarcity or abundance of female candidates thus has a clear influence on celibacy levels among men, which is not surprising. However, the evolution of the two phenomena, though sharing the same turning points, is not analogous. The female candidates are in greater or lesser demand according to whether they face nuptiality conditions of larger or smaller male cohorts. To measure the volume of the male candidacies available to these female candidates, we sum them and calculate the mean. The risk of a "marriage squeeze" is a direct function of this mean since it varies directly with the number of competitors and inversely with the number of female candidates they have to choose among. The difference between the two numbers must therefore follow the curve of male celibacy, which is in fact what we observe. Indeed, the parallelism of the

---

[7] But 3 years in the preferences expressed by the attractions, ψ.

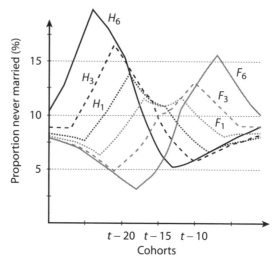

Figure 12.7. Proportion never married by cohorts (noted by their date of birth) in the case of a five-year birth trough, for three mean age differences at marriage of men and women (H_6 signifies male celibacy for a six-year difference, etc.).

movements is remarkable. A symmetrical reasoning can be made for the women: their propensity to marry will rise with the number of male candidates and fall with the mean number of female candidates available to these male candidates. Hence we also observe a remarkable covariation in the difference between these two numbers of candidates and female celibacy.

12.9   Individual Risk

Marriage squeezes at the group level, whether concerning the marriage of blacks and whites, female hypergamy, or the last model with restrictions on the age difference between partners, are merely the possible and particular modalities of a network of individual ties between men and women. To get from groups to individuals we need simply stipulate that there are N_{ij} ties linking the individuals of groups i and j. The probability $m_{ij}(t)$ that a randomly selected tie leads to a marriage between an individual from group i and another from group j is

$$m_{ij}(t) = \frac{N_{ij}}{\sum N_{ij}} \frac{F_j(t)}{F_j(0)} \frac{H_i(t)}{H_i(0)}$$

because the future partners must both be single. All the cases considered thus far can also be interpreted as individual cases since panmictic marriage between certain groups was the rule, so $N_{ij} = H_i(0)F_j(0)$[8] or $N_{ij} = 0$ depending on whether the tie between the two groups is possible or not.

---

[8] Random selection of a tie is not in general equivalent to random selection of an individual. When taking at random a single person, then taking at random a single person of the opposite sex to whom

The total number of marriages becomes

$$M_{ij}(t) = \phi(t)m_{ij}(t) = \psi(t)H_i(t)F_j(t).$$

When the ties between individuals in two groups are no longer all possible but confined to a small number per individual, celibacy might be expected to increase, since a random factor is added to the squeeze. The situation is in fact much more complex and at times the opposite can even occur. This can be verified with the initial model of black and white populations. In the panmictic case, the proportion never marrying stood at 37% in the two groups for which marriages were subject to a restriction. Let us assume that instead of ties between all the individuals of two adjacent groups we have only one single tie, i.e., that the total population is made up of chains separated by ties between four persons, each belonging to one of the four groups:

H_{B1}	$\cdots\cdots$	F_{B1}	$\cdots\cdots$	H_{W1}	$\cdots\cdots$	F_{W1}
H_{B2}	$\cdots\cdots$	F_{B2}	$\cdots\cdots$	H_{W2}	$\cdots\cdots$	F_{W2}
H_{B3}	$\cdots\cdots$	F_{B3}	$\cdots\cdots$	H_{W3}	$\cdots\cdots$	F_{W3}
$\vdots$						
H_{Bn}	$\cdots\cdots$	F_{Bn}	$\cdots\cdots$	H_{Wn}	$\cdots\cdots$	F_{Wn}

The two individuals at the endpoints never marry if the middle tie is selected first, i.e., in one in three cases. Consequently, random celibacy is 33% instead of 37% when all ties were possible in the initial example with blacks and whites. This result is quite close, but slightly unexpected since one might have thought that the random celibacy would be in addition to the celibacy produced by the group situation. In fact, the restriction on the number of ties operates as much for the individual as for his or her partners, and the one very nearly cancels out the other. In the case where

---

he or she is linked, and marrying them, the probability $p_i(t)$ of selecting a single person from group i is $p_i(t) = H_i(t)/\sum H_i(t)$ and the probability of their having a tie with a single person from group j is $q_{ij}(t) = (N_{ij}/\sum N_{ij})(F_j(t)/F_j(0))$, whence a probability of marriage between members of group i and group j of

$$m_{ij}(t) = p_j(t)q_{ji}(t) = \frac{N_{ij}H_i(t)}{\sum H_i(t)\sum N_{ij}}\frac{F_j(t)}{F_j(0)}.$$

In the case of panmictic mating for the groups sharing the ties, we get

$$m_{ij}(t) = \frac{H_i(0)F_j(0)H_i(t)}{\sum H_i(t)H_i(0)\sum F_j(0)}\frac{F_j(t)}{F_j(0)}$$

$$= \frac{H_i(t)F_j(t)}{\sum H_i(t)\sum F_j(0)},$$

whence $M_{ij}(t) = \phi(t)m_{ij}(t) = \psi(t)H_i(t)F_j(t)/\sum F_j(0)$. As a rule, the result is not identical to that from random selection of the ties. In addition, it assumes that one of the two sexes takes the decision. Weighting by the inverse of $\sum F_j(0)$, we again have the formula for the random selection of ties.

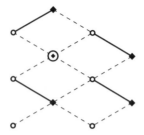

Figure 12.8. Schematic of a "squeeze" in a network of marriage candidates. Squares represent men, circles represent women, light lines represent marriages, and heavy lines represent marriages contracted. The man surrounded by a circle remains single because all his possible partners have married.

Table 12.11. Permanent celibacy in the various types of group, by number of individual ties.

	Proportion never marrying (%)		
Number of ties	Extreme group	Intermediate group	Central group
1	36.6	0.0	16.7
2	40.7	2.0	13.9
3	40.4	1.1	11.7
4	40.0	0.6	10.2
5	40.0	0.3	9.0
10	40.0	0.0	6.0

each individual has exactly two ties with the members of each adjacent group, a change occurs. In the two groups at the endpoints, celibacy amounts to 38%, but celibacy of 2.9% also appears in the two central groups. This is explained by an individual-level squeeze, as can be seen in figure 12.8. A candidate from the central group is the victim of a squeeze because the two possible candidates from the other central group have already formed a union (they each had four possibilities), while the two candidates from the group at the end of the chain have married the other possible candidate (which they could not have done with a single tie).

The individual squeeze becomes more acute when we raise the number of groups to six. When the group-to-group ties are arranged in a hexagon, celibacy is nonexistent in the case of a group but stands at 11% when each individual has a tie with one individual in each of the two adjacent groups. If the six groups are set out in a line, as for the example of the three social classes with female hypergamy operating, we obtain the proportions never marrying reported in table 12.11 for the extreme, intermediate and central groups, by the number of ties between individuals from adjacent groups.

Despite its position, the central group experiences a high level of celibacy as long as the number of interindividual ties remains low. The proportion never marrying still stands at around 10% for five ties between individuals of two adjacent groups, i.e., ten ties or possibilities for the members of the central groups. The presence of available single persons in the groups with which one has ties does not help for there are no interindividual ties with them.

12.10 Equivalence between Number of Individual Ties and Speed of the Group Process

If, in the differential model, the individuals of both sexes remained unmarried, the total possibilities for marriage between two adjacent groups would be

$$N = kTH_i(0)F_j(0),$$

since, at any point in time, the possibility exists of $k \, dt \, H_i(0) F_j(0)$ marriages. Now, if every individual from group i has n ties with n individuals of the adjacent group j, the total number of possibilities for marriage between the two groups is

$$N = nH_i(0)F_j(0).$$

The relationship between the attraction k and the number of individual ties n is thus very simple:

$$n = kT.$$

Thus, being single at age 50, which was used to define permanent celibacy, can be interpreted equally as a particular coefficient of attraction k and as a particular number n of ties between individuals. The equivalence of the two formulations can be verified directly on the system of differential equations for the $H_i(t)$ and $F_j(t)$:

$$dH_i(t) = -k\left(\sum \delta_{ij} F_j(t)\right) dt \quad \text{and} \quad dF_j(t) = -k\left(\sum \delta_{ij} H_i(t)\right) dt,$$

that is, after changing the variable $t = \alpha\theta$:

$$dH_i(\alpha\theta) = -k\left(\sum \delta_{ij} F_j(\alpha\theta)\right)\alpha \, d\theta,$$

$$dF_j(\alpha\theta) = -k\left(\sum \delta_{ij} H_i(\alpha\theta)\right)\alpha \, d\theta.$$

Put $P(\theta) = H(\alpha\theta)$, $Q(\theta) = F(\alpha\theta)$, and $k_1 = \alpha k$. The two systems of equations become

$$dP_i(\theta) = -k_1\left(\sum \delta_{ij} Q_j(\theta)\right) d\theta \quad \text{and} \quad dQ_j(\theta) = -k_1\left(\sum \delta_{ij} P_i(\theta)\right) d\theta,$$

which are exactly the equations when the coefficient of attraction is k_1. The proportion never married at T (by convention age 50 for permanent celibacy) is $P(T)$ or $Q(T)$. Given the preceding, it has the value $P(T) = H(\alpha T)$ and $Q(T) = Q(\alpha T)$.

So the celibacy rates at age 50 for the attraction k are the rates at 50α for the attraction αk. In the case of a finite number n of ties per individual with individuals from the adjacent group, the celibacy rate $C_n(50)$ must also vary like k since $n = kT$. Calculating $H(t)$ for a given attraction, we can verify empirically that the x such that $H(x) = C_n(50)$ vary linearly with n. Indeed, the relationship holds remarkably well from $n = 1$, except that the origin is not exactly 0.

The concept of attraction or speed of nuptiality that was defined by a measurement but remained theoretically unclear, thus acquires a simple and precise meaning when we move from the group level to that of individuals. The coefficient of attraction is quite simply the number of choices possible a priori scaled by a constant factor that depends on the age selected to determine permanent celibacy. This ceases to be necessary when we move from attraction to the number of ties per individual, and permanent celibacy is thus defined without reference to an age limit. Permanent celibacy becomes simply the fact of being not married, since all the possible individuals to whom one was linked are married.

12.11   Networks of Ties

In the previous example we saw the emergence of an individual squeeze that was independent of a group-level squeeze. Celibacy is the result not of an unfavorable overall configuration of permitted unions but of an individual risk. It is dependent on the formation of unions in each individual's immediate vicinity, not on the general organization of society. The celibacy at group and individual levels is compounded, moreover, in the groups occupying extreme positions. Indeed, in that relations between groups are made up of relations between individuals, we may even say that group celibacy is merely the resultant of a parallel series of individual random celibacies. This explains why celibacy levels in the two groups at the ends of the chain are the same in the attractions model and in the model of groups with n ties. This being so, there is no longer any necessity to study nuptiality from the standpoint of groups. It can be approached directly on the basis of the network of possible interindividual ties that may or may not be organized into groups with homogeneous behavior. One could even select a homogeneous situation in which no group exists and where all the individuals have the same configuration of ties.

For this purpose, we have selected a highly schematic representation of a network of ties in which men and women are represented by black and white dots arranged in staggered (quincuncial) form on a plane. The same distribution of ties is used for each sex, with the dots representing the nearest persons of the opposite sex. The ties are randomly selected until no more unions are possible. The result is represented in figure 12.9, where the thin lines are the possible ties and the thick lines are the unions formed. We see that around 10% of the individuals of each sex are victims of a squeeze when each person has exactly five ties.

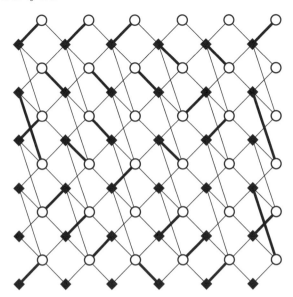

Figure 12.9. Marriages in a regular network of marriage candidates. The squares represent men, the circles represent women, the thin lines represent possible marriages, and the thick lines represent marriages contracted.

Table 12.12. Proportion never marrying by number of ties per person.

Number of ties per individual	Never marrying (%)
1	0
2	13.5
3	12.5
4	9.4
5	8.1
10	5.8
15	4.5

This systematic procedure can be used to explore the intensity of celibacy as a function of the number of ties. This is measured by counting only the individuals inside the square (at least five rows in from the outside) so as to limit the boundary effects, since the persons situated on the outer limit will have fewer ties than those they are linked to, and will thus more often be unmarried. Table 12.12 gives the result from the simulations.

The values obtained between two and ten ties are of interest because they fall within the range observed for celibacy in Western Europe over several hundred years. Furthermore, in surveys on partner selection conducted in the United States and in France (see, for example, Girard 1980), individuals report slightly over three

Table 12.13.

Number	Never marrying		
of ties	M	F	M + F
3	6.2	24.8	15.5
5	3.2	22.8	13.0
10	0.9	20.3	10.6

ties on average in reply to the question about the number of persons they believe they could have married. The percentages are also very close to those we obtained for the case of the central groups in the model with a line of six groups, thereby confirming the preponderance of local versus aggregate ties.

12.12 Imbalances in the Micromodel of the Marriage Market

The individual networks react to the imbalance of the sexes in the same way as the groups, by increasing the intensity of nuptiality for the minority sex, so curbing the increase in celibacy in the majority sex. To show this with the previous simulation all we need do is remove at random a certain percentage of men, in this case 20%, and simulate the process as before. This gives us, in table 12.13, male and female celibacy rates as a function of the number of ties.

If we added together the sex imbalance (20%) and the female celibacy in the case of a balance of the sexes ($0.8 \times 12.5\% = 10\%$), we ought to have 30% of women never marrying for the case of three ties. In fact they account for only half that proportion (15.5%). The shortage of men has considerably limited their risk of a squeeze. The sex imbalance that appeared a priori an inevitable cause of celibacy is to a large degree absorbed by the squeeze that, in its way, creates a localized imbalance. As soon as a union is formed, an imbalance appears next to the male and female partners of the two spouses, increasing the probability of marriage for a partner of the same sex.

With this example we capture the flexibility of the simulation model. The next step is to make it dynamic by equating the x-axis to that of successive ages or cohorts and by randomly selecting from within an age range (for example, the 11 age groups of the age squeeze model). It then becomes possible to track the progression of nuptiality by age as well as the effect of birth shortages and wartime losses on rates of celibacy and mean ages at marriage. Models of this kind have been successfully tested. They extend the field of application of the marriage squeeze concept while producing equivalent results to the model of attraction between age groups.

12.13 Pairings

Another generalization of the networks is in the direction of work on optimization of the pairings between two sets. The problem is stated thus: given n men and n women, the preferences of each as regards couple formation are known. Optimizing the pairing signifies achieving a matching that respects these preferences as closely as possible, for example, by minimizing the sum of the ranked preferences of each sex for all the unions formed. Although apparently distinct from nuptiality, this problem offers a number of interesting perspectives for its study.

A heuristic device makes the relationship with nuptiality a little clearer. We rank all possible unions in increasing order of preference, i.e., MN if we have M men and N women, and we form the unions beginning from the lowest value and excluding couples in which one of the partners was previously married. An example of this method is given in figure 12.10. The black squares represent men and the white circles represent women. The potential value of a union is proportional to the straight-line distance between the two points representing the two partners. We calculate the distances between all the black squares and all the white circles and rank them in order of increasing magnitude. We begin forming the unions from the lowest value and indicate it by a line on the diagram. For 100 unions, this algorithm gives a remarkable result. The first 35 unions are the best for both members of the couple formed. Up to the 63rd union, for both members, it is at worst a third-best choice. Not until the 79th union do more remote choices appear (10th for the man and 4th for the woman). For the last 10 unions, all the choices are made further than the 20th preference for both the man and the woman. This rather singular pattern is clearly visible on the diagram. We see that most unions are made over short distances, but that 10 of them involve large distances.

This very simple model presents a number of interesting aspects. It is quite logical to choose the unions by increasing order of distance. Even if the objects were elementary particles subject to Brownian motion, the encounters would, on average, occur faster the closer the particles. The result is also easy to interpret in terms of permanent celibacy. If we assume, for example, that the union can only occur if at least one of the partners classes the other in the top n, the example in the figure gives celibacy levels as a function of this number n in the top row of table 12.14.

In the case of a sex imbalance, the preferences of the minority sex are respected significantly more than those of the other sex. We performed a simulation comparable with the last one but with 100 men for 90 women. The results, reported in figure 12.11 using the same rules as in the previous figure, show that unions between distant partners—i.e., long lines—are half as numerous. The second row of table 12.14 gives the proportion of unions in which both partners have made choices higher than n (because the best choices were no longer possible). We see that the proportion has fallen substantially compared with the case of equal numbers of both sexes. This is a further example of differences in numbers being absorbed by celibacy.

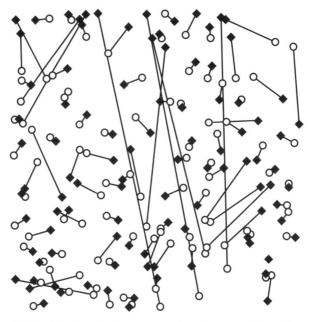

Figure 12.10. Marriages in the network of marriage candidates. The squares represent the men, the circles the women, and the lines the unions formed.

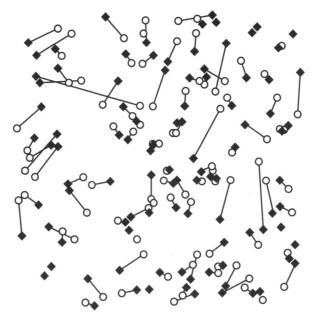

Figure 12.11. Marriages in the network of marriage candidates. The squares represent the men, the circles the women, and the lines the unions formed. Men are 10% in excess of women.

Table 12.14. For each person, the order of preference (i.e., distance) of all his or her possible partners are ranked by order of preference n. After pairing, the table gives the percentage of couples where both partners have a rank order for the other greater than n: i.e., if $n = 4$, both the husband and wife would have preferred 4 or more persons to the actual partner if one of these 4 or more were free.

n	2	3	4	5	10	20
Celibacy model 1	28%	23%	19%	18%	16%	10%
Celibacy model 2	17%	12%	12%	11%	7%	5%
Celibacy model 3	13%	12%	8%	8%	7%	3%

The hypothesis that marriage preferences are described by the proximity of points lying in a plane is arbitrary. Does it influence the result? To find out we first experimented with the distances in spaces of n dimensions (up to 50), which did not cause any significant variations to appear, merely a slight fall in celibacy levels. By contrast, if the distances are selected at random, the level falls considerably. We showed this by ordering at random, for every individual, all the individuals of the opposite sex, and then taking as the value of the union the sum of the ranks of the man for the woman, and of the woman for the man. Armed with these values for all possible unions, we then made the pairings as before in increasing order of values. The result appears on row three of table 12.14. Well-matched unions are more frequent with unordered preferences than with the order, however weak, that a distance creates. This interesting outcome is explained by the local fluctuations in the numbers of each sex. In the case of distances, couples tend to form within limited areas. The members of the majority sex are subject to a localized squeeze and at average distances because unions have been formed in other local groups. An imbalance in the opposite direction is the only means by which they can realize their union. In contrast, when preferences are completely random there is a sense in which everyone is at the same distance from everyone else. There are no local concentrations of individuals since the essential property that defines distance $(d(a,b) < d(c,b) + d(c,b))$ is lacking.

At this stage of the models we see that there are no longer any defined groups nor any dichotomy between unions that are possible and not possible. Marriage squeezes are operating in the pure state. They took the principal role because the implicit reference was the European marriage pattern—as John Hajnal termed it—in which, except for strong incest prohibitions (forbidden degrees of kinship), marriage is based on a wide and relatively free choice. Two consequences of this model are, first, as Hajnal showed, relatively high levels of permanent celibacy for both sexes combined with small spousal age differences, and, second, as Louis Henry showed, the damping of short-term variations in the numbers of marriage candidates. Non-European marriage forms that include preferential unions and polygamy do not follow the models that we have presented. However, the principles of these models can be applied to them and many results probably hold. It is, for example, straightforward to consider groups of marriageable individuals based on moieties or on marriage rules, before turning to the level of individual variations.

Without embarking upon modeling exercises of this kind, it can be noted, conversely, that universal marriage is virtually impossible to achieve if individuals are left to choose freely. There is a sense in which permanent celibacy is the price to pay for freedom of choice. The societies that aspire to universal marriage are thus obliged to develop subtle rules and be extremely attentive to the possible combinations, a task that falls to matchmakers but also to all the members of a society in which future unions are constantly being planned. In western societies particular importance has been placed on love, and thus on the individual's inner freedom. Paralleling this, in the other societies it is probably the union itself that has received greater emphasis.

12.14 Appendix

12.14.1 The Mathematics of Louis Henry's Circles

Continuous notation is used with the following variables: $K(t)$ is the sum of candidates of the sex in excess supply at t; $P(v, t)$ is the density of candidates waiting since time v at t; $u(t)$ is the instantaneous proportion of candidates who continue waiting (the same for all the waiting times by assumption); a is the constant density of entries of candidates of sex in undersupply; A is the initial surplus (at duration 0 and at time 0).

We immediately have the following relationships:

$$u(t) = 1 - a \, dt / K(t),$$

hence

$$P(v, t) = P(0, t - v) \exp\left(- \int_{t-v}^{t} \frac{a}{K(x)} \, dx \right)$$

and

$$P(0, t - v) = \begin{cases} a & \text{if } v < t, \\ A & \text{if } v = t, \\ 0 & \text{if } v > t. \end{cases}$$

If we assume that the persons still unmarried give up at the end of time T, we can express $K(t)$ as follows:

$$K(t) = \int_{0}^{T} P(v, t) \, dv.$$

Two cases must be distinguished:

(i) $t < T$: no unmarried person still waiting has yet left the circle. $K(t)$ thus remains equal to the initial surplus, A. $u(t)$ is therefore constant and equal to $1 - a/A$ dt, and $P(v,t)$ is a decreasing exponential function with exponent a/A. In annual discrete notation it is replaced by a converging geometric series, as was shown in the text. The mean age of the unmarried persons (or their mean length of waiting time) increases.

(ii) $t > T$: the unmarried persons still waiting start to leave the circles, first at the point in time $t = T$ those who provided the initial surplus A, then, for $t > T$, the density corresponding to those who reach the duration T, hence $P(T,t)$. So we can write

$$\frac{\mathrm{d}K(t)}{\mathrm{d}t} = -a \exp\left(-\int_{t-T}^{t} \frac{a}{K(x)} \, \mathrm{d}x \right).$$

This integrodifferential equation for $K(t)$ is not solved by standard functions. It is, however, sufficiently simple for it to be seen that the return to equilibrium is very slow. But it is ineluctable since there is no stable solution, because $K(t) = b$ would mean that d$K(t)/$dt was equal to $-a \exp(-aT/b)$, which contradicts the constancy of $K(t)$.

13

The Laws of Migration

Marital choice was modeled at the end of the last chapter by using an allocation process. At each stage, one person among those still available for marriage was randomly selected and mated with the nearest single person of the opposite sex. We illustrated the method by representing the unmarried of both sexes as points on a plane whose two dimensions represented not a real space but the action of two selection criteria, for example, age and wealth. Different criteria and different spaces could be imagined that would be further still from a concrete representation of space. But perhaps we were overcautious when stressing the artificial character of this representation. In certain real-world situations space can be the direct cause of the distance between partners. For example, in rural societies of small landowners, it made good sense for spouses to be neighbors since in that way the pieces of land they inherited or received through dowries or marriage settlements could be worked as one, and kin could be mobilized to provide extra labor during the busy periods of tilling and harvesting. Marriage acts provide a valuable source for studying this situation that leads to "marriage migration," when either the female or male partner goes to live in the other's place of residence (virilocality and uxorilocality).

13.1 The Gravity or Pareto Law of Marital Distance

Research along these lines using French civil status registers was conducted by two demographers, Luu Mau Tranh and Jean Sutter (1963) when they were investigating "isolates" from the perspective of population genetics. They found the same pattern that sociologists such as James Bossard (1932) had earlier brought to light for marriage migration in the United States. Such migration decreased in frequency as a function of distance. Plotting the distance between the partners' places of residence against the frequency of marriage (table 13.1), we obtain a remarkable constant slope over 2–30 km on a double logarithmic scale (figure 13.1).

In fact, marriage numbers are not plotted directly against distance in figure 13.1 because not all destinations, and hence not all distances, represent the same number of possibilities. Assuming a uniform distribution of the population, we calculate by simulation the distribution $\phi(d)$ of the distances d between each potential partner,

Table 13.1. Number of marriages by distance from partners' place of residence, Finistère, 1911–12.

Distance	Number of marriages
2–3	122
3–4	201
4–5	148
5–7	141
7–10	51
10–15	53
15–20	29
20–30	44
30–60	14

whatever the form of the territory (in the 2–30 km range, $\phi(d)$ is very nearly linear). Dividing the number of marriages $M(d)\Delta d$ in which the partners live at a distance between d and $d + \Delta d$ by the proportion of future partners living at this distance whatever their location $\phi(d)\Delta d$, we isolate the "pure effect" of distance, which is a power function as we saw in figure 13.1[1]:

$$M(d)/\phi(d) = K/d^{\gamma}.$$

It is in this sort of operation that the gravity law works best (Luu Mau Tranh (1964) and later Daniel Courgeau (1970) calculated $\phi(d)$ under the assumption of equal density in a homogeneous space.

The slope obtained reflects one of the most striking and constant patterns relating migration to distance, namely the decrease in the volume of migration in inverse proportion to a power of distance. The first to give it a precise formulation seems to have been the English geographer of German origin, Ernst Ravenstein, who, in an article for *Geographical Magazine* in 1871, noted the inverse relationship linking the distance and migration flows between two places. Many others worked on the question between the 1920s and 1960s, including Young (1924), Zipf (1941, 1949), Stewart (1948, 1950), and Warntz (1966). A number of writers took this pattern as proof of a social physics and even founded a school with this name. Efforts to explain it were also numerous. For many writers this consisted simply of making a crude analogy with Newton's law of gravitation, which can be written

$$M_{i,j} = kP_i P_j/d_{i,j}^{\gamma},$$

where k and γ are constants, P_i and P_j the populations at origin and destination, and $M_{i,j}$ the flow of migrants between the two places. Others such as Zipf detected in

---

[1] In the present case, $\phi(d)\Delta d$ is approximately equal to the surface of the circular band corresponding to the distances indicated in table 13.1, hence to the difference of their squares.

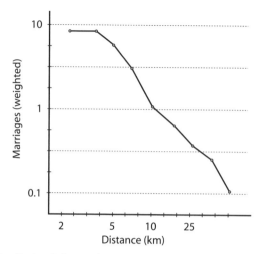

Figure 13.1.   Ratio of observed to possible marriages as a function of distance between the partners' places of residence, Finistère, 1911–12 (log–log scales).

this the effect of the principle of least effort though did not put forward a convincing model. The appearance of a power of distance is curious since diffusion processes usually have a negative exponential component (for instance, in random walks). The diffusion of plants, insects, and animals in fact follows negative exponential distributions of the gamma or Gaussian class. By linking the gravity model to the marriage market, we will open a useful possibility for explanation.

13.2   Migration as an Allocation Process

At the end of the last chapter we used a nearest-neighbor decision model after random selection of the candidate who decided to marry. We examined the rank order of this choice for both partners in the context of marriages squeezes, i.e., that occurred because their first choices had already been taken by others, but it is equally straightforward to work on the distances separating future partners, which in this case is the length of the lines connecting the points that represent them. It is not hard to imagine that their position on the plane of the diagram is also their position in real space, their place of residence, or their landholding. Using the same procedure as with Sutter's empirical data, therefore, the two distributions $M(d)$ and $\phi(d)$ were calculated by simulation of a large number of marriage markets, each containing 100 single men and 100 single women randomly distributed over the square of the diagram. For each market, we first calculated all the distances between the positions of a male and a female candidate, to calibrate $\phi(d)$. Then we randomly selected all the candidates in succession and assigned to them the nearest remaining single candidate of the opposite sex, so as to calibrate $M(d)$. Plotting the logarithms of $M(d)/\phi(d)$ against those of d gives the result shown in figure 13.2, and in table 13.2

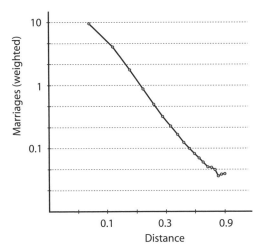

Figure 13.2. Relationship between the ratio of observed to possible marriages and the distance between the partners' homes in the nuptiality model of figure 12.11 (log–log scale).

we indicate the values of $M(d)$, $\phi(d)$, and $M(d)/\phi(d)$ as functions of distance, d. The strictly linear decrease signifies that the relationship between marriage and distance follows a gravity or Pareto distribution. There are slightly fewer migrants at the very beginning than the formula predicts, while fluctuations appear at the end, since very few marriages occur at these distances. The square within which the partners were distributed has a side dimension of 1 and the scale for the distances goes from 0.04 to 0.9 on the diagram.

Since application of the simple allocation process to the male and female candidates yields a gravity distribution, it is tempting to transpose it to internal migration in general. In any migration there is a place of origin and a place of destination, yet equally there is a person located at the origin and a possibility for residence at the destination, and therefore a supply and demand for spatial mobility. Hence supply can be equated with one sex and demand with the other. The model that adjusts supply to demand operates on the same principle as that for male and female candidates (in the next chapter we will see how to get closer to the process and how it differs from the marriage market). One of the candidates for migration decides to move at a given point in time (this person is randomly selected from among all the demands) and receives the possibility of residence or establishment still available nearest to his or her current residence. In this case, the allocation model shows us that migration takes place in conformity with the gravity law.

13.3 A Concrete Example of Migration under the Gravity Law

The French census of 1911 offers a valuable data source for the study of internal migration, and for empirical verification of the gravity law model in particular. The

Table 13.2. Simulation of marriage migration $M(d)$ by distance d: frequencies $M(d)/\phi(d)$ in relation to total possible migratory moves, $\phi(d)$.

d	$M(d)$	$\phi(d)$	$M(d)/\phi(d)$
0.04–0.08	83 527	240 500	0.347 31
0.08–0.12	51 219	452 880	0.113 10
0.12–0.16	24 653	642 120	0.038 39
0.16–0.20	12 457	806 140	0.015 45
0.20–0.24	7 181	952 180	0.007 54
0.24–0.28	4 426	1 063 800	0.004 16
0.28–0.32	3 059	1 159 980	0.002 64
0.32–0.36	2 194	1 250 680	0.001 75
0.36–0.40	1 575	1 314 740	0.001 20
0.40–0.44	1 212	1 350 100	0.000 90
0.44–0.48	975	1 369 040	0.000 71
0.48–0.52	791	1 377 940	0.000 57
0.52–0.56	654	1 375 260	0.000 48
0.56–0.60	505	1 349 120	0.000 37
0.60–0.64	484	1 309 520	0.000 37
0.64–0.68	415	1 251 160	0.000 33
0.68–0.72	292	1 184 740	0.000 25
0.72–0.76	294	1 107 260	0.000 27
0.76–0.80	275	1 017 580	0.000 27

published output includes a table that classifies all residents by their department of birth and their department of current residence, giving a total of 87×87 migration flows. There is a slight loss of accuracy compared with the example of marriage migration, since the unit of subdivision is the department, not the commune, but there are substantial benefits in that the totality of flows is known, whereas Sutter had information on the marriages concluded in one department only. This offers improved possibilities for studying the influence of distance on migration flows. The potential migration between departments i and j can in fact be measured as the cross-product of the total in-migration (immigration) to j and the total out-migration (emigration) from i. For the observed migration we then have

$$M_{i,j} = k E_i I_j f(d_{i,j}).$$

Taking logarithms of both sides, this becomes

$$\log(M_{i,j}) = \log k + \log E_i + \log I_j + \log f(d_{i,j}).$$

When the values for all the migration flows out of or into a given department are plotted, the two scatters of data points are close to lying on a straight line. The function f can be equated to a negative power of distance, hence to a gravity function:

$$f(d_{i,j}) = \frac{1}{d_{i,j}^{\gamma}}.$$

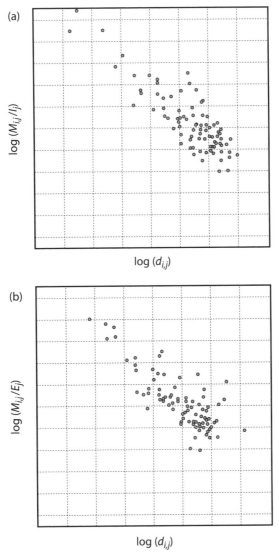

Figure 13.3. Out-migrations from the Doubs department to all the others (the flows are divided by the population of the department of destination; the two coordinates are logarithmic).

This can be seen from the two examples given in figure 13.3, representing out-migration from the Doubs department to the other 86 departments, and in figure 13.4, representing out-migration from the 86 departments to the Indre-et-Loire department. The logarithm of distance $d_{i,j}$ is plotted on the horizontal axis, and the logarithm of actual migration divided by potential migration $M_{i,j}/(E_i I_j)$ is plotted on the vertical axis.

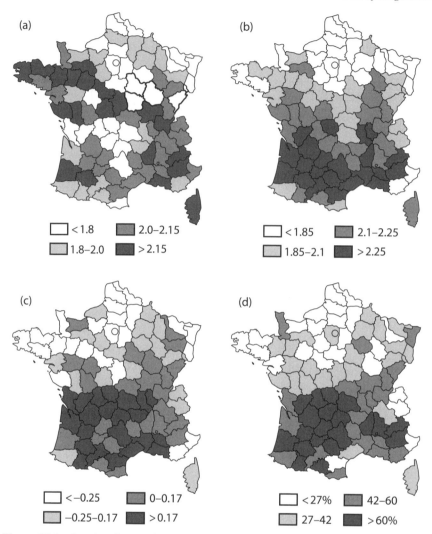

(a)

$\square$ < 1.8   ▨ 2.0–2.15

▨ 1.8–2.0   ■ > 2.15

(b)

$\square$ < 1.85   ▨ 2.1–2.25

▨ 1.85–2.1   ■ > 2.25

(c)

$\square$ < −0.25   ▨ 0–0.17

▨ −0.25–0.17   ■ > 0.17

(d)

$\square$ < 27%   ▨ 42–60

▨ 27–42   ■ > 60%

Figure 13.4. In-migrations to the Indre-et-Loire department from all the others (the flows are divided by the population of the department of origin; the two coordinates are logarithmic).

With the exception of migration to Paris and the contiguous Seine-et-Oise department, all the departments of origin and destination follow the gravity model. For inward migration, 45 of the 87 correlation coefficients between the logarithms of distance and of attraction $M_{i,j}/(E_i I_j)$ exceed 0.85 and all the others exceed 0.8, except that for Paris, which is 0.7. The fit is equally good for out-migration (65 correlation coefficients above 0.85). The values of the exponent for distance vary widely between departments, ranging from −2.7 (Gironde) to −1.4 (Nord and Alpes-Maritimes) for inward migration, and from −2.4 (Basses-Alpes) to −1.5 (Cantal) for out-migration. The more negative the exponent, the more the intensity of migration declines with

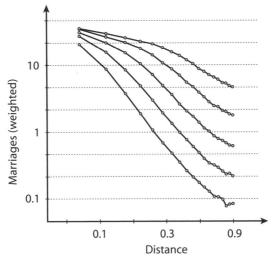

Figure 13.5. Relationship between the frequency of actual to possible migratory moves and distance for several values of the number of a priori possibilities per migrant.

distance and, hence, the more local in character the migration. This indicates that Bordeaux (Gironde) draws migrants from the surrounding areas, in contrast to Nice (Alpes-Maritime) and Lille (Nord), where the migrants travel long distances.

13.4 Explaining the Variations in the Exponent for Distance γ

The foregoing explanation is based on the coincidence of two maps, not on a model. In the case of marriage it produces a gravity law distribution with a single value for the exponent γ. How can it be modified so as to transform γ into a variable parameter for in-migration as well as for out-migration? Given the simplicity of the procedure, the only parameter that can be manipulated is, as in the case of marriage, the number of ties, i.e., the number of migration possibilities for each migrant. The distance exponent γ is in fact highly sensitive to this parameter, as can be checked in figure 13.5, where it varies from 6 to 100 possibilities per migrant. We used exactly the same method of allocation by random selection of the migrant and migration to the nearest possibility. In practice, the location of 5000 out-migrants and of 5000 in-migration places was randomly selected at constant density, then for each one we selected N possibilities at random and performed the allocation process as described earlier. The resulting network is rather muddled and cannot be represented in the way that marriages were in figure 12.9, but the role of N is particularly clear. The values of γ for each N in figure 13.5 are the following:

N	6	12	25	50	100
γ	−1.6	−2.2	−2.8	−3.1	−3.6

So if migration occurs according to an allocation mechanism, each migrant must have a choice between a reasonably small number of destinations ranging between 5 and 20, values that correspond to the observed γ. It seems odd that the most steeply negative curves correspond to the largest number of possibilities, given that the historical tendency is for the steepness of slopes to diminish and consequently for migrants to travel longer distances. Modernity would thus be associated with a reduction in the number of possible choices. But the reasoning can be reversed. As the economy becomes more diversified, so migrants become more specific in their demands and so the number of places suitable for them declines. Simultaneously, falling transport costs and times enable the migrant to make more preliminary contacts and reach a final decision without the fear of someone else taking the place first. The "squeeze" arises from the lack of general information about the market and thus about the state of competition.

13.5   General Simulation of Internal Migration

The best way to test the applicability of the allocation model to migration is by comparing it directly with actual observations. We have simulated the internal migration observed in France in 1911 by adapting the parameters of the allocation model to the empirical situation. We first distribute 10 000 destination places between the departments in proportion to the total I_j observed in each, and 10 000 points of origin in proportion to the total out-migration (emigration) E_i in each department.[2] We then select at random for each out-migrant N possible destination places among the 10 000. Thereafter, we follow the exact procedure for the allocation model. All the migrants are in turn randomly selected and allocated to the nearest possible place among the N not yet filled. Since the only variable parameter is the number N of possible places for each individual, it was selected so that the mean of the exponents γ obtained by regression on the simulated migration flows was the same as the mean of the exponents γ obtained by regression on the observed migration flows (-2.05). This requirement was satisfied by a value of $N = 15$ (the mean of the γ is then -2.1). A good fit for the simulated flows is obtained for 62 of 87 departments: the correlation coefficient between the logarithms of the in-migration rates and of the distance is over 0.70. The gravity law gives a good account of the allocation phenomenon. Of interest is the variability in the values of the exponent for distance for each department. They are situated between -1 and -2.9, which is a slightly larger range than that of the coefficients obtained for the observed flows. Thus, the value of γ in each department depends as much on the number of possibilities for

---

[2] The exact coordinates of each origin and destination point were obtained by randomly selecting a commune of the department in proportion to its population in 1911 and assigning the coordinates of the commune's *chef-lieu* (main settlement) to the point. This procedure offers the advantage of taking into account towns and cities as well as the spatial continuity of the rural population, some communes being adjacent to a neighboring department.

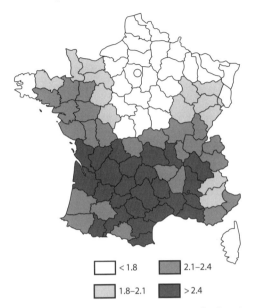

Figure 13.6. Values of the distance exponent γ for in-migration to each department, obtained by simulation in the allocation model.

migration, N, of each individual as it does on that individual's position in the system as a whole. Some migrants have no difficulty finding a close destination because places in the locality are plentiful, others on the contrary have to look further afield because demand exceeds the supply of locally available places. The strength and regularity of the phenomenon can be seen when the values of γ for migration flows in each department are displayed on a map (figure 13.6). Unable to find vacancies at a short distance, large numbers of migrants from the south of the country arrive in the north, with the consequence that the coefficients γ for the departments to the north of the La Rochelle–Geneva line are less negative than those to the south. By symmetry, in the south, the coefficients are strongly negative because local migrants have quickly taken the few available places. It is remarkable that the map of the simulated coefficients is similar to that of the observed coefficients (their correlation is 0.743) and equally regular. From this we infer that if total out-migration and in-migration by department are known, i.e., $87 \times 2 = 174$ numbers, we can reconstitute a close approximation of the $87 \times 86 = 7482$ elementary flows between all the departments.

The good quality of the reconstitution is apparent when we compare the value of the observed attractions for a given department j $(M_{i,j}/E_i)$ and those simulated by the previous model. Figure 13.7 shows the results from this comparison for the Finistère and Marne departments. The similarity of the attractions (and hence of the flows, since they are obtained by multiplying the latter by total out-migration, E_j, from each department i considered) is clear. But these maps reveal a phenomenon of

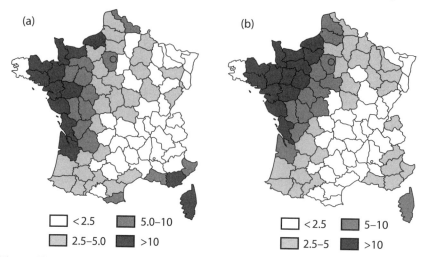

Figure 13.7.   (a) Observed attractions of Finistère department on migrants from the other departments (scale multiplied by a constant coefficient). (b) Simulated attractions of Finistère department on migrants from the other departments (same number of departments by category as for the map of observed attractions).

greater interest concerning the logic of the gravity model. If the gravity model gave a perfect fit, the attractions ought to be equal for equal distances from the department being studied. In fact, we see that distortions appear in the simulation as well as in reality, and that in both cases they resemble each other. For example, migrants to the Finistère come from the Atlantic coast and even from Provence, more than from central France, even though the latter is nearer. This being so, the irregularities in the gravity law are explained by the system as a whole. Rather than a mysterious law that dictates a course of action to individuals through some unspecified channel, we are dealing with a system of spatial interactions of which the gravity law is a by-product. A further proof of this relationship comes from examining the residuals of the gravity law. Their geographical distribution is similar in the simulation and in reality, as can be seen in figure 13.9 for the Marne department.[3] In its capacity to explain migration, the allocation mechanism is superior to the gravity law, since the deviations from the latter are the same in the model as in reality.

13.6   Migration Balances and Chaos

The preceding results concern out-migration and in-migration flows. More commonly, however, attention focuses on their balance in each place i, $S_i = I_i - E_i$, or between two places, $s_{i,j} = M_{i,j} - M_j$. It is not possible to relate the migration balance (net migration) to total out-migration and in-migration for the place

---

[3] The comparison is less convincing for a number of southern departments, where the gravity law gives a relatively less good fit ($r < 0.75$).

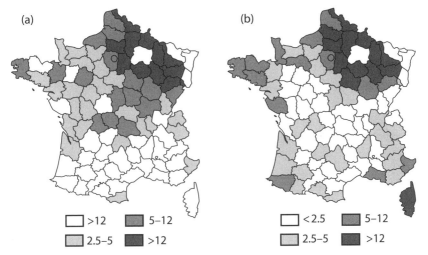

Figure 13.8. (a) Observed attractions of Marne department on migrants from the other departments (scale multiplied by a constant coefficient). (b) Simulated attractions of Marne department on migrants from the other departments (same number of departments by category as for the map of observed attractions).

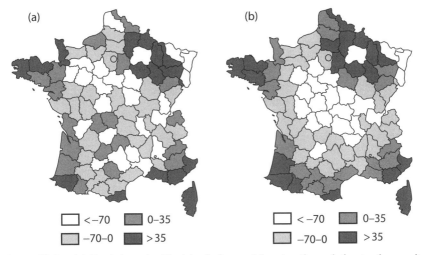

Figure 13.9. (a) Deviations (residuals) of observed in-migration relative to the gravity law for the Marne department (scale multiplied by a constant coefficient). (b) Deviations (residuals) of simulated in-migration relative to the gravity law for the Marne department on migrants from the other departments (same number of departments by category as for the map of observed attractions).

under consideration since these both enter into the formula. So we divide it by the total populations of the origin and destination, thereby obtaining quantities suitable for comparison. Because of how they are defined, migration balances vary more than migration flows. The view is often expressed that the flows reflect sociological constants while the balances reflect economic contingencies. This is incorrect. Migration balances are invariably patterned too, but differently from flows. In figure 13.10(a) we have represented the distribution of migration balances with the other departments for the Manche department, though any other department has an analogous structure. There are large negative balances (net losses) for the departments situated in the direction of the zones of high in-migration (the main urban centers) and strongly positive ones (net gains) as we move toward the zones of high out-migration. Thus, the Manche department receives migrants from all the departments to the west of it, and sends migrants to all the departments situated between it and Paris. It also has large positive migration balances with the departments of the Massif Central, sources of heavy out-migration, and negative ones with two growth zones of population growth, the coastal plain of Provence and Lorraine. Analogous behavior would be observed if another department been chosen, for example, the Tarn. This department receives migrants in large numbers from the Massif Central, a zone of out-migration, but loses migrants to the two population growth poles of southern France, the Garonne valley and the Mediterranean coastal plain. The regularity is no longer based on mathematics—as was the case with the gravity law—but rather on logic. The balance between two departments is generally to the advantage of the one with the larger overall balance. The exceptions are the departments that "screen" a city and thereby intercept the migration flows running in its direction. What are in effect migration paths thus become established, following the coastlines and main rivers. They are a reminder that Ernst Ravenstein, who pioneered research in this area, frequently employed the river metaphor to illustrate how migratory flows run toward the cities, depositing silt along their way as they gain in volume.

The strength of the mechanism is confirmed when we compare the results from the simulation (figure 13.10(b)) for the Manche department. They have the same overall structure, but major inversions occur in the immediate surroundings, with a swing from large gains to large losses for the departments of Loire-Inférieure and Maine-et-Loire. A priori it seems likely that the allocation mechanism cannot integrate phenomena of territorial continuity, such as lines of communication to Paris or the Loire valley, through which a homogenization of the positive and negative balances occurs.

However, there is probably a simpler reason. If we perform the simulation of the allocation while changing the number of migration possibilities per individual, major inversions occur, particularly in the vicinity. A high number of migration possibilities for each potential out-migrant (we set $N = 75$ in figure 13.10(c)) has the effect of reorganizing the results in the departments around the Manche department in a way that is closer to reality. Conversely, however, with a small number of possibilities ($N = 5$) the distribution of migration balances with the Manche department (figure 13.10(d)) becomes closer to that for overall balances.

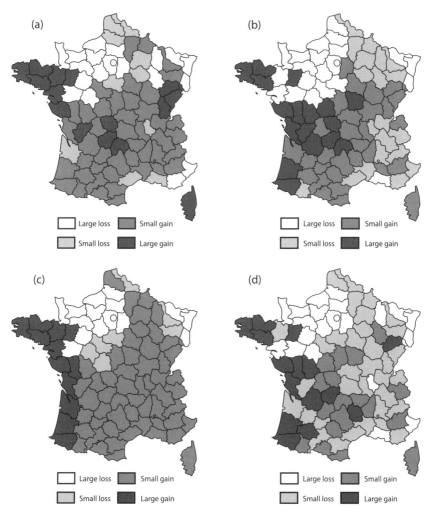

Figure 13.10. (a) Observed net migration balances of the Manche department. (b)–(d) Simulated net migration balances of the Manche department for, respectively, 15, 75, and 5 migration possibilities per person.

There is no necessity for the number of possibilities per individual to be fixed, or even fixed within a given department. In the experiment we have just conducted, varying this number led to a chaotic regime. When the mean number of migration possibilities is varied, the net balances for some departments close to the Manche department swing from strongly negative to strongly positive. Repeating the experiment for all the departments, the same instability is almost always found. The limits of the model have undeniably been reached, but probably also those of the possibility for explaining the observed behavior. The model informs us on the limitations of a causal schema for explaining the observed migration balances. It produces an ordered distribution of the balances that is close to reality, and also a "seed" or starting point for the instability that, once its magnitude increases, develops into a chaotic regime. The model leads, therefore, to the limits of rational explanation.

The allocation model is simple and each of its hypotheses can naturally be made more complicated, for example, by assuming that the same individual makes several successive moves or by using a probability distribution for the number of possibilities offered to each migrant. In the tests that have been performed, none of these modifications significantly improves the fit to the data. Thus the simple allocation model satisfies our requirements, and in addition provides material for a discussion of the general migration system. Because the model accurately replicates the distribution of the flows (approximation to the gravity laws and similarity of the distributions of the deviations from these) and that of the migration balances (a logic of blocs with positive or negative balances and localized contrasts), it might appear that the question of the spatial distribution of migratory movements has been answered. In fact, everything depends on the level of observation adopted. At levels that are higher (international migration) or lower (local distributions of migrants), other forces come into play. These have given rise to very different theories, particularly at the local level—Samuel Stouffer's theory of intervening opportunities, Törsten Hägerstrand's theory of migrant networks, and finally, again from Stouffer, twenty years after his first attempt, the theory of opportunities and competing migrants.[4] Our exposition of them, though still relating to France in 1911, will also involve a change of level. We will use observations at a much finer level than the department thanks to the census that gives the department of birth for the inhabitants of the eighty *quartiers* or neighborhoods (administrative areas) of Paris.

13.7 The Attraction of the Neighborhoods of Paris and Intervening Opportunities

Comparison of migration flows from the departments to Paris uses the same method as for interdepartmental flows. We calculate a coefficient of attraction $k_{i,j}$ for neighborhood j on department i by a relative frequency ratio

$$k_{i,j} = M_{i,j}/E_i I_j,$$

where $M_{i,j}$ denotes the number of persons in neighborhood j born in department i, E_i the total number of migrants from department i to Paris, and I_j the total

---

[4] Despite its important place in social, economic, and political reality, the case of international migration will not be examined here, since there is no satisfactory theory for dealing with it. The theories of internal migration of Stouffer and Hägerstrand are of some use for its analysis but cannot encompass the far-reaching political and historical causes implicated. The simulation model at the end of this chapter could, however, be transposed to the international level since it introduces and formalizes the idea of "migration waves."

number of persons in neighborhood j born outside of Paris.[5] When the flows from the same department are being compared, it is not necessary to divide by E_i since it is constant for all the flows compared, and we multiply by a constant factor in such a way that the sum of the attractions for all the neighborhoods equals 1000. In figure 13.11(a),(b) we represent the distribution of migrants from the Aisne and Mayenne departments within the eighty neighborhoods (aptly named *quartiers* since these are formed by subdivision into four of the twenty arrondissements) of Paris. In both cases, it is in the outermost neighborhoods nearest to these two departments that their out-migrants are concentrated, as if the migrants had come directly by the highways and stopped almost as soon as they entered Paris.[6] Thus, for migrants from the Aisne, the mean value of the 10 highest coefficients of attraction is 21 and for the 10 lowest, 9. If migration had conformed to a gravity law of exponent -2 (which is the mean for interdepartmental migration), this would signify that the square of the ratio of the distances to these two groups of neighborhoods would be $21/9 = 2.333$ and hence that the ratio of the distances would be 1.53. This would require the least attractive neighborhoods to be 50% further from the Aisne department than the most attractive ones, which is not the case (the distances between the 80 neighborhoods and the Aisne vary by only a few percentage points). For the Mayenne department, the differences are even larger—mean value of 26 for the 10 top attractions and 7 for the 10 lowest—although the distances separating the various neighborhoods and the Mayenne resemble each other more than is the case for the Aisne, which is closer to Paris.

The gravity law is therefore disqualified. The fact nevertheless remains that both examples demonstrate a preponderant role for the distance between the neighborhoods and the two departments. The gravity form is unsuitable not because it gives too much importance to distance but, on the contrary, because it gives it too little. In a landmark article published in the *American Sociological Review* in 1940, Samuel Stouffer took this conclusion—which he reached when working with statistics of residential relocation within Detroit—as the basis on which to propose a rather different schema for explaining the spatial pattern of migration in contexts with large differences of population density. He made the hypothesis that migration between two places was directly proportional to the employment opportunities at the origin and destination (which can be interpreted as E_i and I_j) and inversely proportional to the opportunities in between, O_{ij}, i.e., those situated at a distance from the origin less than that of the destination. Stouffer also expressed his rule in mathematical

---

[5] One of the simple justifications for this formula runs as follows. If the town of origin is divided into two equal portions, migratory moves will also be divided by 2, so $k_{i,j}$ is a function of $M_{i,j}/E_i$. If the same is done for the destination town, it will be deduced that $k_{i,j}$ is a function of $M_{i,j}/I_j$. Hence it is a function of $M_{i,j}/E_i\,I_j$.

[6] In chapter 15 we shall see that geographers sometimes use population processes based on diffusion limited aggregation (DLA), which is analogous to this behavior, to explain the growth and form of urban agglomerations.

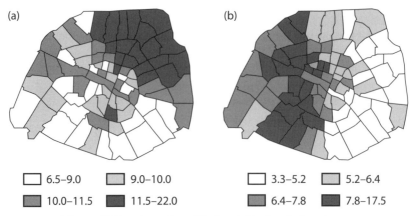

Figure 13.11. Attraction of Paris neighborhoods for migrants from (a) the Aisne and (b) the Mayenne departments.

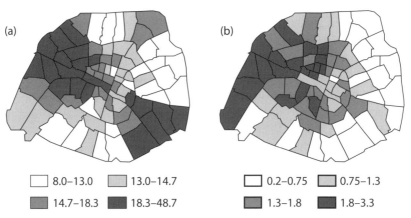

Figure 13.12. Attraction of Paris neighborhoods for migrants from (a) the Nièvre and (b) the Alpes-Maritimes departments.

form

$$M_{i,j} = k E_i I_j / O_{i,j}.$$

In practice, these opportunities are equated with in-migration to the intermediate locations. Because the intervening rural regions situated between the Aisne or Mayenne departments and Paris are lightly populated compared with the capital, they represent few opportunities. By contrast, at the distance of Paris, the intervening opportunities increase substantially since they begin to include the inhabitants of the capital, thereby reducing the number of migrants given by the formula. For this to be halved it is enough that the in-migrants to Paris be equal in number to the in-migrants from all the regions that are nearer to the Aisne than to Paris, which as a minimum is the case. For other departments, however, Stouffer's model does not work well.[7] In figure 13.12(a) and (b) we have represented the attractions for migrants born in the Nièvre and Alpes-Maritimes departments. A proportion of the migration from the Nièvre appears to progress according to the intervening opportunities mode in the southeast of the capital, but another proportion, on the contrary, comes in from the west, which is the most distant part of Paris for migrants from the Nièvre, as if they skirted around the city before entering it. For migrants from Alpes-Maritimes, the Stouffer model is quite simply reversed. The proportion of migrants from this department is highest in the neighborhoods situated in the northwest of the capital, which are the furthest of all from Nice (the *chef-lieu* of the department) that lies to the southeast. The differences in attraction are even larger than for the case of the Mayenne and Aisne departments: mean coefficient of attraction 3 for the 10 lowest, and 26 for the 10 highest.

13.8 Hägerstrand's Networks

We are left with Törsten Hägerstrand's theory to help resolve these difficulties. In a detailed study published in 1957, the Swedish geographer explained the irregularities in migration within Sweden by means of a distinction between active and passive migrants. The former actively seek out new experience and settle when they find an opportunity, while the latter move to be with a migrant who is already established in a place. Using simulation techniques and observations, Hägerstrand showed that concentrations of migrants thus form in a largely unordered way across a grid in which distance continues to play some role, notably for migrants of the active type. Such an idea is hard to prove or disprove since we do not know which migrants were active and which passive. It does, however, have logical consequences that enable it to be tested. If Paris contains few centers of migration from any given department, and if passive migrants significantly outnumber active migrants, we ought to observe concentrations around these poles and a decrease in the proportion of migrants as we move further away. As an example take the cases of the Savoie and Somme departments. The Savoyards had occupied certain specific trades (connected with the Hôtel des ventes, for example) since the Ancien Régime, and were concentrated in the center of the Right Bank (1st, 2nd, 3rd, and 4th arrondissements), with extensions toward the affluent neighborhoods of the west and the Left Bank (6th and 7th). The population of Picards originating from the Somme department resided mainly in two parts of Paris: in the northeast (10th, 11th, 18th, 19th, and part of the 20th arrondissements) and in the affluent neighborhoods of the center (6th near the Seine, 7th, and 1st). The coherence of the groupings can be measured statistically by

---

[7] When in-migrant density (a) is the same everywhere and thus equal to that of out-migrants, for a surface of origin E_i and of destination I_j we have $M_{i,j} = kE_i I_j/(\pi d^2)$, hence a gravity law model of exponent -2, which appears satisfactory, but it is not possible to obtain another exponent like those observed in many circumstances. Basically, Stouffer's law is conceived for territories where density varies greatly.

calculating the autocorrelation of the attractions for the 80 neighborhoods for a given department of birth.[8] The autocorrelation values of the attraction for each department are relatively high (over 0.6) in the northeast, west, and southwest of the country, and low in the Massif Central, Burgundy, Franche-Comté, and Dauphiné (generally below 0.4). The hypothesis of diffusion from a limited number of centers is plausible, therefore, though it is not blindingly obvious.

Another cause of diffusion is the length of time since the migration occurred. The earlier the first active migrants arrived, the longer they have had to spread all across Paris, and the passive migrants with them. The intensity of the differences of attraction by neighborhoods should therefore be inversely related to the length of time since the inward migration occurred. This can be measured by relating the attraction of the ten most attractive neighborhoods to that of the ten least attractive neighborhoods. The geography of this indicator reveals large differences between the departments in the extreme south, where the ratio exceeds 2.5, indicating strong differences of attractiveness between neighborhoods, and the departments to the north of the Le Havre–Geneva line, where on the contrary the contrasts are nearly all below 1.7. This distribution is similar to that compiled by Bertillon for the birthplaces of deceased Parisians in 1833. Relating the number deceased for each department to the population of that department in 1801 (the earliest base of sufficient reliability and that corresponds here to a mean age at death of 32, which is not too far from the reality in this period), we obtain a map similar to that of the differences in attractiveness and on which the Le Havre–Geneva line also establishes a clear division. With the exception of Cantal, all the departments to the south of the line have sent few migrants compared with those to the north. These indirect observations do not form a clinching argument. Fortunately, a simpler solution is at hand, since when the maps of the coefficient of attraction for each department are drawn, the poles are visible to the naked eye: they are the railway termini and the center of the city.

13.9   Attraction of the Railway Stations and City Center

What fixed the position of the first immigration poles in Paris were the means of transport used and the period during which migration occurred. Mention was made above of the possibility of arriving by road and thus of poles being created at the gates through which migrants entered the city. This may have been the case for migrants coming from the Aisne and Mayenne departments. But by 1911 the railway had been in existence for several decades, so migrants could also have come in via the Paris mainline stations. Prior to the existence of the stations, the city was more compact. In the early nineteenth century, as in previous centuries, migrants entered directly at the city center, on the inside of the so-called Farmers-General Wall, beyond which

---

[8] Autocorrelation is a correlation in the usual sense of the term but calculated on all the possible pairs of neighborhoods with a common boundary.

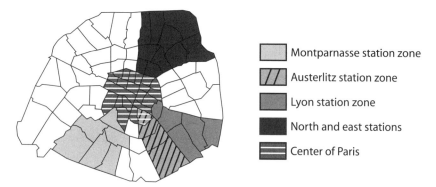

Figure 13.13. Zones of influence of Paris railway stations and of the historic center.

Paris barely extended at this time. The existence of such poles around the stations is tested for simply by assigning to each station a zone comprising the neighborhood in which it is situated, the neighborhood it adjoins going toward the center, and those in the same direction leading out of the city (figure 13.13). Thus, for the Gare d'Austerlitz we have taken the Jardin des Plantes section of the 5th arrondissement and all of the 13th arrondissement. We have done likewise for the Gare de Lyon and Gare Montparnasse. The zones of influence of the Gare du Nord and Gare de l'Est have been combined, as they are very close together. Lastly, the center of Paris has been defined by the first four arrondissements on the Right Bank, by the neighborhoods bordering the Seine in the 5th and 6th arrondissements, and by the Invalides neighborhood (7th). Next we calculated the coefficient of attraction for each department of each sector thus defined (migrants originating from this department in the sector divided by the total number of migrants in the sector), and related this to the attraction of all 80 neighborhoods on the department. On a map of France (figure 13.14(a)) we have indicated which of the sectors, railway station or city center, has the strongest coefficient of attraction on each department. On the same map we have shown the contemporary limits of the railway networks serving each station. We see that they occupy almost exactly the zones of attraction for migrants by the station considered or by the city center. We also see that the zone where the city center attracts more than any station is the extreme southeast and southwest, which is where the differentiations between neighborhoods are largest (though where the gravity model and that of Stouffer predict they should be smallest). Contrary to what might be expected, the oldest migration had not spread through the Paris urban space but had remained localized in the center. More exactly, in the absence of any subsequent wave of migration, this early migration had become fossilized. Subsequent migration waves were settled in successive layers like the skin of an onion, each one filling the niches left free by the previous one. Consequently, the departments from which migration is directed most at the center of Paris are not those which have sent migrants to Paris for longest, but on the contrary those where

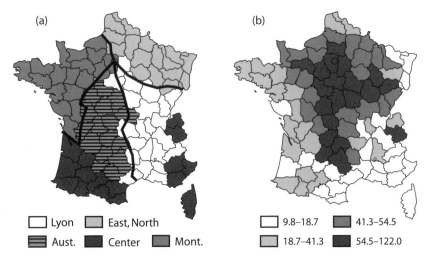

Figure 13.14. (a) Railway stations attracting most migrants from each department and limits of the railway networks for the stations. (b) Rate of migration to Paris (total migrants to Paris divided by total persons born in the department).

out-migration was limited and that had not yet come under the influence of Paris. This is confirmed by drawing the map (figure 13.14(b)) of the intensity of migration to Paris (migrants to Paris as a proportion of all the persons born in the department in France as a whole). With the exception of Savoie, the zones of weak migration are those where the pull of the city center is strongest.

The following scenario can be developed. In the eighteenth century, all migrants arrived in the central part of Paris, a city that was not yet growing rapidly but whose center was best suited to receive immigrants (supply of rooms to rent, proximity to work, just as present-day immigrants in the Paris region are more centrally distributed than the general population of the Ile-de-France region). The second half of the nineteenth century brought the growth of migration from particular departments and regions, for example, the Aveyron, Centre, and Touraine. These migrants could no longer be contained in the center and, depending on the rate of their arrival and on the presence of core groups of innovators, they spread across the growing capital city. These different migratory movements were competing with each other for territory, and together they formed a complex system that cannot be reduced to the poles that we examined above as discrete entities, on the implicit assumption that the position of each was determined by the railway station of arrival and without attention to the competition that could develop between candidates who were in oversupply.

13.10   Paris in Rings

A simple way to trace the growth of Paris is to divide the city into concentric rings or zones. As there are eighty neighborhoods the number of zones is necessarily

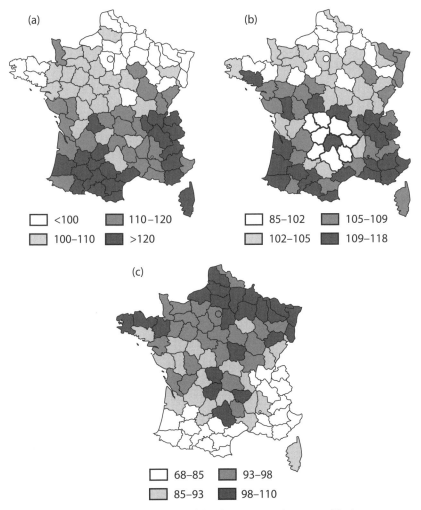

Figure 13.15. Attraction of the three concentric zones of Paris:
(a) city center; (b) intermediate zone; (c) outer zone.

limited. We have drawn three only: the center in the form defined above, then the outer zone comprising all the neighborhoods on the outer limit of Paris (marked by the present-day *périphérique* or ring road) and lastly, between them, the intermediate zone. The same method as for the attraction of railway stations was used, calculating the relative attraction of each zone for each department. Figure 13.15(a),(c) displays the distribution of relative attractions for the city center and the outer zone. Both exhibit a patterned structure that allows the tactics of the departments in competition to be made out. The dominant departments for the outer zone are all those to the north of the Loire and Seine rivers, forming a large circumflex-shape limited at its base by the Nantes–Paris and Paris–Besançon axes. By and large these are the oldest migration waves, which can be assumed to have begun using road communication. Those involved have not got as far as the central area, probably because it was already occupied by earlier waves of migrants, but also because the points of entry in northern and eastern Paris are further than the others from the center of the city. The city is denser in this direction, and crossing it and colonizing it takes longer. The outer zone also contains an above average proportion of population originating from the Massif Central, and in particular from the ring of departments encircling the Cantal department. These departments are also those where out-migration was practically nonexistent until the mid nineteenth century but subsequently expanded rapidly. Migrants from here had no existing core groups to count on for support and were probably obliged to occupy the residential niches that remained in the outlying neighborhoods. Expressed more vividly, they may be said to have spilled out of their traditional spatial context and spread until finding available places, where they created new cores of population.

The description can be refined by using the relative attractions of the intermediate zone (figure 13.15(b)). The ring of departments around the Cantal department is again apparent but this time has the lowest levels of attraction, as if migrants from here had failed to conquer space near the center and been relegated to the margins. Conversely, the other departments to the south of the Loire are strongly represented in the intermediate zone of Paris, into which their migrants had probably spread from the center, where their precursors had settled. This tactic probably remained possible thanks to the moderate scale of the migration, in that the first migrants to the center originating from the same department could provide accommodation for the relatively small numbers of new arrivals from their family or village. A particularity of the intermediate zone must be noted. This is the band, two departments wide, running horizontally from Nantes and Vendée to Doubs and Jura. Migrant numbers from this region also grew considerably, but they could still be distributed between the three zones without spilling over, notably because of their location in western Paris, a relatively undeveloped area, distant from the main railway stations, and that witnessed intense building activity in the late nineteenth century to provide dwellings for a new bourgeoisie and for the services and tradesmen needed to maintain it.

13.11   Immigration to Paris: A Narrative

Enough elements are now available to produce a narrative account of the succession of migratory waves. In the seventeenth century, around 500 000 inhabitants were concentrated in what we have labeled the city center. The main migration flows in the early nineteenth century came from northeastern France, from the Cantal department and, to a lesser degree, from a handful of departments in the center of the country such as Nièvre, Allier, and Loir-et-Cher, as was proved by the distribution of deaths established later by Bertillon. Subsequently, migrants arrived from western France and then from the central band situated on the Nantes–Besançon axis. The departments surrounding the Cantal were the next to join the movement. The occupation of Paris through immigration can now be described since a temporal division can be associated with the geographical division. The first to arrive, before the advent of the railways, were migrants from northeastern France, who came by road. They settled in the neighborhoods close to their points of entry to the city, which accounts for their peripheral location. This also indicates that once their number exceeded a certain level, they could not be accommodated by their fellows who were already present and instead moved on and created new poles of immigrant population. Following them were the migrants from western France. They too settled in peripheral locations, near to the city gates at which they had arrived. Fewer in number, however, they maintained a long-standing pattern of city center residence, more so, proportionally, than migrants from the northeast. Migrants from western France had also begun to make use of the railway, via the Montparnasse and Saint-Lazare stations, whose sectors stand out distinctly. Slightly later, there was an increase in migration from the central Nantes–Besançon band. These migrants used the railway more than their predecessors had, and for this reason settled in the intermediate ring between the city center and the periphery. Migration from this source benefited in particular from the development of western Paris. The fourth wave of immigration came from the Massif Central. Except for those from the Cantal department, these immigrants had little urban space in which to establish themselves since the previous waves already occupied the intermediate ring and the city center. They had no choice but to take up residence in the neighborhoods bordering the present-day *périphérique* (ring road). The last migrant group, that from the south, whose migration was still moderate, retained its central pattern of settlement, extending it into the new western neighborhoods while diversifying slightly in the vicinity of the railway stations (Gare de Lyon and Gare d'Austerlitz) that serve the south. An astonishing parallelism in fact exists between the residential localizations in the departments of the same latitude, symmetrical relative to the Massif Central, for which the attractions of the neighborhoods are identical when the sectors of the Gare de Lyon and of the Gare d'Austerlitz are exchanged. This symmetry persists when the stations no longer play a role in the extreme south. It then becomes virtually an identity, as in the case of the departments of Alpes-Maritimes and Pyrénées-Atlantiques, for example (figure 13.16(a),(b)). This symmetry is in fact a strong justification for the migration narrative. The departments with an analogous position in the population process react in the same way, irrespective of their culture or their sociological specialization.

13.12 Simulation of Urban Immigration

A juxtaposition of snapshots has gradually been transformed into a narrative. How valid is this mechanism? Is it merely one among countless others or does it possess

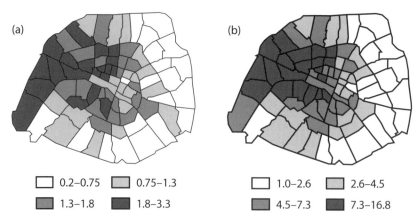

(a)		
☐ 0.2–0.75	▨ 0.75–1.3	
■ 1.3–1.8	■ 1.8–3.3	

(b)		
☐ 1.0–2.6	▨ 2.6–4.5	
■ 4.5–7.3	■ 7.3–16.8	

Figure 13.16. Similarity in attractions of Paris neighborhoods when influence of railway no longer felt: (a) Alpes-Maritimes and (b) Pyrénées-Atlantiques.

a dominant logical coherence? We can try to find the answers with a simulation. The same hypotheses are used as for the migratory movements and applied to a group of fictitious individuals, and the result is compared with the observed distributions of migrants by neighborhood. The quality of the simulation is judged on two criteria: the results must conform to the observations, and its mechanism must be as simple—as parsimonious—as possible.

A simulation along these lines is not hard to construct. It uses the main features from the preceding narrative: the role of the historic city center and of the railway stations and their localization, a succession of migratory waves culminating at particular stations, diffusion away from the initial poles. A single assumption, which is in fact implicit, will be applied: either the immigrants do not already have somewhere to stay, in which case they take accommodation in the vicinity of the station they arrive at, or they know someone in Paris hailing from their region, in which case they look for residence close to this person. This can be the "kin connection," the link with family members already resident at the destination, though more broadly it may involve simply long-standing friends or acquaintances, what are sometimes referred to in French as *pays* (compatriots). The general idea is similar to Hägerstrand's concerning active migrants (the first arrivals) and passive migrants (the followers on, attracted by the precursors and who settle after them). Like Hägerstrand, we take a grid of 50×50 cells that is held to represent the city of Paris. Each cell is a dwelling that can be occupied by one person only. At the start point, the city center, represented by a square of 10×10 cells in the middle of the grid, is occupied by migrants from four regions distributed at random and in roughly equal numbers (for each of the 100 squares of the center, the region of origin of the occupant is selected at random, with equal probability).

Around this initial core, we put three stations. That in the southeast corner represents Gare du Nord and Gare de l'Est; the second, in the middle of the west side, is

Gare Montparnasse; and the last, in the southwest corner, stands for Gare de Lyon and Gare d'Austerlitz. We then simulate three migration waves in strict succession, each of 400 persons, the first culminating at Gare du Nord and Gare de l'Est, the second at Gare Montparnasse, and the last at the two southern stations. The course taken by each of the three waves is simulated in the following manner: each migrant has his or her own trajectory. In half of the cases, the migrant will belong to the current migratory wave and thus originate from region one. He (or she) will arrive at the Gare du Nord and will seek out the first available cell by means of a random walk (i.e., at each step, one of the four squares adjacent to the cell containing the migrant is selected at random; if this new cell is not occupied, the migrant stops there, otherwise random selection of cells continues until an empty one is found). These, then, are the active migrants, and the only constraint placed upon them is their place of arrival, i.e., the start point for their search for resources in the city. The other half of the migrants are attributed the passive role of making contact with one of their fellows. The assumption is also made that they are divided equally between the four regions of origin. The region of origin is selected at random, and then the person who will be the correspondent is randomly selected among all the migrants from this region who are already resident. The newcomer is then put at the abode of the correspondent, from where he makes a random walk to find a free cell in which to settle. The cell of the correspondent thus plays exactly the same role for the passive migrant as the location of the railway station does for the active migrant. When the 400 migrants of the first wave, and hence of the first period, have been distributed, the operation is repeated with the migrants of region two, putting Gare Montparnasse in the place of Gare du Nord, and to conclude, the third wave with the southern stations. No wave comes from the fourth region but a constant and weak inflow.

When the process is complete, the spatial distribution of migrants from the four regions is indicated in figure 13.17. We see that the places of origin are mixed together but that some are preponderant in certain locations. To make this clearer we have divided the city into 8 × 8 large squares containing 25 cells and counted the proportion (percentage) of migrants originating from each of the four regions. We have then drawn the corresponding maps for each region (figure 13.18), which are the analogues of the maps of the attraction by neighborhood of Paris for immigrants from a given department studied at the start of the chapter. We observe that the distribution of migrants from the first three regions that supplied migratory waves is roughly the same as that in reality of migrants from the northeast (analogues of region one in the simulation), from the west and the central band (analogues of region two). Migrants from region three, the most recently arrived, behave in the same way as migrants from the Massif Central and settle on the periphery. But the most interesting result concerns region four, from which there was no migratory wave, simply a steady arrival of passive migrants. It is seen that the majority of these reside in a sector to the north of the center, which is the most distant area from the three railway

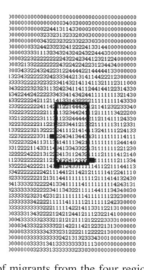

Figure 13.17. Distribution of migrants from the four regions (corresponding to numbers 1–4; the city center is indicated by the dark rectangle and the railway stations by the black squares).

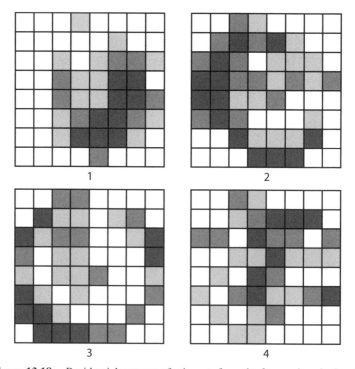

Figure 13.18. Residential patterns of migrants from the four regions in the city (the numbers of the figures correspond to those of the regions).

Table 13.3.

Migrants from	Zones			
	Center	First	Second	Outer
Region one	25	41	32	18
Region two	24	22	40	30
Region three	30	18	24	44
Region four	47	29	27	14

stations and so has not been subject to demographic pressure from them. This is the analogue of Paris's northwestern neighborhoods for migration from southern France, a migration that had not yet developed into a wave but merely provided a continuous stream of passive migrants who were diffused across the remaining free space.

The similarity between the results obtained and the description we have given of migration to Paris can be checked by classifying the migrants from the four regions in concentric zones (square-shaped) of five cells in width around the central square of 100 cells. This gives the attractions (calculated to give the same total number of migrants in each region) in table 13.3.

These characteristics are very nearly those of the types of migration profiles for Paris. In particular, we see that the central position of migrants from region four is due to this region not having produced a migration wave, although this does not prevent migrants spreading into the first two zones. We also see how the third wave of migrants, sandwiched between the first two, has no alternative to residence in the outer periphery. The only significant deviation of the simulation from the observations concerns the weak attraction of the outer (periphery) zone for the first migration wave, whereas in reality the opposite is the case. This is due to the hypothesis of arrival via the railway stations. This defect could be overcome by introducing a specification that allows for arrival by road, for example, by taking the outer limit of the city as the start point for the random walks. We have not introduced this behavior, for while it is always tempting to make new hypotheses that will increase the realism of the simulation and improve the quality of its results, this is done at the expense of parsimony.

More generally, the simulation accurately reproduces the settlement in "onion skin" form that was the image we gave for regional immigration in the neighborhoods of Paris. It is even possible with the simulation to observe phenomena that were not included in the narrative account. Thus, migrants of the first wave do not spread uniquely around the Gare du Nord with an extension toward the periphery, but a group of them goes across the city center and settles in the diametrically opposite sector in the first zone. In fact, most of the distributions of coefficients of attraction by neighborhood for the departments of the northeast, from the Somme to the Meuse, present this particularity. The other types of migration (West, central band, Massif Central, and South) exhibit no such bipolar pattern, any more than do regions 2, 3, and 4 in the simulation.

This simulation validates a simple general idea. The individuals are all in competition for their residential location. They make use of certain advantages—their family and friends—and are subject to determinisms of a more general nature, such as their place of birth or the railway station through which they arrived. These very simple constraints suffice to create large differentiations and organize a geographical distribution of regional origins within Paris itself. It is remarkable that the overall structure of regional residential patterns within Paris *is* determined by such a small number of spatial and temporal constraints. The hypotheses in the simulation can each be criticized for their almost caricatural simplicity: the random walk hypothesis (why not a different process, such as the Lévy flight that will be used in chapter 14, why not preferred directions for moves?); the fact that the three successive waves are of equal size, and that they succeed each other without overlapping; the 50:50 division between active and passive migrants; the hypothesis of one rather than several correspondents for the passive migrants; the flat and isotropic territory of the 50×50 checkerboard and its 10×10 central zone. The list could be extended but the point is clear already. That good results are obtained with a simulation that is so schematic, so simplistic, and so remote from the complexity of the real world, is therefore astonishing. But it is also a powerful argument in favor of analyzing migration as a system of spatial interactions and not as a consequence of mathematical laws. This simulation is merely one among the millions that are possible, almost all of which, however, would give similar results. Behind the simulations, a structural stability is ordering migrant destinations within the capital. What we have found is not the archetype of this structure, but merely one of its facets, which we sought to capture by using simple techniques. The random walk is the simplest and most widely studied of the stochastic processes, particularly in the form of Brownian motion. The decision to have the same number of migrants in each wave and a 50:50 distribution between active and passive migrants is an application of d'Alembert's principle of indifference. The checkerboard pattern and the attribution of one cell to one person constitute the simplest of urban geometries, and so on.

The result of the simulation does, however, supply one profoundly significant piece of information on the migration process. Whereas migration is generally studied from the angle of occupation, sex, and age, these characteristics have not been considered here. The broad outline of the spatial distribution is thus explicable without reference to the regional occupational groups that are familiar in the history of immigration to Paris such as masons from Limousin, chimney sweeps from Savoie, coal merchants from Cantal, café keepers from the Lot and Aveyron, or housemaids from Brittany. Not that these characteristics were without importance for the lived experience of migration and for its social and political consequences. But for what concerns us here, the spatial distribution of migrants within Paris, we find that the more impersonal and general processes that impose their spatial constraint take no account of these subtler social distinctions. Ultimately, spatial phenomena have primarily spatial explanations.

The analyses and models reviewed above, however, are based on an implicit postulate. The total number of out-migrants from a given place and of in-migrants to a given place is a fixed and immutable quantity that is unaffected by the allocation of places of origin and destination. This postulate was accepted because our starting point was marriage models in which marriage was virtually universal. Excessive distance between partners was invoked, however, to explain the frequency of permanent celibacy. So, in the same way, it is not certain that *ex ante* desires to migrate and to receive migrants are verified *ex post*. It may be that their revelation, or else the allocation mechanism, discourages some out-migration, and hence some in-migration. For example, it is not at all certain that the total volume of desired moves will be equal to the total volume of migrants desired in the country under consideration as a whole. Indeed, it would be extraordinary if they did. In other words, total volumes of out-migration E_i and of in-migration I_j are also interacting with, and adjusting to, each other. The opportunities for out-migration from one place and the competition for moves to another place may modify *ex ante* decisions. Stouffer was again among the first to incorporate this competitive dimension, with the model of "intervening opportunities and competing migrants" he put forward in 1960. The next chapter will build on this premise and show the various solutions whereby a match is achieved between total out-migration and in-migration in the same way that the volumes traded on a market are brought into balance.

14

The Four Forms of Internal Migration

The modalities of the migration process are numerous: active and passive migrants, chain migration, stepwise migration, migration networks, temporary, seasonal and journey-to-work migration, and so on. For the purpose of formal modeling of human mobility, however, we are left with only four forms: push and pull, gravity (Ira Lowry 1966), and entropy (Alan Wilson). Each of these types is easily characterized by a mathematical formula, but it is more difficult to explain their relationship to each other and their respective positions within the general category of migration. In a remarkable study, William Alonso constructed a typology that classified the four forms simply as a function of the outflow and inflow elasticities. Unfortunately, Alonso's approach is weakened by two internal inconsistencies. While staying true to his brilliant intuitions, we put forward an alternative framework in which the four forms are not four distinct modalities of migration but four related stages in its construction.

14.1 The Four Forms of Migration

Begin by defining the notation: M_{ij} denotes the migration flow from locality i into locality j; v_i represents the number of people who initially decided to migrate from locality i and w_j the number of vacancies initially available for in-migrants at locality j; t_{ij} represents the attraction of j for i, which is described as being proportional to the number of migrants who decide to move from i to j if the sizes v_i and w_j were all equal.

The first, "pull" form of migration assumes that all the vacancies w_j offered at j will be filled when the constraints are met, i.e., from i proportionally to the expected outflow v_i and to the attractions t_{ij}:

$$M_{ij} = w_j v_i t_{ij} \Big/ \sum_k v_k t_{kj}.$$

By construction, the total inflow into j equals w_j. However, the total outflow from i to all destinations j is not necessarily equal to v_i.

The second form, symmetrical vis-à-vis the first, is "push" migration. This time it is the total outflow v_i expected at i that occurs in proportion to the vacancies at

j, w_j, and to the attractions t_{ij}:

$$M_{ij} = w_j v_i t_{ij} \Big/ \sum_k v_k t_{kj}.$$

As in the previous case, the fact that the flows out all of the localities i satisfy the formula.

The third form of migration is the gravity-model form, built on the premise that the conditions of outflow from i, of inflow to j, and of attraction are the only influences on migration, independently of any other possible migration between all the localities i and j. Hence it is written

$$M_{ij} = w_j v_i t_{ij}.$$

The "gravity" label is usually applied to this model because the attraction t_{ij} is very often a function of distance, and more specifically a negative exponential function of the distance between i and j. The early authors who fitted this model (Reilly 1931; Zipf 1941; Young 1924; Stewart 1948) frequently obtained an exponent with a value of -2, which made migration comparable in formal terms with gravitational force in Newton's formula, with the w_j and v_i being assumed to play the role of masses.

The fourth, "entropy" form postulates migration between all the localities i and j, such that all the predicted outflows, and no more, occur and all the offered vacancies/available opportunities, and no more, are filled, while respecting the proportionality of the flows to the numbers leaving and arriving and to the attraction. This is achieved by a double proportionality of the migration flows out of i and into j

$$M_{ij} = \frac{w_j v_i t_{ij}}{O_i C_j},$$

where O_i and C_j are two factors, one depending on i, the other on j, determined by the conditions imposed:

$$O_i = \sum_j \frac{w_j t_{ij}}{C_j} \quad \text{and} \quad C_j = \sum_i \frac{v_i t_{ij}}{O_i}.$$

In the appendix (section 14.11.1) we show that this system has a single solution and indicate how it is related to a maximum likelihood estimation.

Although these four models use the same elements, at first sight there is no connection between them. True, one might note that the entropy model retains the offers of origin and the demands of destination, that the push–pull models retain only one of them, and the gravity model none at all. But this is a fairly superficial observation. When we speak of linking these four forms to each other we in fact mean finding intermediate forms. This was the achievement of William Alonso.

14.2   The Alonso Model

In Alonso's conceptualization, migration decisions and the supply of destination vacancies are made to vary as a function of the opportunities available and of the degrees of competition existing. We will adopt a general formulation to develop it, and then revert to the specifications used by Alonso. The assumption is made that each would-be migrant has O_i destination opportunities, O_i being greater or less than unity. If $O_i < 1$, a proportion of individuals abandon their project and only $f(O_i)$ decide to migrate. If $O_i > 1$, new candidates for migration come forward proportional to $f(O_i)$. The same reasoning applies for the destination, hence for in-migration. But here we are dealing with immigrants in competition for the same vacancy, as a proportion C_j, per vacancy offered. Similarly, if this proportion is less than 1, vacancies will be withdrawn from supply, while on the other hand, if it exceeds 1, new vacancies will be offered, in both cases as a proportion $g(C_j)$. It can be seen that f and g are two contracting functions about 1. If $O_i < 1$, $f(O_i)$ will also be less than 1 but greater than O_i, and if $O_i > 1$, $f(O_i)$ will be less than it but greater than 1. The same conditions are set for C_j and $g(C_j)$. They can be summarized in set theory notation by

$$f(A) \subset A \quad \text{and} \quad g(A) \subset A \quad \text{with } 1 \in A.$$

Concretely, f and g measure the elasticity of migration supply and demand, respectively. This elasticity can vary, though Alonso takes it as constant.

Under these assumptions, migration, which a priori would be $M_{ij} = w_j v_i t_{ij}$, will be modified (reduced or increased) in the proportion $f(O_i)/O_i$ at the origin and $g(C_j)/C_j$ at the destination. Thus it will be

$$M_{ij} = t_{ij} v_i w_j \frac{f(O_i)}{O_i} \frac{g(C_j)}{C_j}.$$

By construction, total outflow from locality i will be $v_i f(O_i)$, and total inflow to locality j will equal $w_j g(C_j)$. Expressing these two identities on the basis of the migration flows M_{ij}, we obtain two series of formulas with which to determine the values of the O_i and the C_j:

$$O_i = \sum_j w_j t_{ij} \frac{g(C_j)}{C_j} \quad \text{and} \quad C_j = \sum_i v_i t_{ij} \frac{f(O_i)}{O_i}.$$

It must be stressed that the O_i and the C_j are not determined a priori but depend directly on the values taken by the other parameters v_i, w_j, and t_{ij}. They express the overall interactions in the system of n localities under consideration.

14.3 Constant Elasticities

Alonso took particular functions for f and g, those corresponding to a constant elasticity:

$$f(O_i) = O_i^\alpha \quad \text{and} \quad g(C_j) = C_j^\beta.$$

These two functions meet the required conditions as they are contracting about 1 when $0 < \alpha < 1$ and $0 < \beta < 1$.

Migration flows then take the form $M_{ij} = t_{ij} v_i w_j O_i^{\alpha-1} C_j^{\beta-1}$ and the relations between opportunities and competition become

$$O_i = \sum_j t_{ij} w_j C_j^{\beta-1} \quad \text{and} \quad C_j = \sum_i t_{ij} v_i O_i^{\alpha-1}.$$

By taking simple values—the simplest possible, in fact—i.e., 0 or 1, for the exponents α and β, we get the four forms of migration.

(i) $\alpha = 1$ and $\beta = 1$. The migration formula is written

$$M_{ij} = w_j v_i t_{ij}.$$

The opportunities and competition are total out-emigration and in-migration calculated from the v_i and w_j: $O_i = \sum t_{ij} w_j$ and $C_j = \sum t_{ij} v_i$. This is logical since with elasticity equal to 1, the answer is exactly equal to demand for both outflows and inflows.

(ii) $\alpha = 0$ and $\beta = 0$. The migration formula becomes

$$M_{ij} = w_j v_i t_{ij} / (O_i C_j),$$

i.e., exactly that in the case of entropy. In the absence of elasticity, the predicted outflows and expected inflows do not change and have exactly this volume. The opportunities and competition are the two series of coefficients solving the equations:

$$O_i = \sum_j \frac{t_{ij} w_j}{C_j} \quad \text{and} \quad C_j = \sum_i \frac{t_{ij} v_i}{O_i}.$$

We have already encountered this system and discussed it in relation to the entropy model, for which we know that in general there is a unique solution.

(iii) $\alpha = 0$ and $\beta = 1$. In this case migration is written

$$M_{ij} = w_j v_i t_{ij} / O_i,$$

with $O_i = \sum_j t_{ij} w_j$, which, after substitution into the previous formula, gives

$$M_{ij} = w_j v_i t_{ij} \Big/ \sum_k w_k t_{kj}.$$

This is the formula for "push" migration. In this case, the outflows are those that were expected (hence zero elasticity) and the vacancies at the destination adapt exactly, hence elasticity is equal to 1.

(iv) $\alpha = 1$ and $\beta = 0$. This case is symmetrical to the previous one, with $M_{ij} = t_{ij} v_i w_j / C_j$ and $C_j = \sum_i v_i t_{ij}$, hence substituting into the migration formula we have

$$M_{ij} = w_j v_i t_{ij} \bigg/ \sum_k v_k t_{kj}.$$

This is the formula for "pull" migration, in which the elasticity of inflows is zero and that of outflows is equal to one.

The four forms of migration are thus the four cases that enclose the model, forming the four extremities of the domain of possible values of α and β. Within this domain, a system of migration flows M_{ij} is obtained with any pair of values α and β. Our objective has thus been reached. The models can be linked to each other through a continuous number of intermediary models. The four forms of migration produce an infinite number of forms depending on the differences in elasticity at the origin and destination.

14.4 The Alonso Model as an Individual Process

The previous model can be criticized for being a macroscopic and static equilibrium model, whereas migration is an individual process. Can such a process be modeled? The answer is yes, if we postulate that the actual physical move is preceded by an exchange of information between those wishing to migrate and those—friends, family members, firms, or government bodies regulating mobility—with vacancies available to accommodate them. We shall therefore attempt to establish a connection between the *ex ante* knowledge of individuals and their subsequent decision to migrate. To do this we simplify the model to two localities, hence to two flows, and consider just one of them (as they are strictly independent in the Alonso model), which we denote M. These migration flows will depend similarly on four simple quantities, v, w, O, C, which are analogous to the same quantities with subscripts i and j. Finally, t_{ij} is no longer needed since only a single flow is being considered. Reasoning will be on the general form with the f and g functions, not on the particular case of constant elasticities that is solved immediately. Hence we have

$$M = vw \frac{f(O)}{O} \frac{g(C)}{C}.$$

M is also equal to total migration at the origin, $vf(O)$ and, at the destination, to $wg(C)$. Start from any two values of O and C that consist of immediate representations that individuals have of the opportunities and competition, and call them O_i and C_i. A priori, migration M calculated from these values and migration at the destination $wg(C_i)$ will not be equal. We call k_2 the amount by which migration M exceeds or falls short of migration counted at the destination, both calculated with

O_i and C_i. We have

$$k_2 = \frac{M}{wg(C_1)} = \frac{vf(O_1)}{O_1 C_1}.$$

Put $C_2 = k_2 C_1$. We immediately have $C_2 = vf(O_1)/O_1$, which is exactly the recurrence formula used to calculate O and C from each other alternatively. The competition that was originally perceived at level C_1 modifying the vacancies offered proportional to $g(C_1)$ is now perceived at level C_2, giving a new appreciation of the modification $g(C_2)$. So we replace C_1 by C_2 in the formula giving M and then turn to the other side, that of outflows and opportunities, and repeat the reasoning. These successive iterations converge and it can be verified empirically that the convergence is rapid (section 14.11.2). An individual behavior can therefore lead to the Alonso model. Before going any further, it must be noted that this reasoning is only valid if we first accept the initial formula specifying migration M as a function of O, C, u, w, and the possibility of progressively correcting expectations at the origin and destination, for example, by means of letters, messages, and telephone calls between those wishing to leave and those who potentially will receive them.

A faster reasoning that leads to the same result is to say that, knowing $M = vw(f(O_1)/O_1)(g(C_1)/C_1)$ and the inflow $wg(C_1)$, we take C_2 such that the two are equal, hence

$$wg(C_2) = vw\frac{f(O_1)}{O_1}\frac{g(C_2)}{C_2},$$

or, after simplifying, $C_2 = vf(O_1)/O_1$. Repeating the operation at the origin gives $O_2 = wg(C_2)/C_2$, and so on. These are still the formulas of the algorithm. This second approach is more logical and faster than the first but since we no longer describe how the value C_2 is reached, the individual viewpoint is lost.

14.5 The Model's Inconsistencies

The elegance of the solution produced by Alonso no doubt explains why we have disregarded difficulties at several points in the reasoning. These will in fact raise awkward and probably insurmountable problems.

Let us start with a dimensionality issue. What would happen to the formulas if we measured migration not by numbers of individuals but by thousands of individuals, i.e., if we change the unit of measurement? To answer this we will limit ourselves to the simple case used in the previous section. We denote the measurements in thousands by subscript 1. We will have $M_1 = 0.001M$, $v_1 = 0.0001v$, and $w_1 = 0.001w$. We copy these equivalences into the formulas used to define migration. At the destination, we will have $M_1 = w_1 g(C_1)$ and $M = wg(C)$. Hence, $0.001M = 0.001wg(C_1)$, that is, $M = wg(C_1)$. From this we derive $g(C_1) = g(C)$. Since the function g is monotonic increasing, $C_1 = C$. The same reasoning can be applied for O_1 and O, leading to $O_1 = O$. Now take the formula giving the migration flow directly

$$M_1 = v_1 w_1 \frac{f(O_1)}{O_1} \frac{g(C_1)}{C_1}.$$

Replace the terms with subscript 1 by the corresponding terms without a subscript (that is, measured by numbers of individuals, not by thousands). Depending on the identities obtained for O_1 and C_1, we get

$$0.001 M = (0.001v)(0.001w)\frac{f(O)}{O}\frac{g(C)}{C},$$

hence $M = 0.001vw(f(O)/O)(g(C)/C)$, or one thousandth of the normal value. The same discrepancy would appear no matter what the change to the measurement unit. As regards dimension, therefore, Alonso's formulas are not coherent. This is a fatal defect for a theory. One might hope to avoid it by reintroducing the attraction t_{ij} with a dimension inversely proportional to the measurement of the number of individuals. But the difficulty then arises of not knowing which argument to use for the dimensions of this quantity, bringing the realization that it was introduced hastily without reflection on its status.

In fact, attempts to rescue the theory are pointless since it is undermined by a second and certainly more serious inconsistency. To show this, let us take the simple case already used in the previous sections and put $v = w$. Alonso's constant elasticity assumption is also adopted. It is then easy to calculate the values for opportunity O and competition C:

$$C = vO^{\alpha-1} \quad \text{and} \quad O = vC^{\beta-1},$$

whence we derive

$$C = v^{\alpha/(\alpha+\beta-\alpha\beta)} \quad \text{and} \quad O = v^{\beta/(\alpha+\beta-\alpha\beta)}.$$

From this we deduce the value for the migration flow

$$M = vv^{\alpha\beta/(\alpha+\beta-\alpha\beta)} = v^{(\alpha+\beta)/(\alpha+\beta-\alpha\beta)}.$$

So, although there is an overall correspondence between the desired outflows and requested inflows, the interplay of opportunities and competition will modify them significantly. If, for example, $\alpha = 0.5$ and $\beta = 0.5$, the exponent of v will be 4/3. If $v = 27\,000$, then $M = 810\,000$, which is totally excessive. It is not feasible to postulate a subtle adjustment of supply and demand through the circulation of information and at the same time obtain this distortion in which the notion of reception capacity w and that of numbers leaving v become largely meaningless if they can simultaneously be multiplied by a factor of 30.

14.6 Find the Mistake

We must start again from the basic formula for migration

$$M_{ij} = t_{ij} v_i w_j \frac{f(O_i)}{O_i} \frac{g(C_j)}{C_j}$$

and examine each of its elements separately.

The sizes or volumes v_i and w_j constitute a basic piece of information. They can be understood in the following way: if one starts with as many places of origins as there are individuals, those with the same coefficient of attractiveness t_{ij} can be put together.

The coefficients of attraction t_{ij} raised a problem of dimension. However, if they are symmetrical ($t_{ij} = t_{ji}$), they take a relative value for the aggregate flows. If we wish to give them an absolute value, they can be divided by the sum of the v_i or w_j.

The real problem probably comes from the simultaneous multiplication of the flows by $f(O_i)/O_i$ and $g(C_j)/C_j$. One of the two reductions could suffice on its own since individuals may anticipate that those proposing vacancies will reduce or increase their supply and, conversely, that those looking will take account of the opportunities available. The reason for the double reduction is probably to be sought not in a rational behavior but in a tradition established by the two seminal articles by Samuel Stouffer on "intervening opportunities" and "competing migrants." In his numerical application, Stouffer proposed dividing the opportunities existing in one locality by these two quantities. Alonso uses the same terms of opportunity and competition as Stouffer and performs the same divisions.

The problem appears most clearly at the level of the process, not of the final equilibrium formula. Three processes are in fact possible:

(i) The process as it has been described, with a comparison of migration flows M and, alternatively, the total inflows and outflows at one locality. From the discrepancy between the two we derive new values for C_n or O_n and enter these into the migration formula. This process is convergent, but it assumes what it is supposed to explain, i.e., the migration formula. The process is in fact independent of the point of origin that may be different from the product of v and w. Since this point of origin does not have to be selected, the algorithm gives a variable result, as a function of its point of origin, as for any linear convergent series.

(ii) An alternative reasoning is possible. At each stage, the flow M is compared with the inflows and outflows alternatively. Instead of redefining C_n and O_n, we seek to eliminate the remaining discrepancy by setting $C_{n+1} = M_n/(wg(C_n))$. We apply the contracting function g to this discrepancy C_{n+1} and multiply migration flow M by this proportionality factor $g(C_{n+1})/C_{n+1}$. We do the same on the side of outflows. This in fact corresponds to making migration equal, alternatively, to inflows and then to outflows.

(iii) A variant of the preceding process is to compare migration not at the present stage of the inflows but at their initial stage, w, from which to derive the new value of C (then do the same thing for outflows and for O). It can be shown that in the two latter cases the result no longer depends on the initial state, though unfortunately the migration flow oscillates between a final value for outflows and a final value for inflows. An example will be found in the appendix (section 14.11.3) for the case of constant elasticity.

This situation is more serious than it appears, since choosing a priori the quantities t_{ij} generally prevents a solution in which inflows and outflows would correspond, i.e., in which, after changing the v_i and w_j, the push and pull constraints could both be satisfied. All the push movements from the places of origin would have to correspond to the opportunities at each destination, and vice versa. This is written

$$\sum_i w_j v_i t_{ij} \Big/ \sum_k w_k t_{ik} = w_j$$

i.e.,

$$\sum_i \left(v_i t_{ij} \Big/ \sum_k w_k t_{ik} \right) = 1.$$

Each of the denominators depends only on the subscript i and can thus be written A_i setting $a_i = v_i / A_i$. A matrix condition defining the a_i is obtained by multiplying the unit vector by the inverse of the matrix for the degrees of attraction t_{ij}. The result is not necessarily positive. In the appendix (section 14.11.3) counterexamples are given for the case of three localities with migration flows between them. So the idea must be abandoned that after a process of adjustment between the supply of migrants and vacancies for them, the new values of w_j and v_i converge to an equilibrium. Such processes are generally unstable and yield chaotic results, which is not surprising since the equations for the process are quadratic, as, for example, in the dynamic processes that engender chaos (that of Lorenz, for instance). In fact, even if a solution existed, it would depend only on the values of t_{ij} and not on the v_i and w_j that would play no further role, which is unrealistic. Hence there is a latent contradiction between the three initial elements that characterize migration flows. The most fragile is the attraction t_{ij} that depends not on the characteristics of the two localities considered but on their spatial position. However, countless empirical observations have confirmed the generality of the gravity model, i.e., of the formulas in which attraction is a function of distance, and more exactly a simple function, since it varies as a negative power of distance.

14.7   Saving the Spirit of the Model

It would be a pity to abandon the Alonso model on account of the inconsistencies exposed above. The model introduces two valuable ideas that are worth retaining and developing in a slightly modified formalization. The first is that of not keeping the intentions v_i and w_j fixed *ex ante* and instead having their interaction lead to an *ex post* equilibrium in which the sum of outflows decided will equal the sum of vacancies made available. The second involves distributing the flows M_{ij} in such a way that when summed at localities i and j they give the sum of outflows and inflows *ex post*. Alonso actually refers to the distinction between *ex ante* and *ex post* in support of his reasoning that, far from undermining, it strengthens. We will examine these two ideas, not simultaneously like Alonso but in two separate stages.

14.8 Determining Inflows and Outflows *Ex Post*

Denote the above by capital letters, V_i and W_j. To obtain them from the v_i and w_j *ex ante*, we expose the principle of an adjustment model for the case of single migration M. Denote by v, w, V, W the inflows and outflows *ex ante* and *ex post* in this case, and form a sequence obeying the following rules: at each stage, the inflows and outflows are compared with the inflows and outflows at the preceding stage and the difference between the two is reduced by means of the contracting functions f and g used earlier. In this way, the interval containing the inflows and outflows at one stage is necessarily contained within the interval of the preceding stage. It is then easy to show that the sequence converges to an equilibrium point that is the *ex post* value of V and W (they must be equal).

In mathematical notation it is written

$$v_n = v_{n-1} f(w_{n-1}/v_{n-1}) \quad \text{and} \quad w_n = w_{n-1} g(v_{n-1}/w_{n-1}).$$

Ultimately, $w_{n-1}/v_{n-1} = 1$ and the two equations become identities.

This simple reasoning cannot be extended to the case of n localities on account of the chaotic system encountered in the last section. But this adjustment process can be applied to each migration treated in isolation. It is assumed that an initial decision is taken for a migration between locality i and j and that, secondarily, the adjustment of supply and demand is achieved by constraining the predicted outflows and inflows, as was done for the case of a single flow in isolation. For the case where the elasticities are constant, we end up with

$$M_{ij} = w_{,j} v_i t_{ij} \left/ \left(\left(\sum_k v_k t_{kj} \right)^{\alpha/(\alpha+\beta)} \left(\sum_k w_k t_{ik} \right)^{\beta/(\alpha+\beta)} \right) \right. .$$

By construction, the new values of v_i and w_j will be obtained by summing all the flows M_{ij} for the origins i and the destinations j, respectively.

It is perhaps correct to assume that migrants each have a specific destination in mind that they try to obtain in preference to all others. From the opposite side, however, those offering vacancies in the urban destination tend to be less set on any particular locality of origin, except in the case of family migration or of using established migrants' contacts (i.e., in the case of passive migrants). An alternative and more balanced hypothesis assumes that a proportion p of the persons of locality i will migrate as part of a push migration and that the remaining proportion, $1 - p$, will be drawn from the outside, i.e., in a pull migration. In this case, by definition of these two migration types, the flow between locality i and locality j will be the sum of these two push and pull migrations:

$$M_{ij} = w_{,j} v_i t_{ij} \left((1-p) \middle/ \left(\sum_k v_k t_{kj} \right) + p \middle/ \left(\sum_k w_k t_{ik} \right) \right).$$

In the same way as in the previous case, the total inflows and outflows in all the localities are reconstituted by summing these elementary flows.

Other methods can be imagined for combining push and pull effects, and hence for remaining within the approach developed by Alsonso. In every case, however, the gravity-model formulation, that is, the proportionality of the flows to the new sizes of origin and destination, W_j and V_i, and to the attractions t_{ij}, will be lost. Restoring it requires calculation of new flows M_{ij} such that they are proportional to the outflows, inflows, and attractions, W_j, V_i, and t_{ij}, and that the summations by origin and destination are equal to the corresponding outflows and inflows. This is recognizable as exactly similar to Wilson's statement of the problem, i.e., the entropy model. On this subject, attention must be drawn to an important point that was previously left vague: the entropy model can only be solved if the total sum of outflows V_i is equal to the total sum of inflows W_j. It was wrong therefore to include the entropy model in the Alonso typology, since this condition would have to be met, which it is not in the general case when, as Alonso reminds us, outflows and inflows *ex ante* are fixed by local conditions independently of the overall equilibrium.

14.9   The Entropy Model as a Process

It remains to explain what simple migration behavior is described by the entropy model. To do this we need simply imagine that, initially, migrants aim for the vacancies j from i proportional to $t_{ij} W_j$. If the sum of these planned flows does not equal the outflows V_i, they readjust their objective proportional to M_{ij}, such that

$$V_i = M_{1,i} \sum_j t_{ij} W_j V_i,$$

that is,

$$1 = M_{1,i} \sum_j t_{ij} W_j.$$

We then turn our attention to the inflows, for which an analogous reasoning leads to reevaluating the intentions proportional to N_{ij}:

$$W_j = N_{1,j} \sum_i t_{ij} W_j V_i M_{1,i},$$

that is,

$$\frac{1}{N_{1,j}} = \sum_i t_{ij} V_i M_{1,i}.$$

At the following stage we obtain

$$V_i = M_{2,i} \sum_j t_{ij} N_{1,j} W_j V_i,$$

that is,

$$\frac{1}{M_{2,i}} = \sum_j t_{ij} N_{1,j} W_j.$$

What we have here is exactly the algorithm for solving the entropy model that converges to the equilibrium solution. The result can therefore be justified by behavior comprising a succession of adjustments. Note that the limits M_i and N_j are the inverses of the opportunities and competition defined earlier.

14.10 The Value of Conceptual Migration Models

The foregoing development has many consequences and at several levels. First, it shifts the study of internal migration away from an overly simple dilemma between push and pull. Indeed, instead of push or pull migration, commentators frequently speak of push or pull effects. All possible combinations of intensity for the two effects are imaginable in the formalization offered here. At a very general level this makes it possible to get away from the simple ideas of invasion (the push effect only) and of recruitment (the pull effect only). Adding to this first advantage is the possibility of abandoning the *ex ante* quantities, v_i and w_j, in favor of *ex post* quantities that express the outcome of the confrontation between supply and demand. The situation here is in fact reminiscent of equilibrium in a market. In the simple case of a single migration M, the two problems can be equated simply by assuming that the number of outflows *ex ante* is an increasing function of a price p that summarizes the conditions at the origin, and likewise for the number of inflows, a decreasing function of this same price, so that $v = f(p)$ and $w = g(p)$, with the unique equilibrium being established at the point of intersection of the rising and falling curves. Finding the equivalent in market terms for the system of migration flows between n localities is more difficult but can be done by setting restrictions, t_{ij}, on accessibility.

A second benefit from this method lies in introducing the idea of a process that leads to equilibrium rather than postulating this equilibrium on mathematical grounds. In other words, the equilibrium is derived from the behavior of the actors as formalized by the rules of the process.

A third, more concrete advantage is that of allowing examination of prospective questions of the form: What migration flows might result if openings (for example, jobs) are provided in a locality or on the contrary if they are shut down? How would the system as a whole react to a local disturbance? This is easily operationalized by considering that the last known flows give the *ex ante* values of the outflows v_i and inflows w_j and allow direct estimation of the t_{ij}.

But the most valuable feature of this method is its classificatory dimension. Alonso's method permitted the establishment of a simple typology of the four migration types and the introduction of an infinite number of intermediate types, and with this method too it is possible to attribute a place to each type and produce intermediate types. But the way this is done is very different, hierarchical rather than typological. The four models can in fact be considered as belonging to three different stages in the formalizing of migration flows. The first model, the gravity model, is simply a statement of measurement: if the coefficients of attraction t_{ij} of m persons to n positions are identical because the former live in a given locality and the latter are in another given locality, the migration flow will be proportional to them and to the product of m and n through a simple effect of statistical concentration in the two origin and destination localities. Thus the gravity model describes not a form of behavior but a category of measurement, a metrological formula.

The second stage is the passage from the outflows and inflows *ex ante* to their *ex post* values. It is here that a compromise is selected between the push effect and the pull effect, of which the extreme cases are the flows labeled push migration and pull migration. At this stage therefore we recover two of the four forms of migration but also and most importantly the possibility of introducing intermediary forms through the choice of the functions f and g, the simplest of which adopt Alonso's constant elasticity assumption.

Lastly, once the outflows and inflows *ex post*, V_i and W_j, have been obtained, the entropy model is applied. This fourth form is in fact a mode of distributing between the different localities in a way that respects the values t_{ij}.

The four extreme cases of the Alonso model, located at the four extremities of the domain $\{0 < \alpha < 1, 0 < \beta < 1\}$, have thus been replaced by a sequence of three stages. The first serves to set the measurement mode (metrology) through the gravity model. The second determines the volume of outflows and inflows with the division between push and pull effects. The third and last, the entropy model, allocates the elementary flows between any locality i and any locality j while respecting the constraints from the first two stages.

A large literature has been devoted to evaluating the capacity of the various migration models to describe reality. It has been seen here that these models are viewpoints on migration. They are not mutually exclusive but combine to form a whole, in the way that architectural drawings made to show plan, section, and elevation complement each other. But instead of producing several spatial views, they supply several temporal views, so many stages in the process of forming and formalizing migration.

14.11 Appendix

14.11.1 Entropy Model

The system of equations for O_i and C_j is solved by using the two sets of equations in turn, to obtain the opportunities from the competition, then the competition from the new values for the opportunities. The proof of the convergence of the iterations and of the uniqueness of the solution in the general case was given in a different context by Baccharach in 1967. There is an analogous system of equations when we wish to estimate exact marginal distributions from observed distributions when the coefficients of distribution for each category are known. For example, assume that the distribution N_{ij} of social categories by region is known and that fertility has been measured separately by region F_i and by social category H_j. If we want to eliminate the bias produced by the social differences between regions and obtain the unbiased fertility values Φ_i and Ψ_j, we have the following systems of equations, under the assumption that relative fertility differentials by social class are the same in all regions, so that fertility is the product of Φ_i and Ψ_j:

$$F_i = \Phi_i \sum_j N_{ij} \Psi_j \bigg/ \sum_j N_{ij} \quad \text{and} \quad H_j = \Psi_j \sum_i N_{ij} \Phi_i \bigg/ \sum_i N_{ij}.$$

This system reduces to that of opportunities and competition simply by changing N_{ij} to $F_i H_j n_{ij} / \sum N_{ij}$. It will also be noted that the first iteration corresponds to the standard population method, often used in statistics to compare indicators measured on populations with different structures.

But the value of the entropy model goes beyond this. It can be derived from a maximum likelihood estimation and thus be considered as the result of an optimization. Indeed, this is why it was given this name. Alan Wilson derived the entropy model as the most likely allocation of migration flows subject to constraints on v_i and w_j and to an additional constraint fixing the total transport cost C from the elementary costs, c_{ij}, of each migration:

$$\sum_i \sum_j c_{ij} M_{ij} = C.$$

This property is demonstrated by seeking the maximum likelihood of the distribution of migration flows when the individuals are assumed to be subject to a multinomial distribution allocating them between all possible migration flows. Its end result is to establish a ratio between the c_{ij} and the coefficients of attraction t_{ij} from the formulas given earlier for the general model

$$t_{ij} = \exp(-\lambda c_{ij}),$$

where λ is a constant fixed by the system of equations. The costs c_{ij} comprise the transport and expenditure occasioned by the residential relocation. If they differ sensibly according to the pair of localities considered and if the coefficient λ is not too small, the t_{ij} vary considerably between pairs of localities, which is consistent with observations that show orders of magnitude ranging from 1 to over 1000.

The main difference between the entropy model and previous models is that the coefficients t_{ij} are no longer given a priori but are modified by the numbers present. It can be imagined, as Sullivan (1971) proposed, that optimization applies not to the probability of observing such or such allocation of migration flows (maximum likelihood) but to the total cost of migrating that must then be minimized. The problem in this case is one of linear programming (optimizing a linear function of variables, the migration flows M_{ij}, subject to a set of linear constraints). The solution will be a point on the convex hull defined by the functions and will therefore comprise a certain number of zero migration flows, something that has never been observed. Sullivan overcame this problem by assuming migration flows to be organized into a series of separate markets corresponding to each occupational activity, i.e., labor markets that are compartmentalized and not the same. The solution that yielded a zero migration in one market could yield a positive migration in another, so that the sum of migration flows for all the markets together became positive. This is ingenious, but no such compartmentalization has ever been observed, even when data are available on a specific occupation, of zero migration flows between two sizeable localities. Moreover, it is difficult to imagine what mechanism could constrain total migration to respect this minimum cost objective. The operation of an invisible hand is not a possibility. The minimization constraint is more realistic than that of fixed total cost set by Wilson but it leads to a dead end, while his idea produced a tendency to maximization of entropy comparable with that observed in gas mixtures. It seems more realistic to relate migration to a constrained maximum disorder—which is what entropy measures—than to an unlikely order imposed by linear programming under the constraint of minimizing the total cost of migration.

14.11.2 Instability of the Processes Corresponding to the Alonzo Model

In the last two alternatives of the Alonso model, the process does not stabilize and oscillates between two values, one for inflows, the other for outflows. Show this for the case of constant elasticity. At each stage, the ratio of migration M to inflows or outflows, alternatively, is calculated, using the relation $C_{n+1} = M_n/(wg(C_n))$, respectively O_{n+1}, then, applying to this difference C_{n+1} the contracting function g, we multiply migration M by this proportionality factor $g(C_{n+1})/C_{n+1}$ (the same for $f(O_{n+1})/O_{n+1}$). Because f and g are the powers α and β of the O and C, the sequence of migrations and the inflows and outflows thus calculated is the product of powers of initial M, v, and w. Let a_n, b_n, c_n be these powers for the outflows, and d_n, e_n, f_n for the inflows. Applying the formula first to the outflows and then to the inflows, we have

$$a_{n+1} = (d_n - a_n)\alpha, \quad b_{n+1} = (e_n - b_n)\alpha + 1, \quad c_{n+1} = (f_n - c_n)\alpha,$$

and

$$d_{n+1} = (a_{n+1} - d_n)\beta, \quad e_{n+1} = (b_{n+1} - e_n)\beta, \quad f_{n+1} = (c_{n+1} - f_n)\beta + 1.$$

Grouping two by two the equations of each line in the same position, we obtain three double sequences (a_n, d_n), (b_n, e_n), and (c_n, f_n). The 2×2 matrices that define these sequences have two characteristic values with modulus less than unity. These sequences converge therefore to their constant terms that are represented by the corresponding capital letters. These terms are zero for the first sequence, which means that the power of M in the formula for inflows and outflows tends to zero, and thus that the influence of the initial condition M disappears. For the second double sequence, the constant terms B and E must satisfy

$$B = (E - B)\alpha + 1 \quad \text{and} \quad E = (B - E)\beta,$$

that is,

$$B = \frac{1 + \beta}{1 + \alpha + \beta} \quad \text{and} \quad E = \frac{\beta}{1 + \alpha + \beta}.$$

Similarly, for the third double sequence we will have

$$C = \frac{\alpha}{1 + \alpha + \beta} \quad \text{and} \quad F = \frac{1 + \alpha}{1 + \alpha + \beta}.$$

If it is recalled that B and C are the powers of v and w in the expression for outflows and E and F those of the expression for inflows, it can be seen that they do not coincide and that the migration flow M oscillates between the two values.

The same result would be obtained, and more simply, if the third process is used.

14.11.3 Impossibility of Equilibrium under Push and Pull Conditions in the Case of Three Localities

Designate by a, b, and c the three attractions between, respectively, localities 1 and 2, 1 and 3, and 2 and 3. Begin from the formula that is to be verified in the case of equilibrium,

$$\sum_i \left(v_i t_{ij} \Big/ \sum_k w_k t_{ik} \right) = 1,$$

and put $A_i = \sum_k w_k t_{ik}$. The equation becomes

$$\sum_i \frac{v_i t_{ij}}{A_i} = 1$$

and, when setting $X_i = v_i / A_i$,

$$\sum_i X_i t_{ij} = 1.$$

Let there be three equations to determine the three values of the three X. The system has a simple solution that gives

$$X_1 = \frac{b+c-a}{2bc}, \qquad X_2 = \frac{a+c-b}{2ac}, \qquad X_3 = \frac{b+a-c}{2ba}.$$

For the solution to exist, the three Xs must be strictly positive, which is not the case for all the possible values of a, b, c. For some values of the attractions, therefore, there is no equilibrium.

14.11.4 Adjustment of Outflows and Inflows for a Single Migration Flow

Start from the intended outflows v and the expected vacancies at destination w and assume that we are in the case of constant elasticities α and β. On each side, the interaction of supply and demand will play out at constant elasticity, in such a way that the numbers of out-migrants and expected vacancies will adjust to the values:

$$v_1 = w^\alpha v^{1-\alpha} \quad \text{and} \quad w_1 = v^\beta w^{1-\beta}.$$

From these new values we will proceed in the same way. As the values v_i and w_i fall strictly between v and w, a convergence will occur to a limiting value that is identical on both sides. If we name $E(n)$ and $F(n)$ the exponents of v and w in v_n and $G(n)$ and $H(n)$ their corresponding items in w_n, we will have the following relations:

$$E(n+1) = (1-\alpha)E(n) + \alpha G(n),$$
$$G(n+1) = \beta E(n) + (1-\beta)G(n),$$

and similar relations for the F and H when changing α and β.

These are two-dimensional linear sequences for which we verify that the two characteristic values are 1 and $1-\alpha-\beta$. The latter is less than 1 because α and β both are, so, ultimately, the exponent will be the value of the coefficient of the characteristic value unity. It can be determined by setting the two equations of the sequence for the first two values. Letting a and b be the coefficients of the two characteristic values, for $E(0)$ and $E(1)$ we have

$$a+b=1 \quad \text{and} \quad a+b(1-\alpha-\beta) = 1-\alpha t.$$

So the coefficient a of the characteristic value unity is equal to $a = \beta/(\alpha+\beta)$, and, for the exponent c of w at the limit of the number of vacancies expected, in the same way we find $c = \alpha/(\alpha+\beta)$. Ultimately, therefore, the outflows and the expected places have the same value, which is the geometric mean weighted by α and β of the initial v and w.

It might be thought that this very simple method could be extended without difficulty to the case of n localities, but in section 14.11.3 it was seen that unfortunately this is not so.

15
Densities

On the face of it nothing could be simpler than population density. It is obtained by dividing total population by an area of land. Population density thus measured is 110 inhabitants per square kilometer in France and 32 in the United States. Things become more complicated when it is noted that this is an average figure masking wide regional and local contrasts, as between Paris and the sparsely populated French regions or between the east coast megalopolii and the Rocky Mountains. It might be thought that the size of the differences could be accounted for by using an index of variability, for dispersion or concentration, but this is impossible because geographical territory is continuous in nature and can be subdivided in countless and equally legitimate ways. Consider the example of the Lorenz curve commonly used to measure the degree of concentration or dispersion and construct it for France by using the population of each of the country's 36 525 communes (the smallest French territorial and administrative subdivision) at the six censuses between 1962 and 1999. After ranking all the communes in order of decreasing density, we calculate for each rank the percentage of total population and total surface represented by the population of the communes of higher rank, i.e., of higher density. These pairs of values are plotted on a graph. In figure 15.1 we see the high degree of dispersion of the population, with 80% of the inhabitants concentrated in 20% of the territory. Note also that the curves for the six censuses are not strongly differentiated, thus preventing an analysis of their variation through time.

But why use the population of the communes rather than of some larger unit? Larger administrative subdivisions in France include the cantons, each of which comprises ten or so communes, and the departments, each containing four hundred communes on average. Using these subdivisions and the 1999 census figures, we obtain the Lorenz curves of concentration in figure 15.1(b). Compared with figure 15.1(a) the situation is completely changed. The three curves are now clearly differentiated. The degree of concentration is much less marked at the level of the departments than at that of the communes, and the cantons are in an intermediary position. The subdivision used thus has a major effect on the result obtained. The earlier statement that 80% of the population lives on 20% of the national territory is only meaningful with reference to the division by communes and is no longer true at the level of cantons and departments. Taking an extreme case, if France was

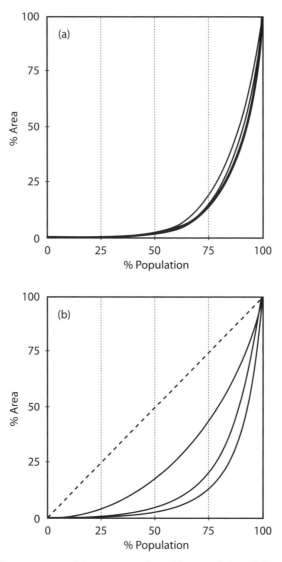

Figure 15.1. Lorenz curves of the concentration of the population of France. (Communes are ranked in order of decreasing density. The *x*-axis shows the percentage of the population inhabiting communes where the density is above a certain value, and the *y*-axis the percentage of the surface of these communes.) (a) At the six censuses, 1962–99. (b) Subdivided in hierarchy of communes, cantons, and departments, 1999. (From Le Bras 1996a.)

divided up into the 551 billion square meters that comprise its territory, fewer than 60 million of these square meters would contain at least one individual. More than 550 billion would thus be left empty, so it could be claimed that 100% of the French population occupies less than a one-thousandth of the territory (under the division by square meters).

The same argument rules out the other measures of concentration or variability, including variance, entropy, and the Gini coefficient. While such indices are of use for characterizing a finite set such as the distribution of individual incomes, they cannot function in a continuous situation like that of a geographical territory. Demographers and geographers have thus tended to characterize concentration by other means. In particular, they have referred to the "rank-size" rule or distribution, a remarkable regularity whereby the population of any city is proportional to a (negative) power α of its rank-order in terms of population. We will first give empirical confirmation for the rule, then examine a number of possible explanations for it. After showing their limitations we will put forward a method of measurement and explanation: multifractal analysis, of which the rank-size rule is a possible consequence.

15.1 Examples of Rank-Size Distributions

The first account of the rank-size rule was given in a short article by Auerbach published in 1911 in the German geographical journal, *Petermans Mitteilungen*. Originally signalled as a curiosity, the rank-size rule gained prestige through the research of Georges K. Zipf, who used it in the geopolitical analyses of his *National Unity and Disunity* published in the United States in 1941. Zipf found that the rule obtained for states that were "healthy," for example, the United States (figure 15.2) but did so less well for states that were unstable, for example, the Weimar Republic, Germany. The subsequent course of the war led Zipf to move away from interpretation along these lines. In his great work, *Human Behavior and the Principle of Least Effort*, published in 1948, he adopted a positivist approach, advancing numerous instances of the rule for population distribution but also for migratory movements, marketing networks, word frequencies in the language of normal and psychotic individuals, in literary texts, and so on.

The quality of the rank-size distribution can be judged by fitting it to the population of the 36 525 communes of France in the censuses taken between 1954 and 1999. Figure 15.3 displays the six curves obtained when the 200 largest communes are rank-ordered by their population $P(n)$ on the y-axis (logarithmic scale) and by their rank in population size n on the x-axis (logarithmic scale also). The linear relationship of the logarithmic coordinates is written

$$\log(P) = \alpha \log(n) + \beta,$$

i.e., $P = e^{\beta} n^{\alpha} = K n^{\alpha}$.

The values of α and the quality of the adjustment for logarithms (correlation coefficient r) are indicated for each census in table 15.1.

Unsurprisingly, the linear adjustment of the curves in figure 15.3 is of excellent quality (r higher than 99% in absolute values) and the exponent is declining. This indicates a fall in concentration brought about as the population of the large communes sprawls across the surrounding territory.

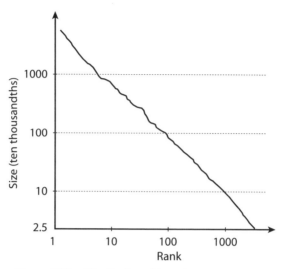

Figure 15.2. Distribution of American cities, rank on
x-axis and population on *y*-axis, 1939. (From Zipf 1941.)

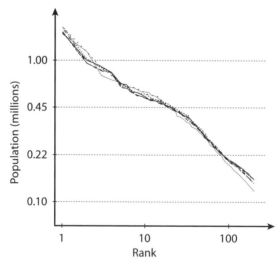

Figure 15.3. Distribution of French communes by their rank and
population (log–log scales) in the six censuses between 1954 and 1999.

15.2 Explaining the Rank-Size Rule: Gibrat and Simon

Zipf naturally examined the question of why such a rule was so widely and closely
respected. In the highly detailed *Human Behavior and the Principle of Least Effort*
he remains at the level of argument by analogy or even of parable, like that of the
craftsman's tools arranged so that the most frequently used is the most accessible.

Table 15.1. Rank-size distribution (α is the exponent of rank and r is the coefficient of correlation between the logarithms of rank and population) for the 200 most populated communes in the last six censuses.

Census (year)	α	r
1962	−0.681	−0.990
1968	−0.647	−0.991
1975	−0.623	−0.990
1982	−0.609	−0.990
1990	−0.602	−0.991
1999	−0.607	−0.992

In fact, the rank-size rule can be accounted for exactly by using simple processes: the lognormal model studied by Gibrat (1931) and an accumulation model proposed by Herbert Simon. The lognormal distribution is the multiplicative version of the normal distribution. The latter gives the distribution of the sum of small deviations or independent errors, while the lognormal distribution is the result of multiplying small independent increments of growth. For example, if localities of identical size have their populations increased (or decreased) at random by between a few per thousand and a few percent each year, after 100 years they will be lognormally distributed. The highest values in a lognormal distribution conform closely to the rank-size rule. To show this we again use the case of the communes in France and assume that each had an initial population of 100 inhabitants. Over a period of 50 years, the increase or decrease for each is randomly selected from a distribution of 100 values spread uniformly between +6 and −6%. This range was chosen so as to give a slope equal to that observed in reality, i.e., of −0.61, which is easy since if all the increments increased by unity are raised to the power of k, the exponent of the rank-size rule is also multiplied by k. Thus we need simply work from an initial distribution of increases and scale on the basis of the result. With this procedure we obtained a coefficient $\alpha = -0.611$ and a correlation $r = -0.993$, which are exactly the values observed in 1999. The curve corresponding to the 200 most populated communes at the end of the process is drawn in figure 15.4. By a happy chance, this curve, as well as exhibiting correct linearity, reproduces the minor irregularities in the curve actually observed in 1999: a slightly too large population for the first commune,[1] a constant-slope line from the 50th commune onward. It might be thought pointless to look any further. We need merely accept the premises, namely that cities develop independently of each other. Their population results from the conjunction of numerous factors in multiplication, each of low amplitude. Through a limited first-order expansion, the logarithm of the population is then the

---

[1] Geographers refer to a "primate city" often found to be above its rank size and explain this by its role as the capital, which is both obvious from the viewpoint of observation and problematical from that of the concrete and measurable reasons that lead to this situation.

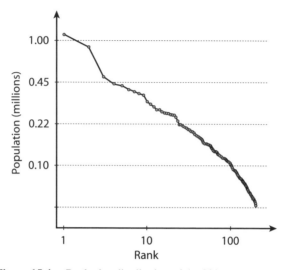

Figure 15.4. Rank-size distribution of the 200 most populated
urban areas among 35 000 generated by multinomial simulation.

sum of these multiplicative factors reduced by unity. By virtue of the law of large
numbers, it obeys a normal distribution and, reversing the operation, the population
obeys a lognormal distribution from which the rank-size rule derives.

This schema is applicable to growth in urban populations, but it does not account
for the many other instances where the rank-size rule is found to obtain, notably in
statistical linguistics. Herbert Simon put forward a simple but ingenious model on
this topic in 1954. He assumed that language initially comprised n separate words
with equal probability of occurring but that as words are chosen, so their probability
of being chosen again increases. This model is simple to simulate. We assign a series
of n grid squares and put into each its rank order (i.e., from 1 to n). One of these, i, is
randomly selected on an equal probability basis. Next, p new squares are added, p
being given by a probability distribution $f(p)$, and in which is entered the number
of the selected square, i. The procedure is iterated this time from $n + p$ squares.
After a fairly large number of draws (running into tens of thousands), a reasonably
stable distribution is obtained whose elements conform closely to the rank-size rule
for over 50% of the population. The value of the coefficient α of the rank-size rule
is highly sensitive to the initial number of possible words n and to the distribution
$f(p)$. For a uniform distribution between 0 and 9 duplications of the selected word
and 1500 possible words, $\alpha = -0.62$ ($r = -0.976$) for the 200 most common
words representing 76% of the total number of words at the end of the process. If
the number of permitted words rose to 5000 with the same distribution $f(p)$ for the
duplications, α would fall to -0.37 for the 200 most frequent words, and, for 1000
possible words, would rise to -0.71. In figure 15.5 we plot the distribution of the
200 most frequent words for the case of 1500 possible words.

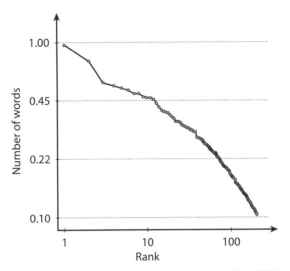

Figure 15.5. Distribution by rank and population of the 200 largest communes of the 35 000 generated by Herbert Simon's model (log–log scale).

The process imagined by Herbert Simon is in fact very close to the lognormal case. At each drawing, independently, the probability of increasing relative to the stock of each word is the inverse of the total number of words already present (original and previously drawn words), and since the selection is random, the increases are mutually independent. The model can also be given a spatial transposition by assuming that each possible word is a commune with a single inhabitant and that the successive drawings in which it comes up have the effect of increasing its population by that amount.

15.3 Communes and Agglomerations

The preceding elements give the impression that the problem is solved. Scant attention has been given to the geographical subdivision, however, with the commune being accepted as the appropriate unit although this was criticized in the introduction to this chapter. A more legitimate choice would be the agglomerations (or urbanized areas), which correspond to units with a real human and economic as opposed to legal basis. Thus, for example, the communes of Paris, Nantes, and Lille would be replaced by the agglomerations of those cities. But how concretely are actual agglomerations to be defined? This is a difficult question in human geography. Many national statistical offices use the criterion of urban continuity (when no building or dwelling is situated more than 200 meters from its nearest neighbor). Such a definition is inflexible and requires blind acceptance of the list published at a particular point in time by the statistical office. A reasonable alternative is to start from the smallest known administrative subdivision and group with it all the

Table 15.2. Rank-size distribution (α is the exponent of rank and r the coefficient of correlation between the logarithms of rank and population) for the 200 largest urban areas in 1999 for different values of density threshold used to define the agglomeration.

Minimum density (inhabitants/km^2)	α	r
1000	−1.11	−0.980
500	−1.08	−0.996
250	−1.08	−0.998
150	−1.14	−0.996
100	−1.21	−0.997
75	−1.30	−0.997
50	−1.36	−0.996

contiguous units in which density exceeds a certain threshold d_0. But the question then arises of which threshold to choose. When in doubt, a range of thresholds can be experimented with. For France we have chosen them running from 50 to 1000 inhabitants per square kilometer, which is a wide range but allows the stability of the results to be tested. In each case, we have brought together all the adjacent communes in which the density exceeded the value in question (in 1999) and fitted the rank-size distribution for the 200 largest agglomerations.[2] The results appear in table 15.2.

The adjustments are excellent, with r consistently above 0.99 in absolute values. The corresponding curve is drawn in figure 15.6. The relevance of varying the threshold is clear from the change in the exponent α for rank of the rank-size distribution. Extremely stable between 250 and 1000 inhabitants per square kilometer—which closely matches the minimum densities observed in agglomerations—it then climbs steadily. Also, these values for α are much higher than in the case of the distribution of communes (from −0.61 to −0.68) indicated in table 15.1. In addition, in practically all known cases, those supplied by Zipf, for example, the values for α are close to unity. This rise in the values from around 0.6 to around 1 is explained by the fact that several communes are combined in one agglomeration, thus increasing the surface area. There is in fact a linear relationship—known as allometry—between the logarithm of the population and that of the surface area of agglomerations. (The relationships between the different rank-size distributions depending on the subdivision used are studied in the appendix (section 15.10.1).)

---

[2] The territory was first placed on a lattice containing 400×400 square cells. Each cell was assigned to the commune whose center (*chef-lieu*) was closest to the center of the square. This procedure is analogous to Voronoï cells in crystallography and makes it possible to apply "cellular" grouping algorithms, i.e., procedures based on a few systematic rules. In the present case, each square constitutes an agglomeration if its density exceeds the threshold. The four adjacent squares are then examined and those with a higher density are selected, then the research is iterated to these new squares until none are left.

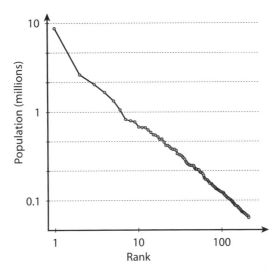

Figure 15.6. Rank-size distribution of the French urban areas at the 1990 census.

While the rank-size rule is satisfactory for describing reality, it is less useful for explaining it. The Gibrat and Simon models start out from a set of identical elements, portions of territory or words, that all contain the same number of occurrences or of individuals. Now the essential point is this: because the different places or words are completely unconnected (this is the independence assumption), there is no reason to group them in one way rather than another. They have no spatial reference in reality but form lists. In order to obtain the equivalent of agglomerations the only solution is thus to group them into equal-sized "bundles," each containing the same number of units or, if they are elementary cells, to divide the whole into squares containing $m \times m$ elementary cells. This forming into groups has been carried out for squares of different sizes in the case of the multinomial distribution studied earlier, which, it will be recalled, produced the same rank-size distribution as the communes of France. The grouping into squares is to some degree a substitute for the grouping of communes into agglomerations. Table 15.3 reports the results corresponding to the different sizes of group formed varying from 1 (the case studied already) to 400 (20×20).

Needless to say, the same by no means trivial problem would arise with Simon's model. Not only is α falling rather than rising in it, but there is no longer even a zone of stability within which its values stay more or less constant, as is the case for empirically observed agglomerations. If no equivalence is possible between the observations and the Gibrat and Simon models, this is because the latter lack any spatial component. Their data, either individual income or words, are not linked by any relations, architecture, or organization; they possess no spatial structure. The rank-size rule is not the end result of simple stochastic processes but is the expression of a coherent spatial pattern. This indeed is why it has been studied so

Table 15.3.   Rank-size distribution (α is the exponent of rank and r the coefficient of correlation between the logarithms of rank and population) for the 200 largest agglomerations of
the multinomial model (Gibrat) with different values for density threshold defining the urban
area.

Number of cells grouped	α	r
1	−0.61	−0.993
4	−0.56	−0.993
9	−0.53	−0.995
25	−0.42	−0.995
64	−0.32	−0.997
100	−0.27	−0.997
225	−0.22	−0.964
400	−0.17	−0.941

often and why Paul Krugman wrote recently that it is perhaps the most mysterious of
socioeconomic regularities. To explain the rank-size rule it is necessary to include
spatial relations in the analysis. The first way to do this is by not piling up the
new items all in the same point, as occurs in the Gibrat and Simon processes, and
instead spreading them out across the territory, giving them a degree of mobility.
Not total mobility, since that would again result in an absence of spatial structure,
but partial mobility, within the limits of neighborhoods or finite random walks. The
first models developed along these lines successfully simulate the distribution of
the spaces occupied though do not give a satisfactory explanation for differences of
density.

15.4   Models of Spatial Population Distribution

The most common models describe the gradual occupation of a territory, the spread
of an epidemic or, at the cellular level, of a tumor. A detailed examination of these is
beyond the scope of the present work. We will merely summarize their basic principle
to show that they have no connection with the rank-size rule, being concerned
principally with occupation of space and not with differences of density. In all
of them space is reduced to a regular grid or checkerboard in which one square
represents the possible habitat of one, and only one, person or family.

   The simplest model of cellular growth, for instance, starts from a "seed" constituted by a first family. The families that descend from it will seek housing in the
immediate neighborhood and so on from one grid square to the next. When no more
neighboring squares are available, the new family is not founded. It can be shown
that in the absence of obstacles represented by prohibited squares, growth in the total
population is concentric in form (excepting random fluctuations) and the increase

in the radius is regular (linear) over time. The famous "wave of advance" model developed by Ammerman and Cavalli-Sforza (1979) to account for the spread of agriculture in the Neolithic period conforms to this schema. Grid squares of the neighborhood need not be immediately adjacent to an occupied square but can be nearby cells, for example, those accessible by a short random walk, on the model of Brownian motion. The squares whence a square that is still empty can be reached make up the "population front." This model has been used to study the spread of farming in the Neolithic period, and even today describes Brazil's Amazonian frontier.

The percolation models are slightly more sophisticated, introducing a constraint into the simple growth model. In the course of population distribution, a grid square that becomes the neighbor of one occupied by the last family to be established has a probability p of being neutralized (if not, it can be occupied by a neighboring family). The Eden model, one of the earliest to describe the growth of tumors and infections, operates on this contagion and immunization mode. When the population has reached a large size, the model is similar to a percolation: the proportion of empty squares is close to p and they are distributed almost at random. Only almost at random, because squares that become completely surrounded by immunized squares, without being immunized themselves, can then no longer be affected. Percolation models describe a wide variety of physical and biological phenomena, including phase frontiers, the position of products in close contact during chemical reactions, the spread of forest fires and of epidemics with immunization, the location of naturally occurring oil and gas accumulations.[3]

The growth and percolation models do not take densities into account. A square in the grid may be empty or occupied, but in no case are n individuals or families crowded into the same square. The phenomena described by the models are in fact independent of density. In the Neolithic period, land either was farmed or was not; and there were not yet any large human agglomerations. In a similar manner, when considering cellular growth, it is not possible to place more than one cell at the same point. These models are clearly intended for modeling the occupation of space, not the growth or distribution of population. This point is even clearer with the diffusion-limited-aggregation (DLA) models. In these, the new occupants come not from the inside but from the outside. Each diffuses randomly (by Brownian motion) until they enter a grid square adjacent to one that is already occupied, and at this point they stick. Beginning from an initial seed, the occupied surface thus spreads in branch-like forms, similar to those observed in electrolysis (the same principle holds at the atomic level). Geographers have used this model to describe the spatial growth of a city, the expansion in its surface area, though not in the number of its inhabitants.[4]

[3] For an exposition of these models, see Vicsek (1994).
[4] See, in particular, the works of Michael Batty, including *Fractal Cities* (Batty and Longley 1994).

These spatial models were never intended to represent or explain differences of density on territories that have been settled for hundreds of years, so it is an illusion to expect that they will open up avenues for our investigation. It is preferable to look instead in a more remote domain, that of astronomy. This discipline has to address the issue of the density of matter, and hence the distribution of stars, galaxies, and galactic clusters, for which useful models are available.

15.5   Models of the Distribution of Stellar Matter: Curdling and Lévy Flights

Matter is distributed very unevenly in the universe. If it were otherwise, the light from the stars would be equivalent to that from the sun and there would be no night. To represent the variations in stellar density, the cosmologist Fred Hoyle developed a model for formation of the universe through a condensation process. Under this, an initial cloud of particles was condensed into successive clumps of much higher density, which in turn were condensed into clumps, and then clumps of clumps, becoming ever more compact and isolated until they attain the size of stars and their sideral neighborhood has been emptied. For complex and questionable reasons Hoyle postulated that at each stage, condensation occurred in five clumps so that after n stages there were 5^n clumps. Benoît Mandelbrot (1983) took up the idea and developed a two-dimensional version to which he gave the name "curdling." Initially, matter is scattered uniformly across a square with a side of length A. The majority of the matter is then condensed into p squares, of the much smaller size A/n, such that $p(A/n)^2 \ll A^2$, or equivalently $p \ll n^2$. The position of these squares is selected at random from inside the large square. The procedure is repeated for the squares p and so on. We can transpose the procedure to population by making the assumption that in the final stage the clumps are not stars or planets but human beings and that the diagram represents their position on the territory at a given point in time. Curdling becomes stochastic if the number of clumps after each division is made to depend on a probability distribution. It can be shown that the scatter of points thus obtained is self-similar, i.e., that it is similar to one of its own components, which is logical given its mode of generation.

Mandelbrot constructed another, more subtle, model to account for the distribution of matter in the universe. He called it the "Lévy flight" after the mathematician Paul Lévy (1965), who had established its theoretical bases. The model combines two fractal mechanisms: an extended random walk and a "devil's staircase," the stochastic version of the Cantor set. To obtain the Cantor set, start with a straight-line segment and from the middle of it remove a segment of length $1 - D$. Then do the same with the two segments that are left, i.e., remove from the middle of them a fraction of their length, $1 - D$, and so on. At the end of n stages, there remain 2^n tiny segments of length $((1-D)/2)^n$. The intervals between the segments are distributed

Figure 15.7. Distribution of densities simulated by a Lévy
process ("flight"). The darker the gray, the higher the density.

according to a geometric distribution: a proportion $D((1 - D)/2)^{p-1}$ are of length
$((1 - D)/2)^p$. Mandelbrot's idea was to make the random walk so that each point
reached was followed a jump of p points in the walk, p being a random variable
distributed according to the intervals in the Cantor set. As a random walk in the
plane has fractal dimension 2, it is shown that this new walk has the dimension $2D$.
Depending on the choice of D, the remaining points form a more or less compact
cloud in which the aggregations are visible to varying degrees. Like Hoyle's cloud,
that of the Lévy flight is self-similar, since it replicates any of its parts. Figure 15.7
represents an example of such a cloud with dimension 1.26, which is the dimension
found for the distribution of matter in the universe. Though it does not resemble
any real distribution of densities, the diagram has many of the attributes of one.
Concentrations of population stand out clearly against a background of low densities. The sequential procedure used also brings out the lines of denser settlement.
The correspondence between this model and empirically observed distributions is
verified by checking whether its agglomerations are distributed according to the
rank-size rule. Agglomerations can in fact be manufactured by using the position of
the points of the Lévy flight in the plane. The procedure is the same as in the case of
the data for France, with space treated as a grid framework. The points contained in
each elementary square are counted and groups are formed from all the neighboring
squares in which the density (i.e., the number of points they contain) is above a
certain threshold. It is verified (table 15.4) that the agglomerations simulated in this
way follow the rank-size rule for thresholds situated between one half and twice the
average density (the parameters of the model are calibrated to the French data by
taking the same average density, and it is again the 200 largest agglomerations that
are considered).

We observe that the rank-size rule is followed precisely in the neighborhood of
the average density threshold. Its coefficient becomes increasingly negative as the

Table 15.4. Rank-size distribution for the 200 largest agglomerations produced by a Lévy flight for different thresholds of density defining the agglomeration (α is the exponent of rank and r the coefficient of correlation between the logarithms of rank and population).

Minimum density (inhabitants/km^2)	α	r
200	−0.76	−0.996
160	−0.95	−0.997
120	−1.18	−0.995
100	−1.28	−0.991
80	−1.17	−0.972

threshold adopted falls and is situated in the region of −1, which are all properties of the observed data. However, if the rank-size rule is fitted to the basic squares or their systematic grouping into squares independently of the distribution of densities, the fit obtained is less good and the slope is less steep. This is clear evidence that the Mandelbrot models still lack the capacity to describe major contrasts of density. On the other hand, the existence of self-similarity is extremely interesting since it is consistent with a well-known model of settlement patterns, Christaller's network of central places.

15.6 Christaller's Central Places

Using the example of the towns and cities—or more exactly the "central places"—in southern Germany, Christaller showed in 1931 that they were differentiated by the number of "central" functions—of an economic, cultural, religious, commercial nature—that they combined.[5] The more central functions a town contains, the higher its position in the urban hierarchy and the larger its population. Assuming an entirely uniform land surface, the central places are organized evenly across space in a way that maximizes access to the populations. The towns of the highest order are spaced furthest apart and arranged in a regular pattern either hexagonal or squared. Occupying an intermediate position are the second-order towns, more numerous and more closely spaced, followed by the still denser network of third-order towns, and so on. If the different agglomerations are placed at the nodes of a geometrical lattice that doubles in density at each stage, each time we drop one level in the hierarchy, the territory covered is four times smaller and there are four times more central places of the kind considered. If the population of the central place is proportional to the size of its hinterland, we can write that at rank p in the hierarchy, the town's population is $P(p) = P(1)/4^p$, and that there are $4^p N(p)$ towns of rank p. The number of towns of rank p or above is thus $(4^{p+1} - 1)/3$, this being the sum of a

[5] See Christaller (1931). A fractal interpretation of it is given by Arlinghaus (1985).

geometric series with common ratio 4. We can write that, excepting a small residual, $P(p) = 12(N(p))^{-1}$, i.e., the rank-size rule of coefficient -1, and thus very close to the coefficient obtained earlier for the distribution of agglomerations in France. But the hypothesis made about the population of the agglomerations of level p in the hierarchy has another meaning: it renders the Christaller model self-similar. For if we take a central place of some rank p, its hinterland will be exactly that of the first-order central place multiplied by a factor of $1/4^{p-1}$. Thus the Christaller model is self-similar both in its geographical organization and in terms of densities. We will verify that the same strong property is also observed in empirical data.

15.7 Fractal Relations and Density Thresholds

Let us start again with curdling in the simplest version of it given by Hoyle. At each stage, matter is condensed into p clumps each occupying a space k times smaller. The proportion S of the space occupied by the matter thus obeys a power law. At the nth division we have $S(n) = (pk)^n$. If space is divided into squared cells of area $E(n) = k^n$, the relationship between the baseline measure and the number of squares occupied $N(n)$ is written

$$N(n) = k^{-n}(pk)^n = p^n,$$

hence $\log(N(n)) = n \log(p)$. Replacing n by its value

$$\log(N(n)) = \log(E(n)) \log(p)/\log(k),$$

which is the usual way of defining the fractal dimension $D = -\log(p)/\log(k)$. This reasoning is analogous to that followed for Christaller's network. Can similar relationships be established for the observed data on densities? A closely related way of asking the question is: does the fixed and densest proportion p of the population follow a power law, which characterizes a fractal set? In the case of the Hoyle cloud, because all the clumps are of the same size at a given stage, the answer is immediate: irrespective of the proportion p chosen, the area containing it evolves as a power D of the measurement unit, the square $E(n)$. This can be written as $D(p) = K$, a constant. What happens in reality when we wish to analyze communal population densities in France in 1999?

To get back to the case of curdling, at each fixed and densest proportion p of the population, we calculated the portion of the surface area occupied when space was divided into squares with sides varying from 1/400 to 50/400 of the length of the original square, i.e., taking a baseline area varying from 1 to 2500. If the densest population distribution is self-similar, as in curdling, we must find a relationship giving the fractal dimension that is written here, denoting by $S(n)$ the number of squares of size $n/400$ occupied by proportion p of the population among the $160\,000/n^2$ possible squares:

$$\log S(n) = -K \log(n^2/160\,000),$$

Table 15.5. Fractal dimension K of the fraction of territory containing the densest proportion p of the total population and goodness-of-fit.

p (%)	$1 - K$	% residual
95	0.045	0.001
90	0.075	0.0002
80	0.132	0.0001
70	0.190	0.0002
60	0.251	0.0006
50	0.319	0.0012
40	0.360	0.0026
30	0.487	0.0062
20	0.617	0.0131
10	0.784	0.0151

i.e.,

$$\log(S(n) \cdot 160\,000/n^2) = (1 - K)\log(n^2/160\,000).$$

This relationship is conformed to exactly by the values for p between 10 and 95% of the total population. Table 15.5 presents the least-squares estimation of $1 - K$ and the goodness-of-fit (sum of squares of deviations over sum of total squares).

The adjustment is exact up to low percentage values of the population concerned. But, unlike in curdling, the fractal dimension varies with the percentage of the population considered.[6] Self-similarity persists, that is to say, that the same table will be obtained if attention is limited to only a part of the territory. The population has a multifractal distribution. This can be verified experimentally by a simple procedure: take a square of any reasonable size inside the territory; divide it into four equal subsquares and calculate the proportion of the population of the initial square contained in each subsquare. Whatever the size of the original square, the proportions in the four subsquares are, on average, constant (the average is calculated by placing the proportions in increasing or decreasing order, since the subsquares are in no particular order).

A total of 10 000 random drawings were made of squares with the original square varying in size from 2 to 140 km (equivalent therefore to areas varying in a ratio of 1 to 4900). In table 15.6 we see that, regardless of the size of the original square, the four subsquares, from the most populated to the least populated, retain virtually the same proportion. Thus the relative variability of the densities is independent of scale over a large range of surface areas.

---

[6] From the table it can be seen that the variation of $1 - K$ by p is very even. When a function $f(p)$ is fitted to it, we obtain an approximation of the Lorenz curves relative to the baseline area measure E: $\log(S(p)) = kf(p)$. When the population fraction p is over 50%, $f(p)$ is linear, so that the Lorenz curves can be represented by exponentials. Below 50%, however, this approximation is inexact and hence is not suitable for giving a general formula for all the Lorenz curves.

Table 15.6. Average distribution of population between the four subsquares from an original square of an area varying from 4 to 10 000 km², France, 1999.

| Area of initial square (km²) | Proportion of population in each subsquare: | | | |
	Most dense	Second	Third	Least dense
4	38	26	20	16
16	42	26	19	14
100	44	25	17	13
400	45	25	17	13
1 600	43	25	18	13
10 000	45	23	18	14

Table 15.7. Average distribution of the population between the four subsquares of an original square with a surface area varying between 4 and 10 000 km², in the case of a lognormal distribution.

| Area of initial square (km²) | Proportion of population in each subsquare: | | | |
	Most dense	Second	Third	Least dense
4	73	19	6	2
16	64	22	10	4
100	51	25	15	9
400	43	25	18	13
1 600	37	26	21	17
10 000	32	25	23	21

The property brought to light here is remarkable. It is not usually encountered. For example, if we go back to Gibrat's lognormal distribution used earlier, although it conforms to the rank-size rule, the contrasts in density diminish with scale, as is seen on table 15.7, where we have applied the same procedure as in the preceding one.

Since the squares in the lognormal model are treated independently of each other, the larger the size of the initial square, the closer we get to the average values. The Lévy flight model, by contrast, is remarkably independent of scale, but the percentages, and hence the differences of density, are much more compact than in reality since the averages for the four subsquares in the example in figure 15.7 are 30, 26, 23, and 21%, respectively. Here again we see the inability of this class of models to produce an adequate concentration of matter (or population). Since the

curdling model directed us toward self-similarity in the distribution of densities, it
is logical to use it as the basis for reproducing the observed variability.

15.8   The Multifractal Model

In the Hoyle model and in curdling, not all matter was condensed.[7] Part of it remained
inert at low densities in the space left empty by condensation of the remainder. A
more uniform mode of condensation can be imagined, so that at each stage density
is generalized whatever its level. A way of doing this is with the method of four
subsquares used to highlight the scale invariance of the observed densities. Assume
that we have a priori the four proportions that divide the matter in a square between
its four subsquares and draw at random which square will receive which proportion.[8] Begin with a single square, for example the 400 × 400 grid used to divide up
France, then repeat the operation this time from the four subsquares, i.e., dividing
the 200 × 200 squares by four and so on. At each stage and in each subsquare the
division is done at random and with the same four proportions. After seven or eight
stages, the matter is distributed very unevenly. The map of densities obtained reflects
the technique used, however, in that it makes conspicuous the first divisions of the
square that provided the boundary for all the subsequent divisions. To avoid this
drawback and the arbitrariness of such boundaries, the position of each square at
each stage must be drawn at random. The population it contains is then calculated
and distributed according to the four proportions fixed at the outset. By applying
this procedure, figure 15.8 is obtained, which closely resembles a map of population
density. It is simultaneously disorganized and balanced, in the sense that concentrations of different sizes are distributed across the whole of the space and it is possible
to imagine that they are agglomerations. The four proportions were adjusted so as to
obtain the same values as in reality. This gave the four values (53, 23, 13, and 10%)
that were used at each division into subsquares. The map obtained in figure 15.8 can
then be analyzed in the same way as the real map or as the lognormal map from the
previous section. The result obtained appears in table 15.8.

The result is very stable and very similar to the series obtained for France. The
model fits the data better than those of Mandelbrot, Gibrat, and Simon. Since the
population, and hence the density, in each elementary square is known, it is possible
to calculate the rank-size distribution for the 200 largest agglomerations with different values for the minimum density threshold used for forming the agglomerations,
as was done for France. Table 15.9 presents the result of these calculations.

The adjustment is precise (correlations higher than 0.99), though the values for
the slope are slightly below those obtained for France. Similarly, the relationship

---

[7] For a more complete discussion of the multifractal model and of the ways for testing it, see Le Bras
(1996a,b).

[8] To be more exact, we randomly distribute the four proportions between the four subsquares, i.e.,
attribute each of the proportions to one and only one subsquare.

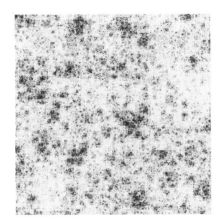

Figure 15.8. Distribution of densities simulated by a
multifractal process (the darker the gray, the higher the density).

Table 15.8. Average distribution of the population of the four subsquares from
an initial square varying in area between 4 and 10 000 km² (multifractal).

Area of initial square (km²)	Proportion of population in each subsquare:			
	Most dense	Second	Third	Least dense
4	44	27	18	12
16	43	27	18	12
100	43	27	18	12
400	43	26	18	13
1 600	43	27	18	12
10 000	41	27	19	13

Table 15.9. Rank-size distribution for the 200 most populated agglomerations from the
multifractal model for different values of the density threshold defining the agglomeration (α
is the exponent of rank, r the coefficient of correlation between the logarithms of rank and
population).

Minimum density (inhabitants/km²)	α	r
1000	−0.81	−0.995
500	−0.87	−0.995
250	−0.91	−0.994
150	−0.98	−0.998
100	−1.10	−0.997
75	−1.23	−0.993

Table 15.10. Fractal dimension K of the fraction of territory containing the most dense proportion p of the total population and quality of the adjustment.

p (%)	$1 - K$	% residual
95	0.048	0.001
90	0.075	0.0016
80	0.121	0.0019
70	0.165	0.0043
60	0.210	0.0056
50	0.260	0.0075
40	0.315	0.0089
30	0.384	0.0099
20	0.471	0.0107
10	0.600	0.0117

between the surface area occupied, the size of the unit used and the most dense proportion of population p, yields results that are analogous both for their precision and for the $1 - K$ values of the fractal parameter by the values of p, as can be seen in table 15.10, whose similarity to table 15.5 can be established by comparison.

The similarity in the behavior of the two series—that observed for France and that simulated using the multifractals—and the accuracy of their adjustment support the multifractal model, although there is still disagreement at values for $1 - K$ of below 20% or thereabouts in the model.

The mathematical behavior of the multifractal models is reasonably well understood. It is known that in the neighborhood of a point X, the density $d(X)$ varies with the scale of the measurement E (for example, the radius of the circle drawn around X) of the area according to a power law:

$$d(X) = K(\alpha)E^{\alpha}.$$

It is also known that the density of points $S(\alpha)$ for which α is the exponent, varies as a function of the scale E according to a distribution

$$S(\alpha) = KE^{-f(\alpha)}.$$

It is verified that the densities in France conform reasonably well to the distribution of $d(X)$ and $f(\alpha)$ can be calculated with a Legendre transformation.[9] The graph of the function $f(\alpha)$ according to α is often called its multifractal "spectrum."

15.9   The Generality of the Multifractal Model

Some discussion of the multifractal model from the previous section is in order. It does not signify a subordination of reality to the model; instead the model offers a

---

[9] The formulas and results for France are in Le Bras (1996a).

means of access to this reality. It can do this because it captures one of its essential elements: the interdependence of densities across the territory as a whole. This fundamental aspect was absent from both the Gibrat and Simon models. The Lévy flight model was based on a relationship of proximity because it was underpinned by a random walk, but this was not a relationship in two-dimensional space. Two points that were close could be separated by a large number of stages. In contrast, the multifractal model incorporates spatial interdependence by its very principle, which consists of subdividing from a whole. In this sense the densities are not absolute but become relative to each other. They no longer depend on one single place but on space as a whole. In a word, they are the result of interactions in a dynamic system. Naturally, it is not at all certain that they were constructed in the way that was simulated with the multifractal model—by random selection of squares and of their allocation into four subsquares—but the scale independence of the variability in the subsquares observed suggests the action of some deep structural tendency, bringing concentration and dispersion into equilibrium. The multifractal model supplies an entry point for a better exploration of this tendency, since the model's simplicity leaves considerable scope for additions or for more precise specifications. For example, the poorer quality of the adjustment at the level of the highest densities could prompt an examination of whether the four proportions do not change in the zones of high density. To test this, the analysis performed for France as a whole is repeated for a single agglomeration (the result exhibits a tiny change). Another question is: might there not be two multifractal distributions, one for urban centers, the other for rural areas? Empirically, it can be shown that the sum of two multifractal distributions of different parameters is no longer multifractal, which disqualifies the idea and reinforces the impression of being faced with a structural behavior underlying sociability.

More generally, the multifractal model integrates a set of regularities up to now observed separately: Lorenz curves, rank-size rule, evolution of densities with distance from a given point, constant effects of scale changes. These various aspects are not at present unified. The fact that they occur together in the multifractal model is encouraging in terms of the search for a synthesis.

15.10 Appendix

15.10.1 Correspondence between the Rank-Size Distributions

Three different rank-size distributions have been encountered for the same phenomenon, the distribution of the population of France in the 1999 census. The most immediate is obtained by using the population of the communes. The relationship is not perfectly linear but slightly convex, so that the slope increases slowly with the number of communes, as can be seen from tables 15.11 and 15.12.

Table 15.11.

Number of communes used	r	α	Percentage of population concerned
200	−0.952	−0.61	28.4
1 000	−0.992	−0.74	51
2 500	−0.994	−0.83	65.1
10 000	−0.995	−0.95	86.2
25 000	−0.992	−1.08	97.6

Table 15.12.

Number of communes used	r	β
200	−0.982	−0.29
1 000	−0.946	−0.33
10 000	−0.993	−0.41
25 000	−0.971	−0.54

Similarly, the surface area of these communes varies as a function of their rank order according to a relation $s = Kn^\beta$. The exponent β varies with the number of communes considered (ranked in decreasing order of their population).

The two distributions—surface area and population—can be linked together by assuming that each commune is divided into a number of portions equal to its surface area and that the population of these portions is that of the commune divided by the number of portions dS. The differential element dS on the x-axis replaces the element $dn - 1$ since dS portions replace one commune. Because dS follows a rank-size distribution of parameter β we have

$$s = dS = Kn^\beta.$$

When $\beta > -1$, and remembering that $dn = 1$, a first approximation can be obtained by integrating the differential relation, which gives

$$S = K_1 n^{\beta+1}.$$

The population P' that corresponds to this new unit of surface is, as we have seen,

$$P' = \frac{P}{dS} = \frac{kn^\alpha}{Kn^\beta} = K_2 n^{\alpha-\beta}.$$

Expressing n as a function of S from the first relation, we obtain a new rank-size distribution that is written

$$P' = K_3 S^{(\alpha-\beta)/(b+1)}.$$

Table 15.13.

S	α' calculated from the α and β	α' observed with division into squares
200	−0.46	−0.51
1 000	−0.62	−0.61
10 000	−0.93	−0.89

The slope α' of this distribution thus has the value

$$\alpha' = (\alpha - \beta)/(b + 1).$$

This relationship may be verified by dividing up the communes into squares and calculating directly the rank-size distributions corresponding to the S first squares. The formula is seen to be a reasonably good approximation (see table 15.13).

The same result cannot be obtained for the agglomerations, since the large disproportion in the areas covered has the effect that the surface areas vary nearly as fast as the populations. Regardless of the density threshold used, from 50 inhabitants/km² to 1000 inhabitants/km², the exponents α and β are in the vicinity of 1, with the second less negative, so higher than 1 by between 0.15 and 0.25. In this case, the "elementary portions" no longer have the same order as the agglomerations, since a large agglomeration can have a lower density than a small one. Hence the relationship is not observed. This could in fact be anticipated, for when β approaches −1, the denominator of α' gets small and must be counterbalanced by a numerator that is also small, hence α and β must be similar.

Conclusion

Demography is often presented as a science of measurement, a sort of land surveying applied to populations. We have shown that this aspect, though real, is secondary. Demography is a science of processes. If concerned only with measuring, it would not need to look further than population censuses and their outputs of age pyramids, densities, and breakdowns of populations by sex, marital status, economic activity, and household type. There would be no discussion of mortality, fertility, nuptiality, and migration. Not that we are dismissive of censuses. They are a source of indispensable data for demography and for many other branches of scholarship and public administration, and census taking calls for conceptual precision and logistical sophistication and for the elaboration of rigorous and unambiguous categories. Little of this has found its way into the present volume. Just two or three age pyramids, no study of the active population, not a single typology of families and households, nothing about the practical aspects of data collection. Why go over again what excellent specialists have already dealt with in excellent books better than this author ever could have written?

A science of processes signifies first process, then measurement of process. Two objections immediately come to mind. One is that many other sciences make extensive use of processes. The other is that defining a process is a theoretical, not empirical, action; it establishes a model that contains an element of arbitrariness. We will address the second criticism first. Demography constructs the simplest processes imaginable. Illustrating this, demographic man is often likened to a lottery participant whose life seems to be spent drawing black or white balls from urns containing them in different proportions. The first processes studied here were the most elementary possible. These had the individual man confined to his lifeline where the only risk he faced was that of ceasing to exist. Death and the life table gave specific form to this elementary process that applies to any nonrenewable event such as first marriage, birth of first child, onset of permanent sterility, and the like. Similarly, fertility represented a simple renewable event, childbearing, that can provide the prototype for any series of events subject to renewal such as migration, marriage, and divorce. In both of the cases that provide the subject matter for the first two chapters of part I, observation was assumed to be complete. Every lifeline was observed without interruption—up to death in the case of mortality, from puberty to age fifty in that of fertility.

The question of measurement was only introduced in chapter 3 via discussion of censoring and once the first two processes, renewable and nonrenewable, had been formalized. The term "censoring" is aptly chosen for communicating the idea of an aggression done to the model by the real world. Measurement and observation are not benign. They have the effect of amputating the process, of removing portions from it that often prove hard to reclassify. An accusation routinely made against models is that they oversimplify reality by omitting many supposedly less important details. With demography we are forced to take the opposite perspective. The model is definitely not a pure product of the intellect. It is based on the world of reality, though the elements it takes from it are imprecise. Stones fall earthwards, the stars turn in the sky, women between ages 15 and 50 give birth to children, the risk of dying is higher in early childhood and old age. Formulating a model under such loose constraints is to commit an act of force on a par with the creation of a concept. At this point the barrage of observations comes into action. This is necessary and unavoidable but harsh in its effects. We showed this in the short but crucial chapter that follows on from the study of censoring and is its ultimate development (chapter 4), dealing with the passage from longitudinal to cross-sectional or period forms of analysis.

The period approach is generally introduced in an innocent manner via the device of the "fictitious cohort," the adjective making inquiry into the fiction itself unnecessary. By defining the period approach using a system of censoring, we showed on the contrary the extreme brutality of the procedure. Demography without period analysis is of historical interest only. Accessing the period approach is vital for the discipline and it achieves this without regard for the cost, though it subsequently dissimulates this to the point of employing identical or near-identical terms—life expectancy and average number of children, for example—for longitudinal and period approaches alike. It is this demographic "novel" that had to be broken, dismantled, opened up to scrutiny. Paradoxically, this can be a way for period analysis to find a new dynamic. In the last two chapters of part I we illustrate this by studying the nature and effect of demographic changes that combine discontinuities of speed and magnitude—of timetable and intensity in demographic terminology. Without our close attention to the censoring that produces the period distributions and the associated indices, these last two chapters of part I could not have been written. There was no qualitative discussion of changes in the timing of demographic behavior; instead they were introduced in precise form into microsimulations of fertility and into equations for mortality change.

The primacy of processes is illustrated more forcefully still with the focus on populations in part II. Fundamentally, change in a closed population occurs through a process of renewal, or more accurately of replacement, since renewal assumes that every entity is sooner or later replaced by another but by one only, whereas in demography it may be replaced by one or several or none. The early population analysts (not yet called *demographers*) did not know how to establish a numerical relationship between the fertility of couples and the growth of populations. Through an examination of the first population projections we saw that the solution was found in the interwar period by means of the female fertility function and stable-population theory. Thus it was logical to begin part II, devoted to populations, with methods of projection and then to move on directly to stable populations and their logical generalization, weak ergodicity. But just as the "fictitious" cohort has never prefigured any real future population, so the stable population remains a virtual horizon that will never be reached. On the contrary, the life of real-world populations is dominated by fluctuations. Partly this is because of changes affecting nondemographic factors, but partly too because of demographic constraints and imbalances. Hence it appeared necessary to go beyond the stable equilibrium viewpoint and to focus attention on modes of fluctuation in constrained demographic structures. This question formed the subject of the third chapter in part II. With it comes an echo at the population level of the issues of short-term change reviewed at the end of part I. The stable population corresponds to the fictitious cohort. With it the movement of variation across time subsides. The age pyramid of a population no longer depends on its past but is entirely determined by its given schedules of mortality and fertility conditions. When we go beyond this stage and shift the emphasis to fluctuations, the dynamics of the replacement process again come into play. Pushed to the extreme we enter the zone where convergence no longer occurs and then the zone where chaos begins.

Parts 1 and 2 in fact correspond to a conventional division that Louis Henry expressed in the title of his demography textbook: analysis and models. Analysis covers the study of individual-level processes; models cover population dynamics. But individuals and populations remain mutually isolated from each other, as if lacking the means to interact. Of course, each death concerns one single individual and childbirth is considered only from the viewpoint of the mother. But the fiction of the isolated subject becomes untenable when working on marriage or migration. It takes two to get married, and two separate locations with two separate populations are needed to say that a migration has occurred. Human mobility and nuptiality cannot be translated into the lifeline model and represented on the Lexis diagram, and for this reason they have been largely neglected in the standard treatises on demography. Specialist research on them has frequently been conducted outside of demography. Migration is an important topic of study in geography, as marriage is in anthropology and sociology. To restore them to their rightful place in demography, a simple process needed to be found, as was done for fertility and mortality. This role was fulfilled in part III by the method of allocation. It was introduced tentatively via the traditional contrast between panmictic mating and homogamy, and was then given a progressively more refined formulation, particularly in relation to female hypergamy. The critical change came in the first two chapters of part III, at the junction of the chapter on nuptiality and that on migration. The simple switch from a random selection of the order in which prospective marriage partners and migrants reach their decision, to the optimization of their choices from this point on, established a natural continuity between the polar opposites of homogamy and panmictic mating. The allocation model thus plays the same founding and central role in the study of interactions in demography as construction of the period form does in the analysis of lifelines or the stable population in population dynamics.

The third process is not as well-known or firmly established as the previous two. But it has the immense advantage over them of bringing geographical space into demography. This clearly occurred when studying the distance between the places of residence of the two spouses, which had an immediate transposition in terms of migration. With the introduction of space comes the realization that demography has flourished while neglecting it almost completely. The discipline has reduced space to the homogeneous interior of administrative and political subdivisions—states, regions, departments, communes. Yet an individual's spatial location is a fact of greater immediacy than his or her age, sex, or marital status. The prime element of demography is not the individual lifeline as defined and studied in part I, but a more complex lifeline, that of every individual's trajectory in real space. This is the approach Törsten Hägerstrand sought to popularize from the 1950s in the Swedish "Lund school" of geography. Geographical information systems and satellite tracking hold out the prospect of new sources of observation for developing demographic analysis with a spatial dimension, as outlined in the last chapter of part III.

In summary, demography is indeed a science of processes at each of the levels considered—individuals, populations, networks of interaction. The importance accorded to dynamic models and to their macro- and microlevel simulations is ample evidence of this. But there remains the second objection to this definition of the discipline, namely that most of the other social sciences also make use of processes. Hence this would not be a discriminating criterion. In demography, however, processes exist in their pure state and make a minimum of assumptions about human behavior. Demography can be said to be the social science that draws on psychology the least. Compare it with economics, for example, which is highly schematic but whose theory of utility heavily relies on psychological elements, or indeed with sociology, where functionalist and pragmatic assumptions abound. All of this is absent from demography. This is both a strength and a weakness. A weakness because it means that we can scarcely expect explanations for population facts, and a strength because the intervening mechanisms are set out simply and precisely. The field's concern is with inner details, not with ultimate ends or first origins. This is a question again present in the work of William Petty, the true founder of demography under the name of *Political Arithmetic*. In one of his *Essays* he tried to find the total number of humans who had ever lived and would have lived up to a certain period. To establish this he started from Adam and ended with the Last Judgement, at which time "the Earth will be full, that is to say, that there will be two men for each acre of cultivable land." The parenthesis opens with Adam and closes with the Apocalypse. Since Petty, however, demography has concentrated on the bit in-between. It views populations as having no origin and no destination (which perhaps accounts for the recurrent anxieties—in threatening though never explicit terms—concerning population explosion and extinction).

As a science of processes, demography puts forward simple, general models free of frills or pretensions and that are easily applicable by other disciplines. In this respect demography represents a genuine science of processes. This characteristic was seen in action in the two chapters on economics. It would be wrong to conclude from this that demography is a science with the same objectivity as physics or astronomy. This was the dream of many scholars, and it is noteworthy that among the early population specialists there were several astronomers: Halley, Deparcieux, Quetelet, Verhulst. But, however simple the assumptions underpinning demographic processes, they exist nonetheless, setting up an insurmountable limit that is made manifest in the notion of population. Except for the world population—which is that of a biological species— all other populations are cultural constructs. Horde, tribe, people, nation—none has any natural foundation. The result is a high degree of uncertainty caused by the lability of the groupings that are formed and designated as populations. Either a geographical definition of populations is used, in which case migration immediately becomes an obstacle, or else a hereditary definition is used, so that intermarriage is the obstacle. In nearly every population, the situation is further complicated by membership rules that combine criteria of descent and residence and have varied over time. From this point of view the ideological use of demography can prove pernicious. It tends to provide a basis and justify the existence of hypothetical populations by the simple fact of treating them as populations that are strictly closed or subject to perfectly specified exchanges. The objection will be made that all the social sciences define their base groups since that is what they work on: firms and states in economics, ethnic groups and peoples in anthropology, classes and societies in sociology, languages and dialects in linguistics. But the danger is greater with demography. Because its processes are simpler, more general, more homogeneous, and less dependent on psychology, their quality rubs off on their object and risks communicating to populations with no precise definition a misleading semblance of reality and permanence. Demography appeared to occupy a place on the frontier of the social sciences, in direct contact with biology and political science—as its founding work, published in 1661, states openly in its title: *Natural and Political Observations*—but is in reality subject to the fundamental dilemma that faces the social sciences: how to fill the space between language and mathematical formalization, between "seme" and "matheme" to imitate a sentence by Alain Badiou when situating philosophy in a similar perspective.

References

Aalen, O. 1978. Non-parametric inference for a family of counting processes. *Annals of Statistics* 6:701–26.

Alembert, J. d'. 1761–1780. Traité de l'inoculation. In *Opuscules Mathématiques* (7 volumes). Paris: David puis Briasson.

Alonso, W. 1973. National interregional demographic accounts. A prototype. Institute of Urban and Regional Development, University of California, Berkeley, Monograph 17.

———. 1974. Policy oriented interregional demographic accounting and a generalization of population flow models. Varsovie, Polish Economic Association.

Ammerman, A. J., and L. Cavalli-Sforza. 1979. The wave of advance model for the spread of agriculture in Europe. In *Transformations, Mathematical Approaches to Cultural Changes* (ed. C. Renfrew and K. L. Cooke). New York: Academic Press.

Arlinghaus, S. 1985. Fractals take a central place. *Geografika Annaler* B 67(2):83–88.

Arrow, K. J. 1962. The economic implications of learning by doing. *Review of Economic Studies* 29(3):155–73.

Auerbach, F. 1911. Das Gesetz der Bevölkerung-konzentration. *Petermans Mitteilungen* 59:74–76.

Bähr, J., C. Jensen, and W. Kulls. 1992. *Bevölkerungsgeographie*. Berlin: W. de Gruyter.

Batty, M., and P. Longley. 1994. *Fractal Cities*. New York: Academic Press.

Beaumel, C., L. Doisneau, and M. Vatan. 2003. *La Situation Démographique de la France en 2001*. Paris: INSEE.

Becker, G. S. 1964. *Human Capital*. New York: Columbia University Press.

———. 1993. *A Treatise on the Family*. Cambridge, MA: Harvard University Press.

Bernoulli, D. 1760. Essai d'une nouvelle analyse de la mortalité causée par la petite vérole et des avantages de l'inoculation pour la prévenir. In *Histoires et Mémoires de l'Académie des Sciences* (published in 1766), volume 2, pp. 1–79. Paris: Imprimerie Royale.

Bhrolchain, M. N. 1992. Period paramount? A critique of the cohort approach. *Population and Development Review* 18:599–629.

Blanchet, D. 1991. *Modélisation Démo-économique*. Paris: PUF-INED.

Bongaarts, J. 1978. A framework for analyzing the proximate determinants of fertility. *Population and Development Review* 4(1):105–32.

———. 2006. How long will we live? *Population and Development Review* 32(4):605–28.

Bongaarts, J., and G. Feeney. 1998. On the quantum and tempo of fertility. *Population and Development Review* 24(2):271–91.

———. 2002. How long do we live? *Population and Development Review* 28(1):13–29.

———. 2003. Estimating mean lifetime. *Proceedings of the National Academy of Sciences (USA)* 100:13 127–33.

Bongaart, J., and R. G. Potter. 1983. *Fertility, Biology and Behavior: An Analysis of Proximate Determinants of Marital Fertility*. New York: Academic Press.

Boserup, E. 1965. *The Condition of Agricultural Growth*. London: Allen and Unwin.

Bossard, J. H. 1932. Residential propinquity as a factor in marriage selection. *American Journal of Sociology* 38:219–24.

Boulding, K. 1955. The Malthusian model as a general system. *Social and Economic Studies* 4(3):195–204.

Bourgeois-Pichat, J. 1960. Vieillissement de la population et systèmes de retraite. *Population* 45:850–64.

Bourgeois-Pichat, J., and S. A. Taleb. 1970. Un taux d'accroissement nul pour les pays en voie de développement en l'an 2000. Réve ou réalité? *Population* 25:957–74.

Bowley, A. L. 1924. Births and population in Great Britain. *Economic Journal* 34:188–92.

Brass, W. 1971. On the scale of mortality. In *Biological Aspects of Demography* (ed. W. Brass). London: Taylor and Francis.

Brossard, J. H. 1932. Residential propinquity as a factor in marriage selection. *American Journal of Sociology* 38:219–24.

Cannan, E. 1895. The probability of a cessation in the growth of population in England and Wales during the next century. *Economic Journal* 5:505–15.

Carnes, B. A., S. J. Olshansky, and D. Grahn. 1996. The search for a law of mortality. *Population and Development Review* 22(2):231–64.

Carrothers, G. A. P. 1956. An historical review of the gravity and potential concepts of human interactions. *Journal of the American Institute of Planners* 22:94–102.

Chiang, C. L. 1978. *Life Table and Mortality Analysis*. Genève: OMS.

Christaller, W. 1931. *Die Zentralen Orte in Süddeutschland*. Iéna, Germany: G. Fischer.

Coale, A. J. 1972. *The Growth and Structure of Human Populations. A Mathematical Investigation*. Princeton University Press.

Coale, A. J., and P. Demeny. 1966. *Regional Model Life Tables and Stable Populations*. Princeton University Press.

Coale, A. J., and J. Trussell. 1974. Model fertility schedules: variations in the structure of childbearing in human populations. *Population Index* 40:185–258.

Cohen, J. E. 1995. *How Many People Can the Earth Support?* New York: W. W. Norton.

Cohn, N. 1957. *The Pursuit of the Millennium: Revolutionary Millenarians and Mystical Anarchists of the Middle Ages*. Oxford University Press.

Courgeau, D. 1970. *Les Champs Migratoires en France*. Paris: PUF-INED.

Cox, D. R., and D. Oakes. 1984. *Analysis of Survival Data*. New York: Chapman and Hall.

Cox, P. 1970. *Demography*. Cambridge University Press.

Daston, L. 1988. *Classical Probability in the Enlightenment*. Princeton University Press.

Demeny, P., and G. McNicoll (eds). 2003. *Encyclopedia of Population*. New York: Macmillan Reference.

Deparcieux, A. 1746. *Essai sur les Probabilités de la Durée de la Vie Humaine*. Paris: Guérin Frères.

Droesbeke, J. J., B. Fichet, and P. Tassi. 1989. *Analyse Statistique des Durées de Vie. Modélisation des Données Censurées*. Paris: Economica.

Easterlin, R. 1975. An economic framework for fertility analysis. *Studies in Family Planning* 6(3):54–63.

Easterlin, R. 1980. *Birth and Fortune*. New York: Basic Books.

Elandt-Johnson, R. C., and N. L. Johnson. 1980. *Survival Models and Data Analysis*. New York: John Wiley & Sons.

Euler, L. 1760. Recherches générales sur la mortalité et la multiplication du genre humain. *Mémoire de l'Académie Royale des Sciences et Belles Lettres de Berlin* 7:144, 175.

Feichtinger, G. 1979. *Demographische Analyse und Populationsdynamische Modelle*. Grundzüge des Bevölkerungsmathematik. Springer.

Galton, F., and H. W. Watson. 1874. On the probability of extinction of families. *Journal of the Royal Anthropological Institute of Great Britain and Ireland* 94(2):138–44.

Gabriel, K. N., and I. Ronen. 1958. Estimates of mortality from infant mortality rates. *Population Studies* 12(2):164–69.

Gibrat, R. 1931. *Les Inégalités Économiques*. Paris: Sirey.

Gini, C. 1924. Premières recherches sur la fécondité de la femme. In *Proceedings of the International Mathematical Congress, Toronto*, pp. 889–92.

Girard, A. 1980. *Le Choix du Conjoint*. Paris: PUF-INED.

Glass, D. V. 1936. *The Struggle for Population*. Oxford: Clarendon Press.

Goldstein, J. R. 2006. Found in translation? A cohort perspective on tempo-adjusted life expectancy. *Demographic Research* 14(5):71–84.

Goldstein, J. R., and K. W. Wachter. 2006. Relationships between period and cohort life expectancy: gaps and lags. *Population Studies* 60(3):257–70.

Gompertz, B. 1825. On the nature of the function expressive of the law of mortality. *Philosophical Transactions of the Royal Society of London* 115:513–85.

Graunt, J. 1661. *Natural and Political Observations... Made upon the Bills of Mortality*. London: John Martyn.

Guérin-Pace, F. 1993. *Deux Siècles de Croissance Urbaine: La Population des Villes Françaises de 1831 à 1990*. Paris: Anthropos.

Hägerstrand, T. 1957. Migration and area. In *Migration in Sweden: A Symposium* (ed. D. Hannenberg, T. Hägerstrand, and B. O. Odeving), pp. 27–158. Lund Studies in Geography, Serie B.

Hajnal, J. 1953. Age at marriage and proportion marrying. *Population Studies* 7(2):111–36.

———. 1965. European marriage patterns in perspective. In *Population in History. Essays in Historical Demography* (ed. D. V. Glass and D. E. C. Eversley), pp. 101–43. London: Edward Arnold.

Halley, E. 1693. An estimate of the degrees of mortality of the mankind. *Philosophical Transactions of the Royal Society of London* 17:596–610.

Harris, T. E. 1963. *The Theory of Branching Processes*. Englewood Cliffs, NJ: Prentice Hall.

Heffer, J. 1989. Du pull et du push. In *Les Immigrations Européennes aux Etats-Unis (1880–1910)* (ed. R. Rougé), pp. 21–48. Paris: Presses de la Sorbonne.

Hartshorne, R. 1939. *The Nature of Geography*. Lancaster, PA: Association of American Geographers.

Henry, L. 1957. Fécondité et famille. Modèles mathématiques. I. *Population* 12(3):413–44.

———. 1961a. Fécondité et famille. Modèles mathématiques. II. *Population* 16(1):27–48.

———. 1961b. Some data on natural fertility. *Eugenics Quarterly* 8(6):81–91.

———. 1971. Pyramides, statuts et carrières. I. Avancement à l'ancienneté, sélection. *Population* 26(3):463–86.

———. 1972. Pyramides, statuts et carrières. II. Avancement au choix. *Population* 27(4/5):599–636.

———. 1984. *Démographie. Analyse et Modèles*. Paris: INED.

Hicks, J. 1973. *Capital and Time: A Neo-Austrian Theory*. Oxford: Clarendon Press.

Hinde, A. 1998. *Demographic Methods*. London: Arnold.

Hobcraft, J., J. Menken, and S. Preston. 1982. Age, period and cohort effects in demography. *Population Index* 48(1):4–43.

Inaba, H. 2007. Effects of the age shift on the tempo and the quantum of nonrepeatable events. *Mathematical Population Studies* 14(3):131–68.

Johnson, D. G., and R. D. Lee. 1987. *Population Growth and Economic Development: Issues and Evidence*. Madison, WI: University of Wisconsin Press.

Johnson, R. A. 1980. *Religious Assortative Marriage in the United States*. New York: Academic Press.

Kannisto, V. 2000. *The Advancing Frontier of Survival. Life Tables for Old Age*. Odense University Press.

Kaplan, E. L., and P. Meier. 1958. Non-parametric estimation from incomplete observations. *Journal of the American Statistical Association* 53:457–81.

Karmel, P. H. 1948a. An analysis of the sources and magnitude of inconsistencies between male and female reproduction rates. *Population Studies* 2(2):240–73.

———. 1948b. The relation between male and female nuptiality in a stable population. *Population Studies* 1(4):353–87.

Keyfitz, N. 1978. *Applied Mathematical Demography*, 3rd edn. New York: John Wiley & Sons.

———. 1981. The limits of population forecasting. *Population and Development Review* 7(4):579–93.

Keyfitz, N., and J. Gomez de Leon. 1980. Considérations démographiques sur les systèmes de retraite. *Population* 35:815–36.

Klein, J. P., and M. L. Moeschberger. 2003. *Survival Analysis. Techniques for Censored and Truncated Data*. New York: Springer.

Kuczynski, R. 1928. *The Balance of Births and Deaths*. New York: Macmillan.

Laslett, P., and R. Wall (eds). 1972. *Household and Family in Past Time*. Cambridge University Press.

Le Bras, H. 1968. Nouvelles table-types de mortalité: présentation. *Population* 23:739–44.

———. 1969. Retour d'une population à l'état stable après une catastrophe. *Population* 24:861–96.

———. 1971. Equilibre et croissance de populations soumises à des migrations. *Theoretical Population Biology* 2:100–21.

———. 1974. Populations stables aléatoires. *Population* 29:435–64.

———. 1976. Loi de mortalité et âge limite. *Population* 31:655–92.

———. 1977. Une formulation générale de la dynamique des populations. *Population* 32(Special Issue):261–93.

———. 1983. Fluctuations et croissance des populations soumises à une contrainte. *Population* 38:311–42.

———. 1984. L'horoscope des populations. *Vingtième Siècle* 1(1):75–87.

———. 1985. Les jeux du hasard et du mariage. *Démographie et Sociologie*, pp. 183–206. Paris: Presses de la Sorbonne.

———. 1990. Population et migrations. In *Encyclopédie Économique* (ed. X. Greffe, J. Mairesse, and J. L. Reiffers), pp. 1233–74. Paris: Economica.

———. 1993. Simulation of change to validate demographic analysis. In *Old and New Methods in Historical Demography* (ed. D. Reher and R. Schofield), pp. 259–80. Oxford: Clarendon Press.

———. 1994. *Les Limites de la Planète, Mythes de la Nature et de la Population*. Paris: Flammarion.

———. 1996a. *La Planète au Village: Migrations et Peuplement en France*. Paris: Éditions de l'Aube.

———. 1996b. Histoire et systèmes démographiques. *Annales de Démographie Historique* 31:359–72.

Le Bras, H. 1996c. *Le Peuplement de l'Europe*. Paris: La Documentation Française.

———. 1997. Fertility and the conditions of self-perpetuation: differing trends in Europe. In *Family and Kinship in Europe* (ed. M. Segalen and M. Gullestrad), pp. 14–33. London: Pinter.

———. 1998. Un compte des étrangers au Monomatapa. In *Le Démon des Origines*. Paris: Éditions de l'Aube.

———. 2000a. Passé simple et présent recomposé. *Le Genre Humain* 35:91–100.

———. 2000b. *Naissance de la Mortalité. L'Origine Politique de la Statistique et de la Démographie*. Paris: Gallimard.

———. 2005. Mortality tempo versus removal of causes of mortality: opposite views leading to different estimations of life expectancy. *Demographic Research* 13:615–40.

Le Bras, H., and J. C. Chesnais. 1976. Cycle de l'habitat et âge des habitants. *Population* 1(2):269–98.

Le Bras, H., and G. Tapinos. 1979. Perspectives à long terme de la population française et leurs implications économiques. *Population* 34(Special Issue):1391–452.

Ledermann, S. 1969. *Nouvelles Table-Types de Mortalité*. Paris: PUF.

Lee, E. T. 1992. *Statistical Methods for Survival Data Analysis*. New York: John Wiley & Sons.

Lee, R. D. 1986. Malthus and Boserup: a dynamic synthesis. In *The State of Population Theory* (ed. D. Coleman and R. Schofield). Oxford: Basil Blackwell.

———. 2004. Reflections on inverse projection: its origins, development, extensions, and relation to forecasting. In *Inverse Projection Techniques: Old and New Approaches* (ed. J. Vaupel, E. Barbi, S. Bertino, and E. Sonino). Demographic Research Monographs. Berlin: Springer.

Leslie, P. H. 1945. On the use of matrices in certain population dynamics. *Biometrika* 13:183–212.

Lévy, P. 1965. *Processus Stochastiques et Mouvement Brownien*. Paris: Gauthier-Villars.

Lexis, W. 1875. *Einleitung in die Theorie der Bevölkerungs-Statistik*. Strasbourg: Trübner.

Lopez, A. 1961. *Problems in Stable Population Theory*. Princeton Office of Population Research.

Lorimer, F. 1954. *Culture and Human Fertility*. Paris: Unesco.

Lotka, A. J. 1924. *Elements of Physical Biology*. New York: Williams and Wilkins,

———. 1939. *Théorie des Associations Biologiques*. Paris: Hermann et Cie.

Lowry, I. S. 1966. *Migration and Metropolitan Growth: Two Analytical Models*. San Francisco, CA: Chandler.

Lutz, W., J. Vaupel, and D. Ahlburg (eds). 1998. *Frontiers of Population Forecasting*. Special issue of *Population and Development Review*.

Luu Mau Tranh. 1964. Distribution théorique des distances entre deux points répartis uniformément sur une surface. In *Les Déplacements Humains* (ed. J. Sutter). Paris: Hachette.

Luu Mau Tranh and J. Sutter. 1963. Contribution à l'étude de la distance séparant les domiciles des époux. In *Les Déplacements Humains* (ed. J. Sutter). Paris: Hachette.

McDonald, P. 2006. Low fertility and the state: the efficacy of policy. *Population and Development Review* 32:485–510.

Makeham, W. M. 1860. On the law of mortality and the construction of annuity tables. *Journal of the Institute of the Actuaries* 13:325–58.

Malthus, T. 1798. *An Essay on the Principle of Population*. London: J. Johnson.

Mandelbrot, B. 1983. *The Fractal Geometry of Nature*. New York: W. H. Freeman.

Massey, D. S., and J. E. Taylor (eds). 2004. *International Migration*. Oxford University Press.

May, R. 1973. *Model Ecosystems*. Princeton University Press.

Modigliani, F., and A. Ando. 1963. The life-cycle hypothesis of saving: aggregate implications and test. *American Economic Review* 53(1):55–84.

Moffat, C. B. 1903. The spring rivalry of birds: some views on the limit to multiplication. *Irish Naturalist* 12:152–66.

Namboodiri, K. 1991. *Demographic Analysis: A Stochastic Approach*. San Diego, CA: San Diego Academic Press.

Nelson, R. R. 1956. A theory of low level, trap in underdeveloped economies. *American Economic Review* 46:894–908.

Niehans, J. 1963. Economic growth with two endogenous factors. *Quarterly Journal of Economics* 77:349–71.

Norton, H. T. J. 1928. Natural selection and Mendelian variation. *Proceedings of the London Mathematical Society* 28:1–45.

Notestein, F. W., I. B. Taeuber, D. Kirk, A. J. Coale, and L. K. Kiser. 1944. *The Future Population of Europe and the Soviet Union: Population Projection 1940–1970*. Genève: Société des Nations.

Odum, E. P. 1971. *Fundamentals of Ecology*. Philadelphia, PA: W. B. Saunders.

Oly, J. C. 1924. Verandering in geboorte en sterfte. Raakt Nederland overbevolkt? *Het Verzekerings-Archief* 5:149–70.

Pearl, R. 1925. *The Biology of Population Growth*. New York: Alfred Knopf.

Petty, W. 1682. *An Essay Concerning the Multiplication of Mankind*. London: J. Nourse.

———. 1683. *Another Essay in Political Arithmetic*. London: Pardoe.

Phelps, E. 1961. The golden rule of accumulation: a fable for grown men. *American Economic Review* 51:638–43.

Pressat, R. 1979. *Dictionnaire de Démographie*. Paris: PUF.

Preston, S. H., P. Heuveline, and M. Guillot. 2001. *Demography, Measuring and Modeling Population Processes*. Oxford: Blackwell.

Quetelet, A. 1835. *Sur l'Homme et le Développement de Ses Facultés, ou Essai de Physique Sociale*. Paris: Bachelier.

Ravenstein, E. G. 1871. *Geographical Magazine*. (Later published in 1876 as *The Birthplaces of the People and the Laws of Migration*. London: Trubner.)

Reilly, W. J. 1931. *The Law of Retail Gravitation*. New York: W. J. Reilly.

Rogers, A. 1968. *Matrix Analysis of Interregional Population Growth and Distribution*. University of California Press.

———. 1975. *Introduction to Multiregional Mathematical Demography*. New York: John Wiley & Sons.

Ryder, N. B. 1964. The process of demographic transition. *Demography* 1:74–82.

———. 1965. The cohort as a concept in the study of social change. *American Sociological Review* 30:842–61.

Samuelson, P. 1975. The optimum growth rate of a population. *International Economic Review* 16:531–38.

———. 1976. The optimum growth rate of a population: agreement and evaluation. *International Economic Review* 17:516–25.

Sauvy, A. 1928. La population française jusqu'en 1956: essai de prévision. *Journal de la Société de Statistique de Paris* 70(12):321–29.

Schoeni, R. F., Liang, J. Bennett, H. Sugisawa, T. Fukaya, and E. Kobayash. 2006. Trends in old-age functioning and disability in Japan, 1993–2002. *Population Studies* 60(1):39–54.

Schultz, T. W. (ed.). 1974. *Economics of the Family: Marriage, Children and Human Capital*. University of Chicago Press.

Shaw, C. 2007. Fifty years of United Kingdom national population projections: how accurate have they been? *Population Trends* 128:8–23.

Sheps, M. C., and J. A. Menken. 1973. *Mathematical Models of Conception and Birth*. Chicago University Press.

Siegel, J. S. 2001. *Applied Demography*. San Diego, CA: San Diego Academic Press.

Simon, J. L. 1977. *The Economics of Population Growth*. Princeton University Press.

Simpson, T. 1742. *The Doctrine of Annuities and Reversion*. London: J. Nourse.

Sismondi, S. de. 1827. *Nouveaux Principes d'Économie Politique*. Paris: Delaunay.

Solow, R. M. 1956. A contribution to the theory of economic growth. *Quarterly Journal of Economics* 70(1):65–94.

Sraffa, P. 1960. *Production of Commodities by the Mean of Commodities*. Cambridge University Press.

Stewart, J. Q. 1948. Demographic gravitation: evidence and applications. *Sociometry* 11(1/2): 31–58.

———. 1950. The development of social physics. *American Journal of Physics* 18(May):239–53.

Stoto, M. 1983. The accuracy of population projections. *Journal of the American Statistical Association* 78(381):13–20.

Stouffer, S. A. 1940. Intervening opportunities: a theory relating mobility and distance. *American Sociological Review* 5:845–67.

———. 1960. Intervening opportunities and competing migrants. *Journal of Regional Science* 2:1–26.

Sullivan, P. O. 1971. Linear programming as a forecasting device for interregional freight flows in Great Britain. *Regional and Urban Economics* I 4:384–97.

United Nations. 1982. *Model Life Tables for Developing Countries*. Population Studies 77. New York: United Nations.

Van Dalen, P., and K. Henkens. 2007. Longing for the good life: understanding emigration from a high-income country. *Population and Development Review* 33(1):37–65.

Vauban. 1933. *Ecrits de Vauban* (ed. E. Coornaert). Paris: Alcan.

Vaupel, J. W. 1997. The remarkable improvement of survival at old ages. *Philosophical Transactions of the Royal Society of London* B 352(1363):1799–804.

———. 1998. Demographic analysis of aging and longevity. *American Economic Review* 88(2):242–47.

Verhulst, P. F. 1838. Notice sur la loi que la population suit dans son accroissement. *Correspondance Mathématique et Physique* 20:113–21.

———. 1845. Recherches mathématiques sur la loi d'accroissement de la population. *Nouveaux Mémoires de l'Académie Royale des Sciences et Belles Lettres de Bruxelles* 18:1–38.

Vicsek, T. 1994. *Fractal Growth Phenomena*. London: World Scientific.

Vincent, P. 1945. *Potentiel d'Accroissement d'une Population*. Paris: Berger-Levrault.

Wachter, K. W. 2005. Tempo and its tribulations. *Demographic research* 13(9):201–22.

Wachter, K. W., and C. E. Finch. 1997. *Between Zeus and the Salmon: The Biodemography of Longevity*. Washington, DC: National Academy Press.

Wachter, K. W., and P. Laslett. 1978. *Statistical Studies of Historical Social Structure* (ed. K. W. Wachter, E. Hammel, P. Laslett, R. Laslett, and H. Le Bras), chapter 7. New York: Academic Press.

Warntz, W. 1966. The topology of socio-economic terrain and spatial flows. *Papers and Proceedings of the Regional Science Association* 17:47–61.

Weibull, W. 1951. A statistical distribution of wide application. *Journal of Applied Mechanics* 18:293–97.

Wilson, A. G. 1970. *Entropy*. London: Pion.

Wilson, A. G., and M. L. Senier. 1974. Some relationships between entropy maximizing models, mathematical programming models and their duals. *Journal of Regional Science* 14:207–16.

Wrigley, E. A., and R. Schofield. 1981. *The Population History of England 1541–1871: A Reconstruction*. London: Edward Arnold.

Wynne-Edwards, V. C. 1962. *Animal Dispersion in Relation to Social Behavior*. London: Oliver and Boyd.

Xie, Y. 1990. What is natural fertility: the remodeling of a concept. *Population Index* 56:656–63.

Young, E. C. 1924. *The Movement of Farm Population*. Ithaca, Cornell Agricultural Experiment Station, Bulletin 426.

Yule, G. U. 1906. On the changes in marriage and birth rates in England and Wales during the past half century. *Journal of the Royal Statistical Society* 69(1):88–147.

Zimmermann, K. F. 1995. European migration: push and pull. *Proceedings of the World Bank, Annual Conference on Development Economics, 1994*, pp. 313–42. Washington, DC: World Bank.

Zipf, G. K. 1941. *National Unity and Disunity*. Bloomington, IN: Principia Press.

———. 1949. *Human Behavior and the Principle of Least Effort*. Cambridge, MA: Addison-Wesley.

Index